God's Messenger: J. F. Riemenschneider
and Racial Conflict in 19th Century New Zealand

God's Messenger:
J. F. Riemenschneider and Racial Conflict in 19th Century New Zealand

Peter Oettli

HUIA

First published in 2008 by Huia Publishers
39 Pipitea Street, PO Box 17–335
Wellington, Aotearoa New Zealand
www.huia.co.nz

ISBN 978–1–869693–20–6

Copyright © Peter Oettli 2008
Cover design: Tim Hansen
Cover image: Untitled (Riemenschneider's Mission Station, Warea) (1852),
Joseph Jenner Merrett. Collection of Puke Ariki (A81.105).

All rights reserved. No part of this publication may be reproduced, stored in a retrieval system, or transmitted in any form or by any means, electronic, mechanical, including photocopying, recording or otherwise, without prior permission of the publisher.

National Library of New Zealand Cataloguing-in-Publication Data
Oettli, Peter H., 1940–
God's messenger: J. F. Riemenschneider and racial conflict in
19th century New Zealand / Peter Oettli.
Includes bibliographical references and index.
ISBN 978–1–869693–20–6
1. Riemenschneider, J. F. (Johann Friedrich), 1817–1866.
2. Missionaries—New Zealand—Taranaki—Biography.
3. New Zealand—History—1840–1876.
4. New Zealand—Race relations.
I. Title.
266.41092—dc 22

Published with the support of Puke Ariki and District Libraries, New Plymouth, and

To my wife

Contents

Foreword		*ix*
Acknowledgements		*xi*
1.	Missionary in the Making: North Germany, 1817–1842	*1*
2.	Strife at Sea and on Arrival in Nelson, 1843	*26*
3.	In Search of a Mission Field: From Nelson to Motukaramū, 1844	*45*
4.	A Bleak and Lonely Post, Mid-1844 to Mid-1846	*57*
5.	Mission Station at Warea, Mid-1846 to the End of 1847	*79*
6.	Losing an Assistant, Gaining a Wife, 1848–1850	*96*
7.	Crisis in Bremen and for the Preacher of Taranaki, 1851–1853	*118*
8.	Puketapu Feud, 1854–1857	*131*
9.	Rift between Riemenschneider and his People, 1857–1859	*149*
10.	War and Exile, 1860	*164*
11.	Final Parting from Taranaki and New Beginning in Otago, Mid-1860 to Mid-1863	*182*
12.	Teacher, Pastor, Counsellor, Builder, 1863–1864	*203*
13.	A Legacy in Taranaki, 1846–1862	*215*
14.	At Rest, 1865–1866	*223*
Bibliography		*235*
Index		*249*

Foreword

THE HISTORY OF THE Christian mission to New Zealand is full of interesting and colourful characters. There are the prominent leaders, such as Bishop Selwyn and his Catholic counterpart, Bishop Pompallier; there are controversial figures such as William Colenso and Thomas Kendall; then there are the quiet scholars whose work has lived on into the present day, such as William Williams, whose dictionary is still the definitive dictionary of Māori and Robert Maunsell, who translated the Old Testament into Māori. Finally, during the wars of the 1860s, there are strong supporters of the Māori cause, such as Octavius Hadfield, as well as missionaries who sided with the Pākehā settlers and, in two cases, Carl Silvius Völkner and John Whiteley, paid for it with their lives.

Their stories have been told, in some cases several times, and the missionaries deserve to be remembered and celebrated as an important part of the history of New Zealand.

Johann Friedrich Riemenschneider has had two biographers, both of whom competently told part of his story. The first, L. Tiesmeyer, in his 1875 biography, based his work on Riemenschneider's copious writings, but he was unable to place the missionary's life and work in the context of New Zealand history and society. The second biographer, William Greenwood, who wrote in 1967, was well versed in 19th century New Zealand ecclesiastical history, but could not read German, so had to depend on someone for a loose translation of the Tiesmeyer biography and the few English documents that he was able to find.

As a consequence, Riemenschneider and his contribution to the history, particularly of Taranaki and Otago, is not well known, and on the few occasions that he is mentioned in books on New Zealand history, he is described as a Lutheran (which he was not), or as a traitor to the Māori cause in the wars of the 1860s, which he definitely was not.

The present biography seeks to correct the record as far as possible. Like so many 19th century New Zealand missionaries, Riemenschneider saw his work crumble before his eyes when war polarised and scattered his congregation. But the missionary has left a rich legacy, not only in his work, but also in his records that provide an insight into the conditions under which he worked and into the wider context of life in rural New Zealand around the middle of the 19th century. If this new biography contributes to a wider appreciation of the work of the German missionary and to the social history, particularly of Taranaki and Otago, it will have achieved its purpose.

Acknowledgements

Behind every book there is a story. This one begins long ago, at the pōwhiri graciously extended to the 1986 annual conference of the New Zealand Association of Language Teachers, of which I was President at the time. The conference was held in New Plymouth. After the pōwhiri, over a cup of tea, one of the Māori elders present, Mr Maurice Walden, drew my attention to a set of papers of a 'German Missionary' who had worked in Taranaki in the mid-19th century. They were in the Taranaki Museum (now Puke Ariki) in New Plymouth, he told me. I could not resist but went to take a look at the papers, which turned out to be microfilms of the originals in Bremen, Germany. I am deeply indebted to Mr Walden for his comment. The transcribed papers and this biography go back to our conversation, more than 20 years ago.

This book, like so many histories, relies heavily on material held by libraries, archives and museums. I would like to acknowledge with gratitude the invaluable help and advice I received from so many dedicated professionals over many years of work. The then Taranaki Museum kindly lent me the Riemenschneider microfilms on long-term loan, and I received a great deal of assistance and encouragement from the staff. I am particularly grateful for their most generous help with the illustrations for this book. Other New Zealand libraries whose staff assisted me include the Alexander Turnbull Library, Wellington, the Hocken Library and the Library of the Settlers' Museum in Dunedin, the Nelson Provincial Museum, the Public Library, the University Library and the library at the Auckland Institute and Museum. Special thanks must go to the librarians at my 'home' library at the University of Waikato in Hamilton. In Europe, I would like to particularly acknowledge the Bremen State Archive, where the original Riemenschneider papers are held. There, I not only received valuable help with finding the relevant material, but one of the archivists, Mrs Dorothea Breitenfeldt, even taught me how to tie a proper archivist's knot, so that I could return the papers in the same order in which

I had received them! Other libraries and depositories of material, and other individuals to whom I am indebted, are acknowledged in the references.

Apart from the professional assistance, I also received financial assistance for a visit to Bremen to work with the original papers. I am indebted to the Claude McCarthy Foundation for awarding me a Fellowship in 1990–91 that made the visit possible. I would also like to express my gratitude to the North German Mission, the society that originally sent Riemenschneider and his brother missionaries to New Zealand. During my stay in Bremen they very generously gave me free lodging in their guest flat that is attached to their offices, as well as access to their own library and the materials that they have deposited in the Bremen State Archive. At the other end of the production process of this book, I would like to thank Puke Ariki and District Libraries, New Plymouth, and the Ministry for Culture and Heritage for grants towards publishing.

Finally, there are a number of individuals, without whom this book would never have appeared. The Rev. Alan Leadley of Hamilton provided valuable suggestions and encouragement in nudging the manuscript towards publication. In particular however, Mr Kelvin Day of Puke Ariki was a steadfast and warm supporter of my work, both professionally and also personally. To them, my warm gratitude.

My most valuable and constant supporter however was my wife. She accompanied me on some of my research trips and assisted with the chore of wading through mountains of archival material. She patiently and critically read every version of every chapter and supported me unwaveringly in difficult times. So to her, in Riemenschneider's native language, *recht herzlicher Dank*.

Peter Oettli

Chapter One

Missionary in the Making: North Germany, 1817–1842

ON THE HILLSIDE overlooking the small coastal settlement of Port Chalmers in the South Island of New Zealand, in the old cemetery behind the Iona Presbyterian Church, there is a grave that has been restored by the Dunedin City Council. The faded inscription on the stone reads:

BY
THE MAORIES OF OTAGO
IN MEMORY OF
THEIR MINISTER
REV. J. F. REIMENSCHNEIDER
WHO DIED 25 AUGT 1866
IN THE 51ST YEAR OF HIS AGE.

SOUND THE GOSPEL TRUMPET
UNTIL THE STRONGHOLDS OF
SIN AND SATAN IN ALL PARTS
OF THE WORLD SHALL FALL.

The man who lies buried there, in a double grave with his sister-in-law, was born in 1817 in the North German city of Bremen. Together with three others he left his homeland, aged 26 years, full of anticipation, to be a missionary among the New Zealand Māori. For 23 years he toiled at his vocation with selfless dedication until ill health, continual overwork, privations and bitter disappointment combined to bring about his early death, just a couple of weeks after his 50th birthday.[1]

*

---

1. The inscription on the grave stone although well-intentioned, is wrong on a number of counts – a fact that has been pointed out several times. See, for example, Hardwicke Knight, *Otago Peninsula: A local history.*, 2nd edn, Broad Bay, Dunedin: Allied Press, 1979, p. 115.

Riemenschneider's life is a remarkable story about a remarkable man. It begins in the city of Bremen, situated on the river Weser in the north of Germany. The city as it was in the first half of the 19th century, with some of its leading figures and its religious and social institutions, is one of the keys to an understanding of the missionary in New Zealand. It was there that he received his vocation, and the values instilled in him in his formative years determined how he would interact with people from a different culture and how he would seek to make sense of the new world.

The 'Free Hanseatic City of Bremen' was the title assumed upon the dissolution of the Holy Roman Empire of the German Nation in 1806. It reflects a history of over a thousand years. The word 'free' refers to the fact that Bremen was independent and self-governing, not subject to a territorial lord or a prince of the church. Although the city had been founded by an Archbishop, its citizens over the centuries gained more and more power in the governance of the city. By 1358, when Bremen joined the Hanseatic League, it was the wealthy merchant families, not the Archbishop, who ruled. The Hanseatic League, the name of which Bremen proudly carries in its official title to this day, was a commercial and political association of north German towns and mercantile organisations. The League became a major political and economic force in North Germany and the Baltic from the 13th to the 15th centuries. It was in the 15th century that Bremen built its most impressive civic building, the *Rathaus* (city hall), with the stone statue of Roland, a symbol of freedom and independence, on the market square in front of it.[2] Both the Rathaus and the statue of Roland survived the destruction of the Second World War – they still stand as symbols of the proudly independent city–state and the wealth of the Bremen merchants.

In the early 19th century, public life in the city was dominated by trade and commerce, and by a determination to guard its independence and to seize commercial opportunities. It was still small, with about 36,000 inhabitants,[3] and it had a proud tradition, with a history of successful resistance to a series of would-be invaders. Many of its merchants were open to the new opportunities in overseas trade offered by the liberation of North Germany from French domination and the defeat of Napoleon in 1814–15 and, as a result, change was in the air.

What did not change, however, in spite of the French occupation and the spread of the ideals of the French revolution, was the strictly hierarchical and paternalistic structure of public and family life. In 1814 and again in 1826 the

---

2. The 'Roland' was a statue of a knight in armour with a naked drawn sword. It is found in many market squares of German towns, particularly in the north. It is a symbol of the town's rights and privileges, particularly those of administering justice and regulating commerce.
3. Herbert Schwarzwälder, *Geschichte der freien Hansestadt Bremen*. Bremen: Röver, 1976, Vol 2, p. 86.

Senate of the city carefully and in great detail specified the precise order in which members of the various social classes, from the senators to the burghers (citizens), were to be arranged in formal processions. In both instances the clergy were ranked very highly, immediately after the members of the Senate and the judiciary.[4] For young Riemenschneider, who came from a burgher class background, any aspiration to join the exalted ranks of the clergy must have seemed an impossible dream.

For an understanding of the religious climate at this time, some background history is necessary. The year of Riemenschneider's birth, 1817, marked the 300th anniversary of Martin Luther's act of posting the 95 Theses on the church door at Wittemberg. Luther, although arguably the most significant figure, was by no means the only 16th century reformer. John Calvin in Geneva and Huldrych Zwingli in Zürich also broke with the Catholic church. While these reformers agreed on many issues, they also had some fundamental differences, particularly in their interpretation of the sacraments. Ever since the Colloquy of Marburg – a debate between Luther, Zwingli and other Protestant theologians – had taken place in 1529, there had been two Protestant churches in German-speaking Europe; the Lutheran church and the Reformed church. They were divided mainly by their interpretation of the sacrament of communion. While Luther adhered to the Catholic teaching, which held that the bread and wine literally turned into the body and blood of Christ at communion, the Reformed theologians argued that the substance of bread and wine remained unchanged – that they were only a symbol of Christ's body and blood.

Johann Friedrich Riemenschneider was baptised on 7 September 1817 in the church of St Stephani, one of the Bremen parish churches. It was in this church that he received his religious education, and was confirmed and nurtured in the faith until his departure for the North German Mission Society's training institution for missionaries. This church still stands and continues as a place of regular worship just as it was in his day. Unlike the perishable wooden churches that Riemenschneider would build in New Zealand, its spire has survived, even if the rest of the building could not withstand the human violence of war. But at least parts of the church were re-built after it was extensively damaged by bombing during the Second World War.

St Stephani is one of the older churches in Bremen. Founded in 1139, its pastors and its congregation made a significant contribution to the at times turbulent ecclesiastical history of Bremen and North Germany. The Lutheran reformation in the first quarter of the 16th century was followed by the change to the Reformed persuasion in the second half of the same century. This change distinguished the theological orientation of all Bremen churches

---
4. Schwarzwälder, *op. cit.*, pp. 92 f.

from that of the churches in the surrounding countryside, which remained Lutheran; and aligned them with the Reformed Protestantism of East Frisia, the Netherlands, Hesse and Nassau.

The next major shift in theology that affected St Stephani, particularly, was the advent of Pietism in the early 18th century. The orthodox theologians and the city's rulers regarded this religious movement, which had its roots in England and the Netherlands, with suspicion. Yet the movement found strong support among the burgher classes. A reaction to the strict formalism and intellectual elitism of the theologians and pastors, Pietism emphasises individual Bible study, personal piety and experience of the faith, combined with a repudiation of the material world. One of the most important European theologians of Pietism, Friedrich Adolf Lampe (1683–1729), was pastor at St Stephani from 1709–1720 and his influence on the congregation went far beyond the period of his ministry. One of Lampe's innovations was the introduction of discussion groups after divine service, where members of the congregation were invited to share their reactions to the sermon, their experience of the faith and their insights into Scripture.[5] Riemenschneider would no doubt have participated, in a later era, in these group activities.

In 1809 the first preacher of the revivalist movement, Hermann Müller (died 1839), was called to St Stephani.[6] The revivalist movement, which had its roots in Pietism, was a reaction to both rationalistic theology[7] and the French occupation of the German states, including Bremen.[8] It stressed the

---

5. Such meetings became a feature of many revivalist Evangelical movements, including Methodism. "The weekly class meeting for the exchange of spiritual experience [established in 1742] was the essence of Wesley's system for building up those who had been awakened by preaching." (D. W. Bebbington, *Evangelicalism in Modern Britain. A history from the 1730s to the 1980s*. London; Boston: Unwin Hyman, 1989, p. 24).
6. Louis von Zobeltitz, "Theologische Hauptströmungen in St Stephani von der Reformation bis ins 19. Jahrhundert". *850 Jahre St Stephani-Gemeinde*. Bremen: Steintor, p. 48.
7. Rationalistic theology developed from the 18th century Enlightenment philosophy. It subjected every religious truth to the critique of reason and was one of the major directions of protestant theology in 19th century Germany.
8. In the course of Napoleon's conflict with England (whom he sought to conquer by a blockade of the European continent), Napoleon had occupied the cities of the Hanseatic League in 1806. While leaving the cities of the Hanseatic League their political autonomy he took steps to strip them of their wealth. In December 1810 the Hanseatic towns (Bremen, Hamburg and Lübeck) were annexed by France. Napoleon's treachery (he had assured the German Reichstag in 1806 that he had no interest in annexing any territory north of the Rhine), together with the extensive French plundering of the cities' wealth, fed the resentment against the French.

At the same time it inspired a form of German nationalism and fuelled the revival movement, which saw the French occupation as God's punishment for what was seen, by the revivalists, as a departure of the rationalists from the Bible as the supreme and exclusive revelation of God. The French occupation of Bremen was lifted in 1813, and at the Congress of Vienna (1815), Bremen regained its status as a free Hanseatic city. (Cf. Kurt von Raumer and Manfred Botzenhart, *Deutsche Geschichte im 19. Jahrhundert. Deutschland um 1800: Krise und Neugestaltung. Von 1789 bis 1815*. Wiesbaden: Akademische Verlagsgesellschaft Athenaion, 1980, pp. 256–265.

place of the Bible as the only valid guiding principle for the Christian life and placed a new emphasis on concepts such as sin, justification and repentance (which had been largely rejected by the rationalist theologians).

Müller is regarded as 'the father of the revivalist movement in Bremen',[9] but his theological orientation was not the only one represented by the clergy of St Stephani. For almost 30 years he shared the pulpit of the church with rationalist preachers. Revivalism received a major boost in 1827, however, with the appointment of Friedrich Ludwig Mallet (1792–1865). Mallet had been brought up by Müller following the death of his father, and had been ordained by him in 1815. He became pastor at another Bremen parish church, St Michaelis, until his call to St Stephani by which time he had already established himself as a renowned preacher. A Bremen newspaper, commenting on his appointment to St Stephani, called him 'one of the greatest preachers in Germany'.[10]

Hermann Müller was to become a pastor to the young Riemenschneider, who received his initial religious instruction from him. In one of Riemenschneider's rare personal comments in a letter from New Zealand, written in October 1856, he pays tribute to Müller's pastoral care for him when he was a young boy:

> … since from my earliest childhood the love for Christ and His Gospel and the fear of God had been kindled in me by my dear, upright parents according to their circumstances and ability, and by my teachers (later in particular by my dear, old and unforgettable Pastor Müller …[11]

The two clergymen who appear to have been most influential in Riemenschneider's later development (and later in his work as a missionary) were Mallet and Georg Gottfried Treviranus (1788–1868), who had been called to the parish church, St Martini, in Bremen in 1814.

Throughout his life, Mallet was a courageous fighter, both for his strong patriotic ideals and for his theology. For him the word of the Lord was not restricted to an interpretation of the Bible. He saw contemporary issues as revelations of God's work in the world and felt that they were appropriate subjects for sermons. This stance involved him on a number of occasions in major controversy. On Ascension Day 1842, for example, the neighbouring city of Hamburg suffered a catastrophic fire in which a quarter of the town was

---

9. Otto Wenig, *Rationalismus und Erweckungsbewegung in Bremen. Vorgeschichte, Geschichte und theologischer Gehalt der Bremer Kirchenstreitigkeiten von 1830–1852*. Bonn: Bouvier, 1966, p. 202.
10. Friedrich Prüser, *Achthundert Jahre St Stephanikirche. Ein Stück Bremischer Geschichte*. Bremen: Arndt Verlag Melchers & Boettcher, 1940, p. 518.
11. RP X, 83. The majority of the Riemenschneider papers have been transcribed by the author. The references refer to the volume and page number of the typed transcript. Thus RP X, 83 refers to Riemenschneider Papers [transcript], vol. X, p. 83. Unless specified, the original text is in German, and all translations are by the author.

destroyed, leaving 20,000 people homeless. In his sermon on the following Sunday, 8 May, Mallet interpreted the fire as an act of God to remind his people to repent of their arrogance and worldliness. It is not surprising that the sermon was publicly criticised by the Hamburg clergy and that, in the last few months before Riemenschneider's departure for New Zealand, his teacher and sponsor was involved in an acrimonious quarrel in the press.[12]

Georg Gottfried Treviranus never achieved the fame of Mallet as a preacher. His congregation in the parish of St Martini was dwindling because the area in which the church was situated was gradually being transformed from a residential into a commercial district during his ministry. Treviranus's strength lay in his pastoral ministry. Since his parish duties were not as onerous as those of some of his fellow pastors he was able to found and administer a large number of church societies, which united the particular revivalist elements in the various Bremen parishes. Some of them are of particular interest. Among them is the *Bremer Jünglings – und Gesellenverein* (Bremen Youth – and Journeymen's Association). It had been founded by Mallet in 1834 and the young Riemenschneider was a member.[13] While he was not involved in the beginning, Treviranus later conducted the weekly Monday Bible groups for the association. From 1834, Treviranus was also the leader of the Bremen Sunday School.

Of more significance for Riemenschneider's later career is Treviranus's involvement in the Mission Society that was founded in 1819, the first such society in North Germany.

As can be seen, the young man's early religious instruction was firmly in the revivalist tradition and he was taught by some of its most prominent and forceful exponents in Bremen. He had learned to take the Bible as the guiding principle for his faith; above all he had been firmly grounded in a religion of the heart rather than a religion of the mind. He had also learned to stand firm when confronted with teachings or attitudes that did not conform to his understanding of his faith. All these qualities would accompany Riemenschneider, shape his views and motivate his actions on his life's journey as a missionary in New Zealand.

The church and its pastors were one very important influence in the formation of the future missionary's character and his faith. The other important factor was his family and he gratefully acknowledged this.

Johann Friedrich Riemenschneider was born in Bremen in midsummer, at one o'clock in the afternoon on 6 August 1817.[14] His father, Anton Conrad

---

12. See Wenig, *op. cit.*, pp. 138 f.
13. See L. Tiesmeyer, *Eine deutsche Missionsarbeit auf Neu-Seeland. Lebensgeschichte des Missionars J. Fr. Riemenschneider.* Bremen: W. Valett & Co., 1875, pp. 4 f.
14. For information on the Riemenschneider family history I am most gratefully indebted to Christa Lütjen of the *Gesellschaft für Familienforschung, E. V.*, Bremen.

Riemenschneider, had been born in Bremen and baptised in the church of St Stephani. His son would later also be baptised at the same church. Anton Conrad's mother, Anna Dorothea Leonore Riemenschneider (née Fronen) came from Lüneburg, ca. 150 km. east of Bremen. Johann Friedrich was the first child of the marriage, which had been celebrated in St Stephani five years earlier, on 26 October 1812. The marriage certificate makes interesting reading. The list of witnesses show the social milieu in which the couple moved: Johann Hinrich Sanders, aged 60, peddler; Johann Friedrich Schneppel, aged 47, clothes mender; Johann Friedrich Riemenschneider (the eldest brother of Anton Conrad), aged 36, saddler. The bride, whose parents had both died by the time she was married, and whose father's occupation is given as 'Invalid', could not recall the names of her grandparents. The certificate ends with the words: 'I [the officiating registrar] and all the parties have signed this except for the bride who cannot write'.[15]

At the time of Johann Friedrich's birth his father was 36 years old, and his mother had just turned 41, although this is not certain, since the records give her date of birth as 'ca. July 1776'. The household was situated in one of the poor districts of Bremen, the parish of St Stephani,[16] at 47 Pelzerstraße. This street no longer exists, having been obliterated in the bombing during the Second World War in which more than two-thirds of the houses in Bremen were destroyed.

When Johann Friedrich (his friends used the colloquial abbreviation Fritz)[17] was 16 months old, his mother gave birth to a second son, Justus Werner, who died four days later. In August 1820 a sister, Anna Metta, was born. It is likely that she may have been chronically ill or handicapped in some way. There appears to be no civil record of her marrying and on one occasion Riemenschneider, in a letter from New Zealand, refers to her as 'my suffering sister'.[18] After the missionary's death, his widow writes to Bremen inquiring whether Anna Metta is still alive. In her letter to the North German Mission Society she comments: 'Poor thing. I believe she is a great invalid'.[19] A further indication that Anna Riemenschneider may have been handicapped is that she does not appear to have been able to contribute economically to the family.

Riemenschneider's father, Anton Conrad, is described in official documents as an 'artisan weaver, also casual labourer'. His weaving trade would have placed him into an occupation that was steadily losing out in the struggle for economic survival in the first half of the 19th century. During Napoleon's blockade of the European continent, England and Ireland had continued

---

15. *Zivilstandsregister Bremen, Heiraten*, 1812/473. [Translated from German.]
16. Schwarzwälder, *op. cit.*, p. 86.
17. See RP I, 61, 62.
18. RP V, 101.
19. RP VIII, 267.

their transition from manual weaving to machine manufacture and from linen and wool to imported American cotton, which was cheaper and easier to work with. When the blockade was lifted, cheap British textiles flooded the German market and ended the livelihood of the traditional handloom weaver.[20] The household would therefore have been very poor and this is confirmed by the very few remarks that the adult Riemenschneider makes about his childhood.[21]

The marriage certificate describes Riemenschneider's mother as a seamstress. She would certainly have had to contribute to the family income, as was common in poor families. Young Johann Friedrich would also have had to do his share of looking after the household as soon as he was able. There are some indications that he had acquired some skills in cooking and housekeeping. It appears that among the group of missionaries sent to New Zealand by the North German Mission Society he was initially the only one who knew how to cook a meal.[22]

There is very little information about Riemenschneider's schooling. His parents could not afford to send him to one of the many Bremen schools that charged fees. So the boy had to attend a so-called *Freischule*, one of eight schools that had been established in 1823 for 'poor children'. The education offered by these schools was not of a very high standard but it was considered 'appropriate for the class of children that belongs there'.[23] The school Riemenschneider attended was most probably the one in the *Öhlmühlenstraße*, a short distance on the way to the centre of Bremen from the St Stephani church. Before being able to attend the *Freischule*, Riemenschneider would have had to learn the basics of reading, probably at a so-called *Klippschule*. Children were not admitted to the *Freischule* until they had acquired the rudiments of reading, by which time they had usually reached the age of eight.[24]

In addition to the *Freischule*, the young boy also appears to have attended the Sunday School of St Stephani. Unlike today's Sunday schools, these were remedial schools in which, in addition to religion, Christian volunteers taught reading, writing and basic arithmetic in an effort to supplement the tuition provided in the secular schools for the poor.

It was at school that Riemenschneider had his first encounter with the overseas mission of the church. It appears to have made a lasting impression

---

20. See Wilhelm Treue, 'Wirtschafts-und Sozialgeschichte Deutschlands im 19. Jahrhundert'. *Handbuch der deutschen Geschichte*. Ed. Bruno Gebhard, Vol III, Stuttgart, 1960, pp. 314–413, 378.
21. See also note 26, below.
22. RP I, 24. In the joint diary that the missionaries kept when they lived together in Moutere in 1844, Riemenschneider figures as cook much more often than any of his three companions. In the entry for 6 January he notes: 'I therefore looked after the household as is usual when I am here'.
23. Schwarzwälder, *op. cit.*, pp. 112–113.
24. Friedrich Entholt, *Bilder aus der Geschichte des bremischen Volksschulwesens. Ergänzt und fortgesetzt von Hinrich Wulff.* Bremen: G. Winters Buchhandlung (1928), p. 110.

on the young boy. Here is how he describes it:

> I vividly remember how in my ninth year of age (that was 1826) Mr Meierdirks, who was my dear schoolteacher at the time, read to us one afternoon one of the first 'Bremen Mission Journals' which contained an article about West Africa and the propagation of the Gospel among the Negroes there. It was the first time that I heard anything about a mission to the heathen, and it was something that was quite overwhelming for me ...

The teacher promised that he would read from further issues of the journal if the majority of the class found it interesting. When this turned out not to be the case the readings were discontinued, much to the disappointment of Riemenschneider. He continues:

> ... my very poor parents and I did not know how the journals could be obtained and I was too shy to ask my teacher for them. But the impressions which I had received from that first journal remained firmly in my mind, and even if my inner vocation does not stem from this point it nevertheless marks the beginning of my inward and heartfelt desire to serve the Lord as messenger of the Gospel, and that preferably in West Africa.[25]

The young boy himself had to work to contribute to the family income. For some years, most probably in his early teens, he worked as an errand boy for the family of a Bremen merchant, E. G. Suffert, and, according to one of his letters, there was at least one other employer after Suffert.[26] Who this other employer was is not known but there are some indications that it may have been a cabinet maker. In the 'Special Instructions' that the North German Mission Society issued to the four missionaries on their departure for New Zealand, there is a comment to the effect that Riemenschneider is not inexperienced in the cabinet making trade'.[27]

With school, and work before and after school, there would not have been much free time. The young man did, however, find time to belong to the Bremer *Jünglingsverein*, which was founded by Pastor Treviranus when Riemenschneider was 17 years of age.[28] This club, the first in Germany, was based on an idea first implemented in Basel. It provided comfortable rooms

---

25. RP V, 294/295. It is interesting to note that Riemenschneider's fellow missionary, J. F. H. Wohlers, was also first attracted to mission work by a pamphlet on missions that he idly picked up in a mill office while waiting for his uncle's corn to be ground. (See Sheila Natusch, *Brother Wohlers. A biography of J. F. H. Wohlers of Ruapuke.* Christchurch: Pegasus, 1969, pp. 28–31.
26. RP II, 29, 77: 'As a lad I was constantly in and out of that family's house, being employed for running errands etc. ... As I grew up more I went to another master, and since Sufferts are society people and I only a poor errand boy any further contact between me and the family ceased.'
27. *Besondere Anweisung für die von der Norddeutschen Missionsgesellshaft nach Neuseeland ausgesandten Missionare Wohlers, Riemenschneider, Trost und Heine,* § 6. North German Mission Society, Papers, Staatsarchiv Bremen (BSA), 7.1025. 81/5.
28. See Tiesmeyer, *op. cit.*

with books, writing materials, etc., mainly for apprentices and journeymen who needed a place to stay when they were not working or sleeping, and whose employers would not let them use their living rooms. It is highly likely that Riemenschneider belonged to the association whose members formed the initial membership of the *Jünglingsverein*, the *Missionsjünglingsverein* (Missionary Youth Fellowship), a club for young men who were interested in missions. So, both at Sunday School and in what little spare time he had, Riemenschneider was in an environment where missions were discussed and supported, and where missionaries were seen as people in the forefront of Christian endeavour.

While Riemenschneider was growing up, the organisation that was to send him to New Zealand was also in its formative years. The founding of the Bremen Mission Society in 1819, and the involvement in this society by Treviranus, the leader of the Bremen Sunday School, has already been mentioned. The Hamburg Society was founded in 1822 and was followed by other such societies all over North Germany. Originally these societies saw themselves as auxiliaries to the established missions in Berlin, Basel and elsewhere. They raised money for these missions, held meetings, organised mission festivals, and some even published newsletters. In this way the mission aspect of the church's work was advanced by dedicated and enthusiastic lay people under the encouragement and guidance of interested clergy. Most of the local mission societies were interdenominational. Although some were based on Lutheran and others on Reformed congregations, the Lutherans accepted Reformed members while the Reformed had no objections to Lutheran members. There was no organisation formally linking the various local auxiliary societies.

Initial moves towards closer relations between the local societies were made by the society of Stade, a small town in what was then the kingdom of Hannover in Lower Saxony. The Stade society invited all the neighbouring societies to their mission festival in 1834. Mallet and Treviranus attended as representatives from Bremen. In the course of the gathering, one of the participants was inspired to become a missionary. The local mission societies did not have the means to train their own missionaries, which meant the candidate would have to go to a mission training institution in Basel or Berlin. In order to maintain links with North Germany the candidate approached the Stade society and asked whether the North German societies could send him into the mission field. The North German Mission Society was subsequently formed, partly as a result of this request, and in its first report the following comment is made:

> [The request] raised the question whether the northern societies had already reached their potential by being mere auxiliary societies for distant societies and

institutes, and whether, if this question had to be answered in the negative, it would not be timely to consider uniting to form an independent society.[29]

After a further meeting in Stade in 1835, the North German Mission Society was formally founded in Hamburg on 9 April 1836. It was initially a small band of six local societies. By 1846 the number had grown to 13,[30] but many other societies, while not aspiring to full membership, sent financial contributions.

As a federation of local societies, the North German Society developed a rather cumbersome constitution. The document that was drawn up stipulated that all member societies had to be consulted in the making of important decisions, such as the choice of candidates for missionary work and the choice of a mission field. Most of these decisions were made at the annual general meeting. An executive committee, the *Verwaltungsausschuß*, based in Hamburg until 1850, was appointed to carry out the decisions of the general meetings. The general meeting, however, jealously guarded its right to make decisions so that the *Verwaltungsausschuß* often could not react with the necessary speed and authority to changing situations in the field. This cumbersome structure would subsequently create problems for Riemenschneider and other North German missionaries in New Zealand and elsewhere.

An important principle underlying the work of the North German Mission Society is enshrined in § 2 of its statutes. The principle anchors the interdenominational stance of the Society by insisting that the denominational differences should not be exported to the mission field, but that 'the churches among the heathen will be formed according to local conditions'.[31]

This principle, while laudable, was to cause major problems for the Society for a number of years, and it appears to have prevented some Lutheran societies from joining – on the grounds that they did not wish to work together with their Reformed brethren.[32]

One of the major questions that faced the new Mission Society was whether to train their own missionaries or ask one of the other societies to accept North German missionaries for training. At the second annual general meeting, which was held in Bremen 19–22 May 1837, it was decided that in order to ensure that future missionaries would see the North German Mission Society as their 'home' society, a training institution should be founded. Johann Hartwig Brauer, then aged 33, a candidate of theology,[33] was appointed

---

29. 1. Bericht der Norddeutschen Missionsgesellschaft, 1837, p. 6. BSA 7.1025. 83/3.
30. Hahn, Ernst Joachim, "Die Geschichte der Norddeutschen Missionsgesellschaft", Dissertation, Tübingen, 1943, p. 11.
31. Quoted by Eva Schöck-Quinteros and Dieter Lenz (eds), *150 Jahre Norddeutsche Mission*. Bremen: Norddeutsche Mission, 1986, p. 1. [Translated from German].
32. Hahn, *op. cit.*, p. 6.
33. A 'candidate' had completed studying theology at university but had not yet been examined for ordination and ordained as a pastor.

as teacher, and the Society opened the doors of its new training institution on 30 October 1837 in a rented house in Hamburg, Stadtdeich 70.[34] The young teacher, now Inspector Brauer, had already made a name for himself in Hamburg's revivalist circles and he appears to have had a strong and rather severe personality. In addition to his teaching duties he took a great interest in the Mission Society and was a member of the *Verwaltungsausschuß*.

The first intake of the training institution consisted of four students, one of whom was Johann Friedrich Riemenschneider. Of the other three, one later left the institution because he was considered to be unsuitable; another, Johann Heinrich Trost, farmer, left because he could not cope intellectually with the work; the third, Johann Friedrich Heinrich Wohlers, farmer, completed the course along with Riemenschneider and they became firm friends. A fifth student, Johann Wilhelm Christoph Heine, shoemaker, joined the institution soon after its establishment and also completed the course.

At the same Bremen annual general meeting at which the decision was made to found a training institution, the 20-year-old Riemenschneider was presented to the meeting as a candidate for training as a missionary. It must have been an ordeal for the young man from a poor family to have to face the delegates, most of whom were clergy or respectable (i.e. fairly wealthy) lay people. Thus, they were socially superior to Riemenschneider and his family – a matter that was important, particularly in Bremen with its strict social hierarchy. Whatever his feelings were, he seems to have acquitted himself well and having his parish minister (Mallet) as sponsor must have been a great help to him. The minutes recorded at this meeting are a dry, matter-of-fact record of what must have been an intense emotional experience for the candidate. Page 12 of the minutes for 19 May 1838 reads:

> Pastor Mallet introduced Riemenschneider from Bremen to the Society as someone who has wished for the last three years to become a missionary, so that the Society could finally meet him.
>
> After a lengthy discussion with him all brothers expressed agreement that he met with their approval. After Pastor Mallet had given more detail about Riemenschneider's conduct, faith, abilities and also his circumstances, and after he had remarked that he had been in close contact with him over the last three years, Pastor Mallet moved on behalf of the Bremen society that Riemenschneider be admitted on probation as a pupil of the North German Mission Society. All deputies agreed unanimously that Riemenschneider should be admitted as a pupil.[35]

The summer of 1837 was Riemenschneider's final one at home in Bremen,

---

34. Like so many buildings associated with Riemenschneider's youth, the building that housed the training institution has not survived the Second World War. It was on the banks of the Elbe River and was destroyed in the heavy bombing raids on Hamburg.
35. BSA 7.1025. 83/3.

and it cannot have been easy. His decision to train for the mission field had a tremendous impact on his family. The departure for Hamburg, and thus the loss of an income, meant that the family was no longer economically viable and Tiesmeyer, Riemenschneider's first biographer, reports that his father at this point entered the poor house while 'Christian friends would look after his mother and sister'.[36] Both parents later died as paupers. The mother's death in 1855 was reported to the authorities by the paupers' warden (*Armenaufseher*),[37] while the father's death six years later was reported by the administrator of the poor house.[38] Like all the other pupils in the training institution, the trainee had free board and tuition but he was not paid a salary even when he was in full-time mission service in New Zealand, until his marriage in 1849. Even then his salary was scarcely sufficient to feed and clothe his family, let alone help his impoverished parents.

The instruction Riemenschneider received at the Society's training institution from Inspector Brauer was obviously different from the rigorously academic theological education given at university to aspiring pastors of the German church. The missionary training at the Hamburg institution was nevertheless broad and intensive. Initially, because there were just four pupils, Brauer could devote his time to individual tuition where necessary. The syllabus was certainly wide-ranging. It included: introduction to and interpretation of the Holy Scripture, biblical history, church history, catechism, religious doctrine, ethics, symbolics, pastoral theology, missiology, biblical geography, general astronomy, comparative geography, general science, anatomy, German, English, arithmetic, elementary algebra, writing, drawing, singing and piano lessons. The latter two were dropped after some time but, for a period, Riemenschneider and Wohlers had some tuition in Latin and the biblical languages of Greek and Hebrew.

The pupils' day at the training institution was carefully structured. In the same report in which Brauer recommends that Riemenschneider be taught the ancient languages he describes the working day at the training institution:

> The pupils get up at half past five when they first of all have to make their beds and clean their rooms. In the meantime water for tea is placed in the hallway so that they can make their morning drink. For each one of them there is a cup as well as milk in a cupboard in the hallway. At quarter to seven we have morning prayers and then class instruction follows without a break until 10 o'clock. Breakfast is eaten next consisting of tea, bread and butter. After that, if it seems appropriate or necessary, class instruction is continued until we have reached the goal set for the session. Next individual students are taught in those subjects which they need to take on their own or separately. Often individual

---

36. Tiesmeyer, *op. cit.*, p. 7.
37. *Zivilstandsregister Bremen, Sterbefälle*, 1855, p. 308, No. 618.
38. *Zivilstandsregister Bremen, Sterbefälle*, 1861, p. 452, No. 903.

tuition starts straight after breakfast. At one o'clock at the latest the teaching is finished, often as early as noon. We generally work until the midday meal at one o'clock or half past one. The meal is finished at two o'clock, and then there is physical work or exercise until four o'clock or longer. At four o'clock water for tea is brought up again and work goes on until eight o'clock. Dinner is at eight o'clock, and consists of tea, bread and butter. At 10 o'clock evening prayers are held, and at half past ten everybody goes to bed.[39]

In addition to the formal instruction the missionary candidates were also given the opportunity to learn public speaking at mission gatherings and they received experience in pastoral work by being invited to make house visits in the Hamburg parish in which the institution was located.

In the papers that have survived, Riemenschneider virtually never comments on his days in the training institution. To obtain some glimpses of him while he was preparing himself for his vocation, it is necessary to read Brauer's reports and the autobiography of one of Riemenschneider's fellow students who was sent out to New Zealand with him, Johann Friedrich Heinrich Wohlers.

Brauer characterises the trainee in his early years at the institution:

Riemenschneider of Bremen, 20 years old, is a lively young man, full of life, full of faith with a sincere heart, and full of enthusiasm for his vocation. In addition to his child-like nature he is also equipped with a particular modesty. This has developed due to the various circumstances of life that he has had to endure. His gifts were somewhat buried but they have come out beautifully and have carved a path for themselves. He is completely sure of his vocation. ... He also possesses a high degree of manual dexterity. He has been a great blessing for the institution and also a great support, since he soon established a close relationship with candidate Wohlers who finds such a prop and encouragement comforting ...[40]

Another report states that Riemenschneider went on a hike with other pupils in 1839 and that in the same year he did not do too well with his arithmetic.[41] In 1841 he seems to have suffered from a liver complaint, as on 15 June of that year he was sent to a spa to take the waters to improve his health. While this seems to have helped somewhat he was excused from some lessons for the rest of the year to prevent any recurrence of illness. This liver complaint would surface throughout Riemeschneider's adult life. It could have been a chronic or recurring condition that would have contributed to his frequent episodes of ill health that were to affect him and his work in New Zealand.[42]

---

39. Bericht des Inspektors über die Bildungs Anstalt der Norddeutschen Missions Gesellschaft am 21. December 1839 (BSA 7.1025. 83/4).
40. Ibid.
41. Ibid.
42. Bericht des Inspektors über die Bildungs Anstalt der Norddeutschen Missions Gesellschaft zum

Wohlers's account provides a more personal view. The farmer, Wohlers, from the village of Hoyerhagen near Bremen and the younger city boy Riemenschneider seem to have struck up a firm friendship almost as soon as they met. In his autobiography Wohlers characterises their relationship:

> At the same time [in autumn 1837] Riemenschneider came from Berlin [Bremen!], and entered as a new pupil. We were soon intimate friends, for we both came from the committee in Bremen, were both of the Weser district, and spoke in leisure hours both the same Bremen Weser low German language. We had both a great desire to learn, and both loved our inspector Brauer in our inmost souls. Riemenschneider had had a better education than I had, and had later and better opportunities for self-cultivation. But yet, by means of the instruction imparted to me in the summer in Hamburg, we both were on a level and made equal progress. In learning our lessons, so far as a matter of understanding them was concerned, I made more progress than he did, perhaps because I had greater health, and could bring greater exertion to bear on them; but in fineness of feeling, and in admiration of all that was noble and beautiful, he was my superior.[43]

By 1838 the North German Mission Society had developed to a point where it now had a constitution, regular financial contributions to its work, a training institution, and some trainee missionaries, but it still did not have a mission field. This deficit had been discussed a number of times. Finally, at the annual general meeting of 1841, which was held in Ritzebüttel, a small hamlet near Cuxhaven and home of one of the constituent societies, a tentative decision was made to establish a field in East India. This had been on the recommendation of Inspector Brauer who had visited England in May of that year to seek the advice of the London Missionary Society, the Wesleyan Missionary Society and the Church Missionary Society (CMS).[44] The Executive Committee of the CMS discussed Brauer's letter on 18 May, 1841 and recorded in the minutes:

> Read a letter from the Rev J. Hartwig Brauer, dated London, the 12th inst., stating that the North German Missionary Society at Hamburg is about to commence Missionary operations, that its attention is at present directed to India, but that it is anxious not to interfere with the present or prospective

---

Schluß des Jahres 1841 (BSA 7.1025. 83/4).
43. *Memories of the Life of J. F. H. Wohlers, Missionary at Ruapuke, New Zealand. An Autobiography*. Translated from the German by John Houghton. Dunedin: Otago Daily Times and Witness Newspapers, 1895, pp. 29–30.
44. There had been close relations between the Church Missionary Society (CMS), which sent the first missionaries to New Zealand, and German interests. Some of the first missionaries that offered to serve with the CMS were German Lutherans and one of the early meetings was hamstrung by the fact that nobody on the CMS committee spoke German, while the German candidates were unable to speak English. See Robert Glen, 'Those odious evangelicals', in: *Mission and Moko; Aspects of the Work of the Church Missionary Society in New Zealand 1814–1882*, ed. Robert Glen., Christchurch: Latimer Fellowship of New Zealand, 1992, p. 28.

operations of any other Missionary Society, and requesting information of the Stations now occupied by the CMS or which it may hereafter occupy, and, in what portion of the heathen world the Committee of the CMS would deem advisable for the North German Society to commence its labours.[45]

By the 1842 annual general meeting of the North German Mission Society, however, Brauer and the members of the *Verwaltungsausschuß*, had changed their minds. Initially, the Chatham Islands, situated some 420 miles south east of Wellington, New Zealand, had been briefly considered at the request of the Hamburg Syndic, Karl Sieveking. He had formed a colonisation company and planned to establish a German colony there after buying the islands from the New Zealand Company for £10,000. The problem was that the New Zealand Company did not have legal title to the islands and the British government, backed by a legal opinion, declared that the Chathams were to be part of the colony of New Zealand.[46]

By the time Brauer and the *Verwaltungsausschuß* proposed New Zealand to the annual general meeting in 1842, this country had become well known as a possible field for missionary labours both in the various member societies and among the wider population of North Germany. In 1838 two Māori sailors who had signed on as crew on the first Bremen whaler to visit New Zealand, had visited Bremen. This visit was well publicised in a series of newspaper articles.[47] Also, a small boy, the son of an Englishman and a Māori woman, had come to Bremen as the guest of the captain of the whaler and had been introduced to the Bible and Mission Society of Stade by Mallet. In 1839 one of the talks given to the Hamburg Evangelical Mission Society was entitled, 'The history of the mission on New Zealand and the Society Islands from their first beginnings to the present day. An overview'.[48]

In May 1839 the Bremen senator W. A. Fritze wrote a confidential letter to the general meeting of the Society, indicating that he was about to send a whaler to New Zealand, and offering to transport missionaries free of charge, if the Society should decide to make New Zealand its first mission field. The only recompense Fritze requested in return for the passage was that the missionaries should act as the ship's chaplains.

While the pupils in the training institution were not considered sufficiently

---

45. CMS Committee Minutes, vol. 20, p. 53 (see Church Missionary Society, Papers, Auckland University Library Microfilm Collection).
46. See Patricia Burns, *Fatal Success. A History of the New Zealand Company*. Auckland: Heinemann Reed, 1989, p. 243; Rhys Richards, 'Plans for a German Colony on the Chatham Islands', in: *The German Connection. New Zealand and German-Speaking Europe in the Nineteenth Century*. Auckland: Oxford University Press, 1993, pp. 46–51.
47. See Peter Oettli, 'Two early Māori travellers in Germany', *Archifacts* (October 1991), 1–11.
48. *Sechzehnter Bericht des evangelischen Missionsvereins in Hamburg, vom Jahre 1839*. Hamburg: Evangelischer Missionsverein, 1839.

trained to be sent out yet, the North German Mission Society did nevertheless have a candidate, a young man by the name of Mengert who had been trained in the Basle Mission Society training institution. On 23 May 1839 the general meeting decided to accept Mr Fritze's offer of free transport to send Mengert to New Zealand. However nothing came of the plan because Mengert failed the examination set by the Society.[49]

Fritze, who was determined to look after the spiritual welfare of his whaler crew, approached another mission society, run by Johannes Evangelista Gossner in Berlin, and Gossner managed to find him a suitable chaplain, named A. W. Müller. Fritze now offered the North German Mission Society Müller's services. Müller, Fritze wrote, could draw up a report about the suitability of New Zealand as a mission field, and to assist with this task he requested that the Society furnish him with a set of questions. A set of 16 questions was therefore prepared and despatched to Müller.

The questions that were formulated were far too broad and complex for the humble young ship's chaplain. For each locality he visited, Müller was to report on how many people lived in the immediate and wider neighbourhood; whether they lived in peace 'among themselves and with others'; how they felt about Europeans; how much contact they had with Europeans; how close did Europeans live to them and what kind of Europeans were they. Question 9 is more specific and asks: 'What vices are rife among the people and are they cannibals?'[50] Müller would have had to have the skills of a trained anthropologist as well as a knowledge of the Māori language, and he would have had to spend a great deal more time than the few weeks that could be spared from whaling to provide adequate answers to the questions posed for him. His report is therefore very cursory and quite inadequate. Müller himself was painfully aware of this and apologises at the beginning of the document, which he sent to the North German Mission Society on 9 March 1842. The report consists mainly of hearsay and rather naive and superficial observations. It did however contain considerable encouragement for the North Germans. Müller writes:

> [In Kororareka][51] no further missionary would find a field of endeavour, but here as well as everywhere we have been, the Germans are loved and desired very much, particularly since the native nation may well have a lot in common with the Germans.[52]

Brauer was well aware of the shortcomings of the Müller report. In his report to the Society's 1842 annual general meeting he remarks: 'It cannot really

---

49. See *Jahresbericht of the Verwaltungsausschuß* for 1840.
50. BSA 7.1025. 81/2.
51. The present-day Russell in the Bay of Islands.
52. BSA 7.1025. 81/2.

be denied that [Müller's] communications have a certain romantic tinge'[53] Nevertheless, he concludes that Müller's comments agree on the whole with the reports of the Wesleyan and Church Missionary Society missionaries. His summary of the situation from his perspective was as follows:

> The undeniable findings of all recent reports about the mission in New Zealand is that amongst the people a great desire for the Gospel has awakened; that a path is being opened for its preaching, often in mysterious ways; that missionaries appear to be necessary in order to direct the stream of life that is beginning to flow into sensible channels; that the political circumstances, at least in the northern island, are turning out favourably, that European immigration therefore is increasing considerably, but that missionary work becomes all the more necessary the more the Europeans become responsible for the introduction of European lusts and vices which spread like a cancer.[54]

In the same report, Riemenschneider's suitability for a posting to New Zealand is assessed:

> For Riemenschneider's physical wellbeing New Zealand, with its German climate, would be suitable. His health would not be impaired as much by mental occupation that is not incessant but interspersed with physical activity, indeed the latter would undoubtedly strengthen him again. He can turn his hand to anything and knows how to make himself very useful in the household, his only problem is he does not know how to deal properly with money. He is a good-natured person and can be very simple and kind-hearted if he is not goaded into giving himself airs by making grandiloquent speeches. Amongst a primitive race his somewhat buried naturalness will appear again and he and Wohlers will be in their proper places in New Zealand.

The annual general meeting accepted the recommendation that Riemenschneider and Wohlers should seek ordination and then be sent to New Zealand as missionaries. They were to be accompanied by two unordained assistants, J. W. C. Heine[55] and J. H. Trost. The latter, after his withdrawal from the North German training institution, had worked in the *Rauhes Haus*, a Hamburg institution for destitute children. Another missionary who was a university trained theologian, was to be sent to India. It appears that the Society felt that Riemenschneider's and Wohlers's training was not up to the intellectual rigour required for converting the Indians, but was adequate for converting the Māori of New Zealand. In addition, a doctor had advised that because of his ill health in the previous year, Riemenschneider was too delicate to withstand the Indian climate.[56]

---

53. *Vorschläge über die erste Aussendung der Norddeutschen Missions Gesellschaft*, BSA 7.1025. 81/5.
54. BSA, *loc.cit.*
55. Heine subsequently passed his final examinations set by the institution but he was not ordained because he suffered from a severe hearing disability.
56. *Monatsblatt der Norddeutschen Missions-Gesellschaft* [henceforth *Monatsblatt*], 3 (1842), 255.

The Society does not appear to have bothered to ask the two ordained missionaries themselves about their views regarding a field for their labours. Neither of them particularly wanted to go to New Zealand. Riemenschneider confessed years later that his goal had always been to bring the Gospel to West Africa.[57]

Wohlers also seems to have had misgivings about being sent to New Zealand. In his autobiography he comments, rather more laconically, 'when at last New Zealand was chosen, I could not rejoice over it'.[58]

The 1842 annual general meeting had made the general decision, and now it was up to the *Verwaltungsausschuß* to put it into practice. A sub-committee was formed whose membership included Inspector Brauer and which reported to the *Verwaltungsausschuß* on 11 August. While Brauer appears to have been well informed about missions in general, the report, on the basis of which the Society took action, contains a major error that was to cause great problems for the missionaries once they arrived in New Zealand. While discussing the question of which island the missionaries should be sent to, and having dismissed the North Island because it had already been occupied by English missionaries, it states:

> The southern of the two large islands, New Munster, on the other hand, has so far not a single mission station, nor a single missionary. So here there is a fine area in which the natives urgently need missionaries ...[59]

This was of course no longer true. The Wesleyan Samuel Ironside had established a mission post in Cloudy Bay, on the north-eastern tip of the South Island in December 1840, while another Wesleyan, James Watkin, had settled as a missionary among the Māori of Waikouaiti, on the east coast, north of present-day Dunedin, six months earlier.[60]

Since 1839, Edward Gibbon Wakefield's New Zealand Company had been advertising for colonists in German newspapers. In that year it had appointed an agent in Bremen and later another in Hamburg. The Hamburg agent, John Nicholas Beit, had recruited a number of German artisans and farmers for Sieveking's abortive Chatham Islands colony, which he had intended to lead. Beit now managed to persuade the investors and prospective colonists to go instead to the British New Zealand Company settlement in Nelson, at the northern end of the South Island of New Zealand. Finally, his propaganda convinced the North German Mission Society to purchase an allotment of land from the Company. Beit himself purchased five allotments, parcels of

---

57. RP V, 295.
58. *Memories of the Life of J. F. H. Wohlers, op. cit.*, p. 37.
59. BSA 7.1025. 81/5.
60. W. A. Chambers, *Samuel Ironside in New Zealand 1839–1858*. Auckland: Ray Richards Publisher, 1982.

which he later sold on to prospective German settlers. The Mission Society's allotment, like all New Zealand Company allotments, was to consist of a one-acre 'town acre' section, a 50-acre 'suburban' or 'accommodation' section and 150 acres of rural land.[61]

With this purchase, the temporal well-being of the missionaries seemed to be assured. The farmer Trost and the shoemaker Heine were given the task of establishing a mission farm, which was to provide food and income for the four missionaries. At the same time it was to provide an investment that could finance the Society's operations in New Zealand.

Because communications between Hamburg and New Zealand were slow and could be haphazard, the Society was anxious to ensure that it should not lose control over any aspect of the mission venture. To this end it issued the missionaries with two detailed sets of instructions, one labelled 'general', the other 'special'. In particular the 'Special Instructions' describe the detail in which the Society wanted to regulate the life and work of its missionaries in an environment about which it had very little reliable information. The instructions require the four missionaries to first of all choose the land, insofar as it had not already been allocated by the Company, and then establish the mission farm. For this task, Wohlers and Riemenschneider are specifically enjoined to participate and not to shirk manual labour under the pretext of their clerical calling. § 6 of the 'Special Instructions' spells it out:

> There will be workers available for wages but in a land where the heathen still have to be led towards civilisation, the preachers must also lend a hand in outward things. By this they will not detract from their office but they will engender trust in themselves and thus also in their office. In this they must not be led astray in any way by the immigrants and argue that their ministerial position amongst them would suffer. They should consider and keep in mind at all times that they are not sent to the settlers in the first instance but rather to the heathen. The apostle Paul, who wove carpets, must be an example and model for the missionaries.[62]

Two years later, after he had established his first mission station in the bush-clad wilderness of the upper Mōkau River on the West Coast of the central North Island of New Zealand, a rather disgruntled Riemenschneider comments on this passage of the 'Special Instructions':

> To be ashamed of [physical] work, particularly here in the bush, would be foolishness. The greatest heathen apostle wove carpets. However I am utterly convinced that if making carpets had been such a hindrance to him in the main

---

61. See Ruth Allan, *Nelson: A History of Early Settlement*. Wellington: A. H. & A. W. Reed, 1965, p. 310-311; Patricia Burns, *op. cit.*, p. 180.
62. *Besondere Anweisung für die von der Norddeutschen Missionsgesellschaft nach Neuseeland ausgesandten Missionare Wohlers, Riemenschneider, Trost und Heine*. BSA 7.1025. 81/5.

purpose of his mission as my current circumstances are, he would very quickly have put an end to that secular business.⁶³

Once the farm has been established, the 'Special Instructions' continue, the ordained missionaries should then move out to live and work among the Māori. In § 11, the instructions order that every week or fortnight the preachers are to return to the farm if possible in order to maintain contact with each other and their assistants. The instructions clearly assume that there would be sufficient Māori to occupy two missionaries within a convenient distance of the farm, and that there would be adequate roads to enable the missionaries to gather regularly at the farm. Neither would turn out to be the case when they arrived in New Zealand.

When the missionaries are together the instructions require that they provide an enormous number of written reports. They ask for copies of a half-yearly financial statement, a quarterly inventory of equipment, a register of new equipment, separate accounts of farm income, copies of individual diaries of each missionary, a quarterly report written by Wohlers, copied by Heine and signed by each of the missionaries, plus a general diary kept by Riemenschneider and signed daily by all present. According to the instructions this diary must contain 'a thermometer reading for morning, midday and evening according to the Reaumur scale, the barometer reading in figures, e.g. 28.1. 27.9. Furthermore the weather and the wind must be entered'.

In addition to breaking in a farm and writing copious reports and diaries, each of the missionaries is assigned a special portfolio. Thus, Riemenschneider is entrusted with the responsibility for the maintenance of the common undergarments, all bed linen and, incongruously, the sacred utensils.

Lest the missionaries should wantonly spend mission funds on personal luxuries the instructions exhort them to live as frugally as possible. § 20 makes it clear that the way of life of the missionaries 'cannot be simple enough'. It advises that the chests in which their equipment is sent out will make excellent wardrobes. § 21 contains the sentence:

> The missionaries are most urgently admonished to treat all things as carefully as possible and to exercise greatest care to keep everything, particularly also their clothing, in the best possible order.

The missionaries were given no salary. In the meantime, the Society regarded the sum of £300 sufficient to meet all their expenses.⁶⁴ To ensure that they had at least something to spend without having to account for every penny, the missionaries were each given five shillings per month as pocket money. As

---

63. RP II, 271.
64. In contrast, the single missionary who was sent to India was granted £150! (Hahn, *op. cit.*, p. 39).

far as the temporal well-being of the missionaries was concerned, the Society had obviously taken to heart a somewhat unkind comment in the sub-committee's report that recommended the posting of the four missionaries to New Zealand:

> ... after the first years [the mission] will not require considerable expenditure, particularly as the pupils [of the training institution] have certainly not been brought up to make great demands with regard to their life style – something that may happen among English missionaries who, without their English *comfort*, do not feel *comfortable* and yet have to be *comfortable*.[65]

The Society was not quite as parsimonious, as may be assumed from the 'Instructions', in purchasing equipment for the missionaries. Nevertheless questions must have been asked, since a report justifying the expenditure was written in October 1843.[66] The report explains that, since the Society did not expect to be able to send anything to New Zealand for at least the next two-and-a-half to three years, and since the missionaries were expected to break in the land to establish a farm and erect a dwelling, the equipment had to be adequate for the task. The missionaries were accompanied by a large number of chests containing farming implements, including a plough with replacement shares, building tools, shoemaking tools and leather for the shoemaker Heine, a modest library and church registers, iron bedsteads and bedding, and clothing according to the station of each missionary – the assistants were given more work clothing and only one black suit, the preachers extra white dickies and two black suits.

The inventory of equipment that was sent with the missionaries makes interesting reading. The book chest, for example, contained, besides devotional, theological and church history texts (including a copy of the Book of Common Prayer), a six-volume history of the world, a three-volume geography text, a 10-volume encyclopaedia, as well as general books on botany, zoology, medicine and a booklet on viticulture.

While the members of the Society were busy writing instructions, and purchasing and packing equipment for the voyage, the missionaries themselves were no less busy with their own personal preparations. Riemenschneider, Wohlers and Heine sat and passed the final examination of the training institution and arrangements had to be made for the ordination of Riemenschneider and Wohlers.

Riemenschneider's ordination does not appear to have presented any problems. After an appropriate examination he was ordained in Bremen on 21 September 1842, in the presence of his friends and family, by his mentor

---
65. BSA 7.1025. 81/5. [Translated from German. The words in italics are in English in the original.]
66. *Bericht über die Ausrüstung der ersten nach Neuseeland gesandten Missionare.* BSA 7.1025. 82/1.

and patron, Pastor Mallet. The ordination did not take place, as might have been expected, in St Stephani, the parish church where Riemenschneider had been baptised and confirmed. The ceremony was held at the Church of *Unser Lieben Frauen* (Our Dear Lady), which the burghers of Bremen had erected as a parish church outside the Bishop's cathedral precinct in the 13th century, and which was used for important civic ceremonies. No record of the ordination service appears to have survived, but many years later, when he almost despaired of the support of his Society and felt very isolated, lonely and depressed in New Zealand, Riemenschneider quotes a few sentences from the ordination sermon:

> Even if you cannot see any fruits of your labour, and even if not a single soul seems to pay attention to your voice – stand fast and remain *faithful*.[67]

The day of his ordination must have been a proud day for Riemenschneider, the son of paupers, who had now become a member of the highly respected clergy.[68] The documents of the North German Mission Society show that his pride did not go unnoticed. In a circular letter about the possible ordination of another missionary, written on 1 September 1848, there is the comment:

> We ourselves experienced with Riemenschneider, who is now worthy, that he had to struggle for almost four years to vanquish his pride, the source of which was mainly in his feeling that he parted from here as a reverend gentleman.[69]

The ordination of Wohlers, a Lutheran, presented some problems but, finally, the Senate of Hamburg agreed that he could be ordained in Hamburg provided that he submitted himself to a further examination and provided that he signed a declaration renouncing all rights to employment as a minister in Hamburg.

While the ordination services had been held in the churches of the ordinands' denomination, the service commissioning them was held in connection with an extraordinary general meeting of the North German Mission Society. It was thus an interdenominational celebration. It was held on 6 October, at 2 o'clock in the afternoon, in the church of the Holy Trinity, St Georg, in Hamburg.[70] In spite of the fact that it was an unpleasant, cold and rainy day,

---

67. RP III, 244.
68. The documents make it clear that Riemenschneider's ordination was not that of a pastor of the German Protestant church, but quite specifically as a 'missionary for the heathen world'. (Letter of 27 July 1842 from the Bremen Commission for Church Matters, BSA 7.1025. 81/5; Riemenschneider's ordination certificate, Heine Papers, Nelson Provincial Museum, folder B).
69. BSA 7. 1025.83/1.
70. The name of the church seems to have caused some problems for the reporter who described the service in the *Bremer Kirchenbote*. In the issue for Sunday, 16 October 1842, p. 162, he gives the church's name as St Georg. Pastor Mallet, who edited the publication and felt that the reporter had not given near enough weight to his sermon, issued a correction in the issue of the *Kirchenbote* for Sunday, 30 October, pp. 171–172.

the church was full and the service was a warm and emotionally charged occasion.[71] The printed order of service is still among the papers of the North German Mission Society.[72] Pastor Mallet delivered the commissioning sermon. His text was from the last two verses of the Gospel according to St Matthew: 'And Jesus came and said to them, "All authority in heaven and earth has been given to me. Go therefore and make disciples of all nations, baptizing them in the name of the Father and of the Son and of the Holy Spirit, teaching them to observe all that I have commanded you; and lo, I am with you always, to the close of the age"'. (Matthew 28, 18–20). The correspondent of the *Bremer Kirchenbote* described the ceremony as a 'heartwarming celebration that will remain unforgettable for all participants'.[73] After the formal service of commissioning, the delegates from the various mission societies who had come to Hamburg for the occasion, gathered at a farewell banquet where more speeches celebrated the momentous occasion.

The next two-and-a-half months were taken up with preparations and leave-taking. The Society also spent some money on the painting of portraits of each of the four missionaries for the training institution. Unfortunately the paintings have not survived. Shortly before the departure of the missionaries, a solemn farewell ceremony took place at the training institution, according to Wohlers.[74] It seems to have been the last official farewell.

Riemenschneider must have taken leave from his friends and family in Bremen when he was there for his ordination. On 31 October he received a last letter from a friend of his, J. H. Schniedewine, which makes reference to the fact that all the pain of parting in person is now behind them. It is a strange letter, full of flowery declarations of Christian love, describing Riemenschneider's calling in rather confused Christian imagery in pseudo-biblical language. What gives the letter its touching pathos is the postscript in which the writer switches to ordinary German and reports how he has just finished writing the letter at Riemenschneider's home and how they are now sitting there thinking of how they could send him a last token of their love and affection. They decided to send him some food, half a dozen of his favourite sausages, and the writer wishes Riemenschneider much enjoyment in eating them by switching language again, this time to *Plattdeutsch*, the low German

---

71. See *Bericht von der am 6. März 1843 abgehaltenen öffentlichen Jahresversammlung des Missionsvereins und der Bibelgesellschaft in Bremen*. Bremen, 1843, pp. 3–4.
72. BSA 7.1025. 81/5.
73. *Kirchenbote*, 16 October. 1842, p. 162. The *Bremer Kirchenbote* was an influential church newspaper. It was sufficiently important to be mentioned and commented on by Friedrich Engels in the literary journal, *Monatsblatt für gebildete Leser*, No. 181, 30 July 1840. Engels considered most of the other Bremen newspapers (apart from the *Bremisches Unterhaltungsblatt*) not even worthy of having their names listed in his article.
74. *Memories of the Life of J. F. H. Wohlers*, op. cit., p. 40.

Bremen dialect, which he and Riemenschneider's parents would have used.[75]

By the day of their departure, Boxing Day 1842, the missionaries had been trained, ordained, equipped and instructed, and they were ready for their first adventure – the voyage to the land of their destiny. This adventure and their arrival in Nelson, they soon found, would turn out to be a nightmare.

---

75. Letter in the Heine Papers, Nelson Provincial Museum, folder B.

Chapter Two

Strife at Sea and on Arrival in Nelson, 1843

RIEMENSCHNEIDER AND his fellow missionaries embarked on the *St Pauli*, a German ship of 380 tons, on a gloomy, cold and damp winter's day.[1] The *St Pauli*, under the command of Captain Schacht, had been chartered by the New Zealand Company to take the German settlers to Nelson. The 17 cabin and 123 steerage passengers had to travel for five hours down the river Elbe on the *Express,* a small steamer, because the *St Pauli* was already anchored that far downstream from the city of Hamburg.

As soon as the passengers had transferred to the *St Pauli*, Wohlers and Riemenschneider carried out their first official duty; they married five couples who had waited until they were embarked to undergo the ceremony in order to avoid having to pay marriage fees. The *St Pauli* spent the following day continuing to take on cargo, which gave the missionaries an extra day to settle in. Riemenschneider and Wohlers, the two 'gentlemen', were accommodated in the cabin, while the assistants Heine and Trost, travelled steerage. The journey down the Elbe River commenced on 28 December 1842 but, because of contrary winds, very little progress was made and by evening the ship had to anchor near Glückstadt to wait for an easterly wind. There was plenty of wind, but unfortunately from the wrong direction. The seas whipped up by a storm resulted in many passengers, including Riemenschneider, becoming seasick while they were still at anchor.

The *St Pauli* managed to leave the Elbe Estuary and reach the North Sea on the third of January 1843 but on the way encountered further storms. On Sunday, 8 January, both preachers were once again too sick to hold a service. A week later, on 15 January, the ship was still in the North Sea, buffeted by severe intermittent gales. Wohlers managed to conduct a short, informal service, while Riemenschneider remained bedridden with seasickness. Finally, on 17 January, almost three weeks after they had left Hamburg, the *St Pauli* at

---

1. *Memories of the Life of J. F. H. Wohlers, Missionary at Ruapuke, New Zealand. An Autobiography.* Translated from the German by John Houghton. Dunedin: Otago Daily Times and Witness Newspapers, 1895, p. 41.

last entered the English Channel. Four days later, on 21 January, they sailed out into the Atlantic Ocean.

There is a brief description of Riemenschneider's of the first few days of the voyage. He wrote a letter to his parents, which was handed to a ship in the Channel, sent to Bremen via England, and subsequently published in the *Bremer Kirchenbote*. On the day on which the *St Pauli* entered the Channel, the missionary writes:

> Our journey has not been the most pleasant so far, even though we have not had any accident. We went to sea on 3 January with a fairly favourable wind, but soon it became unfavourable, and already within the next few days we had storms which have raged repeatedly and several times really dreadfully. The waves broke several times even over the high after deck and it looked as if we were lost.
>
> In one of the storms, which blew from N.W and S.W., our sails and ropes tore apart. In the ship itself, everything that was not firmly secured went topsy-turvy. Our cabin was a scene of dreadful destruction, although people and things frequently fell over each other – something that admittedly happens even with less movement of the ship than was the case during the storm. Still last night one of the small daughters of Mr Beit fell forward with her chair, crashed into another which stood before her, and slid along the cabin with it.
>
> I had been in bed during the whole time of the storms, because I have suffered very severely from seasickness. Already on 3 January, when we reached the sea, I became ill and I have really only been able to get up a bit on the day before yesterday.[2]

Whilst the worst weather was now behind them, they were still experiencing occasional gales and periods of contrary winds in the Atlantic. But the missionaries and their fellow emigrants were to encounter worse problems than those caused by the weather. At dawn on the day the ship entered the Atlantic, Wohlers had to officiate at the burial of an infant. Then a small-pox epidemic spread amongst the steerage passengers, taxing the ship's doctor, Dr J. F. Göders to the utmost. No passengers died as a result of the illness, and fortunately, Heine and Trost were amongst the few steerage passengers who were not infected.

However neither the vicissitudes of the weather nor the widespread illness blighted the voyage as much as the behaviour of the New Zealand Company superintendent, John Nicholas Beit. Unlike other New Zealand Company ships, where the surgeon superintendent was in charge of the passengers, on the *St Pauli,* the two offices of ship's doctor and superintendent were divided among two people. As superintendent, Beit had considerable powers over the passengers. His responsibilities included the supervision of the 'tween deck passengers both with regard to their general behaviour and their overall

---

2. Vol. 12, no. 5, Saturday, 11 February, 1843, p. 20. [Translated from German.]

welfare. The superintendent was also charged with ensuring that there was an adequate standard of hygiene and diet.³ Beit had bought five allotments in the Nelson settlement and travelled in the cabin, together with his wife and 12 children. As soon as he had recovered from an initial bout of seasickness he moved to establish firm control over the emigrants. Already on 8 January he had asked the seasick Wohlers to accompany him to the 'tween deck where he ordered him to admonish the passengers, some of whom had, originally with his permission, stowed their work benches in the 'tween deck. Since this deck was for the accommodation of passengers, New Zealand Company regulations required that such items should be stored below. Beit himself, however had totally disregarded those regulations and had cluttered up the whole of the 'tween deck with his own baggage, once the inspectors of the Company had left the ship in Hamburg.

Every Sunday before the church service Beit mustered the steerage passengers on deck⁴ and there harangued them with abuse, threats and insults. After a number of such incidents the missionaries refused to conduct the service on the grounds that Beit's performances destroyed any worshipful feelings the passengers may have had. The atmosphere on board was further poisoned by a small network of informers who reported any behaviour that they considered subversive to Beit. The superintendent regarded any opposition to himself as an expression of mutiny. He dealt out punishments, such as fines and bread and water diets, at the slightest provocation.

Food was the major source of conflict between Beit and his passengers. According to the published New Zealand Company dietary regulations, each adult passenger was entitled to a daily ration of three quarters of a pound (340 g.) of biscuits, half a pound (227 g.) of meat and half a pound of flour. On four days of the week a quarter pound (114 g.) of rice or barley plus three quarters of a pound (340 g.) of preserved potatoes were issued; on the other three days one third of a pound (151 g.) of dried peas and half a pound (227 g.) of Sauerkraut. The beverage allowance on two days of the week was a quarter of an ounce (7 g.) of tea, on two other days an ounce (28 g.) of chocolate, on the other three, half an ounce (14 g.) of coffee. In addition the emigrants were entitled to a weekly allowance of three quarters of a pound (340 g.) of sugar, half a pound (227 g.) of butter, three ounces (84 g.) of suet, half a pound of raisins, a quarter of a pound of prunes, two ounces (56 g.) of salt, and half a pint (280 ml.) of vinegar. There was a daily allowance of three quarts (3.4 l.) of water.⁵

---
3. See Ruth M. Allan, *Nelson. A History of Early Settlement*. Wellington: A. H. & A. W. Reed, 1965, p. 116.
4. This muster, after which the surgeon superintendent would normally read prayers, was common practice on New Zealand Company ships. The idea was that the superintendent could check on the personal cleanliness of the passengers. (Ruth Allan, *loc. cit.*)
5. See Ruth Allan, *op. cit.*, p. 118. Allan's dietary table does not contain prunes or drinking chocolate.

During the early weeks the seasick passengers had obviously not felt up to eating very much. When their appetites improved, however, Beit refused to part with their entitlement of stores and the passengers went hungry. On 22 January, for example, Heine's midday dinner consisted of three small flour dumplings and ten prunes. According to his copy of the dietary table, which he read out to the hungry steerage passengers, on that day they would have been entitled to ship's biscuit, preserved meat, flour, raisins, rice, preserved potatoes, Sauerkraut, sugar and tea.

The Atlantic crossing, apart from the weather, seems to have been dominated by Beit's despotic behaviour, and the resulting hunger and mistrust that developed amongst the steerage passengers, combined with a decidedly icy atmosphere in the cabin. Conflicts such as this were not unusual for New Zealand Company ships, even though, on the whole they were well run. Even on a well-run ship the confinement of a large number of passengers in a small, cramped, uncomfortable space for months on end was bound to cause friction. Although the *St Pauli* had a competent captain and a good, though not very assertive, doctor, it was disastrously run by Beit. Patricia Burns, in her book on the New Zealand Company, describes the German agent as 'a villain straight out of a Victorian melodrama'.[6] A resident of the Nelson district who was later to achieve eminence, Constantine Dillon, described Beit to his mother in one of his letters:

> [Beit] is the greatest blackguard out of the hulks in the Northern Hemisphere and the greatest out of Norfolk Island in the Southern, and he has been told it 50 times, nay 500 ...
>
> ... he is very plausible, and has a good respectable manner, but at bottom he is an old scamp and what is vulgarly called an old fib.[7]

The seasick Riemenschneider and his fellow passengers must have felt immensely relieved when the *St Pauli* finally reached Bahia, Brazil, on 4 March. The relief was, however, short-lived for the passengers in steerage, as Beit refused to let any of them go ashore. The battle of wits between Beit and his passengers now spread and intensified. The steerage passengers, with the aid of a sailor, smuggled a letter outlining their plight to the British Consul. At the same time they advised Mr F. H. Wolters who was the Hanseatic Consul in Bahia. Wolters asked the ship's doctor, as well as the two missionaries, to visit him and confirm that the complaints of the passengers were justified. When they had done this he wrote a formal letter of protest and selected 11 passengers who were to come ashore and sign it, amongst whom were Heine

---

6. Patricia Burns, *Fatal Success. A History of the New Zealand Company*, Ed. Henry Richardson. Auckland: Heinemann Reed, 1989, p. 245.
7. *The Dillon Letters. The letters of the Hon. Constantine Dillon 1842–1853.*, Ed. C. A. Sharp. Wellington: A. H. & A. W. Reed, 1954, p. 79, letter to his mother, September. 5, 1848.

and Trost. When Beit heard of this he rushed at once to the Consul and tried to have the ship put into quarantine on account of the small-pox epidemic, which he now decided to report, despite the fact that the ship had already been in port for 10 days. His plan did not work. The *St Pauli* was not put into quarantine, particularly since Dr Göders testified that there had not been any further cases of the disease on board for some time and the chosen 11 were able to proceed ashore to formally sign the protest document. On their return Beit assembled them on deck, treated them to yet another of his furious tirades and threatened to fine them for their insubordination. This increased the tension further and during the afternoon Riemenschneider, on several occasions, had to calm down the excited passengers.

The British Consul now also became active in the dispute and sent a commission consisting of his secretary and two sea captains to interview the passengers. Captains Petrie and Selkirk conducted a survey and declared themselves satisfied with the arrangements made by Mr Beit and Captain Schacht for the safety and welfare of the passengers. In addition to the investigation by the nautical experts, the Consul requested a report on the situation from Wohlers, Riemenschneider and Dr Göders. Beit acted on the maxim that the best form of defence is attack. He now lodged a formal protest against the Captain of the *St Pauli*, Captain Schacht, who in turn lodged a counter protest.

The result of all these diplomatic and legal moves was disappointing for the steerage passengers. Their very real and immediate personal concerns had been lost in a diplomatic no man's land between two bureaucrats, neither of whom was willing to exceed what he saw as his jurisdiction. They were Germans travelling on a German ship, with a German captain, and a German superintendent of a subsidiary organisation to the British New Zealand Company. The British Consul felt that he could not do anything for the passengers because they were not yet formally naturalised British citizens. He agreed, however, to send a copy of the protest letter to the headquarters of the New Zealand Company in London, while the Hanseatic Consul undertook to inform the Hamburg authorities. In addition, the British Consul promised to give the missionaries a letter for the Chief Agent of the New Zealand Company in New Zealand, confirming that Beit had been the cause of the problems on board the *St Pauli*. Before the ship sailed three men in desperation jumped ship.

While in Bahia, Riemenschneider's activities included not only visiting consuls (he had been taught English at the Mission Institute), but also calming down passengers and writing reports about conditions on board. Wohlers, in a report on the voyage to the *Verwaltungsausschuß* (executive committee of the North German Missionary Society), written on 24 March 1843, comments:

Riemenschneider, who cannot write well on the ship, even spent several days away from the ship, in order to accomplish his writing tasks in a house [ashore].[8]

The young missionary was also invited to preach in the English church for the German expatriates in the city. According to the summary report he was rewarded for this work with a farewell present of a red easy chair shortly before his departure.[9] Inspector Brauer, in his *Monatsblatt* (monthly mission newsletter) article, simply refers to 'a nice present'. Perhaps the opulence of a red easy chair would be considered too extravagant by the readers of the mission publication on whose donations the Mission Society depended.

The proceedings at Bahia seem to have led to a modest improvement in Beit's behaviour. While the steerage passengers still did not receive any of the 'luxury' food items, and there were still complaints about hunger, Beit agreed to moderate his Sunday morning speeches. The missionaries, for their part, recommended the regular Sunday services. The first Sunday back at sea, 2 April, was a festive occasion for more than one reason. Beit, for once, kept his word and there was no ranting prelude to the church service. Wohlers preached a conciliatory sermon and then baptised a newly born infant. Then it was Riemenschneider's turn to officiate at two weddings. Shipboard romances apparently did occur even in the dark, cramped 'tween deck and even between persons 'no longer young', as Wohlers puts it.[10] According to Wohlers's account, one of the romances had come to light as the result of a disturbance in the 'tween deck when the would-be bride had slapped the face of her married daughter who was opposed to the match.

The double wedding was the last official act that Riemenschneider was able to carry out for some time. Once again he suffered from seasickness and then he succumbed to a Cholera-like epidemic that broke out on board. By Maundy Thursday (13 April) he had sufficiently recovered to conduct the burial of a child who had died and he also officiated at the church service for Easter Sunday.

At some stage during the voyage, probably to relieve the tedium and perhaps to escape the intrigues in the cabin, Wohlers climbed the main mast. Riemenschneider was not amused. He felt that such behaviour was not dignified and in keeping with Wohlers's status as a gentleman. Riemenschneider seems to have been very much aware of his exalted status on board the ship and this affected the relations with his two missionary brothers in the 'tween deck. Two years later Heine reminded him reproachfully of the voyage in a letter:

---

8. Wohlers, Johann Friedrich Heinrich, Letters and Papers, Alexander Turnbull Library, Wellington, Micro-MS 98, reel 1.
9. BSA 7.1025. 82/1. Riemenschneider Papers, RP I, 19.
10. Wohlers Papers, *op. cit.,* p. 57.

Could it be called Christian and fraternal that during the whole voyage, from beginning to end, you spoke with me probably no more than five times except to say hello, even though we had lived in the same house and eaten at the same table for four years? At the time I could think of no reason on your part for such cool behaviour, except that you were ashamed of us because Trost and I were in the 'tween deck, in other words that it was the result of vanity.[11]

Heine's letter indicates that the matter was discussed after their arrival in Nelson and that Riemenschneider apologised.

At dawn on Sunday, 11 June 1843, after some six months at sea, relieved only by a short sojourn at Bahia, land appeared on the horizon. The end of the long voyage was in sight although the landing turned out to be just as frustrating as the departure, when gales and adverse winds had held up the ship. This time the winds were too light and too fickle to permit a direct approach to Nelson. For four days the *St Pauli* drifted and tacked in the Cook Strait area, between the North and the South Islands of New Zealand. At sunrise on Tuesday, 13 June, the missionaries sighted Mount Taranaki, the mountain in whose shadow Riemenschneider would eventually spend the major part of his missionary ministry. Finally, on the evening of Thursday, 14 June, the anchor was let go outside the entrance to Nelson Harbour to await the morning high tide for entering through the shallow channel. As darkness was falling the missionaries and the immigrants joined in singing the hymn *Nun danket alle Gott* in thanksgiving for a safe passage. Across the water lay the land of their destination and of their destiny.

✻

When the missionaries and the immigrants landed in the New Zealand Company settlement of Nelson, they entered a troubled community about to be plunged into a deep crisis. The first settlers had arrived in February 1842 and towards the end of that year the town had experienced a modest, though artificial, economic boom. This was partly due to the fact that the New Zealand Company had not made timely and adequate provision for the settlement of its immigrants. The settlers were trapped on their town sections while they had to wait for the rural land to be surveyed. So, rather than disperse into the countryside and start agricultural production, they remained in Nelson. Those who could afford it, built houses and this activity provided work for the 'labourers' who had come to New Zealand with assisted passages but without capital.[12] The problem was that there were far too many labourers and not enough capitalists able to employ them. During 1843 the New Zealand

---

11. Letter to Riemenschneider, 20 Dec. 1845, BSA 7.1025, 1/2 Heine, Honoré.
12. See Ruth Allan, *op. cit.*, pp. 137–192.

Company, who had guaranteed that these labourers would be provided with work, had to employ more and more of them on relief work, such as building roads and drainage. This was not only demoralising for the workmen, who had, after all, come to New Zealand to better themselves, but it was also a heavy drain on the Company's finances.

The penultimate act of what was going to develop into a major crisis for Nelson took place on the very day on which the two ordained missionaries and Dr Göders landed, on 16 June 1843.[13] The agent of the New Zealand Company, Captain Arthur Wakefield, a number of Nelson's leading 'gentlemen' and 20 labourers, some of them sworn in as special constables, landed from a brig at the Wairau River in Cloudy Bay. The incident, which was later referred to as the Wairau massacre, had many of the ingredients that would later become familiar to Riemenschneider. There was Māori anger about their cavalier treatment by Pākehā,[14] and a dispute about the sale of a parcel of land. There were European attempts to survey it anyway. The response was peaceful but firm resistance by the Māori (in this case the survey party, complete with its equipment, was despatched back to Nelson). This action on the part of the Māori was followed by European attempts to assert their authority at any cost, if necessary by bending the law.[15] In the case of the Wairau land, the Europeans had underestimated the Māori determination to resist, and an armed conflict took place on 17 June in which 22 Europeans, including Wakefield and some of the young colony's most experienced leaders, lost their lives.

However the people of Nelson, the unsuspecting missionaries and the German immigrants who disembarked on 16 and 17 June, knew nothing of this yet. The 'tween deck passengers were landed and accommodated temporarily in New Zealand Company barracks. On leaving the ship they presented Wohlers and Riemenschneider with a letter, signed by all of them, thanking them for their pastoral care and asking them to continue to look after them.

Wohlers and Riemenschneider spent their first day ashore looking for a place to live. According to their description they proceeded to make the acquaintance of the 'more respectable inhabitants of Nelson',[16] who soon offered them a number of properties for rent. Inspector Brauer takes pains in his *Monatsblatt* article to point out to his readers that the missionaries chose a hut on the outskirts of the 'town' because it cost only five shillings per week, rather than renting accommodation in a more convenient location. It would have been easier to be close to the Government offices and the harbour where

---

13. Wohlers, Captain Schacht and Dr Göders had already been ashore on the previous day.
14. Pākehā is the Māori term for European.
15. A full account of the Wairau incident is given in Ruth Allan, *op. cit.*, pp. 241–263. See also Patricia Burns, *op. cit.*, pp. 224–240.
16. *Monatsblatt*, 5 (1844), 159.

their equipment was going to be landed, but the weekly rental in town was expensive at £2.[17] The wooden hut with its lean-to kitchen, was divided into two rooms, and measured 5.2 m. by 3 m. It was owned by Dr J. F. Wilson, the newly appointed coroner and 'medical attendant both at the gaol and for the aborigines'.[18]

On 17 June Wohlers and Riemenschneider, with the help of Captain Schacht and Dr Göders, moved into their hut. They loaded all their cabin luggage onto a hired ox cart, bought a few necessities such as kitchen utensils, and some food items, and then travelled to their first home in New Zealand, helping to push the ox cart when its wheels became stuck in the swamp. Their neighbour, a kindly woman who helped them settle in, cooked their first meal, which consisted of fish and potatoes.

The missionaries now had a busy time ahead of them. First of all, as instructed by the *Verwaltungsausschuß*, they had to ascertain whether the North German Mission Society's land had already been allocated. Accompanied by Dr Wilson, who had 'adopted' the missionaries and helped them with introductions, they visited the New Zealand Company survey office. There they discovered that the town acre and the 50-acre accommodation section had been chosen, while the rural land was still awaiting survey. The town section, lot 1042, on the Waimea Road, near the Van Diemen Street corner, was a fair distance from the port and the settlement. The missionaries consoled themselves with the thought that the street was, after all, the main street leading from Nelson to the fruitful Waimea district. Over time and with more settlers, they felt, the area would become as important in Nelson as was the Steinstraße, a busy access road in Hamburg. The 50 acres of accommodation land, lot 155, was more difficult to inspect. It was situated in the Upper Moutere, 38 km. north-west of Nelson. Wohlers and Trost, who were the experienced farmers among the missionaries, went to look at the land, setting out at dawn on Thursday, 29 June. Hampered by heavy rain, and having to wade through rivers and swamps, the two missionaries took more than a day to reach their property. Once Wohlers and Trost returned, the four missionaries decided to lease the town section to two German immigrants, named Haase and Schneider, and to base themselves on a farm on the accommodation section in the Upper Moutere.

Another important task was the landing and storage of their equipment. Beit, who had filled up the 'tween deck with his own baggage in defiance of New Zealand Company regulations, now tried to ensure that the missionaries' equipment would not be landed until all his own cargo was ashore and housed safely in the New Zealand Company store. Again, Beit used every crafty

---

17. *ibid.*
18. Ruth Allan, *op. cit.*, p. 155.

move he could, but in the end, with the help of Captain Schacht, the Mission Society equipment was landed and stored in the Company shed.

The most important task for the missionaries, however, was to establish what they had come to New Zealand for; a mission among the heathen Māori. Wohlers had encountered his first Māori straight after he landed, on 15 June. They were offering potatoes and fish for sale. Ironically, when Wohlers and Riemenschneider went ashore on the following day, the Māori must have learned that they were clergymen, because as they passed them the Māori whom the missionaries had come to convert from their heathen state, all pulled out their testaments and prayer books. The Māori of Nelson and its district clearly were not virgin territory for the German missionary settlers.

The missionaries' disappointment must have been acute when they realised that they had been preceded by other missionaries. They learned that an Anglican clergyman the Rev. C. L. Reay,[19] had arrived in September of the previous year, followed by a Wesleyan minister, the Rev. J. Aldred[20] who had arrived four months before the Germans. Aldred's Wesleyan chapel was already under construction on its site at the corner of Bridge Street and Waimea Road as the Germans landed, for its foundation stone had been laid on 26 May.[21] The Māori on the coast were being looked after by the Wesleyan missionary Samuel Ironside at Cloudy Bay. The missionaries soon realised that it would not be easy to find a district in which they could work in or near Nelson without trespassing on Anglican or Wesleyan territory. The absence of Māori who were not already under the care of missionaries, as well as the lack of roads and the difficult hilly and swampy terrain made the original plan envisaged in § 11 of the instructions impossible. If they were to work among the Māori they would have to travel far beyond the distances that would permit them to have regular weekly or fortnightly meetings on the mission property. The question was raised and considered intermittently for some years, as to whether New Zealand would be a suitable field for the North German Mission at all, or whether they should move to different territories, such as New Caledonia or Australia.

Dr Wilson, their landlord, took the missionaries to call on the Wesleyan minister, Aldred, and then Mrs Reay, whose husband, the Anglican clergyman,

---

19. C. L. Reay (1808–1846) travelled to New Zealand with Bishop Selwyn after having been accepted for mission service in 1841. He was stationed in Nelson as a priest for both the settlers and the local Māori until 1846 when he was transferred to Te Araroa and Rangitukia, Waipu. He died on 31 March 1846.

20. John Aldred (1818–1894) was ordained in Bristol in 1839 and arrived at Hokianga in the *Triton* on 8 May 1840. He was the first resident Wesleyan clergyman in Port Nicholson (Wellington) before moving to Nelson in February 1843. From 1849 to 1854 he was in the Hutt area to which he returned after five years (1854–1859) in Canterbury. After further service in Wellington (1862) and Dunedin (1864) he retired in 1867.

21. Ruth Allan, *op. cit.*, p. 175.

was absent at the time in the North Island. They received a friendly welcome at both houses. Mrs Reay even allowed the missionaries to use the Anglican church for the confirmation of a boy by the name of Sixtus, whom Wohlers had instructed in the faith during the voyage. This service, which took place on Sunday, 25 June, was the first German church service on New Zealand soil. Riemenschneider, the revivalist Evangelical, preached the sermon while the Lutheran, Wohlers, confirmed the candidate. The singing must have been particularly impressive because the missionaries had written out the hymns and those who did not have hymnbooks were asked to copy them so that they all had a sheet to sing from.[22]

Once they had dealt with the most pressing business of gaining a foothold in Nelson, the missionaries were faced with three major tasks. They had to continue to look after the welfare of the German immigrants for whom they felt responsible, they had to establish a farm as instructed by the Mission Society and they had to look out for a possible mission field. While the first two were most urgent, the third was always in their minds. After all, their instructions had stated specifically that they 'were not sent to the settlers in the first instance, but rather to the heathen'.[23] Since the journey to the accommodation section in the Upper Moutere required a 10-hour trek through hills, swamps and rivers, the missionaries decided to split into two groups for the time being. The first group, consisting of Wohlers, Heine and a hired worker, one of the young German immigrants called Berthold Ullrich,[24] left to establish the farm on 25 July, while Riemenschneider and Trost, who comprised the second group, remained behind in the hut in Nelson to look after the Society's affairs there. At this point Wohlers had formally handed over the responsibility for the Germans to his brother missionary. Both groups were to find their respective tasks extremely difficult.

The immigrants found themselves in a dismal situation. Nelson was in turmoil because of the Wairau affair in which the colony's leader, Captain Wakefield, had been killed. Public meetings were held to express anger at what the public considered to be inadequate measures on the part of the Government representatives to maintain law and order; some of the settlers left, opting either to return to England or to seek their fortune in safer places. Those who remained turned Church Hill, near the centre of the settlement, into a fortress, and for some weeks a force of special constables drilled twice

---

22. *Monatsblatt,* 5 (1844), 171.
23. BSA 7.1025. 81/5.
24. In the transcript of the passenger list of the *St Pauli,* June E. Neale spells the name Ulrich (*Pioneer Passengers.* Nelson: Anchor Press, 1982, p. 177). Brauer, in the *Monatsblatt der Norddeutschen Missionsgesellschaft* uses the spelling Oellrich. I have chosen to use the form in which the name appears in the joint diary of the missionaries.

daily in preparation for defending the town against Māori attack.²⁵ A few days after the German settlers had landed they found themselves in an atmosphere of 'grief, anger, fear, depression and insecurity'.²⁶ They were given temporary accommodation in the New Zealand Company barracks with a fortnight's food rations provided by the Company. As none of them spoke English they could not go out and find work in a settlement that already had a surplus of labourers. Beit, the person responsible for them, abandoned them to their fate while he proceeded to engage in his mercantile pursuits, selling the trade goods that had cluttered up the 'tween deck of the *St Pauli*. When reminded of his responsibilities, he offered the Germans, who had every reason to mistrust him, leases on his land at exorbitant rates. When understandably they failed to respond to this proposition he suggested that they should work at clearing his land. Inspector Brauer, the missionaries' contact at the North German Mission Society, later calculated for the readers of the Society's newsletter, *Monatsblatt*, that the daily rate of pay Beit offered would have bought exactly one two-pound loaf of bread a day!²⁷

Riemenschneider, who had learned English at the training institution, tried to help where he could. He pleaded the case of the Germans with the officials of the New Zealand Company who found that they had no authority to act because Beit could prove that as accredited agent for the Company for the German immigrants they were his responsibility. So the missionary started to look for jobs and managed to place a number of individuals in work. This enraged Beit who threatened to complain about him to the North German Mission Society and tried to spread the rumour that Riemenschneider was, in fact, a sacked preacher.²⁸

When Colonel William Wakefield, the New Zealand Company's agent in Wellington and brother of the slain Arthur Wakefield, came to Nelson in the wake of the Wairau affair, a relieved Riemenschneider felt that at last he could negotiate with a person of authority. By now, the Germans were desperate and running out of food, so they sent 'their' pastor to visit Wakefield and ask for the food rations that Beit had withheld from them during the voyage. Wakefield wrote to Riemenschneider on the evening following their conversation, indicating to him that, while he had strongly urged Beit to hand over the rations, he was in no position to order him to do so. Beit at first appeared to agree to the request but a few hours later he changed his mind.

What now followed is worthy of a scene from a comic opera. The whole group of indignant and hungry Germans went to visit Beit at his residence,

---

25. Ruth Allan, *op. cit.*, pp. 261–269.
26. Ruth Allan, *op. cit.*, p. 264.
27. Vol. 5 (1844), 272.
28. Brauer in *Monatsblatt*, *loc. cit.*

demanding their food. When he refused they started to give loud expression to their anger. The frightened Beit sent for the police. His call appears to have been answered in person by the newly appointed Police Magistrate, George White.[29] White, in turn, wisely sent for Riemenschneider before setting out for the scene of the uproar, knowing he would have to face about a hundred people in an ugly mood and speaking a language he could not understand. By the time the missionary arrived it was all over; the Germans had gone back to the Company barracks after White had assured them that he would help them obtain justice.[30]

By involving the police, Beit had made a tactical error because the quarrel between him and the immigrants, which had so far been a Company matter, now became a police matter. After Riemenschneider had prepared a report at the request of White and after an interview, in which Beit accused the missionary of inciting disorderly behaviour, an order was issued to Beit to hand over the food stores that had been the object of the dispute.

This action however was only a short-term solution to the difficulties of the German settlers. What they needed was an assured future. Colonel Wakefield saw this and he must have realised that Beit's machinations would not provide this. He therefore called Riemenschneider to an interview in which he intimated to him that he was prepared to let the Germans select some land in Moutere that they could cultivate rent-free for the first three years. After that, they would have the right of purchasing the land they had broken in, for £3 per acre. The Company would also provide any settlers who wished to make use of this offer with food for the first few months for which they could pay at a later date. Furthermore, Wakefield offered free transportation from Nelson to Moutere, of the luggage of such settlers. The 13 families that took up Wakefield's offer became the founders of the first German settlement on New Zealand soil.[31] They called it St Paulidorf, after the ship in which they had travelled to New Zealand and the valley received the name Schachtstal in honour of Captain Schacht.

The departure of a number of settlers from Nelson also meant that

---

29. George White had been appointed Police Magistrate after the death of his predecessor, Henry Augustus Thompson, in the Wairau incident. (See Ruth Allan, *op. cit.*, p. 270.)
30. *Monatsblatt*, vol. 5 (1844), 273–274. The confrontation between Beit and the Germans was only one of a number of incidents between disaffected workers and New Zealand Company authorities. On 29 October 1843, the acting agent for the Company in Nelson, Frederick Tuckett, reported that as a result of the riotous behaviour of workers the settlement was 'now in a state of anarchy'. (Ruth Allan, *op. cit.*, p. 280; Patricia Burns, *op. cit.*, pp. 238–239.)
31. The fullest account of the German settlements is found in Ruth Allan, *op. cit.*, pp. 309–352. See also, James N. Bade (ed.), 'The Nelson German ssettlements', in: *The German Connection: New Zealand and German-Speaking Europe in the nineteenth century*. Auckland: Oxford University Press, 1993, pp. 52–59; and Briars, Jenny, and Jenny Leith, *The road to Sarau. From Germany to Upper Moutere.* Upper Moutere and Nelson: Jenny Briars and Jenny Leith, 1993.

Riemenschneider's flock in the town decreased in number. Partly because of this fact and partly because Wohlers, Heine and their worker Ullrich had made sufficient progress with the house in the Moutere, which had reached the stage of being habitable, the decision was made that Trost and Riemenschneider should now join their colleagues. They arrived at the farm on 9 August 1843.

The house certainly was no palace. While it had two living areas, the missionaries at first slept on four bunks in a common bedroom until they were able to add more bedrooms. In addition, the plot on which it stood was prone to flooding.

Even though he had now moved into the country, the missionary did not forget his charges in Nelson, some of whom were beginning to establish themselves in business and trade, while others worked on various relief schemes instituted by the New Zealand Company. Every fortnight, regardless of the weather, Riemenschneider trudged the 10 hours from the Moutere to Nelson to officiate at a church service for the Germans and to look after their welfare.

Apart from conducting worship and spiritual counselling, Riemenschneider continued his self-imposed duties as social worker for the Germans. He organised a relief committee for the shoemaker Körber who lost everything, including his savings, which had amounted to £3, when his house burned down in September or October 1843. The missionary also arranged for the hospitalisation in Nelson of a single man called Fricke who had fallen ill after having moved to the Moutere.

In spite of his many duties both in Nelson and in the Moutere, Riemenschneider found time to establish relationships with a number of prominent Nelson figures. Naturally, the two resident clergymen, the Anglican Reay and the Wesleyan Aldred, were of particular interest to him. In one of his early reports to the *Verwaltungsausschuß* the missionary, who appears to have had a good professional relationship with both of them, wrote down his impressions. Reay, in his view, was 'strictly high-church' to the extent that he regarded other churches, particularly the Wesleyans, with disdain.[32] Some of Reay's critical remarks, although they were made 'only very rarely' gave Riemenschneider the impression that Reay regarded the Wesleyan (but not the German) church as having broken away from the true church and therefore heretical.[33] The Wesleyan Aldred, on the other hand, although 'not as crass as many other Methodists may be', had, in Riemenschneider's view, a 'decided antipathy' for the Anglicans, particularly against the power and 'arrogance'

---

32. Riemenschneider's judgement agrees with that of Captain Arthur Wakefield who had described Reay as 'A very good fellow but a bitter high-churchman'. Ruth Allan, *op. cit.* p. 170.
33. RP I, 30.

of the bishops. Indeed, Aldred went so far as to privately call Reay 'papist' – a view with which the Calvinist reformed German pastor 'could not fully agree'.[34] As he saw it, relations between the two clergymen and the two English congregations in Nelson were decidedly chilly. He had no doubt that this was detrimental to the mission work among the Māori. An interdenominational approach was, after all, part of the philosophy of the North German Mission Society even though the Society was not without its own quarrels between the two denominations which, at a later stage in its history, almost destroyed it. The idealistic and still rather naïve Riemenschneider himself was later to become embroiled in the sectarian conflict. Such conflicts were a feature of the Christian missions to New Zealand in the 19th century.

Riemenschneider's good working relationships with both Nelson ministers helped and nurtured him, not only spiritually, but also practically, because they enabled him to make further contacts in his quest for a mission field. Reay, for example, introduced him to Bishop Selwyn when the latter visited Nelson at the end of 1843.[35] The missionary and the bishop, although not too far apart in their ages,[36] could not have been further apart in background and theological orientation. The German pastor, son of paupers, educated and brought up on charity, and an uncompromisingly revivalist Evangelical in his religious conviction, encountered the upper class, Anglo-Catholic Englishman, son of a QC, educated at Eton and St John's College, Cambridge. According to Riemenschneider's journal, the encounter does not appear to have fazed him:

> Since I happened to be in town when Bishop Selwyn arrived, Reay presented me to him. He received me most kindly and asked me to sit down and we conversed for about half an hour. He asked me about the North German Mission Society, as well as generally about the missionary activity emanating from Germany. He expressed his pleasure that the spreading of the Gospel was now being undertaken from all Christian countries, with such success and zeal. He inquired further about the German congregation in this colony and expressed his regret that we had not been able to find a field of work among the heathen as well. As I know well how strictly High Church he is, I carefully avoided putting a positive question about whether there might still be a place open for us in these islands. However I could not altogether avoid alluding to it gently in the course of the conversation, by pointing out that the large and densely populated districts of the northern island of New Zealand were only sparsely occupied by missionaries. He seemed to understand very well what I was hinting at with these words and replied: 'The large districts of the island are admittedly still occupied frugally with workers, but *all* of them have already been occupied by us, although in parts only nominally.'[37]

---

34. *ibid.*
35. The visit took place from 8 to 13 December.
36. Riemenschneider was 26 at the time, while Selwyn was 34.
37. RP I, 46–47.

Apart from his clerical colleagues, Riemenschneider also established friendly relations with a number of other members of Nelson society. One of them was the Quaker Frederick Tuckett, the chief surveyor of the New Zealand Company. Tuckett had been the acting agent for the Company in Nelson following the death of Captain Arthur Wakefield in the Wairau incident. Consequently, the missionary had frequent contact with him while exercising his role as advocate for the German settlers in their dispute with Beit and in their dealings with the Company. Tuckett, who came to respect Riemenschneider in this role, was also a deeply religious man and felt that the division between the Wesleyan and the Anglican missionaries was a scandal. He became a friend of the North German missionaries, in particular with Riemenschneider, whom he often invited to dinner during the latter's regular visits to Nelson.

Tuckett's relationship with the German missionaries continued past their acquaintance in Nelson. In February 1845 he writes to his brother Francis:

> Mr Riemenschneider has gone to teach Christianity in the interior of the Northern island, south of Taranaki back from Mokau on a native pa on the coast. I sent to him 35 of the second 100 Testaments received from the Bible Society. About 40 I have already sent to Mr Wohlers.[38]

When he finally left Nelson to return to England, Tuckett donated his house and section to the German church. He also sent gifts to Wohlers for his mission station from England for the rest of his life.

Another Nelson family with whom Riemenschneider had close contact was that of Philip Vallé, a qualified road surveyor who had been appointed as superintendent of roading by Captain Arthur Wakefield in May 1843.[39] As was the case with Tuckett, the missionary would most probably have first come in contact with him in his work for the German immigrants, many of whom he placed in relief work, building roads. In December 1843 he writes to the *Verwaltungsausschuß*:

> Whenever I am in Nelson I live with a respected English family called Vallé who have taken me in like an old friend of the family and give me free bed and board. When we first moved into our small cottage in the forest in Nelson, we were neighbours of Vallé, without however getting to know each other more closely. At that time they often sent us presents (without us knowing that it came from them), of potatoes, carrots, cabbage from their garden which were delivered by their little boy. We were not able to find out from the boy who it was and when we asked, 'who is sending this', he always answered just: 'mum and dad'. Finally, Vallé himself visited us and invited us for tea. He is a very experienced and sensible man, and as both he and his wife are Christians, we soon became close friends. When we moved away from Nelson and they heard

---

38. Hocken Library, Dunedin, M 1, 156 ++.
39. See Max D. Lash, *Nelson Notables 1840–1940. A dictionary of regional biography.* Nelson: Nelson Historical Society , 1992, p. 144

that I came to town every fortnight because of my work among the Germans, they offered me a hospitable lodging in their house.[40]

For much of the second half of 1843, Riemenschneider lived on the farm in the Moutere. He shared in the farm work, taught school for the children in the small German settlement, and acted as pastor and preacher for the German settlers. These settlers did not have an easy task. Most of them were tradesmen and not farmers and they did not have the necessary knowledge or the capital to make a success of cultivating the poor soil. In addition, as the result of a surveying error, a drainage ditch that was meant to drain the swampy valley into the Moutere River ended up below the level of that river and thus water flowed into the swampy ground, causing frequent and disastrous floods.[41] Most of the German families barely survived on a subsistence diet. The men working on road projects could only just earn enough money for food for their families. It must have looked to them as if their dream of bettering themselves in a new land would never be realised.

In view of the problems and hardships they had to suffer, it is not surprising that the German settlers became despondent. Riemenschneider's pastoral diary contains numerous accounts of strife and quarrels among the demoralised and disillusioned settlers. There were also disputes between the settlers and the New Zealand Company – an institution that became a convenient scapegoat. The missionary himself responded by analysing the situation of the Germans in the light of his faith and his theological teaching. When he discovered that while he was away in Nelson, some of his parishioners had gone to nearby Motueka to try and buy some potatoes from the Māori on a Sunday, he preached a stern sermon of admonition on the following Sunday taking Isiah 48, 1–11 as his text. His former teacher and pastor, Mallet, had denounced the sins of the citizens of Hamburg when the great fire had ravaged the city in 1842. Now, in a similar fashion, Riemenschneider used his text to point out to his people that their misfortunes were the result of their numerous and grave sins. The scripture passage contained enough ammunition for the zealous young missionary:

> Because I know that you are obstinate,/and your neck is an iron sinew/ and your forehead brass ...
> For I knew that you would deal/very treacherously,/and that from birth you were/ called a rebel
> Behold I have refined you, but not
> like silver;/I have tried you in the furnace/of affliction

It must be recorded, however, that the 'heathen' Māori at Motueka, whom

---
40. RP I, 45–46.
41. Ruth Allan, *op. cit.*, p. 326.

the missionary had come to convert, refused to sell the 'Christian' Germans potatoes on the grounds that it was a sin to trade on a Sunday.

From the very beginning of their stay at the Upper Moutere the missionaries had been greatly helped by the two resident English farmers in the district, W. Dickenson and W. A. Weightman. On Wohlers's and Trost's inspection trip to see the land for the first time, Dickenson had accompanied them with his ox cart and they had stayed at Weightman's house. They appear to have remained good neighbours and on friendly terms for as long as the missionaries stayed in the district.

By the end of 1843 the missionaries had established a tenuous foothold on the land, having cleared and cultivated two of their 50 acres. They had also acquired some cows, which kept on straying because there were no fences,[42] and they had built a modest house. In his *New Zealand Journal* article, William Fox, an agent for the New Zealand Company in Nelson, and later Premier, paints a rather idyllic picture of them:

> [In Moutere] also the German missionaries have a section; one of them [Wohlers] has a taste for agricultural pursuits, and with two schoolmasters of the party [Heine and Trost!] is making a fair progress towards the cultivation of the section. The other [Riemenschneider] is less inclined to agriculture, and attends chiefly to the spiritual affairs of that portion of the Germans who are living in and about Nelson. These gentlemen appear very well qualified for the office they have undertaken, and I am happy to have an opportunity of referring to the interest which they take in the welfare of the German immigrants, and the assistance I have received at their hands, of which, owing to the unfortunate misunderstandings between the German immigrant agent and the immigrants, I have occasionally stood in need.[43]

A very important aspect of the young German pastor's role was that of an advocate and mediator. Time and again he was called upon to represent his congregation, or individual members of it, and to look after their interests. As an advocate for the German settlers, he had negotiated with Beit, Captain Schacht, the Police Magistrate (White), and with the officials of the New Zealand Company. While he did his best to assist his parishioners, he tried to maintain the stance of an impartial pastor who is not only an advocate but also the judge of the actions and demands of his people. Their actions had to comply with his understanding of the teachings of the Bible.[44] His sermon on the breaking of the Sabbath shows that Riemenschneider was not afraid to harshly condemn what he saw as the serious sins committed by his people –

---

42. Dawn Smith, 'Cow herding in the Moutere', *Journal of the Nelson and Marlborough History Societies*, vol. 2, no. 2 (1988), 39–40.
43. *loc. cit.*
44. In the 'Third Report on the Germans' Riemenschneider writes: 'My work is not mine, but *His* work'. (RP I, 56. The emphasis is Riemenschneider's.)

the people whom he loved and for whom he was deeply concerned.

In the circumstances in which he found himself, Riemenschneider was constrained to look after his parishioners' physical as well as their spiritual well-being. The German immigrants turned to him when they needed an interpreter, assistance with finding jobs, or medical attention, and he took care of them to the best of his ability. Another 'secular' obligation that he undertook was teaching school whenever he was in the Moutere.

Fulfilling all these tasks required an enormous amount of work, energy and dedication. His congregation lived dispersed over an area of about 40 km. and could be visited only on foot. He also worked on the farm, where he took responsibility for the household consisting of five adults. In the 'Third Report on the Germans', dated 27 February 1844, he excuses what he considers to be his inadequate reports by describing his duties:

> Certainly, dear fathers, I am weighed down by so many duties, each of which is more pressing than the next, weighing me down that it is simply quite impossible to fulfil them all to my satisfaction and as they should be accomplished. To be a preacher and pastor of a congregation that is spread over an area of 25–30 English miles, and in addition to be schoolteacher, housekeeper, cook, wood chopper, and to look after the cows now and again, and on top of all this to do a lot of writing; if I want to attend to all this with the appropriate faithfulness … it is too much indeed, at least for me.[45]

Riemenschneider, whose health was never very robust, found himself taxed to the limit. What the missionary could not know at the end of 1843 was that all of these roles and the heavy demands made on him were to be the continuing pattern of his ministry in New Zealand.

---

45. RP I, 53.

Chapter Three

In Search of a Mission Field: From Nelson to Motukaramū, 1844

BY THE SUMMER OF 1843–44, no progress whatever had been made towards the main aim of the missionary venture, that of the establishment of a mission station among the Māori. The missionaries had concentrated their energy on establishing themselves in the Upper Moutere, building their modest dwelling and breaking in a small part of their farm. Riemenschneider conducted the majority of church services in the Moutere with Wohlers filling in for him whenever he was away looking after the German settlers in Nelson.

Riemenschneider was charged with keeping the common diary. As required by the 'Special Instructions', he faithfully records day-to-day events on what was, to all intents and purposes, a secular, communal agricultural settlement. For example, a meeting was held on 4 January, and according to the data required by the Society, the weather on that day was mainly fine with some cloud, a strong north east wind and a noon temperature of 18° Reaumur (22.5° Centigrade). One of the main items on the meeting agenda was the question of whether they should employ a boy to look after the cows, which kept wandering off the property, or whether they should carry out that task themselves. The unanimous decision was that they should take turns in looking after the recalcitrant cattle themselves.

The young missionary continued his fortnightly visits to Nelson. There was, however, a change in his lodgings. In a report to the *Verwaltungsausschuß* (executive committee of the North German Mission Society) he alludes to some unpleasantness with Vallé's eldest son, which caused him to leave.[1] He gives no detail in the official report but from later correspondence it appears that some money that he had left in the house had been stolen.[2]

Riemenschneider moved from the Vallé's place to stay at the home of C. F. W. Jung who was a German spice merchant, and who was also cantor

---

1. Riemenschneider Papers, RP I, 71.
2. Riemenschneider to Heine, 3 June 1846, Heine Papers, Nelson Provincial Museum, series A2, folder C.

in the German church. Following repeated invitations, he shifted lodgings again, this time to the house of the Rev. H. F. Butt. He was a former surgeon who had recently married, been ordained as deacon and brought to Nelson by Bishop Selwyn.[3] Butt, like Riemenschneider, was a revivalist, and the two men formed a deep friendship on the basis of their shared understanding of the faith. He also started teaching the missionary some elementary Māori.

Riemenschneider's other close friend, Frederick Tuckett, was instrumental in finally giving the missionaries the first real opportunity of seeking a suitable place for work among the Māori. The gruff Quaker, Tuckett, who had counselled the young German to go and establish himself as a missionary without heeding the opposition from the Wesleyans and Anglicans, was about to set out as chief surveyor of the New Zealand Company to seek a site for a Scottish settlement on the east coast of the South Island. Riemenschneider, on one of his regular visits to Nelson, spent the evening of 30 January with him and in the course of their conversation, Tuckett offered him a place on the ship that was to take the survey party south.

A delighted Riemenschneider returned two days later to the Moutere to inform his brother missionaries of the generous offer. It was a real disappointment to him when Wohlers decided that he would go instead of Riemenschneider. Wohlers had been entrusted by the North German Mission Society with chairing the missionaries' meetings and with responsibility for the most important tasks even though he had not been formally designated the leader of the expedition. Nevertheless, Riemenschneider seems on this occasion to have deferred to his friend as the older of the two ordained missionaries. But this did not happen without an inner struggle, which is reflected in his papers.[4] When he next saw Tuckett, on 25 February, and Tuckett asked him whether he was prepared to accompany him, he did not have the heart to say that it would be Wohlers, not he, who would make the journey.

At the next meeting with Tuckett, on 17 March, the missionary still made no mention of Wohlers going in his place. The matter was now becoming urgent. The ship was due to sail on 21 March and Riemenschneider, in spite of having borrowed a horse to get back to the Moutere quickly, did not arrive there until the morning of the 19th. On arrival, he asked Wohlers once more whether he really wanted to go or whether he would not rather have the

---

3. Henry Francis Butt (1815–1886) arrived in New Zealand with Bishop Selwyn and was sent to Nelson in 1843 and subsequently spent the rest of his life in the northern part of the South Island. He was ordained priest in 1847, became missionary of the Wairau district in 1857 and subsequently was first archdeacon of Marlborough in 1868.
4. Riemenschneider's papers do not mention the fact that there were frequent disagreements between him and Wohlers during their stay in the Moutere. In one of his letters to Riemenschneider, written after the missionary had moved to the North Island, Heine complains that he and Trost were frequently asked to take sides by one or the other ordained missionaries. See Heine to Riemenschneider, 20 December 1845, Bremen Staatsarchiv, 7.1025.1/2.

younger man make the journey. To Riemenschneider's great disappointment, however, Wohlers had not changed his mind and preparations were made for his departure.

The missionaries travelled to Nelson and a surprised Tuckett agreed to take Wohlers instead of Riemenschneider. The ship was not ready to sail, so on Sunday 24 March the missionaries celebrated holy communion with the German congregation. On Wednesday 27 March the ship had still not left port but Riemenschneider had work to attend to in the Moutere and therefore decided to return. The two friends who had spent almost eight years living, training, hiking, working and praying together, took leave of each other. Their hope at this time was that Wohlers would find a mission field in which Riemenschneider could join him as a brother missionary, but in this they were to be disappointed. Many years were to pass before they would meet again, although they kept in touch by correspondence.

The young missionary continued his pastoral work amongst the Germans in the Moutere and Nelson. While the Wesleyans in Nelson had generously made their church available to the German settlers for their divine services, the Moutere had no suitable building for worship and this was causing some problems. Riemenschneider describes the situation in a letter to the church paper in his hometown, the *Bremer Kirchenbote*:

> Here in the Moutere we held our church services for a long time in the hut of one of the Germans. However, when it happened that the people in the village had quarrelled with each other, one or the other stayed away, because he did not want to come into the hut of his neighbour. Finally I began to conduct worship in our house, something that is still happening now. Our space in the house is however so limited that we do not really have enough room, even though we use the largest room, the lounge, for the services. I therefore for quite some time wished to have our own small church in our little German village, particularly since it is very likely that the numbers of its inhabitants will soon increase.[5]

On 21 May the missionary records in the communal diary that he had called a meeting of the Germans in the Moutere to discuss the building of a church. The meeting took place at 4.00 p.m. and was attended by all the men who had settled in the village. The young pastor spoke about the desirability of a proper church and presented a plan, which he had drawn up himself. The project was approved enthusiastically, and the men agreed to get to work at once. They were prepared to devote four weeks to it, provided the New Zealand Company would supply them with food rations, which they would then pay off in instalments once they returned to their work on the roads. The Company agent Fox not only agreed to this, but he also generously did not charge for the food. Riemenschneider raised the money for the materials

---
5. Vol. 14, no. 16, (26 April 1845), 61.

from amongst his friends and acquaintances in Nelson, while his farming neighbour, Dickinson, offered to cart the timber and building supplies free of charge.[6]

The missionary himself laid the foundation stone of the church on 16 June 1844, the first anniversary of the arrival of the Germans in New Zealand. The hymn he chose for the occasion was fitting. It was Luther's 'A safe stronghold our God is still'. On 1 July Dickenson arrived with his ox cart and the normally very austere and abstemious Riemenschneider arranged a celebration dinner party:

> ... Mr Weightman, who had promised to come, arrived and of course Dickinson [sic] was also here. At 5 o'clock the five of us sat down to a *Grand Dinner*. The pig which had been donated for this occasion had been roasted whole and was also served whole.[7]

On 8 July, before sunset, the final roof beams were in place, an event that was celebrated by the community according to German custom, with the hanging on the beams and spars of enormous wreaths, which the women and children had made.[8] According to the missionary, the church, including the vestry, was 15.5 m. long, 6.4 m. wide and 3.4 m. high. The tower on the west side had a height of 12.5 m.[9] This was the first of five wooden churches that Riemenschneider designed and built during his stay in New Zealand. Only one of them has survived. It is the church in Moeraki, inaugurated in 1862.[10]

Despite the careful planning and the hard work, this first German church in the Moutere was never completed. The flood that had necessitated the postponement of the celebration of its roofing over, was the final straw for the handful of settlers. It signalled the eventual abandonment of the unsuitable location and the dispersal of its inhabitants. Four months after the festival no German settlers remained in the village of St Paulidorf.

While the church was being built, the missionaries had other concerns as well. Word had arrived from Wohlers that he had settled on Ruapuke Island,

---

6. *Allgemeines Tagebuch der von der Norddeutschen Missions Gesellschaft ausgesandten Missionare Wohlers, Riemenschneider, Trost & Heine, auf der neuseeländischen Station in Moutere Disctrict*. Nelson Provincial Museum, Heine Papers; also RP I, 118–119.
7. *Allgemeines Tagebuch*.
8. There is some doubt about the exact date of the celebration. Ruth Allan, *Nelson. A History of Early Settlement*. Wellington: A. H. & A. W. Reed, 1965, p. 326, cites an article in the *Nelson Examiner* according to which the 'consecration' was postponed because of a major flood from 7 July to 9 July. In his report to the *Verwaltungsausschuß* Riemenschneider gives the date of 7 July (RP I, 119) while the diary entry describing the event is dated 8 July. Since the diary entry is the most immediate record, and since it is also supported by Heine's diary, I have considered it to be the most reliable.
9. RP I, 119.
10. The church has been shifted twice and now stands in the old quarry historical reserve. Hardwicke Knight writes that it was built by the Anglicans (*Church Building in Otago*. Dunedin: H. Knight, 1993), but see chapter 12: Teacher, Pastor, Counsellor, Builder, 1863–1864.

a small island in Foveaux Strait, but that there were not enough Māori living on the island to warrant more than one missionary. Riemenschneider would now have to look elsewhere for a mission field, but his wings were clipped, as he put it, by a lack of money available for travelling. He was rescued by a fortuitous event, which he and his brother missionaries interpreted as divine intervention. After a year's service with the missionaries the farmhand, Ullrich, had decided to go and work for the neighbouring farmer Weightman. Ullrich's annual wages for his work with the missionaries, all of £15, had been drawn from the bank in cash but he did not want to use the money immediately, asking instead that it be paid to his mother in Germany. This meant that the Society could use German funds for payment, and thus the missionaries decided to invest this unexpected windfall of £15 in a journey for Riemenschneider to search for Māori who had not yet been claimed by either the Wesleyans or the Anglicans. Like Wohlers, he did not take much time to prepare for his departure:

> Even though it was in the middle of winter and the rainy season was at hand, I began to make preparations for the journey. I had a small travelling tent made from 10 yards of shirting, and purchased a billy, a lamp, spats and some provisions for the journey, as well as shirts, tobacco, pipes etc for the natives, whose services I would need as porters for my luggage, and got ready to set out.[11]

During his frustrating year searching for a suitable place to work as a missionary, Riemenschneider had tried hard to get as much information as he could about possible fields. He had asked Aldred, the Wesleyan minister, without success, to get him information from his brethren when the latter went to the annual meeting of Wesleyan missionaries in Wellington. He had tried to find out about prospects in Tasmania and New Caledonia but again had not obtained any concrete information. The problem was that even if he had, it would have taken more than a year to get permission and resources from the Society to make such a move. Finally, he now planned to explore the Lake Taupō area in the interior of the North Island, no doubt encouraged by the chief surveyor Tuckett's repeated insistence that if he felt called to be a missionary he should follow his call and not be put off by denominational jealousies.

When the missionary declared his intention to travel to the North Island his farmer neighbour and friend Weightman offered to come along as a travelling companion. Riemenschneider gladly accepted the offer and started to inquire about passages to Port Nicholson (Wellington), which was to be the starting point for their overland journey. There was, however, no shipping available for that destination, but instead they discovered that the barque *Urgent* was due to sail for Sydney via New Plymouth in late August. The missionary

---

11. RP I, 129.

decided to take this opportunity of crossing Cook Strait, particularly since the overland route into the interior of the North Island was going to be shorter from New Plymouth than from Port Nicholson.

On Sunday, 5 August, Riemenschneider preached for the last time for his Nelson congregation, and the service was followed by a tearful farewell. The final communion service at the Moutere took place on the following Sunday, but on 19 August the missionary was still in the Moutere, conducting a final meeting with the Germans at which he formally handed over their care to the two missionary assistants, Heine and Trost, and left detailed instructions about the conduct of the congregation's affairs.

Riemenschneider and Weightman finally sailed on the evening of Monday, 27 August, and a south south-west gale that night forced the missionary – never a good traveller by sea – to retire to his bunk. On the following morning shortly before noon he caught his second glimpse of Mount Taranaki in whose shadow he was to spend the next 16 years. 'Just as if [the mountain] wanted to greet us', he writes in his travel report, 'it took off its dense veil of clouds for a few minutes, and revealed itself to our gaze in its whole, most majestic splendour and sublimity'.[12] After another uncomfortable night anchored in the roadstead of New Plymouth, the two travel companions went ashore on the morning of Wednesday, 29 August. In a letter to his parents, published by the Bremen church paper, *Bremer Kirchenbote*, Riemenschneider describes his first couple of hours in the North Island:

> The first thing that I now did [after landing in the New Zealand Company surfboat] was to take lodgings in a guesthouse and have a hearty meal. I felt all the more inclined to do so because since my departure I had taken neither solid nor liquid refreshment because of my seasickness. Then I took a walk. The town has been founded only a few years ago and is therefore still quite insignificant. The houses are built mainly of wooden boards.[13]

His first impressions of the town and its inhabitants do not seem to have been favourable. In his journal, which clearly was not meant for publication, he records:

> The first thing which confronted us on landing in New Plymouth, was a certain small town quality. The inhabitants, consisting of all classes, who rarely get to see strangers because of the lack of a port here, had gathered in large numbers on the beach and looked at us with such inquisitiveness as if they thought we were flying Eskimos. We sought lodging for the time being in a second class hotel where we enjoyed good service and comfort.[14]

---

12. RP I, 136.
13. Vol. 14, no. 50 (24 December 1845), 199.
14. RP I, 137. The hostelry in question was the Seven Stars Inn, 'Mr George's Public House, where it is decent and cheap' (Riemenschneider to Heine, 10 Oct. 1844. Heine Papers, Nelson Provincial Museum, series A2, folder C).

It should be noted that in 1844 the settlement of New Plymouth had a population of about 1,155 inhabitants, compared with ca. 2,915[15] in Nelson.

While the missionary was unimpressed by New Plymouth, the town seems to have felt pretty indifferent in turn towards him and his travelling companion.

> On the day of our landing Weightman and I, after being pressed hard by our captain, allowed him to introduce us to the aristocracy of New Plymouth, the greatest part of which was assembled in Devon's Hotel. They welcomed us with cold politeness. The politics of this colony were being discussed most animatedly here. After a short time we withdrew from this company. Next morning I delivered two letters of introduction which I had received before my departure from Nelson from Colonel Wakefield and Mr Fox, the two main agents of the New Zealand Company in Wellington and Nelson, to Mr Wicksteed, main agent in New Plymouth. But as I did not find him at home I handed the letters as well as my card to Madame W. But I have never received a reply of any kind. Another letter from the Rev. C. Reay in Nelson I delivered to the Episcopal clergyman in New Plymouth, the Rev. Mr Bolland. Both he and his wife received me most graciously and both Weightman and I were invited for a meal.[16]

At the home of the Bollands, Riemenschneider met the Rev. Richard Taylor[17] who was up from Whanganui, most probably to celebrate communion for the settlers, an office Bolland was unable to perform, as he had not yet been ordained as a priest.[18] The missionary appears to have been favourably impressed by Taylor; he devotes several pages in his report to Bremen describing the dinner conversation, which he enjoyed with the Anglican missionary.

Riemenschneider's initial contacts with New Plymouth society thus appear to have been, not surprisingly, with the clergy. The fact that he was not welcomed with open arms by the 'aristocracy' of the settlement may have made him feel less than charitable towards them. After all, in Nelson he had been recognised by society both as a reverend gentleman and as the advocate for the German settlers. This gave him a certain status, which he

---

15. *Statistics of New Zealand for the Crown Colony Period, 1840–1852.* Auckland: Department of Economics, Auckland University College, 1954, p. 8. A note on the figures for Nelson states that A. S. Thomson (*The Story of New Zealand*, London: John Murray, 1859) gives 3,036 inhabitants for Nelson. However, that total included '20 sailors and 101 Germans', which were deducted.
16. RP I, 137–138.
17. Richard Taylor was born in Letwell (Yorkshire) on March 21, 1805. He served in Sydney under Samuel Marsden from 1836 to 1839 and in the northern part of the North Island of New Zealand from 1839 to 1843. In that year he was sent to Whanganui in which area he worked until his death on October 13, 1873. Richard Taylor held an M. A. degree from Cambridge and he was a tireless traveller.
18. Bolland was ordained a priest on 22 September, 1845. (See Margaret H. Alington, *Goodly Stones and Timber. A History of St Mary's Church, New Plymouth*, New Plymouth: The Church, 1988, p.112).

clearly enjoyed.[19] His initial comments to the *Verwaltungsausschuß* (executive committee of the North German Mission Society) on the leading figures of New Plymouth are therefore somewhat scathing:

> In general, as far as the aristocracy of this place is concerned, they appear to frequent Devon's Hotel often. Apart from that, the good form and good taste which one otherwise is entitled to expect (and finds more or less everywhere among the higher classes), appears here to be extremely feeble and flat. For example I saw a well regarded gentleman pass my lodgings several times daily, dressed in a coarse woollen jacket and with a short clay pipe burned brown in his mouth. Another young gentleman, who is regarded as a merchant of some property, recently came to blows with another man to the great amusement of a growing crowd of people on the open road not far from my lodgings.[20]

The local Māori were involved in the seasonal task of potato planting, and it took Riemenschneider nine days to find a group of Māori guides and luggage carriers who were willing to take him inland in search of a field for his labours.

Richard Taylor, who was one of the most avid travellers amongst the Church Missionary Society missionaries, advised the newly arrived missionary that there were two major routes from Taranaki to Lake Taupō. One of them led south along the coast and then by canoe up the Whanganui River, while the other, which was shorter, involved travelling north along the coast and then a canoe journey up the Mōkau River. Riemenschneider would have preferred to travel the longer route, up the Whanganui, because Taylor was returning to his mission station at the mouth of that river, and they could have travelled together for part of the way. When he finally found a group of eight men, they were not willing to go to the Whanganui but were by choice travelling the Mōkau route. The missionary decided to grasp the opportunity, and he engaged their services for the cost of one shirt and 10 plugs of tobacco each. The chief whose canoe they would use for the journey up the Mōkau River was to receive a woollen blanket in addition. Riemenschneider also engaged a European interpreter whom he does not name. In spite of his lessons with Reverend Butt, in Nelson, he had not made any significant progress in the Māori language.

The overland trek from New Plymouth to the mouth of the Mōkau River was not easy for the city dweller, even though his fortnightly walks from the Upper Moutere to Nelson must have served as useful training. The travelling party used the beach as a road where possible, wading through the many rivers

---

19. In a rather acrimonious letter that Heine wrote to Riemenschneider he comments: 'People here say that you do not like it in Motukaramu, but that if you could visit as many gentlemen there as you could here you would be quite happy there'. (Letter of 20 December 1845, BSA. 7.1025.1/2 Heine, Honoré.)
20. RP I, 138–139.

and streams that drain the North Taranaki hinterland, and went inland or over the cliffs where necessary.

On climbing the spectacular White Cliffs, south of the Tongapōrutu River, called Parininihi by the Māori, the missionary was most probably unaware of the fact that these cliffs formed the northern boundary of the Taranaki tribes who sometimes describe their area as 'Parininihi ki Waitōtara', from Parininihi to Waitōtara.[21] He was now entering the territory of the powerful Tainui tribes, one of which, the Ngāti Maniapoto, occupied a large area that included, on its southern boundary, the Mōkau River. He comments, however, that the chief in his party of Māori, who was sick, was opposed to taking any rest periods in the Taranaki area. Apparently he feared that if he died before reaching Ngāti Maniapoto territory his bones would be made into fishhooks by the Taranaki people against whom his tribe had periodically waged war.[22]

Before he reached Mōkau, however, Riemenschneider encountered a European who had apparently 'married' a Māori woman. The missionary was not impressed. He writes in his report:

> At Tongaporutu, where we rested for half a day because of our Te Turu,[23] we found an English Dr of Medicine living among the natives in a wretched house built of reeds which has neither door nor windows or even contains the slightest bit of furniture. He seems to live entirely by his shotgun. I don't know what caused this gentleman to live here in the wilderness. (I have however learned this much, that the daughter of the chief there has to serve him as the victim of his bestial lust.) I had to give medicine to several sick persons, as the doctor who lives there was indeed a doctor, but not a pharmacist as well.[24]

At two o'clock in the afternoon of 11 September the party arrived at the Wesleyan mission station near the mouth of the Mōkau River. After an initial failure it had been re-opened six months before the missionary's visit and was now in the charge of a catechist, a lay missionary teacher. Riemenschneider must have been delighted to discover that this Wesleyan missionary was, in

---

21. Evelyn Stokes, *Mokau. Maori cultural and historical perspectives*. Hamilton: University of Waikato, 1988, p. 15.
22. RP I, 148. Riemenschneider would not have known at this stage that turning an enemy's bones into fishhooks was the worst insult that Māori could offer to a slain foe, and that this had indeed been done to two Te Āti Awa chiefs by the Ngāti Ruanui in the 1830s. (See John Houston, *Maori Life in Old Taranaki*. Wellington: A. H. & A. W. Reed, 1965, pp. 59–60).
23. Riemenschneider never gives the name of the chief. He states that he belonged to the Waikato tribe and that he was a baptised Wesleyan. He further writes that he had been under the impression that the chief's name was 'Te Turu or Te Tuturoi' because the other Māori had used that term, which the missionary understood to mean, 'the sick one'. According to the Williams dictionary (H. W. Williams, *Dictionary of the Maori Language*, 7th edn, Wellington: GP Publications, 1992), the Māori term for a sick person is tūroro. Riemenschneider, who did not know the language at this stage, may well have misheard or made a mistake in his transcription. See RP I, 143.
24. RP I, 148.

fact, a countryman of his, Henry Cort Schnackenberg. Schnackenberg, a Hanoverian who had learned the trade of ropemaker in Australia,[25] was five years older than Riemenschneider while the latter, unlike Schnackenberg, was trained and ordained. These differences in age and status did not prevent the two Germans from becoming close friends.

After a rest day at Schnackenberg's the missionary and his party continued their journey up the Mōkau River by canoe. The craft measured 5.5 m. with a beam of just over 0.9 m. It must have sat very low in the water and this would present problems later when the party was negotiating the numerous rapids that lay ahead of them. It contained three passengers (Riemenschneider, Weightman and the interpreter), eight paddlers, all of the Europeans' luggage, and provisions for the passengers and crew for eight days. Before their departure Schnackenberg, who spoke Māori, had warned the travellers that their crew intended to coerce them into paying more than the agreed goods for their services. On the second day of the journey it became clear that Schnackenberg's warning had been right. The paddlers began to ask with increasing ferocity for more payment and, when Riemenschneider refused, became more and more threatening. On the morning of the following day, Saturday, 13 September, the crew mutinied. They emptied the canoe of all the missionary's and Weightman's luggage and were about to abandon the Pākehā to their fate on the river bank. At this point, the sick chief intervened. He refused to enter the canoe, pointed out to the paddlers that the Pākehā were under his protection and that he would stay with them if they paddled away. The crew disappeared and stayed away for some hours, but then came back and resumed the journey with Riemenschneider and his party on board. After they had attempted to overturn the canoe in one of the many rapids, the chief ordered the Pākehā ashore when rapids had to be negotiated while he stayed in the canoe to ensure that the luggage was safe.[26]

Finally, in the early afternoon of Monday, 17 September, the party reached a settlement, which also marked the limit of canoe navigation up the Mōkau River. The young missionary writes down his first impressions in his diary:

> Here, on the right hand side of the river there is a native village the inhabitants of which may number in total 60–80 souls. On the left hand side of the Mokau where we landed a new village is being built. Maori from the most varied areas of the interior are here right now and have put down an enormous potato plantation which they are still busy cultivating. At the same time they have built a Pa[27] here and after a few months, when the produce is ready for harvest,

---

25. See G. E. J. Hammer, *Pioneer Missionary, Raglan to Mokau, 1844–1880. Cort Henry Schnackenberg*. Auckland: Wesley Historical Society, 1991. Proceedings of the Wesley Historical Society (New Zealand), no. 57.
26. RPI, 158–168.
27. A *pā* is a Maori fortress sometimes involving extensive earthworks, such as defensive trenches, a number of levels and palisaded walls. The one whose construction Riemenschneider reports was probably a simpler structure, designed to defend the food crops.

about 150–200 natives will gather in this new settlement and settle down permanently.²⁸

The name of the Māori settlement was Motukaramū and its inhabitants soon made it clear to Riemenschneider that they wanted him to stay as their missionary. At first the missionary would not give a binding answer. After earnest prayer, and an assurance that no other protestant missionaries had claimed the area (the Catholics who had visited the area and made some converts, obviously did not count), he felt inclined to establish himself there, particularly as it appeared to him that the numbers of Māori living in the area permanently would increase.²⁹ At the same time he felt that his journey to Motukaramū had been guided by a number of divine interventions, which gave him an assurance that it was God's will that he should settle there rather than proceed to Taupō as planned.³⁰ His decision, however, was to be subject to a formal *kōrero*, a public discussion of the issue. This took place and the missionary describes the scene in his diary for Tuesday, 18 September:

> At seven o'clock this evening the tent and the area in front of it began to fill with natives who wanted to hear the decision about whether I would stay or go. The chiefs sat inside the tent, the others outside. ... My friend Weightman and I sat on our bedrolls in the back of the tent facing the entrance. In front of us, stuck on a pole, the oil lamp was burning. Weightman sat on my right, on his right the old Christian chief Te Wati. He was wearing a short coat made of dog skin, joined in broad black and white stripes. The interpreter sat on my left and next to him the young heathen chief Mukau, wearing his woollen blanket which hung from his shoulders like a Roman toga. Then, on both sides and in front of us sat the remaining old people, all wrapped in their blankets, and behind them the women and the young folk. Right in the background a large bright fire was burning around which another group had gathered. All the faces were heavily tattooed and could only be recognised when they were close to the lamp. A deep silence fell when I addressed the gathering.³¹

In the course of the discussion Riemenschneider emphasised that he was willing to become their teacher and pastor, but that he was not willing to become *their* Pākehā. In other words, he was careful to assert and maintain his independence and the right of his mission society to confirm his choice of station or to send him elsewhere if they so pleased. The Māori, on the other hand, expressed their wish for a commitment, since the Wesleyan custom of

---
28. RP I, 168–169.
29. This may have been a serious miscalculation on the part of the missionary. The potato plantation may well have been established temporarily to maintain the claim of a particular *hapū* (group of families) to ancestral land, with no intention of permanent occupation.
30. Riemenschneider to Heine and Trost, 10 Oct. 1844, p. 11. Heine Papers, Nelson Provincil Museum, series A2, folder C.
31. RP I, 173.

rotating missionaries every three years was not to their liking. In the end, both sides made cautious concessions. The Catholic Māori, while not agreeing to convert at once, would do so if they found themselves convinced by the new arrival's preaching. They promised to attend his services, even though at this stage in his career, the missionary was unable to conduct services, let alone preach, in their language. Riemenschneider, while pointing to his status as servant of a society that could recall him if it so wished, indicated that it was certainly his intention to stay and that he was prepared to bring more of his people to show that his establishment was intended to be permanent. After two hours of talking the missionary agreed to stay, convinced that the population of the area would increase and that he would be able to establish a mission station of the North German Mission Society without trespassing on the areas claimed by the Wesleyans. The young and inexperienced preacher firmly believed that he had been chosen, and that his choice of a mission field had been God's will.

Chapter Four

A Bleak and Lonely Post, Mid-1844 to Mid-1846

Thus Riemenschneider commenced his work at Motukaramū with great enthusiasm and high hopes. According to the biblical injunction he did not stop to count the cost. At the age of 27 he could not have had a realistic appreciation of the work and of his ability to carry out the duties of a missionary in a remote location, among a people whose language and culture he did not know.

The first weeks were difficult for him. Neither the training in Hamburg nor the experience he had gained while working among the Germans in Nelson and the Upper Moutere had prepared him for living at close quarters with the Māori whom he had come to serve. Privacy was initially an unattainable luxury. The missionary and his companion Weightman were surrounded from dawn to well after dusk by scores of friendly, inquisitive and importunate Māori.

In his early days in Motukaramū Riemenschneider still had not detached himself from his German congregation in Nelson. In a letter of his to Heine and Trost, dated 10 October 1844 (a few weeks after his arrival), in which he asks Trost to join him in Motukaramū,[1] he encloses a pastoral letter, clearly with the intention that it should be read to his German flock. It is a letter in which the young pastor attempts to express loving concern for the welfare of his former parishioners, but there is a strong overlay of stern paternalism, which had been a feature of his own experience as a parishioner in Bremen. It was to become a feature of his dealings with his Māori congregations in the future as well. The letter begins as follows:

> Greetings in advance, my dear congregation,
>
> I believe that I may hope that you are well as far as secular matters are concerned, but how are things spiritually? Who is ruler in your hearts and commands your thinking and your behaviour? Is it the god of this world with his retinue that stifles all buds of truth: hatred, animosity, envy, anger, quarrelling,

---

1. Trost did not arrive until 4 January 1845.

divisiveness etc. What are you striving for in your innermost hearts? Where do you seek your fresh and best treasure? Is it perhaps that you are looking for it in the vain glitter of this poor, transient world and are all your senses and powers devoted to obtaining this?[2]

In spite of this admonishment of his German congregation, Riemenschneider, like almost all of the missionaries of his time, appears to have been unable to disassociate the religious message he preached from the idea that the customs of his European people, which often contravened the teachings of the Bible, were 'Christian'. Māori customs, on the other hand, were 'heathen' even though they were no more irreconcilable with the Bible than those which Europeans practised. This becomes apparent in an incident involving the missionary's friend and travelling companion. Weightman had dropped his shaving pouch while performing his ablutions at the river's edge. The missionary's diary tells the story:

> 30 September, Sunday. ... E Wati's daughter, a grown woman, had the good fortune to bring up the lost article from the depths. However by the end of the day the shaving gear had still not been returned to Weightman.
>
> Now it is a custom with the natives that anyone who finds something which has been lost or fishes it out of the water, claims a right of ownership for it even if the rightful owner is known to them. The Christians however, to which E Wati and his family belong, make an exception to this in that they return the lost article to the owner in return for a high reward, often set above the value of the lost article.[3] The finder of the shaving gear would also have offered back her find under this condition if it were not Sunday when bargaining is not valid. This evening after prayers E Wati showed it to me. It was still as wet as it had been when it was pulled from the river and the pouch, consisting of pressed leather, was completely ruined. Apart from that everything was still in it. E Wati demanded a dress for his daughter as a reward. I replied that I did not have one, also that today was Sunday and not bargaining day. If the pouch has been wet up to now there won't be any harm in it staying wet till tomorrow. Old Te Turu had in the meantime had Weightman called and had told him to offer no more than one shirt.[4]

Riemenschneider then describes the protracted bargaining over the reward that went on through the whole following day. He expresses his bitter disappointment that E Wati, a Christian, engaged in the unchristian practice of haggling.

A major issue and what was to become one of the most fruitful sources

---

2. Heine Papers, Nelson Provincial Museum, series A2, folder C.
3. The custom of restoring lost articles to the owner against a reward was not specifically Christian as Riemenschneider seems to believe. It appears to have been practised in pre-contact times. See Raymond Firth, *Economics of the New Zealand Maori*. 2nd edn., Wellington: Government Printer, 1959, p. 349.
4. Riemenschneider Papers, RP I, 188–189.

of misunderstandings between the missionary and the Māori was, however, the question of land allocation and ownership. Already at the *kōrero* of 18 September, at which the missionary had committed himself to establishing his mission station at Motukaramū, he had been asked to select a piece of ground where he wished to have a house built. On the following day he and Weightman made their choice only to be subsequently told that, since the senior chief, Te Kurī, was absent in Mōkau, it would be best to wait with the allocation of land until he returned as 'he owned all the land in the vicinity'.[5] Riemenschneider does not give any indication that he had an understanding of the Māori system of land tenure in which the tribal land was vested in the chief even though he was not, in fact, the 'owner' of the land in the European sense. Te Kurī returned to Motukaramū on 23 September and at once asserted his authority. There was a repetition of the *kōrero* of the 18th at which Te Kurī welcomed the missionary and accepted the conditions under which he had agreed to stay. When the piece of land that the new arrivals had selected was pointed out to him, however, he stated politely but firmly that the land was his to allocate and that he would find them a different section, which in his view would be more suited to their needs.

Te Kurī was as good as his word. On the following day, together with the two lesser chiefs who in his absence had welcomed the missionary, and including Te Kapa, the tohunga, he took the missionary and his friend across the river and allocated him a building site. This was located on a rise a couple of hundred metres downstream from the village and a short distance downstream and on the same side of the river as the temporary village set up by the new arrivals who had established the potato plantation. Riemenschneider describes the manner in which the verbal agreement was confirmed:

> The three native chiefs and the priest began to pull out the fern on the section and obliged me to do the same because this would give me a right to the land. After we had cleared a good space we stopped and we all sat down in a circle on the ground. Then Te Kurī said to me: 'when the house which you intend to build is complete you shall also have as much land for agriculture as you like. If you wish to buy it, fine; if not, also fine and we will not withhold it from you'.[6]

When the time came for the missionary to make a choice of agricultural land Te Kurī again gave him the freedom to choose but then, after consultation with his people, subsequently assigned him a different plot.

Another area that caused Riemenschneider considerable trouble was that of contracting for goods or services. Always mindful of the need to get the best deal in order to avoid wasting the North German Mission Society's precious

---
5. RP I, 179.
6. RP I, 186.

resources, he haggled hard and mercilessly for the best price, obviously unaware that he was often cutting across Māori customs. After having assigned him a piece of land opposite the village, Te Kurī offered to build a small temporary house for the missionary in the *kāinga* (village). It was planting time and everybody was busy in the fields; so there was not enough spare labour to erect a permanent dwelling for him. The temporary house, a small structure of approximately 4.2 m. length and 3 m. breadth, was completed on Saturday, 6 October. Riemenschneider and Weightman, who had been living in a tent for the three and a half weeks since they had left the hospitable home of Schnackenberg, must have been relieved to be able to move into a house, no matter how small. They would finally be able to stand upright again and have a dry roof over their heads.

There was, however, considerable trouble over the payment. In their initial discussions concerning the project, the missionary and Te Kurī had agreed that 50 men would be required for the building and that the price should be 100 figs of tobacco, i.e. two figs per labourer. After the newcomers' gear had been shifted to the new dwelling, the workers lined up to receive their payment and it now turned out that 112 men had participated, each of whom expected two figs. For a Māori chief this would not have been a problem. He would simply have paid the extra men and his reputation for liberality would have been correspondingly enhanced for having made more workers happy than required originally.[7] However the European missionary, the anxious steward of his Society's resources, viewed the matter quite differently. For him a contract was an agreement in which the precise value of a quantity of goods or services were determined and agreed in advance, and this agreement was binding on both parties. His opinion of the housebuilding deal was therefore that the original contract for 100 figs of tobacco had been broken and it was Te Kurī's responsibility to honour it. This in turn put the chief into a difficult position since he could not offend his workers by paying them less than had been agreed. A stalemate ensued, which lasted most of the afternoon of 6 October. The additional workers were not willing to allow Riemenschneider and Weightman to move into the house until they had received their payment. The missionary indicated that in this case he and his friend would continue to live in the tent. It appears that in the end

---

7. See Raymond Firth, *op. cit.*, p. 313: 'It may be noted in passing that no attempt seems to have been made by the donors of the feast to limit the number of workers who attended – that is the recipients of their hospitality. In the processes requiring quantities of unskilled labour, as in the raising of a ridge-pole into position or the dragging of a log, it was possible to add to the number of workers without obtaining any proportionate increase in the efficiency of the labour, though such persons had to be fed just the same. The thought, however, does not seem to have troubled the Māori. Notions of restriction of the working party in order to obtain the maximum of labour efficiency for the minimum of food expenditure were not characteristic of his economic psychology'.

the astute Te Kurī brought about a compromise solution even though the inexperienced German does not seem to have been aware of it. He presented Riemenschneider with a pig for which the missionary gave him a further 30 figs of tobacco. It is likely that Te Kurī used the extra tobacco to pay the additional workers because soon after the exchange of presents had taken place Te Kurī invited the two Europeans to take possession of their house. In the evening the missionary brought his diary up to date:

> We have now moved into our house but inside it looks very empty and bare because we have no domestic utensils, no door or window, even the hole for the window is missing. However we now have room and a good roof against the rain, something we have longed for for a long time.[8]

Riemenschneider does not appear to have learned anything from this incident, if indeed he would have perceived it as a lesson. When the permanent house on the opposite bank, a structure of 9 m. by 6 m. was ready for occupation on 24 April 1845, a similar quarrel arose about the number of blankets to be given in payment. The missionary had agreed with Te Kurī to barter six but his people insisted on 10. When the house was almost finished Te Kurī invited Riemenschneider to move in. Instead of asking for payment he told him it was his obligation to satisfy the 50 people who had participated in building the edifice, each of whom expected a blanket. The implication was, of course, that the price for the building had now risen to 50 blankets. The chief himself would charge nothing for his labour. When the missionary indignantly refused, claiming, quite rightly from his point of view, that the contract was between him and the chief, Te Kurī indicated that in that case he would rather not wish to receive any payment, not even the six blankets that had been agreed upon. Riemenschneider set the six blankets aside for Te Kurī to collect whenever he wished and finally they were collected when Te Kurī was getting together some goods, which he intended to present to his father Taonui.[9] The new house, while larger, still seemed to lack the comforts that Riemenschneider would have wished for and he comments in one of his reports:

> Life in this house, in the condition in which it was, was less than cosy, particularly in this wintry and unfriendly season. The house resembled nothing more than a barn, it has neither door nor window, floor nor attic and not even a fireplace or chimney. It is as empty of domestic utensils as a bare and swept threshing floor – a wooden box serves as a table, a rough plank as a bench.[10]

No matter what the transaction was, whether it was the purchase of potatoes, timber, pigs, carrying services or canoe trips to Mōkau, the young missionary

---

8. RP I, 193.
9. On the custom of annual presentations to senior chiefs, see Raymond Firth, *op. cit.*, p. 295.
10. RP I, 267.

was unable to come to satisfactory arrangements in advance of the deal and then always bitterly complained about being cheated. The fact that the Māori regarded him, as they did all Pākehā, as rich and therefore fair game for high prices, did not help either.

Another area of conflict was the employment of Māori to assist with labour. Soon after the missionary's arrival, on 8 October 1844, Te Kurī sent the missionary a boy to help with running the mission station. According to him, the boy was about 15, and a *Rangatira* (well-born), a 'native gentleman', as the missionary puts it.[11] Riemenschneider describes him as lazy and indolent. This may have been true but another explanation is also possible. The work that he was asked to perform, such as drawing water, collecting firewood, cooking food, etc., were duties normally assigned to slaves or women and thus not tasks to which a boy on the threshold of manhood, particularly of chiefly rank, would take too kindly.[12] It is probable that the young missionary from an impoverished household, who in his boyhood was asked to perform precisely such menial tasks and who may well not have known about divisions of labour in Māori society, may have misinterpreted the boy's behaviour. The boy's tardiness in carrying out the assigned tasks or his outright refusal to perform them was a source of constant friction. Seven months later, in May 1845, a dispute about the boy picking up his things in order to keep the house tidy, led to him drawing a knife and threatening the missionary. Riemenschneider dismissed his worker and thereafter performed his own chores. Doing menial house work would certainly not have enhanced his *mana* (standing, reputation, prestige) among his prospective parishioners.[13]

Riemenschneider's initial difficulties in coming to terms with the Māori were not helped by a dispute about his right to be in the area. Early opposition came from the superintendent of the Wesleyan district, the Rev. John Whiteley. Whiteley was an experienced missionary who had come to New Zealand in 1832 and had served in a number of stations during his 12 years in the country. On 26 September 1844, about a week after the missionary had made the decision to stay at Motukaramū and found his mission station there, he sent a canoe down the Mōkau River to take a letter to his new friend Schnackenberg. He informed him that he had made up his mind to settle as a missionary at Motukaramū, and asked him to send some necessities, such as paper, ink and tobacco. Schnackenberg and his wife replied warmly and

---

11. RP I, 269.
12. See Raymond Firth, *op. cit.*, pp. 181 f.: 'Hence no man possessed of any self-respect would engage in cooking, nor collect firewood, nor, since the most tapu parts of his person were his head and back, would he carry burdens of cooked food. Such work was left to slaves, who had lost their tapu and to women, who did not have any'.
13. Riemenschneider never mentions Weightman's or Trost's role in household duties, although he was to have problems with Trost's untidiness later. (See chapter 6, below.)

sent not only the requested goods but also a gift of a rooster and two hens, two sets of knives and forks and some spoons with the returning canoe, which arrived on 5 October. In his accompanying letter he wrote that while he personally was delighted to have his compatriot as his neighbour, 'I don't know what our chairman, the Rev. Whiteley, and the other brethren of our society may say about it'.[14] Riemenschneider responded that he had carefully ascertained that there had never been any missionaries to Motukaramū, except for a Catholic priest. Superintendent Whiteley however does not seem to have been convinced. His response to Schnackenberg's announcement, which Schnackenberg copied to Riemenschneider, reads in part:

> The movement of the German missionaries [Whiteley was under the impression there were several] surprises me. It looks as if they wanted to share with you the labours of Mokau where there are scarcely natives sufficient to justify even the settling of one Missionary. You must tell them, that that place is in Mr Miller's circuit, and though he may have never been yet he would visit it if the people were regularly settled there and [he] could reach it in half a day from his place. I think they ought to go to some other places, where the Missionaries are fewer and the wants of the people greater.[15]

From Whiteley's point of view, Riemenschneider's establishment in Motukaramū was indeed an intrusion into Wesleyan territory. However he clearly admits that his catechist (or unordained teacher), Frederick Miller, whose station was closest to it, had not so far visited the *kāinga*.[16] At the same time, only two men served the Mōkau region, with its sparse and scattered Māori population, Schnackenberg at the mouth of the river and Miller at a locality called Whakatumutumu, situated at the confluence of the Mōkau River and the Mangapehi Stream. The mission station, established in 1843, was situated on a narrow plateau halfway up a small hill, the summit of which, on the side where the station stood, was flanked by some spectacular limestone cliffs. Neither Schnackenberg nor Miller had undergone formal training, both were manual workers who were now employed as catechists. Rumours had reached Riemenschneider that Miller was less than assiduous in his work and that he was fast losing ground against the Catholic missionaries who made periodic visits to the area from their base at Rangiaowhia, present-day Te Awamutu. These rumours would certainly have been of concern to Whiteley, since Miller as well as Schnackenberg had been placed on their stations to

---

14. RP I, 202.
15. RP I, 203.
16. In his history of the Methodist Mission in New Zealand, George I Laurenson writes: 'When [Riemenschneider] reached Motukaramū where the Wesleyans had frequently visited during their inland journeys, he decided to establish his Mission there ...' *Te Hahi Weteriana. Three half centuries of the Methodist Maori Mission, 1822–1972*. Auckland: Wesley Historical Society of New Zealand, 1972, p. 113.

ward off possible proselytising. In the week after Riemenschneider's arrival at Motukaramū, Whitely writes to the Secretaries in London:

> The great distance and peculiarly exposed condition of some of our outstations required our attention and we saw that unless some expedient were devised, we should, either through Popery or Puseyism, lose some of our most promising fields. We resolved upon engaging four respectable individuals as Salaried Teachers, to assist us in taking care of these distant places – one was placed at Whakatumutumu, another at Mokau, another at Patea ...
>
> ... We knew that over this part of Zion we were especially made the watchmen, we saw our territories threatened with an invasion both by Popery, Puseyism and the evils of emigration ...[17]

What irked the missionary most was that Whiteley seemed to regard his establishment at Motukaramū as an intrusion, and above all that Whiteley had chosen to use Riemenschneider's new friend Schnackenberg as an intermediary so that the debate that now developed was not a direct discourse between himself and Whiteley. Schnackenberg does not appear to have been comfortable in his role either and he almost managed to get Whiteley to write directly to Riemenschneider when that superintendent spent a night at Schnackenberg's Mōkau mission house shortly before Christmas 1844. Whiteley, who still opposed the German missionary's settling at Motukaramū, but was 'prevented by circumstances' from writing on that occasion, asked Schnackenberg to inform Riemenschneider of that fact, while at the same time wishing him 'blessed success' in his work.[18] In his previous letter Riemenschneider had suggested that he would welcome a personal meeting with Whiteley, and his German friend now informed him that Whiteley was likely to be in Whakatumutumu soon. Schnackenberg's letter reached the missionary on 19 December, and Riemenschneider wrote at once to Miller suggesting that he (Riemenschneider) call at Whakatumutumu to meet Whiteley. On 27 December he walked to Whakatumutumu and reached the station about an hour before Miller and Whiteley. He reports that Whiteley's first words to him were,

> I am very pleased to meet you here, dear brother. I had intended to pay you a visit on my way from here to Kawhia. Your arrival here has saved me this detour and I will therefore be able to get home sooner.[19]

While Riemenschneider was heartened by this friendly welcome he had to wait patiently until the following morning before the question of his mission

---

17. Whiteley to Secretaries, 23 September, 1844. Wesleyan Methodist Missionary Society, Letters to the Secretaries, John Kinder Theological Library, St John the Evangelist Theological College, Auckland.
18. RP I, 211.
19. RP I, 214.

at Motukaramū was raised in conversation. Whiteley spent the evening reading a bundle of letters that his wife had sent on to him from Kāwhia and then, when the two missionaries had gone to their shared single bed together (Miller had only one bed for guests), Whiteley seems to have given his bedmate an impromptu theological examination. In their intimate conversation Riemenschneider explained to the Wesleyan missionary the difference between the Lutheran and the Reformed denomination, and also enlightened him about the North German Mission Society. Subsequent events show that Whiteley must have been satisfied that his German brother was a bona fide and well-trained missionary.

On the next morning Whiteley asked Riemenschneider what his intentions were and under what circumstances he would be prepared to vacate Motukaramū. He seems to have been satisfied with the German missionary's reply that he would leave only under the following conditions: he would have to be convinced that it was God's will that he do so; Motukaramū would remain a source of dispute and friction between his and Whiteley's Societies; and he would have to be satisfied that the pastoral needs of the people of Motukaramū would be met adequately by the Wesleyans. Whiteley now informed Riemenschneider that he had discussed the matter with his colleagues. He had also written to his superior in Auckland, the General Superintendent of the New Zealand mission, the Rev. Walter Lawry. The general feeling was that the German mission settlement at Motukaramū was God's will. Lawry's letter confirming this had been in the packet of letters he had read on the previous evening. He had, however, not informed the anxious missionary until he had ascertained that he was acceptable to the Wesleyans in terms of his theology and training. In accepting Riemenschneider's decision to establish a mission station at Motukaramū and wishing him every success in his labours, Whiteley and his colleagues pointed particularly to the threat of the Catholics whose itinerant priests appeared to make inroads into what they considered was their field of endeavour.

Riemenschneider's relations with his Anglican colleagues were comparatively cordial, since he appeared to present no direct threat to them. Nevertheless, on 3 December 1844, the concerned but not very well informed Church Missionary Society missionary, John Morgan, who was stationed at Ōtāwhao (near present-day Te Awamutu), wrote to his superiors:

> There is another point to which I would beg leave to direct your attention. There are now labouring in New Zealand either two or three German missionaries, belonging (if I am not misinformed) to the Reformed Lutheran Church, and sent out by a Society at Geneva. It does not appear to me advisable that three Societies should labour in New Zealand, and I would therefore beg leave to suggest that an arrangement be entered into with the Geneva Society and the services of their missionaries be transferred to the Church Missionary

Society. The Rev. J. R. Riemenschneider is stationed 3 days journey from this place, in rather a confined sphere of labour, and only three quarters of a day's journey from the Wesleyan Station at Whakatumutumu. I would suggest that he be appointed to supply Mr Spencer's place at Taupo. Mr Riemenschneider's Brethren are stationed in the Middle Island.[20]

A year later, on Saturday 7 December 1845, the German missionaries received a visit from the Church Missionary Society missionary, Richard Taylor, whom Riemenschneider had met at the Bollands in New Plymouth on his arrival in August of the previous year. The newly appointed Sub-Protector of Aborigines for the Western District, Donald McLean, accompanied Taylor.[21] On the following Sunday Taylor and Riemenschneider took the morning service together. Riemenschneider conducted the service and Taylor preached the sermon. The young German comments:

> Here then one could see, for the first time in New Zealand at least, the black gown of the German Protestant Church and the white surplice of the English Episcopal Church, standing fraternally side by side and an Episcopal and a presbyterian[22] minister united in officiating together at one and the same divine service.[23]

The sermon, which is summarised in the report and which apparently gave the German church her due recognition, must have been good because McLean remarks in his journal:

> Crossed the river and with Messrs Riemenschneider and Whiteman [sic] attended native service. Mr Taylor preached and gave us one of the best narrative sermons and as appropriate to the place and people as could well be given and that I have as yet heard him preach.[24]

Taylor's journal entry describing the visit and the German mission station is perhaps less than charitable, even though Taylor found his new colleague 'a mild amiable man but like all Germans is seldom without a pipe in his mouth'.[25] Taylor describes the visit and the German mission as follows:

> We reached Mutu Karamu about 4 the river is here shut in by perpendicular rocks of limestone the natives are principally papists. Hence we crossed the

---

20. Morgan to Church Missionary Society, Alexander Turnbull Library.
21. Donald (later Sir Donald) McLean, born 1820, arrived in New Zealand in 1840. He later became Police Magistrate in New Plymouth, then Land Purchase Commissioner and finally Native Secretary. After being elected to parliament he served as Minister of Native Affairs from 1871 to a year before his death in 1877.
22. Riemenschneider's reference is to the German protestant (Calvinist) rather than the German Lutheran persuasion – not to the religious denomination.
23. RP I, 316.
24. 'Extracts from a journal kept during a visit to the tribes in the interior of the northern island of New Zealand'. Alexander Turnbull Library, Wellington.
25. Richard Taylor, Journal, typescript, vol. 3, p. 191. Alexander Turnbull Library.

river again to Mr Reimenschneider's[sic] station a german Miss^y where we have pitched our tents for the night the air very cold I have a bad sore throat which I caught by sitting in Mr Miller's house in wet clothes. Mr Reimenschneider's house is placed in a commanding position having the Pa of Mutu Karamu only separated by the Mokau, his house is a Raupo one at present without either doors windows floor or chimney and consequently is not the most comfortable one in the world he has neither table chair nor stool, at present; he is sent out together with a farming superintendent by a German Miss^y Soc^y at Hamburg. He has another European living with him and I think if the party had thought less of their pipes (which they smoke from morning to night) and more of their house their situation would not have been so uncomfortable, there is moreover an English carpenter living at the pa, and their means do not appear to be limited. They had no flour and had not the chief's wife sent them a pound or two of sugar in a dirty bag when we arrived, they would not have had any.[26]

Richard Taylor, with the sharp eyes of an experienced missionary, may have come to the conclusion that Riemenschneider's prospects at this locality were not good. He comments in his journal:

> Kuri, the eldest son of Taurui, a papist, is the principal chief. He appears a very respectable man but his wife Rangihuia, a commanding woman, is the main pillar if not the only one of [Riemenschneider's] Maori church, for she only is his follower and she says that she was a papist but her husband paying more attention to another of his wives (for the priests do not compel them to put away any) than she liked to mortify him. She turned over to Mr Reimenschneider[sic] and became his patron. Thus perhaps a trivial misunderstanding may have been ordered for good in founding a Protestant church in the midst of this popish pagan district.[27]

Taylor, who obviously thought highly of Riemenschneider's potential as a missionary, suggested to him, like John Morgan had to his Society a year earlier (and on John Morgan's advice),[28] that he should put himself under the general superintendence of Bishop Selwyn and work in a field assigned to him by the bishop. Unlike Morgan's sentiments, however, Taylor's advice was that the German missionary should retain his links with the North German Mission Society. The rather suspicious Riemenschneider was afraid that such an arrangement could mean that, in time, he might be asked to become an Anglican, and he declined the offer.

As Taylor observes in the diary entry describing his visit to Motukaramū,

---

26. *ibid.* p. 190.
27. *op. cit.*, Journal, vol. 3, p. 191.
28. A year later, in a letter to Riemenschneider in which he renews the offer, Taylor writes: 'In fact it was Mr Morgan, as I told you, who first wished me to speak to you, from a conviction of the mutual advantage, as at present in a country which may be said to be occupied, a new comer is placed in a very unpleasant and unprofitable position. (Taylor to Riemenschneider, 10 Nov. 1846, Auckland City Libraries).

the Catholic church had indeed made major inroads among the Māori of the upper Mōkau region. The Catholics had established a presence on the East Coast with the stationing of Father Viard in Tauranga in March 1840. From there, they had expanded to Matamata where Father Seon was sent in August 1841. Father Seon visited the Upper Mōkau region before Father Pezant replaced him at Matamata in March 1844 and he must have been successful in making converts. Father Pezant reports Catholic congregations when he visited the area for the second time after having shifted the Matamata station to Rangiaowhia.[29]

This visit took place a week after Taylor and McLean had been at Motukaramū, Pezant arriving on Friday, 13 December. Riemenschneider decided to display a studied indifference to the visit and refused to cross the river from his station to the village on Friday and Saturday, telling the astonished Māori that he had no business with the priest. They finally met on Sunday when the German Protestant went across to conduct worship. He reports to his superiors in Hamburg as follows:

> When I arrived in the village, the Roman priest was officiating and he did that in exactly the same house in which we normally have services of worship. All natives with the exception of one family and a few women (Te Rangihui, the wife of the chief, was absent in Maketu) attended the Catholic service. I waited outside until it was finished and then I had an opportunity to see the priest. He approached me apparently respectfully and greeted me in a friendly manner, taking off his hat. I returned this compliment. He then said that he was sorry that he did not understand any German and only a little English. I replied that I could not understand any French and unfortunately so far only a little Maori.
>
> He: 'You are the first German protestant minister whom I have the opportunity of seeing.'
>
> I: 'Really?'
>
> He: 'Since I have the honour to see you here now I take the liberty of remarking that I have heard the natives in this whole area highly praise your love, loyalty and liberality, and that I have noticed everywhere that you are held in high regard.'
>
> I was silent.
>
> He: 'I cannot help admitting that since my last visit here there has been a great change for the better among the natives here.'
>
> Since I had not come here in order to hear French flattery but rather to conduct worship I told the natives to ring the bell rather than answer the priest.
>
> While this was being done the Roman priest began to touch on the differences between the German and English Protestant churches as far as the doctrine of communion is concerned. Perhaps he intended to test whether my teeth were capable of biting. But when he realised that this was not exactly foreign territory

---

29. See 'Letters received from Oceania by the General Administration of the Marist Fathers during the Generalate of John Claude Colin, 1836–1854. Translated by Father R. O'Rielly S. M., Wellington, 1995'. Typescript, Marist Archives, Wellington.

for me and since on this occasion, perhaps for the first time in his experience, his total ignorance regarding the German Protestant church became clearly apparent, he suddenly said while the bell was still ringing: 'I fear that I am detaining you since you are about to begin your service', and left with a bow.[30]

Father Pezant's account of the visit to Motukaramū is rather more laconic:

> Punihangarua and Motukaramu, no baptisms but strengthened the people in their faith, especially the Chief of the last named place. Nga Ture who had a young German Lutheran staying with him. Despite the presence of this young preacher who had stayed for two years this young Chief whom I found very interesting, of majestic bearing, still persevered along with his tribe in the Catholic faith.[31]

The Motukaramū Māori were disappointed that they were deprived of the spectacle of the two missionaries engaging in a religious argument in public. News had spread of a public disputation between Pezant and the Church Missionary Society missionary John Morgan in the Waikato, in which both sides claimed a decisive victory.[32] Some of the Motukaramū Māori had urged Riemenschneider to challenge the priest. Pezant however had virtually no English and at this stage Riemenschneider's Māori was inadequate for a discussion of theological issues.

The fact that in the initial stages of his work the missionary was unable to speak Māori was one of the major hindrances in his work. He does not seem to have made much progress with the language despite his initial work with the Reverend Butt in Nelson. For his journey from New Plymouth to Motukaramū Riemenschneider had engaged the services of an interpreter, but, once the interpreter had departed, the missionary was virtually on his own. Fortunately there was a European carpenter living in Te Kurī's village who had a young son. This boy, Edward Jones, acted as interpreter when required but there is of course no way to gauge the accuracy and skill with which he performed his duties.[33] Riemenschneider's initial attempts at preaching in

---

30. RP I, 327–328.
31. Letters received from Oceania, *op. cit.*, p. 22.
32. See Letters received from Oceania, *op. cit.*, p. 8; RP I, 325.
33. The European, Jones, remains a shadowy figure in Riemenschneider's papers. He seems to have had some contact with him (he made the door and the window frame for the missionary's house), but Riemenschneider initially does not even mention his name, which is taken from the papers of Schnackenberg. In a later report (January 1847) Riemenschneider describes how he treated Jones for an illness that they both thought could be terminal and how Jones dictated his last will and testament to him. He describes Jones as a widower who 'generally lives an impeccable life and has always been friendly and helpful towards us'. (RP II, 39.)
It may well have been through the good offices of Riemenschneider that Jones's son Edward obtained a position in the Schnackenberg household. Schnackenberg writes to Edward's father on 15 October 1846 informing him that his son had been very ill but was now better. In a letter to Riemenschneider, dated 10 August 1847, Schnackenberg informs his friend of the death of Edward.

God's Messenger

Māori were, as he admits himself, failures. He describes his method in a report to his superiors in Germany:

> Finally I decided, with God's help, to attempt to preach in a language of which I had to admit to myself that I did not know. I now drafted my next sermon as simply as was humanly possible in the German language which I then translated into the Māori language as best I could and on Sunday, 20 April, I preached my first sermon on the text Matthew 7, 13–14. In the same way, with much prayer and careful preparation during all the weekday evenings I continued to prepare myself for the Sunday services. Because of my concern that I might speak Maori so badly that the assembly could not understand me, and because of my desire not to leave them completely unfed I attempted to introduce as many passages from the New Testament as humanly possible into the talk and often to assemble the greatest part of it from them, by taking them word for word from Scripture and attempting to join them meaningfully. I soon discovered that my own concoction was not understood as far as the construction of the language was concerned.[34]

Riemenschneider himself was aware that if he wished to become fully effective in his work he would have to become fluent in the Māori language. He therefore asked Reverend Whiteley, during a visit in Kāwhia in January/February of 1845, whether he would be able to stay at the Wesleyan station for a couple of months in order to learn Māori. Whiteley, who was fluent in Māori, issued a warm invitation and on 23 June the missionary set out for an extended stay in Kāwhia. As on the first visit to Whiteley, he travelled via Whakatumutumu. On this occasion he met another Wesleyan missionary, George Buttle,[35] who arrived from Waipā on Saturday, 27 June and with whom Riemenschneider shared the conducting of services in both Māori and English on the following Sunday. On 1 July he continued his journey but he did not arrive in Kāwhia until 6 July 1845 mainly because inclement weather hindered his progress.

Even though Whiteley did not have much time to devote to his language student, the German missionary seems to have made good use of his stay in Kāwhia. In the second half-yearly report for 1845 he describes his activities:

> From the beginning to the end of my stay on his station missionary Whiteley gave me as much help as his extraordinarily limited time permitted. He taught me the necessary pronunciation, read through my written exercises and corrected them and tried to get me on my feet in every way possible. He had also procured for me the Williams dictionary, which had just been published at that time ... Every Sunday I preached on average once in English or in Maori (some Europeans live scattered around Kawhia although there is no actual English

---

34. RP I, 274.
35. Buttle arrived in New Zealand in 1840 and served in Kāwhia, Mōkau, New Plymouth, Raglan and Waipā before returning to England for a few years. On his return to New Zealand he was supernumerary at Ōtāhuhu until his death in 1874.

settlement),³⁶ and in Whiteley's absence I conducted fully, as far as I was able, his functions both on the station at Ahu Ahu as well as in the actual locality of Kawhia, on the other side of the harbour ...

... Whenever brother Whiteley is not absent on his travels he regularly goes across to Kawhia for divine service every fortnight. When it was therefore my turn to deputise for him I set out for the place on Saturday evening with a woollen blanket and provisions, conducted worship on the same evening with the natives who arrived for Sunday and slept in the church. On the following morning (Sunday) at 10 o'clock I then had to preach again for the natives, and at 11 o'clock for the English people. The first and second occasion I did not particularly like the journeys across the water in the admittedly fairly large station boat. However, soon they became a pleasure for me, even though we did not always keep completely dry.³⁷

Towards the end of August 1845 Riemenschneider decided to accept George Buttle's invitation to visit him at Waipā, which could be reached in a day's journey from the head of Kāwhia Harbour.

Another Wesleyan missionary who visited Kāwhia was H. H. Turton.³⁸ While the German missionary does not mention Turton in his report, Turton's diary for Thursday, 4 October, 1845 records:

I also here [at Ahuahu] found the Rev. Mr. Riemenschneider, Lutheran Mssy. who had come from his Station at Mokau – interior to enjoy for a few weeks, the pleasures of civilized life & Xian communion, on the sea coast. Beside himself there is only another German Minister in New Zealand & though they are each endeavouring to do what good they can in their separate localities, yet I am decidedly of opinion that they wld. have been far more successful in enlarging the redeemer's kingdom, had they gone at once amongst the thousands of the South Sea islanders, than they are ever likely to be amongst the few scores to whom their present stations will limit their influence in this country. We shall do what we can to assist them in their "labour of love"; but after all, there is an undefined kind of prejudice existing in the Maori mind against all other denominations than the Episcopalians & Wesleyans wh. I apprehend it will be no very easy task to undermine.³⁹

---

36. In April 1841, Riemenschneider's compatriot and Naturalist to the New Zealand Company, Ernest Dieffenbach, had visited Kāwhia and commented on the European community: 'There are about forty Europeans settled on the northern shore [of Kāwhia harbour], who have lived here for several years past: but the mixed members of this little community do not keep up the best understanding amongst themselves; and it would be well to establish soon some authority at this place ...' (*Travels in New Zealand*. Vol. 1, London: John Murray, 1843 (reprint Christchurch: Capper Press, 1974), 310.
37. RP I, 292–293. Whiteley named Ahuahu Lemon Point because of the lemon trees that he planted there. It still bears this name today. The locality Te Waitere at Lemon Point is named with his Māori name in his honour.
38. Henry Hanson Turton (1818–1887) arrived in New Zealand in 1840 and served on the west coast of the North Island, at Aotea, New Plymouth, Kāwhia and Manukau from where he retired from the Wesleyan mission in 1858. After a short period in England he became a Government agent and interpreter.
39. Turton to Secretaries, May 30, 1846. St John the Evangelist Theological College Auckland, John Kinder Theological Library, Wesleyan Methodist Missionary Society, Letters to Secretaries.

On 28 October Riemenschneider left Kāwhia to return to Motukaramū, travelling with Whiteley as far as Whakatumutumu. The stay had been a profitable one, both professionally and personally. The missionary had not only made progress in the Māori language, but he had also profited from working alongside and observing one of the most experienced and highly regarded missionaries in the Wesleyan mission. His closing comments in the report to the *Verwaltungsausschuß* (executive committee of the North German Mission Society) in Hamburg show how much he had received in personal terms from the Whiteley household:

> My parting from Kawhia and from the Whiteley family was almost as difficult for me as my parting from my parental home. I will always remember with warm gratitude the love which I enjoyed there from all sides to the fullest extent.[40]

In spite of considerable handicaps initially, the missionary had set about establishing himself with vigour and enthusiasm. Once he had taken stock of his situation and the future prospects of the mission in what he believed was an area with an expanding population, he had written to Trost in Nelson to come and join him at Motukaramū. On 14 November 1844 Weightman had left Motukaramū with the letter and with instructions to draw some money for the new mission station. If Trost decided to come to Motukaramū (and he had expressed interest in following Riemenschneider before the latter's departure), Weightman intended to accompany him for a second period on the upper Mōkau. After returning with Trost on 4 January 1845, Weightman stayed until May 1846.

The mission congregation at Motukaramū was much depleted, now that the last of the Māori who had worked on the temporary potato plantation had left on 12 October 1844. The new pastor looked forward to their return to settle permanently in the district and in the meantime he was not short of work. Apart from pastoral duties, Riemenschneider's congregation also expected him to look after their physical welfare and health, even though he had not been given any training in medical care. As early as the day after his arrival in Motukaramū, on 18 September 1844, Riemenschneider notes in his diary:

> Already today I found confirmation of what my friend Butt had told me repeatedly, namely that a missionary on this island had to be a doctor at the same time, since all natives expect it of him. I was literally surrounded by sick people suffering partly from internal, partly from external complaints. I was therefore glad to have some medicine with me.[41]

The medicine that the missionary had brought from Germany did not last long with the heavy demands that were made on his pharmacy. Another factor

---
40. RP I, 300.
41. RP I, 172.

that contributed to the rapid depletion of his supplies was his view that Māori, with their strong constitution, required double or treble the dose of any drugs prescribed for Europeans.[42] He therefore wrote to his friend Butt in Nelson, who was a trained physician, and Butt despatched a carefully chosen selection of drugs with Trost and Weightman when they travelled to Motukaramū in late December 1844.

The missionary comments particularly about the prevalence of venereal disease among women. One of the worst cases he reports concerns a seven year old girl whom he believed he managed to cure. The treatment began with one grain of Calomel every five or six days as well as the application of Mercurial ointment along with a daily dose of rhubarb.[43]

Riemenschneider was also asked to treat a baby born to the chief Te Kurī's wife, Rangihuia, also known as Te Pawa. It was born on 26 May 1845, on the day after the arrival at Motukaramū of Rangihuia's brother, Te Waitara, the chief of Mōkau. It was her tenth confinement but all the previous babies had died within weeks of their birth because, as the missionary reports, the mother did not produce enough milk to sustain the life of the baby. He describes his well meant and desperate measures to save the baby:

> On Monday morning I went again to the village in order to look after the prostrated woman and the baby. The mother still had no milk and they had fed the infant some potato. The mother was well. How I wished that I owned a goat so that I could give the child some milk. However, something had to be done. I returned to my house and roasted some flour to the point where it began to turn yellow, in order to prevent the build-up of acid in the child's stomach, and then made a thin gruel from it, breaking the insipid taste of it with a little sugar. With this I filled a little flask and stuck a feather shaft through the cork around which I wrapped some rag so that it would serve as a teat. When I returned I found that a woman had sucked out the mother and they were just in the process of dribbling it into the child from a leaf. However there was so little milk that my flask was not in the least superfluous. I showed them how to use it and how to prepare the baby food. This was the first time in my life that I fed an infant.[44]

Sadly the treatment was not successful. The baby died while Riemenschneider was absent in Kāwhia where he heard the news on 16 August 1845 and he wrote a letter of condolence and comfort to the grieving parents.[45]

Riemenschneider travelled frequently in the exercise of his ministry. On 28 January 1845, for example, he set out on foot from Motukaramū to go to

---

42. RP I, 230.
43. RP I, 272.
44. RP I, 276–277.
45. While wetnursing was on occasions practised among Māori, particularly for children of chiefs, it does not seem to have been used for any of Rangihuia's confinements. See Te Rangi Hiroa (Sir Peter Buck), *The Coming of the Maori*. 2nd edn, Wellington: Maori Purposes Fund Board; Whitcoulls Limited, 1987, p. 354.

Kāwhia to pay his first visit to Whiteley. He arrived there on the evening of 2 February. On 5 February he began his return journey via Mōkau where he arrived at 9 o'clock in the evening of Sunday, 9 February. The following day he attempted to hire a canoe and paddlers to go up the Mōkau River but was unsuccessful because news had reached Mōkau that a Taranaki woman had been killed. There was a rumour that her kinsmen were on the way to exact revenge, which meant that nobody was willing to leave the settlement. On Tuesday, 11 February The missionary, together with Schnackenberg, accompanied the Māori war party that moved south to meet the expected attackers. When the attack did not eventuate, Schnackenberg and Riemenschneider continued on to New Plymouth where they arrived on Friday evening at 6 p.m. On Tuesday morning, 18 February, at 4.30 in the morning, Riemenschneider set out on his return journey. He reached Mōkau on Thursday, 20 February. There he was held up by the flooded river and did not manage to find a canoe and crew to take him up the river until 10 March. The journey upriver took until midday on 13 March.

On arriving home he found the village deserted and discovered that the people had gone to try and settle a dispute about an eel trap in which they had an interest on the upper Waipā River. Te Kurī's wife, who had stayed behind, was worried about her husband and the situation at Waipā, and urged the missionary to go and intervene in the quarrel. So 24 hours later, at noon on 14 March, the missionary set out again to find his flock. He reached them on Monday, 17 March. On Wednesday morning, having persuaded the chief Te Kurī and his warriors to return, Riemenschneider set out on his own return journey. He called in at the Wesleyan mission station at Whakatumutumu to celebrate Good Friday with the Millers, was forced to stay there over Easter because of inclement weather, and finally reached Motukaramū on Tuesday, 25 March 1845. This whole journey alone had lasted 56 days and in the course of it he would have walked at least 850 km.[46]

Riemenschneider's assistant Trost, who had arrived on 4 January 1845, would run the mission station during the missionary's frequent and often lengthy absences. Riemenschneider's letters to Heine refer to severe tensions between the two Germans in the early stages of their work at Motukaramū.[47] This may explain why there is no mention of Trost and his contribution in Riemenschneider's papers during 1845. It must have been a very hard and lonely time for the simple farmer Trost who had very little English and knew no Māori at all.

One of the major political incidents that affected the missionary and in

---

46. First half-yearly report for 1845, RP I, 240–265.
47. For example, Riemenschneider to Heine, 13 July, 1845 and 3 June 1846. Heine Papers, Nelson Provincial Museum, series A2, folder C.

which he was to some extent involved was the placing of a *tapu*, or ban, on the route from New Plymouth to Kāwhia at the mouth of the Mōkau. A former slave called Piritoko had insulted Te Kurī's father, the great chief Taonui who lived at Paripari.

While some penalty payment from the family of the person who had committed the offence was forthcoming, Taonui did not regard it as enough and the *tapu* remained in force for a number of months. It was becoming increasingly irksome for the people of Mōkau and Kāwhia since it prevented them from sending their pigs to market in New Plymouth. A *tapu*, after all, was a complete block on a piece of land or a river, and passage over it was prohibited, theoretically on pain of death. The *tapu* therefore blocked not only the local Māori but any traffic. Even the postman on his way from Kāwhia to New Plymouth was sent back.[48] Riemenschneider and Trost also suffered, particularly since their work was not prospering at all. The majority of the inhabitants of Motukaramū were Catholic and they had taken to holding their own services from which Riemenschneider was excluded. In a report to the *Verwaltungsausschuß*, which he wrote after he had left Motukaramū, he writes:

> Nobody suffered more during that blockade than we did. For many months we had neither tea, sugar, nor other necessities of life, indeed there was not even a little can of salt in the house so that we could season our dry bread with it. It is *really* hard to live for months without salt. We were in the same situation with regard to tobacco and other things which we use to buy from the natives. In the latter part of the period I could visit my baptismal candidates only very infrequently as I could not pay any people to accompany me.[49]

After some months, Taonui found himself under considerable pressure from his own people to lift the *tapu*. The Te Ātiawa of New Plymouth had invited a large number of Waikato and Ngāpuhi for a feast. The guests could travel as far as the Mōkau River but then the *tapu* barred their further progress down the coast. They began to arrive at Motukaramū in the early days of June 1846 and camped there in the hope that the ban would be lifted. The German pastor finally had enough people to keep him busy and he seems to have enjoyed the experience:

> Motukaramu now resembled a fair with all its noise and din. On Sundays however, as well as in the mornings and evenings everybody gathered in appropriate silence for divine service. During their two week stay at Motukaramu both Episcopal and Wesleyan natives placed themselves in my care as far as divine service and

---

48. Angas, who travelled from Kāwhia to Taupō in October 1844, remarks, 'I have nowhere seen the law of tapu more rigidly adhered to than amongst these wild inhabitants of Mokau'. George French Angas, *Savage Life and Scenes in Australia and New Zealand*: London: Smith, Elder & Co, (reprint Adelaide: Libraries Board of South Australia, 1969), vol. 2, p. 90.
49. RP II, 38.

school were concerned. I therefore found something to do and this gave me no small pleasure. It was a terribly wet and rough time of the year. Because of that many women and children were sick and miserable and I therefore found plenty to do in this respect as well.[50]

Finally, a fortnight after the guests had arrived at Motukaramū, Taonui decided to join them and the journey downriver to Mōkau was begun. Riemenschneider, although weakened by the exertions of the past few weeks and an inadequate diet over several months, decided to go down as well. He then intended to carry on to New Plymouth to fetch some supplies and the money waiting for the missionaries there. Taonui however now refused to budge from Motukaramū and it was not until 2 July that Taonui and his party finally arrived at Mōkau where the locals had assembled as much food as they could to feed the enormous assembly, which the missionary thought numbered about 1,400 to 1,500 people. Schnackenberg was more cautious with his estimate of 1,200. Schnackenberg describes the events of 3 July 1846:

> I was sent for & went accompanied by Mrs. S. and the Rev. J. F. Riemenschneider. On our arrival at the heads I was very much surprised & grieved to find that nearly all our people had their bodies painted, their heads decorated with feathers and armed themselves with muskets. Thus prepared (I afterwards found) for a wardance, the christian natives attended prayers, most of them standing up & leaning on their muskets, while the heathen much in the same posture, remained at a little distance. The sun shone beautiful which gave the whole party a very strange & imposing appearance. Immediately after morning service, about 400 men – Wesleyans & heathens – worked themselves up into the greatest excitement. As I had never witnessed anything of the kind before, and saw at a half a miles distance a body of natives from the interior – Roman Catholic, heathens, church people [i.e. Anglicans] and Wesleyans advance towards us. I became much alarmed and begged of the christian party to remember their profession. They assured me that no fighting was intended, that their muskets were all unloaded and it being only hei wakakite,[51] but I was directed to go with Mr Reimenschneider & stand at a certain distance where both parties would meet. After I had sent Mrs. S. to an eminence in charge of a native, we went trembling and praying to our station. Both parties advanced slowly, headed by their respective chiefs, until they come within a short distance of us, when they commenced running as fast as they could and galloped up close to our heels, but did not hurt us, tho they looked more like fiends than men. Then followed their Wardance, throwing the muskets about and grinning at each other, jumping with a dreadful yell, and stamping as if they were about to swallow each other & the earth with rage. Such mighty execution of their legs, arms, & voice could not be continued long, as when they got

---
50. RP II, 39.
51. Most probably *hei whakakite* – as a display.

out of breath, both parties retreated, then made a second onset and acted the former barbarous ceremony over again.[52]

Riemenschneider spent a total of 12 days with the Schnackenbergs at Mōkau in July 1846 and the loving care lavished on him by his friend and his wife restored him sufficiently for the walk to New Plymouth where he stayed for several weeks. This visit to New Plymouth was to prove one of the turning points in his career.

Already before the *tapu* had been placed on the New Plymouth road, the missionary had come to the conclusion that Motukaramū was not going to be the expanding field for his labours that he had hoped it would become. During his four-month stay with Whiteley in 1845 he had heard rumours that the large group of people who had established potato plantations at Motukaramū and had promised to settle there permanently had now established plantations elsewhere. It became apparent that they had no intention of making Motukaramū their permanent home. On his return to Motukaramū he made further inquiries, which confirmed the discouraging news that Te Kurī and his people at Motukaramū and a small neighbouring kāinga would be the only permanent residents – who altogether numbered about 30 to 40 people. Of these, Te Kurī and most of his people professed to be Catholics. In the second half-yearly report for 1845 Riemenschneider sadly concludes:

> Really only three of my heathen natives at Motukaramu are so far clearly on my side, the wife of the chief and one other couple, and they regularly attend divine service and school on Sunday.[53]

His judgement about the long-term prospects for the Motukaramū settlement proved to be accurate. In 1858 the former Surveyor General of New Zealand, S. Percy Smith, travelled up the Mōkau River with three companions. The party reached Motukaramū on Saturday, 9 January and spent the Sunday there. Smith reports:

> At Mangaharekiekie we had dinner, and at six arrived at Motukaramu, very well pleased to get out of our cramped position in the canoe. Here are about 20 Māories located, mostly old women ...
> ... This place was once a mission station but is now deserted.[54]

In terms of the missionary's personal relationships, Motukaramū was a bleak and lonely post for Riemenschneider. Weightman, who had been a good and

---

52. Cort Henry Schnackenberg, Papers, Hamilton: University of Waikato, letter to Whiteley, 28 September, 1846.
53. RP I, 308.
54. *An 1858 Journey into the Interior*. The diary of S. Percy Smith describing a journey from Taranaki to the Taupo and Rotorua districts. New Plymouth: Taranaki Herald, 1952, p. 8.

faithful friend and companion, had returned to Nelson in May 1846.[55] For almost two years, with only a short break in Nelson, he had stood by him, he had acted as his friend, confidant and on a number of occasions, even as a banker. The missionary sorely missed his company after his departure, although they do not appear to have corresponded frequently.[56] The farmer, Trost, who was considerably older and intellectually clearly inferior to Riemenschneider, does not appear to have been particularly good company and the missionary complains in his letters to Heine about the differences of opinion that hampered their relationship.[57] The lengthy and bitter quarrel with Trost, which was ultimately settled, may explain why the farming assistant, who often had to mind the mission station during his missionary brother's lengthy absences, is hardly ever mentioned in Riemenschneider's papers.

Plagued by loneliness, disappointment and frustration, Riemenschneider had finally decided, after the visit of Taylor (the Anglican missionary) and McLean (the Sub-Protector of Aborigines), in December 1845, to make a major journey to Wellington via Taupō in search of a new field for his labours. The *tapu* incident had frustrated this plan but the incident had, if anything, strengthened his resolve to move to a new area. The old New Zealand hands Whiteley and Taylor, the Wesleyan and Anglican missionaries, had been proved right. Motukaramū, chosen by the inexperienced young missionary without consultation and advice, had turned out to be not viable. His choice had been unwise, but he had also learned many valuable lessons in the painful process of discovering that it was a mistake.

---

55. He subsequently appears to have purchased the North German Mission Society's town property in Nelson. One of the notes in the Heine Papers in the Nelson Provincial Museum reads: 'July 1847 I sold the mission property with the house at Nelson to Mr Weightman. I was forced to do so because of debts £23.6.3; and £22 which Riemenschneider & Trost owed Mr Weightman. Mr Weightman went with Riemenschneider to the North Is. but now returned. As Mr Tuckett had given his section with house to the Lutheran congregation I did not need mine.' Heine Papers, Nelson Provincial Museum, folder D 3.
56. Riemenschneider's letters to Heine contain occasional references to Weightman and requests to Heine to convey apologies for tardy correspondence to his friend.
57. See, for example, letter from Motukaramū, 3 June, 1846, Heine Papers, Nelson Provincial Museum, series A2, folder C.

Chapter Five

Mission Station at Warea, Mid-1846 to the End of 1847

T HE JOURNEY RIEMENSCHNEIDER made to New Plymouth, once the *tapu* had been lifted in July 1846, was not easy. During his stay with the Schnackenbergs at the Wesleyan mission at Mōkau he had recovered to some extent from the privations he had suffered at Motukaramū. Unfortunately, on the onward journey from Mōkau to New Plymouth, the Māori who was carrying his blanket and his warm clothing went astray and the missionary was forced to spend three chilly nights clad only in light clothes, which had become wet. One night was spent in an abandoned hut and the other two in his tent, resulting in an even more arduous trip than normal. By the time the missionary reached New Plymouth he was exhausted. At Waitara he ran into Donald McLean, who had been appointed Police Magistrate for New Plymouth in April. The missionary had become friendly with the young Government official during the latter's visit to Motukaramū, and McLean insisted that his friend should stay at his house. Riemenschneider gladly accepted the offer of hospitality.

Although the missionary had also had pressing invitations from the Wesleyan missionary in New Plymouth, Henry Hanson Turton, to stay with him, McLean had managed to capture him first. While the visit to McLean's home does not appear to have been a complete success, it does not seem to have affected the growing friendship between the two men. Riemenschneider reports to his superiors that because both he and McLean were very busy, the latter,

> ... had arranged a room and board for me in a most respectable house in the middle of town, where, he hoped, I would be more comfortable and less disturbed than the present circumstances in his house permitted. As he hoped that I would not think of returning to Mokau in less than a month or more, he had made arrangements that I could keep the room for my entire stay in New Plymouth.[1]

Since McLean had rented the lodgings by the week, Riemenschneider felt obliged to stay there for at least one week. He found plenty to do. The feast

---

1. Riemenschneider Papers, RP II, 49.

organised by the Te Ātiawa, for which the *tapu* at Mōkau had been lifted, was being held. It is mentioned by B. Wells, an early historian of Taranaki, who reports laconically: 'July. – 400 Waikatos visited the settlement and stayed a fortnight. There was great feasting during their stay. They sold a number of pigs to the settlers. Mr McLean's force contributed much to the maintenance of peace'.[2] Since Riemenschneider knew most of the strangers, 'particularly those from Kawhia, Mokau, etc.', he writes,[3] he spent the week 'supervising' them, as the local Māori had voiced to him misgivings that there could be trouble. The missionary himself felt that any incident that would involve New Plymouth Pākehā authorities 'might be regarded as involving some risk with regard to maintaining the peace between the natives and the Europeans'.[4]

At the end of the week, Riemenschneider moved out of town again, this time to stay at the Wesleyan mission station with the Turtons (the missionary having met the Reverend Turton the previous year in October 1845 in Kāwhia). After his long isolation in Motukaramū, the young missionary must have enjoyed the opportunity to talk in depth with an experienced colleague. He poured out his heart to Turton about the very difficult and depressing situation in which he found himself at Motukaramū and about the need for him to find a new area. Turton's reaction was a complete surprise for the German missionary:

> He offered me as a field for my labours, without imposing any conditions: a coastal strip of 40 English miles, north to south, of the Taranaki District, with all the rights and claims which his society might have and with all the natives who are there in the care of the latter. I expressed my doubts about his authority to make such an offer to me just like that. He was certain, however, that the annual district meeting as well as the committee in England would agree to such a step, and indeed he has got full agreement and ratification of the matter.[5]

Turton felt that a village called Warea, about 35 km. south west of New Plymouth, on the coast, would be the best place for Riemenschneider to settle since it was approximately in the centre of the new district. It was also the seat of one of the senior chiefs, Pāora Kukutai, and because of this, it could be regarded as the 'capital' of the Taranaki tribe.

Turton's colleagues and superiors were not quite as sanguine about his unilateral offer as he had thought and there were some repercussions in Wesleyan circles of which Riemenschneider appears to have been unaware.

Turton was, however, in a difficult situation. He was the only missionary

---

2. Benjamin Wells, *The History of Taranaki*. New Plymouth: Edmunson & Avery, 1878, p. 138.
3. RP II, 49.
4. *ibid.*
5. RP II, 47–48. The translation leaves out a second 'without imposing any conditions' in the first sentence, which is clearly a mistake.

in a very large district, as well as minister to the settler congregation in New Plymouth, and he badly needed some assistance, which the Wesleyans could not provide. Their resources were stretched to the limit and they were under attack from London for spending too much money in their Southern District.[6] More and more Māori who had been taken as slaves by the conquering Waikato and northern tribes such as the Ngāpuhi in the 1830s, were being released by their former masters who had embraced Christianity.[7] They were flocking back to their ancestral lands and thus Turton's congregation in Taranaki was expanding. At the same time, Taranaki had become one of the focal points in the contest for Māori souls between the Anglo-Catholic, Bishop Selwyn, and the Wesleyans. In 1844, Turton had written a number of open letters, which were published in *The Southern Cross*, and in which he accused the Bishop of fostering division between the churches by insisting that Anglican Māori were not to share in worship with non-Anglicans. This had brought about a climate of strong antagonism between Anglican and Wesleyan Māori, which had culminated in the action taken by one village in building a fence across it to separate the two religious denominations.[8] Bishop Selwyn, undeterred by Turton's criticism, had stationed a young clergyman, John Bolland (whom Riemenschneider had met on his arrival in New Plymouth in August 1844), in New Plymouth who saw it as his task to bring as many Taranaki Māori as possible into the fold of the Anglican church.[9] Bolland's rather vigorous advocacy of his church and his denial that the Wesleyan church was a 'true' church[10] seems to have won him converts in the Taranaki area.

Just as the Wesleyan Superintendent, John Whiteley, had finally consented to accept Riemenschneider's stationing himself at Motukaramū in the hope that he would stem the tide of Catholicism that threatened to overwhelm the upper Mōkau region, Turton obviously regarded the entry of a German missionary into the ministry in Taranaki as a convenient way to stop the drift

---

6. See, for example, Whiteley to Secretaries, September 23, 1844, Wesleyan Methodist Missionary Society Papers, containing correspondence between the Secretaries and missionaries stationed in New Zealand. Typescript copy, John Kinder Library, St John the Evangelist Theological College, Auckland.
7. On slavery as an institution among the Māori see Raymond Firth, *Economics of the New Zealand Maori*. 2nd edn, Wellington: Government Printer, 1959, pp. 109–10, 213–16.
8. See Bronwyn Elsmore, *Like Them That Dream. The Maori and the Old Testament*. Tauranga: Tauranga Moana Press, 1985, pp. 53–54.
9. John Bolland (1820–1847) came to New Zealand in 1842. After some training in St John's College he was ordained a deacon and installed in New Plymouth as its first Anglican clergyman on 3 December 1843. He was ordained priest in 1845 and died less than two years later on 29 May 1847.
10. Riemenschneider reports that while he was looking after Whiteley's station in Kāwhia in October 1845 some Māori came to see him to ask whether Whiteley and other Wesleyan missionaries were really proper ministers of the gospel. They claimed that Bolland, on his way home from Auckland, where he had been ordained, had told them that Wesleyan missionaries were not proper ministers, that their titles were only presumptions. (RP I, 313.)

towards Anglicanism without incurring further expense for the Wesleyans.

Another factor which, in Turton's view, made the stationing of a missionary in Taranaki, and particularly in the village of Warea, desirable, was that there had been some kind of religious revival among the Māori of Taranaki between September 1845 and May 1846, which had alarmed the Wesleyan missionary considerably. On his way south from New Plymouth to visit the southern Taranaki mission station of Heretoa to settle the affairs of John Skevington,[11] Turton visited the Māori settlement at Warea and reported as follows:

> Octr. 23rd... On arriving at Warea on my way thither, I was perfectly confounded to hear of certain new & fantastic notions which the people of the place had actually brought themselves to entertain – something, I imagine, of a similar nature to what has recently sprung up in the Principality of Wales.[12] They told me that they had dreamt dreams, seen visions, and received revelations from the Spirit – that they had personal converse with God, seeing Him with their mortal eyes – that Christ had come a second time into the world, and was there, as it were impersonated in the body of *Hakopa* (Jacob), under wh. Māori shape he is hereafter to be worshipped by all nations – that there was no Bible, no sin, no Sabbath, no hell, no Devil, neither a day of Judgement nor a Future State - that they themselves were Angels – that all Ministers were false Prophets, "Speaking lies in hypocrisy" &c. &c. This appears to have been the doctrinal part of their faith. In practice, they went regularly into the bush to receive their revelations – they bowed themselves before Hakopa as the descended Messiah – they went out fishing and did other work on the Sabbath – they packed up their Testaments, and sent them off to *Otumatua* – they rolled their eyes, bowed down their heads, extended their arms, wept like children, & kept reiterating the word "Amen" wh. served alike as an expression of worship, a welcome to strangers, & a blessing on their food. Such is a mere outline of the new *religion* of Warea: equally affecting both Church [Anglican] & Wesleyans, and put forth with an infatuation of feeling perfectly indescribable ...
>
> ... And hence it was that they wrote a letter to Captain Fitzroy, praying him "to remove the Government, and all his white-men to Warea, to the place where Jesus Christ had taken up his abode! This unique epistle, however, was detained at New Plymouth ... [13]

---

11. John Skevington (1814–1845) arrived in New Zealand in 1842. He was stationed at Waipā and then Taranaki South. He died suddenly during a church service at the annual meeting of Wesleyan missionaries in Auckland on 21 September 1845.

12. It is probable that Turton is referring to the so-called 'Rebecca riots', which were directed against road toll gates in 1839 and erupted again in 1842–43. 'The rioters – who wore women's clothes – were known as Rebecca, probably a reference to Genesis 24,60, a verse that claims that the seed of Rebecca shall inherit the gates of those that hate her.' (John Davies, *A history of Wales*. London: Allen Lane the Penguin Press, 1993, p. 378.)

13. Turton to Secretaries, May 30, 1846. Wesleyan Methodist Missionary Society Papers, containing correspondence between the Secretaries and missionaries stationed in New Zealand. Typescript copy, John Kinder Library, St John the Evangelist Theological College, Auckland.

The Anglican, Richard Taylor, who witnessed the movement among his parishioners, called it the 'Warea Delusion' in one of his books.[14] This term appears to have gained some currency among historians of New Zealand religious movements[15] although the Rev. W. C. Cotton, the Church Missionary Society missionary at Hēnui, who described it in September 1845, called it the 'Tikanga Hou' movement, which may be translated as 'new way, 'new doctrine' or 'new truth'.[16]

Riemenschneider accepted the challenge of a new field after making a short visit of inspection on which he was accompanied by Turton. When the two clergymen were halfway to Warea they met virtually the entire population of the village who were driving pigs to New Plymouth to sell in payment for a water mill that they were having built.[17] There clearly was no point in continuing south to visit a deserted village. The missionaries therefore turned back and journeyed with the Warea people to Hauranga where they spent the night together before travelling in their company to New Plymouth. From there, Riemenschneider intended to go back to Motukaramū, gather his belongings and move to Taranaki to take up his new position.

After walking from New Plymouth to Mōkau, and waiting a fortnight at Mōkau for Te Kurī to accompany him up the river, Riemenschneider arrived at his mission station for the last time on Saturday, 21 August 1846. He had decided that his departure would have to be clandestine. The Mōkau *tapu*, which had just been lifted, and an earlier incident in which Te Kurī's wife Rangihuia had placed a *tapu* on the Mōkau River to prevent the Catholic priest from travelling downriver,[18] had made Riemenschneider afraid that Te Kurī could stop him from leaving Motukaramū. If the chief did that, the missionary would have to stay there, a virtual hostage, for as long as it pleased the Māori chief. He thus used the pretext of an extended journey into the interior and the south of the North Island as a ruse to hide the true nature of his departure from Motukaramū. He had intended to go on such a journey anyway before the Mōkau *tapu*, and he had already informed Te Kurī of his plans.

The missionary wasted no time at Motukaramū. On the Sunday, the day after his arrival, he conducted divine service and school. The size of his

---

14. Richard Taylor, *The Past and Present of New Zealand: With its prospects for the future*. London: William Macintosh, 1868, pp. 41–43.
15. See, for example, Paul Clark, *'Hauhau'. The Pai Marire search for Maori identity*. Auckland: Auckland University Press, 1975, p. 105.
16. See Bronwyn Elsmore, *Mana from Heaven: A century of Maori prophets in New Zealand*. Tauranga: Tauranga Moana Press, 1989.
17. For an account of this, as well as two other flour mills built by Māori in Taranaki in the mid-19th century, see Kelvin Day, 'Iwi flour mills', *New Zealand Historic Places*, 55 (September 1995), 26–28.
18. The priest apparently had angered Rangihuia by stating that Protestant missionaries were slaves. (RP I, 259. footnote.)

congregation could have only confirmed his feeling that he was fighting for a lost cause here, and thus strengthened his resolve to depart. It consisted of a total of six people: four from Motukaramū and the two bearers whom he had recruited at Mōkau. After a lengthy discussion with his mission assistant, Trost, the decision was made that Riemenschneider should leave first on his own with some of the mission property, and that Trost would then follow him with the rest, once the new German mission station was established in Taranaki. On Monday, the missionary started to pack:

> I told my two Mokau companions to have the canoe ready for going downriver on Wednesday morning, 25 August, at the same time I engaged my old companion Wiremu for the journey to New Plymouth. I left all my books standing with the exception of the concordance and some others, but I packed my leather suitcase and another chest full of clothing, underwear etc., as much as seven men were able to carry. I intended to take the suitcase to Taranaki but to repack the content of the chests into bags [to be left] in Mokau.[19]

Wednesday was spent haggling and pleading with the two bearers from Mōkau who had now changed their minds about returning and intended instead to go inland to have themselves tattooed. By Thursday morning they had agreed to accompany Riemenschneider but now the price for their services had gone up. They demanded a payment of four shillings in addition to the shirt they had been promised. The missionary writes:

> So I finally agreed on Thursday morning and at 11 o'clock in the morning I took my final leave of my station at Motukaramu, not without an inner feeling of deep melancholy and grievous pain.[20]

Riemenschneider's feelings were understandable. He had commenced work at Motukaramū just under two years ago, full of enthusiasm and with high hopes of being able to establish a flourishing congregation in a district with an expanding population. He now had to accept that the venture had proved a mistake and had resulted in failure. The population of Motukaramū was declining, and he had not been able to persuade the chief, and with him his people, to give up Catholicism. In comparison with his colleagues from other religious denominations who were working in New Zealand, Riemenschneider had admittedly suffered from a number of serious disadvantages. He lacked a support network of experienced missionaries and he had fewer financial resources. Neither a strong faith nor youthful enthusiasm could compensate for lack of experience, a lack of knowledge of the language and culture of the people amongst whom he worked, and the isolation of his station.

---

19. RP II, 59.
20. RP II, 60–61.

Yet the two years had not been wasted. The young missionary had learned a lot about working among Māori, both from the small *hapū* at Motukaramū and from his friend and mentor, Wesleyan Superintendent, John Whiteley. He had also acquired enough of the Māori language to be able to use it with confidence in everyday transactions with Māori and in the much more difficult and demanding area of pastoral care. The German missionary, who had just turned 29, had served his apprenticeship. It had been hard and costly, both in personal and professional terms. Now he was putting it behind him and set out to face a new challenge among a new people.

✣

When Riemenschneider reached New Plymouth, he found that Turton, without consulting him, had decided that the German missionary would deputise for him while he went to the annual meeting of Wesleyan missionaries in Auckland. He had informed the Warea Māori not to collect their new pastor until 19 September 1846.

A party of Taranaki Māori duly arrived on Saturday, 19 September to fetch 'their' missionary. He packed on Monday, 21 September and on the next day they set out for Warea. Halfway to Hauranga, their first overnight stop, the new pastor of Taranaki had his first encounter with the sectarian attitude he would in future have to deal with in his new area. On offering to preach at a Māori funeral he was told politely but firmly by the officiating Anglican Māori teacher that they had strict instructions from the Episcopal clergyman, Bolland, not to permit any non-Episcopal person to conduct divine worship in their village.

Riemenschneider was warmly welcomed when he arrived at Warea. A house was being built for him at an abandoned *pā* site called Tarakihi, about five minutes' walk from the *kāinga*. Since it was not yet finished because the Māori were busy on their fields, the local Wesleyan teacher, Piripi, had prepared his own house in the village as interim accommodation for the missionary. This was achieved by the erection of a dividing wall to make a bedroom and a living room and the addition of a chimney. Riemenschneider describes the welcome in Warea, which was doubtlessly a pleasant experience for him. He clearly enjoyed the attention that was being lavished on him.

> I had already been expected on the previous evening at Warea and when I finally arrived I found many of the natives of the neighbouring villages, both my own as well as Episcopalians, gathered here in order to welcome me as the preacher of Taranaki. As soon as I entered the village I found myself surrounded by a large crowd of people, old and young. All were eager to give me their hand and their *tena koe* (be welcome).[21]

---

21. RP II, 69.

The missionary calls the area to which he was called Taranaki. It is important to distinguish Riemenschneider's Taranaki from the district that is now known by that name. Present day Taranaki (Taranaki whānui) comprises four traditional tribal areas: the Te Ātiawa territory in the north includes Waitara and New Plymouth, while Taranaki proper (Taranaki tūturu) comprises the area south of New Plymouth and around Cape Egmont. The Ngāti Ruanui territory extends down to approximately the Pātea River, while the southernmost Taranaki tribe, the Ngā Rauru, occupy the territory between the Pātea River and the mouth of the Whanganui River. Riemenschneider's ministry from Warea was to the Taranaki tribe. The Wesleyan Woon[22] at Heretoa was the missionary for Ngāti Ruanui while Turton in New Plymouth ministered to the European congregation there and to the Te Ātiawa people. As far as the Anglicans were concerned, Bolland looked after Te Ātiawa and Taranaki, while Taylor from Whanganui ministered to the Ngāti Ruanui. Some of the villages in Taranaki had populations consisting entirely of Wesleyans or Anglicans, others had a mixed population and two separate chapels. When Riemenschneider began his work in Taranaki, Warea was split about half and half.

The missionary had arrived in a district that he saw as vastly more promising than Motukaramū. He had come to settle in a village whose chief, Pāora Kukutai, was a baptised Wesleyan and whose people had received the missionary with joy. There was an existing body of Māori who would see him as their minister; he would not have to try and convert people one by one and persuade them to join his church. True, he had encountered the obstacle of sectarianism already on his way to Warea, but he felt confident in his vocation and in the power of the Gospel to overcome any obstacle. He believed that the time of trial was behind him and he could acknowledge that he had learned valuable lessons from it. Warea was a new beginning, full of hope and promise.

※

Riemenschneider lost no time in exploring and examining his new district. A week after his arrival in Warea, on 1 October 1846, he set out to visit the villages to the south of Warea and to make the acquaintance of his Wesleyan missionary neighbour in Ngāti Ruanui territory, William Woon. Woon, who replaced the recently deceased John Skevington, had arrived with his family

---

22. William Woon (1803–1858), a printer by trade, arrived in New Zealand in 1834 after having served for two years in the Friendly Islands (Tonga). He served in Māngungu, Waimā and Manukau before being appointed to Heretoa. He became Supernumerary in Whanganui in 1853 where he also served as postmaster until his death on 22 September 1858.

only five months ago, on 27 May, so he was still familiarising himself with his district. On the way south, the newly arrived German missionary visited a number of small Māori settlements. In his report he mentions Okawa, Kapoaiaia, Tīpoka and Pungairere, where he spent the first night. The list continues with Te Umuroa, Waiaua, and Ōtūmatua, whose Anglican teacher had specially written to him to assure him of a welcome and where he spent the second night. Most of the Māori settlements were very small indeed. Riemenschneider states that Waiaua was one of the largest settlements with approximately 36 inhabitants.[23] These population figures were a sad contrast to the days before the Waikato invasions in the 1820s and 1830s in which northern tribes using muskets had decimated the population of Taranaki, whose inhabitants up to that point had not access to European weapons.[24] The defeated Taranaki people either fled south or were enslaved by the conquerors. In addition, at least two devastating epidemics, one around 1790, the other in 1820, had taken a heavy toll of the Māori population in this as well as other regions of the North Island. The missionary's travelling companions gave him a glimpse of the former conditions:

> Between Otumatua and Waiaua the natives showed me one of the earlier *Pa* of which they said that previously it had [a population of] 1,500 natives, a greater number than *all of Taranaki* can boast of now. Another *Pa* is supposed to have contained 900 inhabitants and one of the smallest that I have seen here, 300 inhabitants. If we look at the number of the fortresses which are now empty and abandoned, we can conclude from them how densely this part of the island must have been populated before repeated war expeditions from the north and the south and illness raked over it with the dreadful scythe of death.[25]

On Saturday evening, 3 October 1846, Riemenschneider reached the Wesleyan mission station at Heretoa. He seems to have been favourably impressed by the Woons, and in particular by the work of his brother missionary. The German missionary's favourable opinion of the Woons seems to have been reciprocated. On October 5, Woon notes in his journal:

> Spent the Sabbath yesterday at Waitoto among the people and held two services. The German minister being here to see me about the natives at Waiaua, etc. to take charge of them conducted the services on the station, with whom I have been much pleased being very pious and sound in the faith.[26]

In addition to making contact with Woon, Riemenschneider also wrote to his Anglican neighbour to the south, the Church Missionary Society missionary

---

23. RP II, 84.
24. For an account of the Taranaki invasions see John Houston, *Maori Life in Old Taranaki*, Wellington: A. H. & A. W. Reed, 1965, pp. 47–73.
25. RP II, 90.
26. William Woon, Journal, Alexander Turnbull Library, Wellington.

Richard Taylor at Whanganui. He informed him that he had abandoned Motukaramū, where Taylor had visited him together with Donald McLean (at that time the Sub-Protector of Aborigines), and that he would henceforth be stationed in Taranaki. Taylor responds:

> Wanganui, Nov 10th 1846
> My dear Sir
> I was much pleased to hear from you although very sorry to find you had been so unfortunate in your station at Mokau. However we have this great consolation that as we come out as labourers in the Lord's vineyard he will most assuredly guide us into the part he would have us be placed.[27]

Taylor then renews the suggestion he made during his visit to Motukaramū that Riemenschneider should consider placing himself and his work under the superintendence of the Anglo-Catholic Bishop Selwyn.[28] By now however the German missionary was confident that he had found a field that would sustain him and his work, as well as reliable partners in his Wesleyan neighbours, so that he did not need the help of the Bishop, whom he regarded with considerable suspicion in any case.

Once he had returned to Warea from his journey to the Ngāti Ruanui territory in the south, Riemenschneider set about establishing himself as the 'preacher of Taranaki', a phrase that he used often to describe himself and his work in the despatches to his Society. In contrast to the situation at Motukaramū where the inexperienced young missionary had had no readymade infrastructure for his work as a pastor, the Wesleyan missionary Turton had already organised Taranaki, so that when the new pastor arrived there were 12 Māori teachers or catechists in the various villages, who assisted with the pastoral work. In addition to the regular morning and evening prayers, they also conducted Sunday services when the missionary was absent. Riemenschneider himself worked tirelessly, not just in establishing his ministry in this new and promising area but, as will be seen later, throughout his life as a missionary.

The work was hard, both physically and mentally. The lack of success at his first post must have weighed heavily on his mind. He had had no rest between finishing his work at Motukaramū and beginning at Taranaki; the days in New Plymouth had been spent looking after Turton's parish. In addition to fatigue, which sometimes bordered on exhaustion, the missionary seems to have been suffering from repeated bouts of deep depression of which rare glimpses appear in his papers. On Thursday, 30 July 1846, he reports in his diary that on getting up in the morning he was attacked by 'such an unbearable melancholy that I could breathe only with difficulty, even when, regardless

---
27. Taylor to Riemenschneider, Taylor correspondence, Auckland City Libraries.
28. Taylor to Riemenschneider, *loc. cit.*

of the rain, I walked up and down outside in front of the [sleeping] hut'.[29] His depression cannot have been helped by what can only be interpreted as neglect on the part of the North German Mission Society. In a letter written to the *Verwaltungsausschuß* (executive committee of the North German Mission Society) while he was in New Plymouth on his way from Motukaramū to Taranaki he laments about the fact that he has had to go into debt and that no money seems to have come for him and Trost from the Society. He then adds:

> I find it necessary to close for this time because I feel physically very tired, and have a dismal feeling in my mind which for many months now has frequently conquered me and is particularly prevalent now and renders me inept for writing.[30]

Commenting on an illness from which he suffered in his early days in Taranaki he states:

> I didn't fall seriously ill again after that but for a long time afterwards I felt an immense weakness so that after I had carried out my professional duties as best I could, neither strength nor inclination was left for anything else and I was often obliged to lie down in the daytime for several hours.[31]

In a report written in January 1847 the missionary feels the need to justify a visit to New Plymouth over Christmas 1846:

> My indisposition and sitting around alone finally made me sad and depressed and I felt it would be a good thing to run away for a change in order to seek some refreshment and encouragement.[32]

Again, as at Motukaramū, loneliness seems to have been a factor in Riemenschneider's condition. On 27 December 1846 he writes to the *Verwaltungsausschuß*:

> I find so much to do that I can hardly master it with my feeble strength, particularly since my constitution, which was never particularly strong, has been weakened quite considerably by the hardships and deprivations over the last two years. I am really looking forward to the coming of Trost, who has not arrived yet from Motukaramu with our things, so that I can get him to work in this vineyard of our Lord. ... I trust I have a faithful and good companion in him.[33]

Trost arrived at Warea on Saturday, 27 March 1847. He had gradually shifted the mission property to Schnackenberg's Wesleyan station at Mōkau whenever an opportunity arose.

---

29. RP II, 53.
30. RP II, 5.
31. RP II, 11.
32. RP II, 132.
33. RP II, 17–18.

In spite of his physical and mental illness, Riemenschneider felt positive about his new area and about his task. In his first report to the *Verwaltungsausschuß* about his work in Taranaki, which he wrote over a period of about three months, he twice remarks how much at home he feels in Taranaki, in contrast to Motukaramū.[34]

Even the Episcopalian missionary William Bolland's vigorous opposition to his work could not break the young missionary's optimism. While he was at Motukaramū, Riemenschneider had been on friendly terms with Bolland and had even stayed at his house on occasions. Now that they were in opposition in the same field, the friendship seems to have cooled. Bolland, accompanied on this journey by his wife, visited Warea for the first time, about five weeks after Riemenschneider's arrival, on Wednesday, 4 November 1846. He refused the missionary's offer of his house as night quarters, preferring to stay in his tent. He had however told some Wesleyan Māori whom he had met in New Plymouth that he intended to have a discussion with the new arrival about the situation in Taranaki. Theological debates between missionaries of different denominations had developed into something of a spectator sport in the first half of 19th century New Zealand, and there would have been an air of excitement in the village of Warea when Bolland arrived.

Victorian decorum was strictly observed when the two reverend gentlemen met that evening. The Anglican 'had himself announced'[35] at the German missionary's residence at 9 p.m. The discussion lasted three hours and was followed eagerly by scores of Māori who had crowded into the house as spectators. Bolland chided Riemenschneider for having preached to the Anglican Māori whom he regarded as belonging to him. The North German missionary, for his part, insisted that while he did not actively seek converts, he would not prevent anyone from hearing the word of God and would certainly not turn anyone away from his services. After a lengthy debate, which also included, among other things, the question of whether the Wesleyan church was a proper Christian church or not, Bolland offered his colleague the right to hold catechism lessons with the Anglican Māori, provided he left all other duties, such as preaching, administration of the sacraments, etc., to Bolland. When Riemenschneider was not prepared to enter into such a compromise, Bolland stated that in that case he would 'vigorously oppose'[36] the missionary's work in Taranaki and the opponents parted. The verdict of the Māori audience is not recorded by an independent source, and the debate certainly does not seem to have come to its conclusion in Riemenschneider's residence on that evening.

---

34. RP II, 71–72, 105.
35. RP II, 111.
36. RP II, 119.

Ten days later when the Police Magistrate Donald McLean came to visit, the Warea Māori asked him whether Riemenschneider was indeed a legitimate minister of the Gospel or whether he was a Roman Catholic impostor, as Bolland apparently had told them.[37] Bolland also appears to have attempted to forbid 'his' Māori from attending the North German services but in this he was not particularly successful. Riemenschneider spent the evening of 31 May 1847 writing down the content of his debate with Bolland in a report for his superiors in Hamburg. He used as his source (for the account of the November 1846 meeting) his diary in which he had apparently recorded so much detail that he had enough material for 15 pages of writing. At the end of his description he writes:

> In the course of the next reports I may well mention my former opponent once or twice, but then it will stop. I have just received, about an hour ago, the credible but deeply affecting news that Bolland died on the evening of the day before yesterday after an illness of three or four weeks.
>
> Since our conversation of 4 November 46, Bolland and I have never talked a single word about the matter. He did indeed oppose me most vigorously in all the villages where he had *tamariki* [children][38] but I did not take any notice of this. Apart from that, when we met, we greeted each other and shook hands. I don't know yet how his end was. However it happened, his death affects me deeply.[39]

Gradually, the new missionary was becoming established in Taranaki. On 26 November 1846 he moved from Piripi's house in the *kāinga* into his newly built house in Tarakihi. He describes his new abode, the most 'luxurious' house in which he had lived since leaving Nelson:

> In November [1846] the natives went back to building the house which was soon completed. The millwright made two doors and windows for it and a table and four four-legged trestles or stools. The whole house is 20 by 11 feet [6 m. by 3.4. m] and contains two rooms, both however without a wooden floor. As is usual, the house is built of reed internally. Externally and in front it is clad in toetoe.[40] In the front there is a small veranda in order to provide a shield from wind and weather. In front of the house there is a small fenced garden which I established very assiduously and in which I sowed all kinds of garden fruit and vegetable seeds. Unfortunately nothing has come of it as yet as it was already very late in the season and also an extreme drought was prevalent for a long time before and after the establishment of the garden.[41]

---

37. McLean Journal, 13/14 November 1846, Alexander Turnbull Library, Wellington.
38. *Tamariki* is the term missionaries generally use to describe their Māori charges. The term also appears to have been used by the Māori themselves to describe their allegiance to a particular missionary.
39. RP II, 119–120.
40. Riemenschneider refers to *toetoe rakau*, a pampas or swamp grass of the species *cortaderia*. The assignation *rakau* appears to have been applied to several sub-species, provided they were particularly suitable for the cladding of rooves or walls. See James Beever, *A Dictionary of Maori Plant Names*. Auckland: Auckland Botanical Society, 1991.
41. RP II, 133.

Apart from settling into his house and laying out a garden, Riemenschneider also established himself among the Māori congregations in the Taranaki region. There had been warm welcomes for him in Warea and the *kāinga* he visited in his new parish. Now a large feast, a *hākari*, was planned to welcome him to the district as a whole. It may be best to let the missionary speak at length because his report describes the feast with many of its traditional elements and it also reflects the ambivalent attitude of the Calvinist clergyman. He had to find 'redeeming' features in a practice that had been condemned by many missionaries because of the perceived gluttony and sexual licence that may have accompanied the feast and activities.[42] It is well possible that, with the notable exception of the feast that was held in conjunction with a meeting to discuss land matters by the Ngāti Ruanui in May 1854, this was the last feast of such proportions held in Taranaki.[43]

> On Monday, the 1st of June and in the following days the guests gradually came streaming in and in front of the Pa, a number of huts made of foliage and green grass were now erected, so that now it almost looked as if the Israelite feast of the booths were to be held here. On Friday, 4 June, everything was ready for the festival. The dried fish hung on a scaffold, five feet [1.52 m.] high and 66 feet [20.11 m.] long, which had been erected specially for that purpose. Along it were placed, always two at a time, 2,000 baskets in two lines with the most varied foods, of course still raw. The content of each basket weighed *at least* 25 pounds [11.32 kg.], so that now, inclusive of the fish, about 58,000 [26,274 kg.] to 60,000 pounds [27,180 kg.] of food were ready to entertain the guests. There were dumplings as hard as stone (incidentally, they were cooked), made of wheat flour and water, Kumara (a long, sweet, potato-like tuber vegetable), Taro (also a very flowery tuber), pumpkin of various kinds, Karaka (a nut which is very popular with the natives) etc. etc. Ordinary potatoes, which are held in very high esteem in the daily life of the Māori, were considered to be too common in order to be served, although they did in the end come back into favour during the latter parts of the feast.
>
> About 600 to 700 natives had come from Taranaki. Many of my own *tamariki* were missing, as they had not yet returned from their visits to their relatives in Waikato etc. I also missed some of the Episcopals who were not on journeys. I assume they stayed away for other reasons. On Saturday, 5 June about 150–160 natives arrived here from Ngatiawa and Waikato.
>
> My festival work started on midday, Friday 4 June and continued almost without interruption until Saturday evening, 6 June.[44] Even though it may be dull and uninteresting to convey in this report a detailed list of my tasks and

---

42. See Raymond Firth, *op. cit.*, Wellington, 1972, pp. 333 f.
43. Firth, *op. cit.*, p. 330, does not list this feast. If Riemenschneider's figures are correct, and there is no reason to believe that they are not, his feast would have been larger than the feast given by Taranaki and Te Ātiawa in honour of Rewi Maniapoto at Waitara on 28 June 1878. For a description of the quantities of food said to have been consumed at the Ngāti Ruanui feast at Manawapou in May 1854, see John Houston, *op. cit.*, 1965, p. 116.
44. The day should, of course, be Sunday.

activities during the festival, you may nevertheless like to see how ecclesiastical festivals are celebrated among the New Zealanders. For this reason I undertake to write about it in some more detail.

First of all I conducted an examination with my teachers from the various villages. At the conclusion of this, our house filled with candidates for the Lord's Supper, partly to report to me and partly to talk to me about the condition of their hearts. At 4 o'clock in the afternoon the first festival service was held in the Pa which lasted until 5.30 and after that I had further conversations with several of the natives about matters of salvation. The people who had gathered spent the rest of the evening together to go over the sermon which they had heard as a group, as well as to share among themselves their thoughts and spiritual experiences.

Early in the morning of Saturday (5 June) our house was filled again with natives. Those invited from Ngatiawa had also now arrived and many of them came to the station in order to register their intention to partake in communion [on the following day] for which they had received permission from missionary Turton. He informed me of this in a note. Then I conducted confession for several hours. Because of the [limited] time however I was able only to admit my own *tamariki*. As soon as this was finished the bell rang for public worship, after the end of which I first conducted an examination of the baptismal candidates, and then there was confession once again with the Ngatiawa. All this took until 8 o'clock in the evening. Then I still had to make the physical arrangements for the Lord's Supper etc.

First thing on Sunday morning several people arrived who had come to ask or tell me something so that I hardly had time to get dressed.[45] At 9.30 in the morning the general divine service commenced. This time I preached about Luke 14, 16–24, with special reference to the festival and the sacred meal. Then I distributed communion to 80 communicants of which just 40 were my own *tamariki* and at the end of this act I performed holy baptism by immersion in water on four persons. All this took until one o'clock in the afternoon. School was next and as soon as I was finished with the service I was reminded by some people that it was time to start with it, as darkness would overtake us if I didn't.

There were about 265 pupils for reading. I separated them off into several classes, while I let the ignorant and old people off for this time so that they could prepare food for the crowd. I mention in passing that they had only had *one* meal throughout the day and that had been very early in the morning. I had previously given all of them the third chapter of Acts to prepare and now delegated the various teachers to lead in the reading of it while I went for a short stroll. As soon as the reading was finished the various groups gathered and formed a large double circle around me in which I then moved around and asked questions about the chapter which had been read.[46] The answers of several of them were very apt and satisfactory. As soon as we had finished with this the ovens were opened and the densely woven, square baskets which served as dishes were filled with steaming food. Now the natives sat everywhere, scattered in small groups,

---

45. The text has 'undressed'.
46. The original has 'I catechised through the read chapter'.

and tucked in with a will. As I knew that I would do a favour to my dear old Paora as well as to the others, I took part, sitting first with one group, then with another, and joining them in eating a kumara from their baskets.

At 3.30 we proceeded to the general service of worship which lasted until 5 o'clock and concluded the church celebrations of the festival. I preached about Philippians 2, 1–3 and at the end I asked five of the various teachers, one after the other, to pray, which they all did with the greatest earnestness and fervour.[47]

The text for Riemenschneider's sermon at the closing of the celebrations embodies the message that he would preach consistently over the coming years.[48] The two key terms, unity and humility, occur again and again in the teaching and preaching of the missionary.

By the end of 1847 Riemenschneider, together with Trost, had well and truly established himself in Warea. He had a modest house, a garden, and some goats, which Trost had brought down from Motukaramū. He had had a splendid welcome both from individual groups and the Taranaki *iwi* (tribe) as a whole. By his own count, the number of his parishioners had increased from 180 to 224, partly due to his ministry and partly to the return of Wesleyan Māori to Taranaki.[49] Looking back over the past year, the missionary comments:

> ... Since I am in this present field of labour, where I have found both room and work, I can say that in God's name my vocation as missionary to the heathen has really become to me what it should be. I have not felt myself so at home anywhere in a strange country than here, where my flock bind me. My most heartfelt desire and striving is to devote all my time and my powers to my flock. I trust that this has happened so far to the best of my ability.[50]

William Woon, Riemenschneider's Wesleyan colleague and neighbour in the Ngāti Ruanui territory to the south, who had been impressed with the young German missionary on their first meeting, also paints a picture of a successful and established missionary. On 20 September 1847 he notes in his diary:

> On the 12th that excellent minister the Rev. Mr. Riemenschneider arrived here from Taranaki North, and is gone to visit the natives and preach to them at the different places as far as Wanganui. His plans of instruction, doctrines, &c. are much the same as ours, and I can heartily wish him 'God speed.' He is of

---

47. RP II, 150–154.
48. So if there is any encouragement in Christ, any incentive of love, any participation in the Spirit, any affection and sympathy, complete my joy by being of the same mind, having the same love, being in full accord and of one mind. Do nothing from selfishness or conceit, but in humility count others better than yourselves.
49. RP II, 182.
50. RP II, 185.

the Lutheran Church. His humility is deep, and he is at home in his work, the natives having great respect for him.[51]

There were however a number of problems that faced Riemenschneider by the end of 1847 and at the beginning of 1848. He was desperately short of money because none had been sent for some time by the Society and he had to borrow money from the Wesleyan missionary Turton just to pay for his modest daily necessities. The lack of funds also meant that he found it difficult to hire travelling companions and even to dress according to his station. It soon became apparent that he and Trost needed a bigger house than the present tiny two-roomed cottage, which in total was about the size of an average lounge in a modest late 20th century New Zealand house, but without adequate headroom. These difficulties aside, the missionary looked forward with confidence to the new year in which he, together with Trost, would build on the sound base he had established and extend the work of the North German Mission Society among the Māori of Taranaki.

---

51. Woon to Secretaries, *op. cit.*, December 1847.

Chapter Six

Losing an Assistant, Gaining a Wife, 1848–1850

RIEMENSCHNEIDER STARTED the year 1848 with his usual industriousness; he certainly did not take a break on New Year's Day. The diary for the first week of the year gives a good insight into the variety of tasks that the missionary had to carry out. It contains no hint of the major problems he was going to have to face in the months ahead:

> Saturday, 1 January, 1848   From 6 to 8 o'clock this morning I worked on cultivating the piece of land destined for the permanent station,[1] 8 to 9 o'clock, breakfast and morning prayers. 9 to 1 o'clock domestic tasks such as cooking etc. 1 to 4, *raruraru* (trouble, preoccupation) with sick natives. 4 to 7 o'clock gardening, 8–11 o'clock this evening; work on the accounts of the previous years.
>
> A number of Ngati Ruanui natives passed here today on their way to Wareatea, where they intended to hold a lament for a Maori who had died the previous August. From them I heard that the fever epidemic which has broken out several weeks ago in Port Nicholson has spread up the whole coast as far as Ngati Ruanui and has become prevalent in that district. Several persons have died as a result of it. The majority of the natives passing through here had themselves been stricken with the disease to a greater or lesser extent on the way and called here especially to fetch medicine. It appears that the affliction is nothing other than influenza. That it has broken out and spread is no surprise however with the sudden changes in temperature and weather this summer.
>
> Sunday, 2 January   This morning I set out at 4.30 and at 8.30 reached Te Aharoa, 12 English miles distant from Warea. Conducted morning worship and visited the sick. As rain was threatening I set out on my return journey at 10 o'clock. Soaked with rain I reached Tipoka where I conducted morning service and then had my breakfast. At 2 o'clock this afternoon I reached Okawha. I was dry again as the sky had cleared. Held school at Okawha. At 4.30 I arrived back home and from 5 o'clock to 6 o'clock I conducted evening worship here at Warea.

---

1. Āperahama Te Reke, the nephew of the chief of Warea, Pāora Kukutai, had assigned Riemenschneider a plot of land of about an acre three minutes' walk inland from the Tarakihi site where the small house had been erected, on a small rise above the Warea (Te Ikapārua) River.

Pl.1: *St Stephani Church in Bremen* (1991)
Peter Oettli private collection

Pl.2: *Liebfrauenkirche Bremen, the church where Riemenschneider was ordained* (1991)
Peter Oettli private collection

Pl.4: *Ordination Certificate for Rev. Mr F. H. Wohlers and Rev. Mr J. F. Riemenschneider Photograph (S07-236) from MS-319/3. Collection of Hocken Library*

Pl.3: *Holy Trinity St Georg church Hamburg, the church where the New Zealand missionaries were commissioned and farewelled (1991) Peter Oettli private collection*

Pl.5: *The Town of New Plymouth in the Year 1843* (1843)
Emma Wicksteed, lithograph on paper, 1575 x 380 mm, collection of Puke Ariki, New Plymouth (A66.126)

Pl.6: *Whakatumutumu Mission Site* (1993)
Peter Oettli private collection

Pl.7: *Frederick Miller Memorial Cairn at Whakatumutumu* (1993)
Peter Oettli private collection

Pl.8: *From Quarterly Paper of Wesleyan Mission House, London, September 1846, Wesleyan Mission Station, Kawhia, 1845* Reproduced in Morley, William, *The History of Methodism in New Zealand.* Wellington: McKee & Co., 1900: 109

Pl.9 (above): *Whiteley Mission Site, Te Waitere* (2007) Peter Oettli, digital photograph, private collection

Pl.10: *Lemon tree, planted by Whiteley, Te Waitere* (2007) Peter Oettli, digital photograph, private collection

Pl.11: *Reverend John Whiteley* (n.d.)
Photographer unknown, black & white photograph, 175 x 140 mm, collection of Puke Ariki, New Plymouth (PHO2002-736)

Pl.12: *Sir Donald MacLean* (c. 1865)
Photographer unknown, copy negative, reproduced in Sinclair, Keith, *The Origins of the Maori Wars*. Wellington: New Zealand University Press, 1961: 115, Alexander Turnbull Library, Wellington, New Zealand (C-19170-1/2)

Pl.13: *Reverend William Bolland* (n.d.)
Photographer unknown, black & white photograph of original pencil sketch, 186 x 138 mm, collection of Puke Ariki, New Plymouth (PHO2007-068); location of original sketch unknown

Pl.14: *Dr Peter Wilson* (n.d.)
Photographer unknown, hand-tinted ambrotype in gold-painted wooden frame, 155 x 135 x 15 mm, Collection of Puke Ariki, New Plymouth (A77.527)

Pl.15: *Warea Kāinga was situated to the left of Te Ikapārua River mouth, with Tarakihi pā behind (centre left)* (1995)
Kelvin Day, colour positive slide, 35 mm format, collection of Puke Ariki, New Plymouth (PHO 2008–287)

Pl.16: *Untitled (Riemenschneider's Mission Station, Warea)* (1852)
Joseph Jenner Merrett, pen, wash and pencil sketch on paper, 240 x 327 mm, collection of Puke Ariki, New Plymouth (A81.105)

Monday, 3 January This morning Trost left for Waimate. This evening I slaughtered a pig. I struggled almost all day trying to herd the goats. On the one hand they don't know me, on the other they have become terribly wild some time ago.

Tuesday, 4 January to Saturday, 8 January Salted down a slaughtered pig, baked bread, pulled out the weeds, which were taking over in the cabbage patch by the house. Had to run after the goats for several hours each day so that I had to give up working on the land on the new station altogether. Influenza seems to take over in this district as well; I have had patients every day. Trost has arrived back from Waimate tonight (Saturday). I am feeling very unwell and feverish but hope that things will improve tomorrow.[2]

Things did not improve and Riemenschneider spent almost a week in bed. He did get up periodically to dispense medicine to Māori who came from all over the district with empty wine bottles. He filled each bottle with 15 grain Ipecacuanha, 2 grain emetic tartar, added warm water and shook the mixture vigorously. The dose was one tablespoon four times daily 'until it works'.[3] During his illness he was also asked to go and conduct the funeral of one of his parishioners because the relatives insisted that he should be there. The conscientious missionary, whose sense of duty would not allow him to stay on his sickbed, limped to the graveside, about a mile away, with the aid of a stick.

On Monday, 17 January, Riemenschneider's condition still had not improved. He was troubled because news had reached him that a packet of letters that he had sent to New Plymouth for posting had been held up at Ōmata because the messenger had been struck down with influenza and had been unable to proceed. At the same time he was anxious to find out whether money had arrived from Germany for him and Trost. So, sick as he was, he set out for New Plymouth.

In New Plymouth he lodged with his friend and Police Magistrate McLean. Another guest in McLean's house was Dr Peter Wilson[4] and his family who had arrived from Whanganui six weeks previously, and who were having a house built next door. The missionary's bout of influenza continued unabated and he claims that it was the most virulent attack of the disease that he had ever suffered. Fortunately, he was among good friends, and there was no lack of care and attention.

Despite the fact that Dr Wilson felt that it was too early for him to resume his duties, Riemenschneider, determined that his Māori congregation needed

2. Riemenschneider Papers, RP II, 201–202.
3. *ibid*. Ipecacuanha and emetic tartar were used to induce vomiting.
4. Dr Peter Wilson (1791–1863) arrived in New Zealand in 1841. He moved to New Plymouth and in 1848 was appointed Colonial Surgeon to the town and Medical Officer of the newly established hospital, a position he held until his death.

him, and convinced that he was now sufficiently restored, set out again to return to Warea on Wednesday, 26 January 1848. Wilson was right however. It took Riemenschneider another week before he could do a full day's work without having to lie down and rest in between tasks. In the first half of 1848 the missionary suffered from two major relapses of influenza as well as from stomach cramps and what appear to have been migraine attacks. These complaints were joined by rheumatic pains in the back and the hips. It was clear that such poor health meant that he would not be able to continue his work under present conditions.

After much thought and anxious prayer the missionary reluctantly decided to spend £20, which Turton had promised to advance to him, on purchasing a horse from McLean rather than building the new and larger house that had been approved by the mission administration in Hamburg. McLean had offered to sell him a young stallion for the reduced price of £26. Riemenschneider considered that by being able to ride from preaching place to preaching place he would not only cover more ground but would also conserve his strength. He took delivery of the horse in New Plymouth on 30 August 1848, while still feeling ill and suffering pain in his hips. On his very first ride, to McLean's house where he was going to spend the night before returning to Warea, the girthstrap on the horse's harness broke, and the horse shied and threw him. He was not badly hurt but his illness now developed into Rheumatic Fever. The poor missionary was obliged to spend another fortnight as the guest of McLean, receiving the tender care of the other guests, Dr Wilson and his wife.

Riemenschneider's poor health in 1848 can without doubt be attributed to overwork, poor diet, loneliness and depression. A major factor however would have been the anxiety caused by the increasingly bizarre behaviour of his assistant Trost. After his arrival in Warea in March 1847 Trost had spent most of his time setting up the mission station. He built a small oven for baking bread, started to plant a vegetable garden and in June went to New Plymouth to get cuttings of fruit trees. He also made plans for establishing an agricultural training centre for Māori youth and apparently submitted a proposal for such an institution to the *Verwaltungsausschuß* (executive committee of the North German Mission Society). After he had left the mission training institution in Hamburg, Trost had worked in a shelter for endangered young people in that city, and had run their farming enterprise. He therefore felt qualified for the task, which he had set himself. The missionary's companion and assistant had also begun to read the Māori Bible in an attempt to learn the language, which he had not yet mastered. However, Riemenschneider does not appear to have attempted to give him any tuition, and Trost himself was of limited scholastic ability, so the project was doomed to failure. The discouraged Trost soon gave up the hopeless task, and early in 1848 he reverted back to the

German Bible, concentrating particularly on the Prophets and the Book of Revelations. As Trost's English was also barely adequate, isolating him from contact with the missionaries' European friends and acquaintances, he seems to have withdrawn more and more into a world of his own, focused on the Bible and memories of his North German homeland, and isolated himself from his brother missionary as well as his Māori charges.

By the end of 1847 Riemenschneider begins to express the view that Trost was not making an adequate contribution to the running of the station. Trost seemed to think that his reputation would suffer in the eyes of the Māori if he worked on the land or helped his ordained colleague with menial work in the house and the kitchen. He therefore either went for long walks, read his Bible for hours, sat idly in the lounge, smoking his pipe, or lay on his bed. He also stopped attending to the goats, which started to run wild. Early in 1848 Trost informed the astonished Riemenschneider that he was not going to be staying in Warea for much longer. He now started to suffer from the delusion that he had been called to do great things in his homeland and that he was going to be invited to join a ruling council of four governors. All of this, Trost claimed, had been revealed to him and to leading figures in his homeland in dreams.

By April 1848, Trost's increasingly bizarre behaviour, which culminated in a cataleptic trance, and prayers in the missionaries' house at which he addressed the bewildered Māori (who, at his insistence, had hurriedly been called there by his brother missionary), in German. Riemenschneider urgently called New Plymouth for medical help.

On Saturday, 22 April, Dr St George arrived from New Plymouth.[5] Riemenschneider had actually expected Dr Wilson, but according to the missionary, the 'aged and sluggish' Wilson had sent the younger Dr St George who is 'quicker on foot'.[6] Trost ignored him, and in response to questions claimed that he was fine. St George prescribed a journey to distract Trost. He also advised the patient to drink wine or spirits. Neither of these treatments were within the financial reach of the missionaries, so Trost received no treatment for what clearly was a severe psychotic episode.

On Friday, 6 May, Riemenschneider went to New Plymouth via Hauranga where he was occupied with pastoral duties until Sunday. He arrived in New Plymouth in time for the Sunday evening service at which Whiteley preached. After the service the missionary went to the Wilsons, where he lodged, and had a long conversation with Dr Wilson about Trost. The doctor,

---

5. Dr G. H. F. St George (1808–1893) arrived in New Plymouth from England in 1841 and served the New Plymouth community for almost half a century. He was a general practitioner who established a reputation for obstetrics. He supplemented his income as a doctor by farming.
6. RP II, 260.

who had consulted with Dr St George after the latter's return from Warea, explained that the state in which his colleague had found Trost on Maundy Thursday was called catalepsy and that he was convinced of the fact that a major contributing factor to Trost's condition was homesickness. This analysis completely surprised the missionary who had not told St George or Wilson about the delusions in which Trost claimed that he was being recalled to Europe. The nature of the delusions confirmed for Riemenschneider that homesickness was indeed the cause of Trost's condition.

Wilson's diagnosis and explanation did nothing to ease Riemenschneider's burden. The reality was that he was living with a psychotic assistant in the confined space of a tiny house, and there was no effective treatment apart from the possibility of repatriating him. A decision to send him back to Hamburg would however have to come from the *Verwaltungsausschuß* and such arrangements could take a year or more, given the time required for the mails as well as the cumbersome decision-making processes of the North German Mission Society. In addition, the missionary understandably continually vacillated between the realisation that Trost was ill on the one hand, and making moral judgements about his behaviour on the other. Mental illness carried a moral stigma, particularly if it occurred in a missionary. Clearly Riemenschneider was out of his depth and he expresses his intense frustration and despair in his diary:

> The work of the mission has suffered, my health has been affected even more and my worries have increased while Trost dreamt and still dreams through his days in carefree idleness. When he arrived here a year ago our station was admittedly wretched enough, but there was order, cleanliness and regularity in the house and the garden. What has happened since as a result of his help? My blood boils with annoyance when I look at it. The garden has turned into a shameful wilderness, the house is in the most wretched condition and decay both inside and outside. If I didn't, to the best of my ability, maintain order and cleanliness at least *inside* the house and cleaned the table, the cupboard, the door and the windows, we would stick to them and Trost would not think of taking the trouble of soaping and washing them. When I leave the house it is *clean* and then I return to a dirty house. Everything is going backwards instead of forwards.[7]

In June, Trost appears to have gone through a manic phase. He went to bed at seven or eight o'clock, then rose again between 10 and midnight and spent the night reading very loudly from either the bible, or a collection of sermons, or singing and, to the missionary's horror, even dancing. He still did not participate in the running of the household however and when Riemenschneider returned to Warea on 30 September after an absence of more than four weeks he found

---

7. RP II, 269.

a spatula that he had dropped in the bedroom on the day of his departure still in the same position. Trost's behaviour was also beginning to be discussed among the Māori who made no secret of their view that they considered it appalling. Towards the end of 1848 the missionary had reluctantly come to the conclusion that he could no longer afford to have Trost on the mission station, both because of the strain on him and the negative example his bizarre behaviour gave to the Māori.

In November 1848 Riemenschneider wrote to the Wesleyan missionary Turton in New Plymouth and asked him to visit Warea in order to look at the situation and then write a brief informal report on his impressions about conditions at the mission station. Turton obliged on 7 December. After Turton's departure, Riemenschneider wrote a lengthy letter to Trost in which he carefully recorded the history of their relationship and enumerated the 'internal' and 'external' reasons why he had to ask him to leave Warea. On Saturday, 6 January 1849 the missionary gave a copy of this document to Trost in which he asked him to vacate the mission station by 30 January. He himself was going to spend the next fortnight in New Plymouth to give Trost time to pack his belongings and to try and avoid any further friction. When the missionary returned however, Trost had made no move to leave. Riemenschneider therefore decided that he had no option but to move himself. He took up lodgings in a Māori hut in the *kāinga* of Warea where he lived during the stalemate with Trost, which was to last several months. Riemenschneider does not record Trost's feelings in the matter. This was probably due to the fact that Trost was lost in his delusions and that, apart from a sense of grievance that his exalted station did not appear to be recognised by his brother missionary and the Māori, Trost does not seem to have shared his feelings with his companion.

It is remarkable that Riemenschneider managed to continue his work as a pastor and teacher among the Māori during 1847 and 1848 in spite of his frequent illnesses and his problems with Trost. His diary shows however almost undiminished preaching and pastoral activity. He records at length conversations with baptismal candidates, quarrels in which he intervened at the request of his parishioners, and both formal and informal sermons, which he preached in the villages.

Apart from the missionary's pastoral work with individuals and families, there also arose wider issues, which began to affect the life of Taranaki. One of them was the modest re-population of the Ngāti Ruanui, Taranaki and Te Ātiawa tribal areas. Towards the end of 1848 Riemenschneider witnessed what became the best known of a number of migrations of Taranaki Māori who had been displaced by the wars of the 1830s and had fled to the south. They had decided at a *hui* in Queen Charlotte Sound in 1844 to return to their homelands under the leadership of Wiremu Kīngi.[8] The migration was called Te Ruru Kai Mā Heke and it took place over several months. Riemenschneider describes the arrival of the fleet in Warea:

> Finally, on a very beautiful morning on 13 October the fleet appeared. On a wide front we saw the many white sails glide across the sea. I counted 31 large sailing canoes and two large [ship's] boats. The whole scene afforded a most imposing spectacle and more or less resembled a proper naval force in miniature, particularly since muskets were fired from many of the small craft. As soon as they had landed, a camp was erected for the 300 arrivals close to Warea. They only thought of setting sail again in order to camp at two more spots in Taranaki after they had eaten everything which had been given to them as a result of the hospitality of Warea and its surrounding villages.[9]

As Riemenschneider watched the splendid sight of the migration canoes moving north along the coast, he noted that most of the migrants were going to settle on their land on the banks of the Waitara. He could not know at this stage that the land on the Waitara was going to be the issue of contention that would ultimately lead to war and to his expulsion from his post in Taranaki.

Another historical event, which Riemenschneider experienced and described, was the strong earthquake of 18 October 1848, which resulted in major damage to the settlement of Port Nicholson. Also towards the end of 1848 he completed a census of his parish, which he sent to the *Verwaltungsausschuß*. His list reads as follows:[10]

		Men	Women	Boys	Girls	Total
1	Hauranga	10	10	6	4	30
2	Kaihihi	2	1	2	-	5
3	Mokotunu	6	3	-	-	9
4	Warea	18	12	4	3	37
5	Okawha	9	7	9	2	27
6	Tipoka	12	7	5	2	26
7	Te Oharoa or Pungairere	18	14	16	1	49
8	Pukeko	6	5	4	2	17
9	Mautoti	4	4	-	-	8

---

8. See Evelyn Stokes, *Mokau: Maori cultural and historical perspectives*. Hamilton: University of Waikato, 1988, p. 83; B. Wells, *The History of Taranaki*. New Plymouth: Edmudson & Avery, 1878, pp. 145–146.
9. RP II, 300–301. Wells, *loc. cit.*, gives detailed figures for the migration, which are considerably larger than Riemenschneider's. He reports that 587 men, women and children, who travelled in 1 vessel, 4 boats, 44 canoes and 21 horses, undertook the migration. Part of the discrepancy may be explained by the fact that some of the migrants were Ngāti Ruanui and Taranaki, and Riemenschneider may not have seen all the canoes. Also, not all of them travelled by canoe, some came by land, driving their stock north. According to Wells, about 70 of the 587 migrants would have disembarked south of New Plymouth.
10. *Mittheilungen von der Norddeutschen Missions-Gesellschaft* (henceforth *Mittheilungen*), 90 (1850), 26.

Table continued from previous page

		Men	Women	Boys	Girls	Total
10	Te Umuroa	6	4	–	–	10
11	Te Namu	1	1	–	–	2
12	Matakaha or Waiaua	13	14	9	4	40
13	Otumatua	4	3	1	–	8
		109	85	56	18	268

Anybody above 16 years of age was counted as an adult.

These numbers represented an increase from 1847 when the total had been 227. At the same time they show how much Riemenschneider's work was a labour of love. He travelled large distances to minister to very small congregations and even though the faithful from one *kāinga* would on occasion travel to a neighbouring preaching place, the missionary's congregations were still tiny in relation to the effort it cost him to visit them.

Riemenschneider continued to do his duty in very trying and difficult circumstances throughout the year 1848. The difficulties with Trost were very distressing for the missionary. He was clearly unable to cope with them on his own and he continued being housed in a Māori hut. He was fortunate in having good and kind friends and colleagues in New Plymouth and was grateful for the support given to him by his Māori parishioners. What he felt he needed however in order to be more effective in his vocation was a settled household and for him this meant that, at 31 years of age, it was time to seek a wife and helpmeet.

*

In the early months of 1849 Riemenschneider found himself in an unenviable position. He was still temporarily housed in a dilapidated Māori hut in Warea, because Trost had made no move to leave and continued to occupy the mission house, while the difficulties in their relationship continued. There had been no instructions regarding Trost from the Mission Society in 1848 but news had arrived that an assistant, Carl Sylvius Völkner, would be sent out to help him in the mission work in Taranaki. The assistant was to arrive in the following year. Another aspect of his life in which the missionary had received no news in spite of making repeated, and finally somewhat impatient requests, was in the matter of the possibility of his marrying, for which he required the permission and active help of the Society.

Some rather determined attempts had been made by the Māori in Motukaramū during the early days of his stay to provide him with a Māori 'wife'. After all, he was unmarried, and many Pākehā who lived with Māori took Māori wives. Some of the Motukaramū Māori could not understand why the missionary seemed reluctant to avail himself of the domestic help and other comforts, which would gladly be provided by one of their young women. Riemenschneider does not appear to have appreciated the solicitude of his Māori neighbours. At one stage he reports having to use a stick to ward off relatives who were trying to insinuate a young woman into his hut at night after he had politely but firmly declined their offer on the previous day.[11]

Informal arrangements for the possible marriage of the young missionary appear to have been made before his departure for New Zealand. At the end of his first half-yearly report for 1845 he refers to them. In the light of the extreme decorum, which he observes in his writing, and in the absence of any other documentation, the details of the arrangement can only be left to speculation. Riemenschneider writes to his 'fathers and brothers' of the Administration Committee with some warmth: the italics in the text are his emphasis:

> And now, dear sirs, in hastening to a conclusion, I take the liberty of mentioning one point in particular. *It is my earnest wish to have a life-companion at my side soon*, and I therefore renew my urgent request to you, to put me in a position to realise this wish. The prospects, which were put before me in this respect two and a half years ago and the promises, which were made to me, are known to you and don't need repetition here.[12]

The missionary does not appear to have received a response to this request, at least he complains in a letter to the *Verwaltungsausschuß* dated 27 December 1846 that, in spite of several reminders, he has not heard anything on the matter of his marriage for four years. By the time the missionary wrote this letter he had however fallen in love with someone else. In the solitude and loneliness of Motukaramū, a figure from the past seems to have captivated his heart, and the missionary appears to have become almost obsessed with her, even though he had not seen her or had any contact with her since he had left Bremen.

Riemenschneider explains to the gentlemen of the *Verwaltungsausschuß* that, while he was a pupil in the Society's training institution in Hamburg, he had one evening read a newspaper report of a tragedy in Bremen. It described how the three youngest children of a family called Suffert had suffocated while asleep in the nursery, apparently because the nursemaid had neglected to open the vent on the stove. The missionary trainee realised that this was the same family for whom he had been an errand boy when he was young.

---

11. RP I, 194–195.
12. RP I, 286.

He subsequently wrote a letter of condolence to Mr Suffert and had received a grateful reply, which had also contained an invitation to visit them when he was next in Bremen. Thus encouraged, he decided to go and see his former employers, and the visit led to the development of a friendship between the Suffert family and Riemenschneider. Clearly, the former errand boy had now attained a social status as prospective man of the cloth, which made such a social relationship possible.

The object of the missionary's fervent love now was Leonore, the second daughter who had been, as he stresses, his *particular favourite*,[13] and who had been about 13 or 14 years of age at the time of his departure. From Motukaramū, the lonely missionary had already made some discreet inquiries about her through his sister. On the basis of his sister's reply, which he had received three days prior to writing to Hamburg, on Christmas Eve of 1846, he felt that both Leonore and her parents might well be willing to view a possible proposal of marriage favourably.

This time the gentlemen of the *Verwaltungsausschuß* seem to finally have acted, albeit in their usual, ponderous way. Nine months after the missionary had written to them, an extract from the minutes of the *Verwaltungsausschuß* of 21 October 1847 records that the consent of all the constituent mission societies was going to be sought. There could hardly be a more comprehensive scrutiny of a young man's marriage plans than the one employed by the North German Mission. After a voluminous correspondence between head office and the societies all over North Germany, the consent must have been given, but the bureaucratic path of true love did not yet lead to a conclusion, and it certainly did not become any smoother. Inspector Brauer, on behalf of the executive committee of the North German Mission Society, took the important matter in hand. On 28 February 1848, he writes in his report to the *Verwaltungsausschuß*:

> 4. In the matter of Riemenschneider's marriage I have written to Bremen in accordance with the decision. The letters mentioned in connection with the matter have also been sent there. Bremen has replied that it does not consider itself competent to carry out the commission *fully*. As far as I can see that is supposed to mean that the committee does not wish to have the responsibility of making a definite judgement about the girl which Riemenschneider has named. Pastor Treviranus now asks for clear rules of conduct; whether he should give the letters to the father or whether he should first direct a tentative inquiry to the father to whom he has easy access.
>
> It would seem most expedient if Pastor Treviranus visits the father and informs him personally of the content of the letters. If father and daughter are both willing, he should then have an earnest conversation with the daughter in which he should ask her whether she is equal to the task which would become her lot.

---

13. RP II, 29.

Almost a month later, on 23 March 1848, Brauer had further news for the *Verwaltungsausschuß*:

> As far as [Riemenschneider's] marriage is concerned, a letter has been written to Pastor Treviranus according to the decision. He has since handed over the letters and advises as follows: the father had certainly been very much taken aback. He knew that Riemenschneider earlier had considered another girl; his daughter had [then] still been a child [and was] now hardly 18 years of age. Pastor Treviranus doubts very much that anything will come of it.[14]

In April 1848 Brauer wrote a letter to the increasingly impatient missionary. It contained both bad and good news.[15] After long and careful consultation and deliberation, Riemenschneider was finally given permission to marry, but Leonore Suffert had not after all accepted his proposal. The thwarted lover seems to have taken the news philosophically.

Freed from any previous commitments in Germany, Riemenschneider, who was not getting any younger — and who clearly felt that a wife would free him from having to do the household chores and thus enable him to spend more of his time on the important work of the Lord — now lost no time in investigating prospective spouses in New Zealand. His fortunes in his adopted country were initially no better. His approach to Mary Ellen Walsall, the stepdaughter of his fellow-missionary and friend Schnackenberg, was unsuccessful. In June 1849 he reports to Hamburg:

> I thought it best to approach her, first of all, in writing, and in order to prevent any possible future heartache I expressly indicated to her that as the means of German mission societies were not equal to the means of English mission societies, the salary of a German missionary would naturally also be less than the salary of an English missionary, and that, as a married man, I would be able to reckon on £100 Sterling per annum *at the most* ...
>
> ... After a few weeks I received my answer. It was negative! Both Whiteley and Schnackenberg, no matter how much they had wished to promote my case, had felt too many scruples to do so because of my great poverty and paltry prospects and this had determined the girl to whom I had turned, to deny her hand to me. I must confess that this was a severe blow for me. If servants denied their hand to me, because they fear that I cannot provide for them adequately, I seemed to have to give up any further hope to find a life companion.[16]

The poor young pastor was distraught. In his work as a missionary among Māori it was not easy for him to make contact with eligible women and the one with whom he had come into contact and whom he had considered eligible had turned him down. He poured out his heart to God and also to

---
14. Bremen State Archive (BSA), 7.1025. 82/4.
15. The *Verwaltungsausschuß* had to wait much longer! Brauer did not inform it of the negative decision until 21 December 1848.
16. RP II, 348–349. See footnote 29, which records the later marriage of Mary Ellen Walsall.

Dr Wilson and his wife. The Wilsons encouraged him to consider the Woon family at Heretoa. Riemenschneider, who had a very highly developed sense of social ranking, felt that now, after his last proposal had been declined by the daughter of a mere catechist, he would have no chance whatever with the daughter of a fully ordained missionary. However since that was the only objection he could think of, he decided he had nothing more to lose. He would visit Heretoa after all and, if he could muster the courage, present his proposal there. In June 1849 he sent the *Verwaltungsausschuß* a description of his visit:

> In the meantime I committed the matter to the Lord and asked for His guidance and answer. On the second day I was here I gained the certain conviction that I should present my proposal to the parents and lo and behold, on the following day I not only had their consent but also the consent and the hand of the daughter. ... When I first presented my request to my future parents-in-law, I not only told them about my previous failed hopes. I also told them that I was poor, but that I was convinced that my society would not let me and mine, whom the Lord might give me, suffer hunger.[17]

The Woons' eldest daughter was Catherine, who was born in Tongatapu, Friendly Islands, on 9 June, 1833. She had been brought up in a mission house, and was therefore conversant with the life of a missionary and would also know the duties of a missionary's wife. One accomplishment of Catherine Woon, in particular, was going to be a useful skill later in Otago; she was able to play the piano. The instrument on which she learned to play had been carried by Māori on long poles all the way from New Plymouth, over roadless, broken country, 120 km. away.[18]

After informing the *Verwaltungsausschuß* of the happy news of his engagement, Riemenschneider appears to have written only one more letter to his superiors in 1849. He completed it on August 9, 1849, and in it he advises them that he will shortly be going to Wellington to meet his brother missionary Wohlers for the first time since 1845, when Wohlers had left Nelson to search for a mission field, which he established on Ruapuke Island in Foveaux Strait:

> Just as I am writing this I receive a letter from Wohlers, dated 'Wellington, July 20/49'. It almost seems as if I anticipated it when I wrote the above.[19] Wohlers

---

17. RP II, 349.
18. Letter of George Curtis, entry for 10 Jan, 1850, Puke Ariki (formerly Taranaki Museum), New Plymouth, ARC2002-168.
19. In the previous paragraphs Riemenschneider had informed the *Verwaltungsausschuß* that Trost was still living in the old mission house, and that he and Heine had now written him a formal letter dismissing him from the services of the North German Mission Society. Riemenschneider had added that he hoped that Wohlers would be able to visit him in Warea to provide an independent view of the matter.

laments about his single state and his deplorable financial circumstances. He writes that he can't come to Taranaki in order to see me and to take a look at our mission here, as he has no money. At the same time he urgently asks me to come to Wellington in order to meet him there and talk about everything that needs to be discussed. He has now gone to Nelson in order to ordain Heine etc.[20] and in a fortnight or three weeks he will return to Wellington.[21]

In view of the fact that a number of important personal events took place in the second half of 1849 it is frustrating that there is a gap of almost a year in Riemenschneider's correspondence with the Society. The next letter to the *Verwaltungsausschuß* is dated 16 July 1850, although it does contain diary extracts from the middle of May 1850 onwards. In the meantime Riemenschneider had met with Wohlers in Wellington, he had completed the new mission house in Warea, had moved in and married. Trost must have left for Germany sometime in this period as well. A letter recalling him had been despatched urgently by the *Verwaltungsausschuß* in July 1849.[22] The missionary's own papers give no details about these events except for some tantalising glimpses:

> Later, after I had been living apart from [Trost] for the whole of last year, I had to live in the tumult and noise of a rowdy New Zealand village in an old, dilapidated hut, in which the sun shone on me in the day and the moon at night. At times I sat for a week as if I were under a gutter …
>
> … At the same time the days which I from time to time spent with my bride and her parents after my engagement, and the weeks which I used for a journey to Wellington, were periods of spiritual recuperation and refreshment which the Lord, from whom my misery and my sighing were not hidden, graciously granted me.[23]

Trost's departure from Warea is never mentioned directly. On 14 May 1850 Riemenschneider writes in his diary:

> I also received a note from Mr Heskin [a New Plymouth merchant] with the news that Trost has sailed for Wellington in the *Carbon* last Friday.[24]

Riemenschneider records that three days later Mr Heskin wrote again:

> Received a note from Mr Heskin this afternoon. He reports that the *Woodstock* sailed for England shortly before the arrival of the *Carbon* in Wellington. So Trost has missed this excellent opportunity to get home, and it is due to nothing

---

20. Heine left the service of the North German Mission Society and was ordained Lutheran pastor of the German congregation in Nelson on 12 August 1849. Heine did, however, retain some connection with the Society. Inspector Brauer informed Riemenschneider that Heine was going to be the 'agent' of the North German Mission Society in Nelson, without, however, being specific about what precisely this title meant or what duties were associated with the position.
21. RP II, 358.
22. *Mittheilungen*, 80 (1849), 28.
23. RP III, 46.
24. RP III, 3.

except his usual vacillation. If he had the slightest amount of energy he would have got on the way to Wellington at once when I told him three weeks ago that the *Woodstock* was getting ready to sail for England from there. Then he would have arrived there just in time. Now he will have to arrange his travel himself.[25]

Trost must have managed to get away after all, because in December 1850 the missionary remarks at the end of one of his letters:

> I wonder whether Trost has already arrived at home. I would really like to know how the poor man is and whether perhaps his sea voyage and the return to the homeland has been instrumental in him coming right again.[26]

There appears to be no full report of the meeting of Wohlers and Riemenschneider in Wellington. Wohlers describes it briefly in his autobiography:

> In Wellington I had the pleasure of meeting Brother Riemenschneider, who, as he had heard of me through Brother Völkner, had gone there to meet me. He had waited for me for a few days, and had, therefore, soon to start on his return journey.[27]

There are some sources that describe at least some aspects of Riemenschneider's wedding. The records of the North German Mission Society, after noting the circumstances of the missionary's marriage, state:

> ... and thus Riemenschneider became a happy husband, without a house, without furniture, without money. The costs were:
>
> | | |
> |---|---|
> | To the Registrar's office for permit and fees: | £ 3 - 12 - 6 |
> | For an ordinary wedding ring: | £ 0 - 17 - 6 |
> | Gloves etc. for the bride and witnesses: | £ 1 - 4 - 2 |
> | | £ 5 - 14 - 2[28] |

The bride's father, William Woon, gives a slightly fuller account in the entry in his diary for 29 October 1849:

> This has been an eventful week and I have experienced both sorrow and joy. On the 2nd inst. our brother Turton was called upon to consign to the dust of death his beloved wife, which event deeply affected my mind;[29] and today, the 29th,

---

25. *ibid.*
26. RP III, 127.
27. *Memories of the Life of J. F. H Wohlers, Missionary at Ruapuke, New Zealand. An Autobiography.* Translated from the German by John Houghton. Dunedin: Otago Daily Times & Witness Newspapers, 1895, p. 177.
28. North German Mission Society Papers, BSA, folder 83/2. It seems that the 'fathers and brothers' of the Administration Committee were relieved to have the matter settled at last. This is the only example of humour that I have found in the records of the *Verwaltungsausschuß*.
29. In February 1851 the Wesleyan missionary and pastor Turton proposed to Mary Ellen Walsall, the stepdaughter of Schnackenberg who had declined Riemenschneider's offer of marriage. They were married in New Plymouth on 10 April 1851.

my eldest daughter was married by her father to the Revd J. F. Riemenschneider, in the presence of her Mother, brother, sister and several natives in this house, by licence, procured from the Registrar, Capt. King of New Plymouth.

> 'Tell His wondrous faithfulness,
> and sound His power abroad;
> Sing the sweet promise of His grace
> And the performing God.' Psalm 57:2

A month later, the *New Zealander* for 24 November 1849 carried the following announcement:

> *Married*, by l'cense on the 29th of October, at the Mission house, Waimate, Taranaki South, by the father of the bride, the Rev. J. F. Riemenschneider, to Katherine Garland, eldest daughter of the Rev. W. Woon, Wesleyan Minister.[30]

From the bridegroom himself, no description of this important event in his life appears to exist. In his diary for Friday, 17 May 1850, he records laconically:

> A year ago today was the day of my engagement. At that time it looked as if my marriage would be in one and a half years' time. The Lord has provided otherwise. Seven months of married life are already behind me.[31]

More than two years later, in January 1852, the missionary looks back on the events in 1849 and 1850, and describes the initial domestic arrangements, mainly to justify the purchase of another load of timber to finally complete the mission house. He writes:

> When I got married in October 49, our house was still open to all sides and uninhabitable. Until that time I lived in an old, wretched Maori hut in the village in which I had spent the whole year while Trost inhabited our old, small house. So in the meantime I was forced to leave my wife with her parents, while I had to spend most of my time here alone, in order not to neglect my vocational duties among our natives and at the same time to advance our building project ...
>
> At the end of March (50) I had our new house roofed and weatherproof. The living room and the bedroom as well as my small study had been furnished with a decent wooden floor.
>
> In the beginning of April I set out with seven natives in order to fetch my young spouse with her bags and baggage. They included a bed because I did not have one and up to this time I had slept on a sack filled with fern. On 12 April we arrived, my wife on horseback, I on foot. The entire furniture which was now in our house consisted of one old table, two old stools so that we could sit, one chest in which I kept my clothing, some cooking-, eating-, and drinking vessels, and four old, short, planks. Our bedroom had neither a bedstead nor a washing stand, nor anything else except a bare floor and four walls. Our kitchen

---

30. Page 2, col. 1.
31. RP III, 3.

was equipped just in Maori style without table, cupboard or even floorboards. The floor consisted of black, moist earth.

The worst in all this was that at that time I had absolutely no timber in order to make even the smallest bit of furniture, except that I drove four posts into the kitchen floor and nailed two of the planks on them to serve as a table, while I fastened the remaining ones one over the other, tied reeds over and around them, attached a window which I took from the old house after Trost had left and thus made some kind of cupboard for food.

We had to be content with this in the meantime until I could buy two chairs and have them transported here. The floor remained our bedstead in the meantime. In June (50) I hired a small boat in New Plymouth – the only one that can be hired – and loaded it with provisions and some things which I had stored in town since I had come down from Motukaramū, such as the book chest etc. and some timber which I had bought in town. This boat capsized in the surf and the sea claimed half the load. However my book chest (soaked through) and some timber was salvaged.

First of all I made a good, strong bedstead, then a washing stand and, in expectation of the imminent arrival of a small stranger, a cradle. I also made a few bookshelves and a small desk, pieced together from many small bits of timber. We now considered our house well furnished with the exception of the kitchen. This room however remained in a very uncomfortable and uncivilised condition, with the roof as its ceiling, the earth as its floor, without any necessary domestic implements, half full of potatoes and firewood and suchlike things. Finally I managed to have a small Maori hut built outside in the courtyard. I paid £1 for it and it serves as goat stable, woodshed etc.[32]

The pastoral work among the Taranaki people continued and appears to have prospered in 1850. On Saturday and Sunday, 8 and 9 June 1850, a major *hui* (gathering) was held at Pungairere to celebrate the building of a new church, seating 200 people. Riemenschneider, accompanied by his wife, attended and reports that about 500 Māori had gathered for the festival. On Sunday, 9 June, he writes in his diary:

> Today was the birthday of my dear wife. This time [it was] a doubly happy and festive anniversary, as it coincides with the hui.[33]

Being winter, it was very cold however:

> As soon as the day dawned the solemn (?) beating of a shovel called the faithful to the early service. Everything outside was covered with thick frost and it was bitterly cold. When I left the church I defrosted my hands on the warm potatoes which they had brought for our breakfast.[34]

The question mark after 'solemn' is Riemenschneider's. Earlier in the report

---

32. RP III, 286–287.
33. RP III, 19.
34. RP III, 19.

he complains that none of his churches in Taranaki have a decent bell. His complaint was taken up by the editor of the North German Mission Society publication, the *Monatsblatt*, Pastor C. R. Vietor, who promptly launched an appeal among the German mission supporters.

Another pressing need, which the missionary reports in the course of the description of the communion service marking the opening of the church, is for a proper communion chalice and paten. He already had a small set, designed for taking along to visit the sick, but at large communion services he was obliged to use an ordinary plate and (what a scandalising thought for his supporters at home) a beerglass. Again, Pastor Vietor, in his report of the *hui*, asked for donations for the purchase of appropriate communion vessels.[35]

One of the aims Riemenschneider pursued in his pastoral work, and which continually eluded him, was to educate the Māori to conform to his image of sober, sensible and subservient European peasants. In a report written in November 1850 he voices his frustrations at length. He wanted the Taranaki Māori to buy cattle and embark on pastoral farming. But they, for their part, preferred horses because the wealthy Europeans in New Plymouth had them for pleasure.[36] Their antagonism against cattle was so great, Riemenschneider reports, that they prevented their chief Āperahama from accepting a calf that was offered to him as a gift.[37] The Māori preference for horses over cattle was not confined to the Taranaki tribes. The Church Missionary Society missionary John Morgan reports that in the early 1850s, the Waikato Māori in Rangiaowhia (present-day Te Awamutu), owned 56 horses but only 13 cows.[38] Even though the missionary had spent countless hours chasing stray cattle in the Moutere during his brief sojourn on the North German Mission farm there, the city-raised Riemenschneider did not understand that pastoral agriculture requires totally different farming techniques than the ones employed by the Māori. Cattle require fenced pasture, and the application of fertiliser to ensure continued growth of feed. The Māori did not fence their properties, and did not use fertiliser, shifting their plantations periodically to allow the soil to regenerate. Pigs, which were their preferred stock, were allowed to roam and forage for their food.

Another irritation for the missionary was the Māori attitude to clothing. He complains that they wore either filthy blankets, which they would not wash, or else they put on what he considered to be unsuitable and flamboyant

---

35. *Monatsblatt*, 5, 1851, 23.
36. RP III, 100.
37. RP III, 102.
38. See K. R. Howe, "Missionaries, Maoris, and 'Civilisation' in the Upper-Waikato, 1833–1863. A study in culture contact, with special reference to the attitudes and activities of the Reverend John Morgan of Otawhao". Thesis (MA), Auckland, 1970, p. 108.

European clothing, which was not appropriate for their mode of life in the country. The thrifty paupers' son comments:

> How often they have made all sorts of mocking and disdainful comments about me, when they see me walk around in linen trousers and jacket, and even often on Sundays, when I ride from village to village in an old, shabby jacket and linen trousers. I consider it wiser, however, to adapt myself to the length or shortness of my wallet than to pay heed to the remarks of the natives.[39]

The city-bred Riemenschneider, whose knowledge of farming was confined to the brief spell of activity on the mission farm in the Moutere, found it difficult to cope with the fact that his Māori parishioners refused to conform to his idealised view. His vision was of wholesome, simple country folk in the European mould, dressed in simple, practical garments, and engaged in pastoral agriculture. To his great disappointment, the Taranaki Māori had different aims and aspirations.

One of the topics, which the missionary discussed with his congregation, and which also caused him considerable problems, was education. The Society had asked him to report on the possibility of establishing a regular pattern of schooling for the people of Taranaki. Riemenschneider found this discussion, as well as many others, which he conducted at various places, intensely frustrating. The Māori all agreed that it would be a good thing to send their children to school, but they had either refused to send them to an institution that Wesleyan minister Turton had founded in New Plymouth, or else they had withdrawn them after a few weeks. This was because, in addition to normal school lessons, Turton had sought to finance his venture from the proceeds of a farm on which the pupils were expected to work. All of the missionary's arguments that such work was good for the pupils and that they would be able to learn valuable agricultural skills did not find favour. The Māori pointed out to him, not unreasonably, that they could learn all the agricultural skills they wished to acquire by working for the Pākehā farmers in New Plymouth and get paid for their labour as well. They could not see why their children should work for Turton's establishment and not get paid for it.

In Riemenschneider's writings he frequently complains that Māori parents are too indulgent with wayward children. In spite of his repeated exhortations, they did not enforce 'Christian' discipline. The Calvinist missionary preached a stern paternalism with emphasis on control and punishment. On more than one occasion he reports to his superiors in Bremen that he preached many sermons on the Christian way to bring up children with a heavy emphasis on passages of Scripture that advocate discipline. In one such report he quotes the

---

39. RP III, 103.

verses, which he used from the book of Proverbs, for example:

> 13, 24: He who spares the rod hates his son, but he who loves him is diligent to discipline him.
> 19,18: Discipline your son while there is hope; do not set your heart on his destruction.
> 23,13: Do not withhold discipline from a child; if you beat him with a rod, he will not die.
> 29,17: Discipline your son, and he will give you rest; he will give delight to your heart.[40]

The missionary, who saw himself as father of his Māori *tamariki* felt not only justified but compelled by his reading of Scripture to teach such behaviours and attitude. With the same justification he also exhibited precisely such behaviours in many of his dealings with his parishioners, whether Māori or Pākehā. For him it was clearly part of his role as minister and pastor of his flock, as it had been for his parents as well as for his secular and spiritual teachers and role models in Bremen and Hamburg.

In the course of a long report in which Riemenschneider reviews the countless conversations he had with his Māori flock about education, and in which he also tries to analyse what he sees as the failure of the Anglican and Wesleyan attempts to introduce Māori schools in New Plymouth, he comes to the sad conclusion:

> From the short comments above you will already be able to see to some extent why no school system would be able to thrive at this time in this area. The parents deny us any support and any co-operation, the children themselves are unfettered and refuse to respond to discipline and order. There is absolutely no help on the part of the authorities and the parents for the establishment and maintenance of a cohort of pupils. On the contrary, the parents hinder instead of helping by being unfavourably disposed towards a school system, and when they do send their children with their agreement, they are ready at any time to help them throw off the yoke of schooling again.[41]

In spite of his sustained and strenuous efforts, the missionary never managed to establish a formal mission school at Warea. The most he achieved was an informal arrangement, which he describes as follows:

> In the letter before the last I informed you that for some time traces of a eagerness for learning had become apparent among the young native men at Warea and the neighbouring villages, and at Christmastime the total number of my pupils reached 10. For these I conduct a kind of school when they are present in the area; i.e. I teach them as often and as much I can in the time I have available.[42]
> However, in spite of all my efforts I cannot bring any discipline or regularity,

---

40. RP III, 79.
41. RP III, 80.
42. This sentence contains an illegible word and the translation rests on a cautious guess.

in short, no proper system, to bear on the matter and this is the reason why it will not and cannot flourish properly.[43]

His repeated pleas for regular attendance as well as his suggestion that they might wish to build a modest schoolhouse failed. Formal, systematised education along the lines advocated by the German missionary was not a priority for the Taranaki people.[44]

In spite of the frustrations, Riemenschneider educated at least two pupils at Warea who were later to become famous. His favourite and best pupil was Erueti, who later became the leader of the Parihaka movement under his Māori name Erueti Te Whiti o Rongomai. His partner in the non-violent struggle against unjust Pākehā confiscations of Taranaki land in the wake of the wars of the 1860s was Tohu Kākahi, who was also educated by Riemenschneider.

While the Taranaki people were not receptive to a systematic Pākehā approach to education, they could see the value of the knowledge and skills such a system could provide. They certainly appear to have been eager to acquire them as long as it was on their terms rather than in the organisational framework, that the missionary insisted was necessary to ensure progress. Te Whiti seems to have taken the lead in establishing a Māori framework for instruction that proved to be more acceptable and therefore more successful than the German missionary's attempts. In 1857, a few years after his own futile and discouraging attempts to establish a mission school, Riemenschneider comments:

> There are very few among [my congregation] who cannot read in their language and besides this can write and do some arithmetic. And in this respect as well, Erueti's help and example has had a considerable effect. He is keen to learn and has, as I have already said, a bright mind. Therefore he has learned and continues to learn this or that at every opportunity from us. Because of this he has acquired among his people, old and young, a certain superiority, without seeking it, and spontaneously, that is, as it has turned out, he has in a certain sense and to a certain extent become some kind of *village schoolmaster*. In the long winter evenings, sometimes this group, sometimes another, just as they feel like it, gather around him in his hut beside the fire in order to have lessons in writing and arithmetic and suchlike in its light, and to read and search Holy Scripture. This has found imitators and general imitation in other villages. In this way we have here among our people a school after all and an increase in secular learning,

---

43. RP III, 146.
44. Richard Taylor was no more successful among the Ngāti Ruanui people, although he reports that, for a time, young people were taught and boarded by various villages, which took turns to educate them for a month or two at a time. He comes to the conclusion, however, that, 'Day schools for native children will not answer; but only good boarding schools, where children of both races mix together'. (*The Past and Present of New Zealand: With its prospect for the future*. London: William Macintosh, 1868, pp. 40–41, 89.) See also J. M. R. Owens, *The Mediator. A Life of Richard Taylor 1805–1873*. Wellington: Victoria University Press, 2004, pp. 167–8.

even though we neither have nor can maintain a central school institution or a firm and orderly school system here.[45]

Late in 1850 the 'little stranger' for whom the missionary had built the cradle, arrived. As always when he refers to family or personal matters, he is laconic about the event. In his report of 2 November he announces to the *Verwaltungsausschuß*:

> On 6 September the delivery of my wife took place and God has given us a healthy, strong son. On the 15th of the same month he was baptised here by his grandfather and was named after him and me; Friedrich Wilhelm.[46]

Apart from the important personal events, Riemenschneider also had to consider the organisation of his parish in 1849 and 1850. When the Society had written that they were going to send him an assistant, Riemenschneider expressed some doubt whether there were enough Māori in his district to warrant two missionaries. He then suggested that the new assistant should live at Waiaua so that their combined efforts could cover a larger area.

The new assistant, who arrived overland from Wellington after having landed there on the voyage from Hamburg, was Carl Sylvius Völkner. He arrived at Heretoa while the missionary was visiting his bride, on 9 August 1849. Völkner had gone through the Society's training institution in Hamburg, and Riemenschneider had been informed by the *Verwaltungsausschuß* in the middle of 1848 that Völkner had been chosen as his assistant and that he would be arriving as an ordained missionary. However when Völkner arrived in New Zealand he was not ordained and the missionary was informed that the ordination was to take place at a later date. Riemenschneider speculated that the ordination had probably been postponed because the Society had taken his point that Taranaki needed only one missionary and that Völkner's ordination would only take place when he had found a field of his own for his activities. This may well have been so. Another factor could have been that Völkner may have been disciplined shortly before his departure. On 10 October 1848 Pastor Treviranus writes from Bremen to the *Verwaltungsausschuß*:

> I also feel bound to inform you that Völkner has formally proposed to a local girl who is not without means. I have informed her mother that he is not allowed to marry or get engaged without permission from the society.[47]

Völkner commenced his work at Waiaua in December 1849, living in the house of one of the teachers, Tamati, while a house was being built for him.

In March 1850 Völkner left for what was to be a short journey north.

---

45. RP VI, 99–100.
46. RP III, 117.
47. BSA, 1025. 83/1.

He was away much longer than Riemenschneider had expected and finally arrived back in Taranaki on 24 August 1850. He was now convinced that there were not enough Māori for him and the established pastor. In September Völkner visited his senior colleague at Warea and asked his advice. He felt that he should not commit the Society's resources to a building in Waiaua, particularly if in the end a decision would be made to send him to a different post. At the same time, the Church Missionary Society missionary Maunsell at Waikato Heads, whom he had visited on his journey north, was prepared to give him free board and lodging in return for teaching duties in his school. After his discussion with Riemenschneider, Völkner decided to return to live with Maunsell in the meantime, and to look for further opportunities for mission work elsewhere, possibly in New Caledonia. He must have changed his mind, however. Riemenschneider later reports that Völkner spent from August 1850 to the beginning of April 1851 at Waiaua, where he had originally started work.

In the course of 1849 and 1850 Riemenschneider had lost an assistant, and although he gained another, the replacement spent most of his time elsewhere with another missionary. He had travelled to Wellington to meet his brother missionary Wohlers, and on the homefront he had acquired a modest station house, a wife and a child. After the problems associated with the first five years of his life as a missionary, he now badly needed a few years of peace and stability, and the time to consolidate his work.

Chapter Seven

Crisis in Bremen and for the Preacher of Taranaki, 1851–1853

RIEMENSCHNEIDER HAD never enjoyed robust health. Already during his training years in Hamburg he had had to be sent to the seaside for health reasons. The years of hard toil and privations, together with a diet that often consisted of nothing but potatoes and salt pork for months on end, had not improved his physical condition and his earlier visits to New Plymouth to find medical attention during the troubles with Trost have already been mentioned. Another factor in the missionary's frequent illnesses seems to have been that he lacked the patience to wait for a complete cure and tended to return to his duties before he was fully recovered. This had already become apparent in 1848 and his behaviour had not changed by 1851. In a letter of 16 October of that year he reports an incident when he had suffered from a chest infection and abdominal pains. He had been obliged to seek medical advice in New Plymouth and writes:

> I was forbidden any mental exertion and physical work was permitted only if it was very light and not tiring. However rules of this kind don't hold any weight with the life and the varied professional duties of a missionary in New Zealand, who cannot and must not even think of a rest day as long as his legs will carry him at all.[1]

It is not surprising then that Riemenschneider continued to be plagued by frequent bouts of illness over the next few years. Apart from regular attacks of influenza, he suffered from a major illness in March 1854, which kept him in New Plymouth for six weeks. Again, he left for Warea on 20 May, before he was completely recovered.

For the next five months the missionary continued his work in Taranaki but he was continually feeling exhausted and unwell. In addition to his pastoral work the missionary also had to act as a doctor and provide medical treatment during a measles epidemic in Taranaki in August and September

---

1. Riemenschneider Papers, RP III, 237–238.

and which affected his wife and family.²

In spite of his frequent illnesses, which culminated in a collapse in October 1854, Riemenschneider diligently continued with his pastoral duties. He had much to do in promoting what he saw as the path of righteousness among the people whom he called, just as he had his German congregation in Nelson, hard-hearted, worldly and beguiled. In January 1852 he gives a couple of examples of what he means by this:

> Some time ago Poirama, who is one of our natives who particularly prides himself on his Christianity and his love, brought his child, aged about six years, to the station. The boy was ill with a high temperature etc. and he was almost naked. Of course we took the poor boy into our care, gave him medicine and appropriate food and my wife made him a good, long cloak from an old piece of clothing. The boy was soon restored to health and the father was extremely pleased when he collected his son healthy and in addition clothed.
>
> A few hours later this same man came with a load of firewood. I was half inclined to believe that he was bringing this as some kind of expression of thanks, but it soon turned out that nothing could have been further from his mind, and not only that, but when he received payment according to the usual scale he demanded more and called us hard-hearted and unkind because we did not pay a higher price. Of course he was taught his lesson at once.³

Another example, which he provides in the same report, is that of a boy who broke his leg and had to be sent to hospital to have it set. According to the report his father could not find anybody to help him carry his sick child to New Plymouth until the missionary hired a Māori for two shillings and sixpence for this task. Almost every report that Riemenschneider wrote in the early fifties contains one or more bitter complaints about the behaviour of Māori towards him and his family or towards each other.

Some of the disagreements between the Māori parishioners escalated into more serious conflicts that required mediation. In such cases Riemenschneider was often asked to perform a judicial role.

The administration of justice in areas inhabited predominantly by Māori had presented a problem to successive Governors. George Grey had attempted to solve it with his Resident Magistrates Ordinance of 1847. This provided for the appointment of (Pākehā) Resident Magistrates who were to be assisted by Māori chiefs, so-called Assessors.⁴ In May 1852, Paora of Warea was appointed as Assessor with a salary of £10.

---

2. According to Wells, the epidemic was started by a few infected children in the barque *Cornwall* who called at New Plymouth on 18 August. (B. Wells, *The History of Taranaki* New Plymouth: Edmundson & Avery, 1878, p. 118)
3. RP III, 273–274.
4. See Keith Sinclair, *The Origins of the Maori Wars*. Wellington: New Zealand University Press, 1957, pp. 36–37; Alan Ward, *A Show of Justice. Racial 'amalgamation' in nineteenth century New Zealand*. Auckland: Auckland University Press, 1973, pp. 74 ff.

There is, however, no record in Riemenschneider's papers of Paora ever having exercised his judicial office conferred on him by the colonial authorities, and the missionary seems to have continued to act in a judicial role, arbitrating in matters such as petty theft, numerous and often lurid cases of adultery, described in some detail by the zealous missionary, and quarrels about land. As far as possible he used local customary law and the Holy Bible as a guide for his decisions.

One of the major factors that Riemenschneider, like other missionaries, cites as contributing to a decline in moral standards, is the frequent and increasing contact with European settlements. While in his eyes this contributed, on the one hand, to the prosperity and 'civilisation' of the Māori population, it also introduced new 'evils' into rural Māori society. In October 1851 he describes the problem as he sees it:

> Particularly here at Warea the young people were almost as if possessed. With sadness I watched even those who had previously given a good account of themselves now surrender themselves to a wantonness which is afraid neither of God nor of man. At times they came to the station in smaller or larger groups, ostensibly for no other reason but to offend us and to hurt us by their talking and their gestures. If I earnestly reproached them for their godless foolishness, they laughed. If I ordered them to leave, they defiantly replied that this land was their own and that they could send me away, but I could not send them away. So we had to put up with it and content ourselves with showing our disgust at them by silent earnestness.[5]

Part of the missionary's problem was his sincere but naive belief that all Europeans in influential positions thought like he did and that Māori suspicion of their motives was unjustified and perverse. In his December 1853 report he writes:

> They view with contempt and suspicion the Queen as well as the local government and the officials who have done everything possible for their welfare and are prepared to do more in future, who have established free hospitals and care for them, who let them have all protection and freedom and who strive most earnestly to help with the promotion of their civilisation and education in every possible way. They have to share with us the reward of the callous ingratitude of this people.[6]

Riemenschneider the missionary, who had come to bring his beliefs and his values to the Māori and who sincerely believed that they were superior to any other religion and civilisation, was incapable of understanding that what he saw as the blessings of European civilisation might be regarded by another culture with distaste and as a curse.

---

5. RP III, 242–243.
6. RP IV, 167.

As the son of impoverished German city dwellers, Riemenschneider also was incapable of understanding the value that land had in the eyes and the hearts of the Māori. The Māori made attempts to explain their views to him and he faithfully records them in his report to the *Verwaltungsausschuß* (executive committee of the German Mission Society) of 12 December 1853:

> 'If the Europeans had not come into the country, with the exception of the missionaries', [the Maori] say, 'it would have been better for us. Then we would have remained one people and would have eaten our daily bread in peace. The Europeans have brought us much, but along with it also illness and destruction, and in exchange for this they have taken our land and want to take more and more, until they have it all in their power, and we and our children have nothing left but are forced to throw ourselves into labouring and carrying out the trade of the lowest class of the Europeans to find our livelihood. We Maori do not intend to do that. Our land is our greatest good. It is to us like our mother's breast. The Pakeha (Europeans) have enough land, and they have enough wealth from which we can draw all that we desire. Let them be content with what they have, and let them leave us everything else. We do not want them to spread themselves any further across our land'. They advance this and similar other advice and objections.[7]

The Taranaki people, who had suffered from invasions from the north and the south, were of course aware that the Māori people as a whole had not been 'one people' and certainly not always 'at peace' before the arrival of the colonists.

Despite these explanations, the missionary could not understand Māori attitudes to land or to colonisation, at least not at this stage of his life. To him, the arrival of the Europeans in New Zealand, whether they were missionaries or colonists, was part of God's plan, instituted by Him to save the heathen Māori. To rebel against it or even question it was not only foolish, it was blasphemous in his eyes. At the same time, he did not want to take sides and explains his stance to the fathers in Hamburg:

> Right from the start I have made it my firm resolution and principle, not in any way to take part *directly* in any of the land questions that arise between the Europeans and the natives. Only by keeping strictly to this principle of a neutral and impartial independence have I succeeded in securing, so far, the firm trust of this people in every way, and to keep all false prejudice and misinterpretation away from my actions and my teaching.[8]

This 'neutral' position, he continues, gives him the freedom to preach his millennial vision for the Taranaki people:

> Using scripture, reason and experience I continually try to show them God's

---

7. RP IV, 186.
8. RP IV, 186–187.

gracious hand, intention and purpose in the work of colonisation and its spread over this wild land and its physically and spiritually decayed people, so that the desert and wasteland will turn into a flourishing garden; and that its original inhabitants should not only be saved from destruction, but should become a physically and spiritually healthy and happy people, which would enjoy all the blessings of Christian civilisation together with the Europeans.[9]

Riemenschneider's undoubtedly sincere but very naive belief in the blessings of colonisation and the wisdom and benevolence of the Governor, combined with his inability to see in the changing Māori attitudes a move to self-preservation, did not bode well for his work among a people who saw themselves as increasingly threatened by precisely the forces that the German missionary regarded as God's tools for their salvation.

The Māori, while more realistic about the impact of colonisation on their people, were nevertheless prepared to use not only European technology, but also what they considered to be European religious magic to protect themselves against the encroachment of the settlers. In August 1853 the Ngā Māhanga *hapū* (sub-tribe) of Taranaki tried to protect its lands against further inroads by the Pākehā by burying in the ground a copy of the New Testament. In their view, this would be even more effective than a *tapu*. Riemenschneider heard of it on one of his trips to New Plymouth.[10] He stopped and gave the Ngā Māhanga people a stern lecture on their idolatry. This Bible-burying incident was later used by McLean (who had been appointed Land Purchase Commissioner in 1852), in a report to the Colonial Secretary, dated 20 February 1854. McLean and some other contemporary writers connect the incident with the formation of an anti-land-selling league.[11] It is clear from the missionary's account that the incident was a local phenomenon.[12]

Riemenschneider's own search for a small parcel of land for his mission station was not successful either. He had heard that in March 1853 the Anglican Māori in Taranaki had offered the Bishop a plot of 400 acres for the establishment of a mission station. He himself had long felt the need for a piece of land that would belong to the North German Mission Society. Once this land was secured he hoped that he would then not continually be exposed to Māori impositions, which were explained on the grounds that he was on

---

9. *ibid.*
10. The territory of the Ngā Māhanga lies between Warea and New Plymouth.
11. A. J. H. R, 1861, C–1, p. 197.
12. For a discussion of the anti-land-selling movements in Taranaki without reference to Riemenschneider's account of the Bible-burying incident (which was not known to the author), see Keith Sinclair, 'Te tikanga pakeke. The Maori anti-land-selling movement in Taranaki 1849–59', in: *The Feel of Truth. Essays in New Zealand and Pacific history, presented to F. L. W. Wood and J. C. Beaglehole on the occasion of their retirement.* Ed. Peter Munz, Wellington: A. H. & A. W. Reed, 1969, pp. 79–92. See also Peter Oettli, 'The Taranaki Bible-burying incident – A Footnote', *Turnbull Library Record,* 29 (1996), 85–90.

their land at their sufferance and therefore subject to their whims and wishes.

When the missionary made it clear to the Warea Māori that if the Bishop could get land for a mission station he should be entitled to some too, they held a formal meeting on 11 May and agreed to his request. He was finally allocated a plot of about 20 acres across the river from where his present house stood.

On Monday, 15 May 1853 the boundary of the land that was to be given to the Society was cleared with sickles and the land was formally handed over. All that remained to make the transaction legal was that a deed of gift should be signed by all the donors and forwarded to the Government agent. This deed was never signed. On the evening of the day on which the ceremony of clearing the boundary lines had taken place, a rumour reached Warea that the Ātiawa tribe (even though they had no right to it), had sold Mount Taranaki, the sacred mountain of Taranaki and Ngāti Ruanui, to the Government. This rumour, which later turned out to be untrue, caused an uproar and the signing of the document that would have given Riemenschneider title to his station, was postponed and then seemed to have been forgotten.

It appears that Māori disenchantment with European colonisation, fear of total domination by the Pākehā and doubts about the missionary analysis and interpretation of their condition, had certainly contributed to the Bible-burying incident among the Ngā Māhanga. These factors would also have been significant in the rise of a Māori healer and miracle worker, called Mitai, in 1853. Riemenschneider reports that Mitai was a Ngāti Ruanui who had returned from slavery in the Bay of Islands and was making a name for himself in Taranaki. While he did not place himself in direct opposition to the missionaries, he propounded the view, according to Riemenschneider, that while Pākehā doctors understood Pākehā illnesses and could successfully treat them, Māori illnesses were beyond their competence and therefore would have to be cured by Māori healers like himself. When a grandson of Paora, the chief of Warea, returned home ill from a journey to Wellington, the missionary-doctor, although unable to make a diagnosis, nevertheless used every weapon in his medical arsenal to try and effect a cure, without success. He then tried to persuade the young man's relatives to have him transported to the hospital in New Plymouth because his condition was rapidly deteriorating. They refused. Instead, Mitai was secretly called to his bedside, identified a tapu, which the grandson appeared to have unwittingly broken, and successfully exorcised the evil spirit that was tormenting him as a result of his transgression.

One of the features of Riemenschneider's preaching appears to have been a tendency, prefigured in the preaching of his pastors and teachers in Bremen, to interpret natural calamities as punishment from God. On 22 May 1851 he describes a potato blight in Taranaki and comments:

As soon as I became aware of the trouble I earnestly strove to make clear to the natives and to convince them that this is a serious and warning sign for them from the Lord God, with which he admonishes them to do penance and to now earnestly seek and accept the grace of God in Christ which had been offered to them so far but which they had so much neglected.[13]

He records that he made similar comments about influenza and measles epidemics to his Māori parishioners, but does not appear to have seen the strong similarity between the 'heathen Māori' view that breaking a tapu may incur misfortune or illness, and the 'civilised Christian' view that a people's or individual's trespasses are avenged in the same way.

The missionary's religious interpretation of illnesses and epidemics as scourges of the Lord that constituted warning signs for his parishioners (he never interpreted any of his own illnesses in this way!) was complemented by the European 19th century attitude to medicine. Riemenschneider had not received even rudimentary medical training at the mission school. When he discovered that Māori came to him for treatment he eventually purchased a book entitled *Modern Domestic Medicine: A popular treatise illustrating the symptoms, causes, distinction & correct treatment of the diseases incident to the human frame; embracing the modern improvements in medicine. To which are added, A domestic diateria Medica, A copious collection of approved prescriptions etc. etc. The whole intended as a comprehensive medical guide for the use of Clergymen, Heads of families & Invalids. By Thomas J. Graham MD etc. London, 1831.* If this work was not comprehensive enough, his friend Dr Peter Wilson supplemented his medical knowledge in their conversations. In March 1855, Riemenschneider comments on the Māori attitude to doctors, missionaries and health care:

> ... and in all such cases it is we [missionaries], in whom the natives seek refuge. It is admittedly true that the English hospitals in the towns offer them not only medicine and medical help, but also food and care, all of it free and gratis. However their prejudice and their antipathy against these institutions is so great that the majority of them would much rather depart this life without help than bring themselves to go into these hospitals. No matter what we do to get them over such foolishness in their own best interest, it is no use. They cannot bring themselves to have faith and trust in the doctors and they maintain adamantly, against all better advice, that we missionaries alone understand and know how to treat their Maori illnesses; that doctors may well be able to help Europeans, but that they rarely understand how to heal a Maori.[14]

The missionary does not appear to have reflected on the fact that the Māori concept of health and healing was more holistic than the one he had inherited. Māori looking for healing would therefore have had more faith in their spiritual leaders, the missionaries, than the doctors who treated only the

---
13. RP III, 186.
14. RP V, 79.

physical symptoms. Their reluctance to go to a hospital can be explained by Māori teaching on death. Buildings in which people had died became *tapu* (set apart, restricted) and had to be destroyed. A European hospital, in which people died and in which even the beds where they had died were used again, must have been a very threatening place for a 19th century Māori.[15]

Apart from his Māori congregation, which appears to have caused Riemenschneider much heartache in the early 1850s, his assistant Völkner also caused problems. The period from 24 August 1850 to April 1851 was the longest Völkner had spent at his assigned post in Waiaua. He was however not happy there and felt that the number of Māori in Taranaki was not sufficient for two missionaries, particularly since most of them were, at least nominally, converted and thus needed a pastor rather than a missionary. He had not only expressed his views to his brother missionary but had also written to the *Verwaltungsausschuß* asking to be transferred. Early in April 1851, Bishop Selwyn visited New Plymouth. Völkner, who happened to be in town, met the Bishop and must have complained to him because the Bishop, who was about to set off for a journey visiting a number of South Sea islands in July, generously offered Völkner a free berth on his ship, the *Border Maid*.

After consultation with Riemenschneider, Völkner decided to accept the offer and set off for Auckland to join the Bishop's party on 22 April. He subsequently notified the missionary of his safe arrival in Auckland in early June. On 2 July he wrote again, much to Riemenschneider's surprise from Maunsell's station at Waikato Heads.

Völkner cannot have painted a very favourable picture of the North German Mission Society to Maunsell because the latter writes to his superiors, after praising the German's efforts in the Church Missionary Society establishment at Waikato Heads:

> [Völkner] with five of his brethren was sent out to this island by the North German Missionary Society. Since their arrival here now nearly four years ago they have not received any supplies from their Society beyond a few HUNDRED POUNDS. Their letters are scarcely ever answered and the question which they are now anxiously debating is, Is their Society in existence? What is worse, the letters of this young man sent to his friends through Brauer the inspector of the Society are not acknowledged by them, so that he fears that they have been suppressed.[16]

Maunsell's description contains more than a grain of truth, and it is not surprising that on Easter Monday, 12 April 1852, after an absence of nearly a year, Völkner arrived in person in Warea to inform his fellow missionary that

---

15. See Te Rangi Hiroa, Sir Peter Buck, *The Coming of the Maori*. Wellington: Maori Purposes Fund Board; Whitcoulls Limited, 1987, p. 416.
16. Maunsell to the Church Missionary Society, cited by Helen Garrett, *Te Manihera. The life and times of the pioneer missionary Robert Maunsell*. Auckland: Reed Books, 1991, p 177.

he had decided to leave the service of the North German Mission Society and to join the Church Missionary Society as a teacher at Maunsell's station.

Riemenschneider himself had expressed considerable alarm when he received no communication or financial support from Bremen for a long time. He wrote on 16 October 1851:

> ... As far as the uncertainty is now concerned to which I have just alluded, it certainly seems to be of some importance to us. The longer it lasts, the greater are the worries which arise from it. For the question here is: *Does the North German Mission Society still exist or has it really ceased to exist? And in that case, what will become of us and of our mission here*? The last letter which has reached us directly from the Administration Committee and from Germany at all, was written on March 3, 1850, and it arrived here in November 1850. In that I was given to understand that within a short time I might expect something more. However 11 months have now passed already, and not a single line has been received either for me or for Völkner.[17]

Riemenschneider's (and Völkner's) concern was justified. The North German Mission Society was indeed going through a major crisis. On 1 and 2 May 1850 an extraordinary general meeting had been held in Hamburg, at which the question of the continuation of the Society was debated. Things looked bad. A significant number of constituent societies formed by 'strict' Lutherans were leaving the interdenominational federation; interest in the mission cause was waning; the training institution had been closed in 1848 due to financial difficulties and as a result of a crisis of confidence between the pupils and Inspector Brauer. Worst of all, the accounts of the Society were 150,000 Current Mark in deficit. The meeting of the Society made a number of recommendations. It suggested that the seat of its operations should be shifted to Bremen; that the East Indian mission was to be handed over to the American Lutherans; that there should be no change in the basis on which the Society's interdenominational character rested and that there should be a rationalisation of the decision-making process. These recommendations were adopted by the Annual General Meeting on 20 and 21 November 1850. One of the effects of these decisions was that Inspector Brauer left the service of the North German Mission Society at the beginning of 1851.[18]

Between the first and the second general meetings of the Society, it was rocked by another blow that almost brought about its demise. In September 1850 it was revealed that the treasurer of the Society had, over a period of many years, embezzled substantial funds and had brought the enterprise to the brink of bankruptcy.

---

17. RP III, 252.
18. See, Hans Lehmann, *Geschichte des evangelischen Missionsvereins und der Norddeutschen Mission in Hamburg: Ein Beitrag zur Hundertjahrfeier der Norddeutschen Missionsgesellschaft am 9. April 1936*. Bremen: Verlag der Norddeutschen Missionsgesellschaft, 1936, pp. 30–31.

While Riemenschneider was spared the trauma of the individual debates and discussions, he suffered long months of uncertainty and rumours until finally, to his immense relief, he received two letters informing him of the situation in November 1851. In his letter acknowledging the news from the Society, dated 19 December 1851, the missionary gives his superiors a glimpse of his difficult situation in the period of uncertainty:

> In the course of the past winter, when time and again the rumour of the complete dissolution of the North German Mission Society arrived here, I often felt extremely heavy hearted and depressed, particularly when I was travelling on my solitary journeys. I felt a *deep* sadness about the lingering death of an evangelical mission society, and that all the more because it was *my* society and a society of the church of my dear German fatherland.[19]

Through all adversity and uncertainty, he had remained faithful to his German Society, as he would in years to come when his links with his parent Society would again be subjected to severe tests.

The quarrels in Germany did not leave the New Zealand mission completely unaffected however. The strict Lutheran Heine, who had been ordained by Riemenschneider's German mission colleague Wohlers as minister in Nelson and who had acted as 'agent' for the North German Mission Society in New Zealand, wrote to the Society with his resignation in protest at the shift of its leadership to (the mainly reformed) Bremen. He had also written to his fellow Lutheran Wohlers inviting him to do the same. Wohlers declined on the grounds that he saw it as his task to preach the gospel, not to brood on the more esoteric points of denominational doctrine. Editor Pastor Vietor gleefully printed Wohlers's letter in full in the Society's publication, *Monatsblatt*.[20]

One way out for the missionary during the long period of uncertainty about continuing support for his work from the North German Society would have been to follow Völkner's example and find another source of income. The European settlers at Tataraimaka, 22 km. south of New Plymouth, had invited him to shift his station to their locality. They had no clergyman of their own and offered him free land for his station and a church. This was, of course, tempting for the missionary who felt that he was in a precarious situation both with regard to his station at Warea and continuing support from his Society. He comments:

> In many external respects it would be more advantageous and more pleasant to live among Europeans and on our own plot of land, independent of the natives and their narrow-minded toleration.[21]

---

19. RP III, 262.
20. No. 32 (1853), 132.
21. RP IV, 145.

He concludes however that his particular vocation is among the Taranaki Māori and that his move to Tataraimaka, attractive though it might be for him and his family, would make him too much of an 'English pastor'.

In spite of the fact that Dr Wilson strongly advised him to do so, the missionary never took a holiday, although his life at Warea was not without some social diversions and happy family events. The coast road, such as it was, from Whanganui to New Plymouth was used by many interesting travellers, some of whom stayed overnight with the Riemenschneiders. (Socially inferior persons were referred to the Māori *kāinga* for hospitality!) One visitor was the artist J. J. Merritt who visited the station in February 1852 and spent several days there drawing the buildings with Mount Taranaki in the background. In appreciation for the hospitality he enjoyed, Merritt made a copy of his picture for his host, as well as a smaller copy, which the missionary sent to Bremen.

On Saturday, 22 May 1852, the Riemenschneiders' second child, a daughter, was born. Catherine's mother had come to Warea for the confinement and delivered the baby. On Friday, 28 May, her grandfather, who had been feeling rather lonely and sorry for himself in Waimate, came to Warea and baptised her. She received the names of her two grandmothers, Anna Jane.

The addition to the family meant that the mission house was getting very small and at the same time was also getting old and was in urgent need of major repairs. In a report to the *Verwaltungsausschuß*, written between January and March 1854, Riemenschneider describes his house as follows:

> The height of this house from the floor to the roof is seven and a half feet [2.3 m.] because the posts have had to be set two feet [610 mm.] into the ground. The interior dimensions are as follows: Entry hall or vestibule, four feet [1.2 m.] square. Living room, 10 feet [3 m.] deep and 11 feet [3.3 m] long. Study, four feet [1.2 m.] deep and seven feet [2.1 m.] long. Bedroom, 10 feet [3 m.] deep and 11 feet [3.3 m.] long. Kitchen, 12 feet [3.6 m.] square. In the kitchen however a small pantry has been partitioned off, four feet [1.2 m.] deep and seven feet [2.1 m.] long.
>
> Its flimsy and makeshift construction which was inevitable because of the lack of any resources at that time, means that the house, which was built only four years ago, is threatened with imminent and inevitable collapse. *All* the supporting poles have *rotted through* to ground level, and as the house has nothing which supports it either inside or out I can only attribute it to the protecting grace of the Lord that it has held out as well as it does, particularly as it is exposed to storms and weather on all sides.[22]

It would seem that one of the few relatively secure supports for the house would have been the two massive chimneys, built of boulders and local clay.

---

22. RP IV, 241.

By the time Riemenschneider wrote this description, however, he had already had to rebuild both chimneys three times after rain and earthquakes had weakened them and finally caused them to topple.

If the house was becoming dangerous to live in, the missionary was exposed to various dangers when travelling in his parish. On 16 November 1851, a scrub fire, lit by the local Māori to clear land for their cultivations, threatened to burn down the mission house, and the missionary and his family spent an anxious night fighting the flames around them, helped by the Warea parishioners. In February 1852 Riemenschneider was almost killed while warming himself at an open fire in a Māori hut. He discovered to his horror that the barrel on which he was sitting was full of gunpowder! In September 1852 his horse shied and threw him. The injuries he sustained in the fall confined him to his bed for a week. In the following month he came very close to drowning when he was swept off his feet while fording a swollen river and his Māori travel companion also lost his footing.

By the end of 1854 Riemenschneider could look back on a few years of comparative stability. True, there had been ups and downs, both as far as his personal health and the cause of the mission was concerned. On Sunday, 27 August 1854 the missionary could welcome another addition to their family. He had intended to spend the weekend away from home but had been prevented by atrocious weather from leaving. This was fortunate because a second daughter, Emma Eleonora, was born...

> ... apart from us there was not another soul on the station. I myself had to act as midwife and nursemaid. With God's help I was so successful that within an hour the newborn little child had been washed, fully clothed in all its garments, and every other task had been carried out. Already by three o'clock mother and child had been most comfortably settled in bed together and I too could soon after lie down to sleep for the rest of the night.[23]

The missionary family was thriving in New Zealand, the North German Mission Society had weathered a long and painful theological and financial crisis and the preacher of Taranaki could look forward to continued support from Bremen and security in his chosen field of labour. Visible symbols of this support had arrived in December 1852, when a silver communion plate and chalice, two boxes of medicine and, to crown it all, a church bell with the inscription 'From Bremen for Taranaki', had arrived at Warea.[24]

Riemenschneider's mission had found acceptance among the large majority of Taranaki Māori and the sectarian division, which had existed when he arrived, had given way to understanding and co-operation. In November 1852 the missionary was able to report to Bremen:

---

23. RP IV, 304.
24. RP IV, 109–110.

Missionary G[ovett][25] and I have a friendly relationship. He has expressly permitted his natives to attend our preaching and teaching sessions, and this has contributed substantially to spread our effectiveness more generally over the whole population of this district. There seems to be a complete end to the quarrelling and fighting about denominational differences. Two churches are standing side by side in fraternal unity, differing only in their form of worship. Apart from that they are one in one faith and in one Lord.[26]

As far as his European friends were concerned, he had become a respected member of the New Plymouth clergy and society, being invited, for example, to preach the sermon at the annual meeting of the New Plymouth Friendly Society on 27 December 1853.[27] The Māori respected him and in his rather stern and Calvinistic way he felt that he had now been accepted as their father, mentor and guide. He had finally established a home, he lived in comparatively settled domestic circumstances and was fully absorbed by the work he had come to do, to be the Preacher of Taranaki.

---

25. Henry Govett (1819–1903) was a cousin of the Episcopalian missionary, William Bolland, who had come out to New Zealand with him. After having farmed for some time in Taranaki, he studied theology and also learned Māori. He was ordained priest by Bishop Selwyn in 1847 and appointed vicar of New Plymouth after Bolland's death, at whose funeral he officiated. In 1859 he was appointed the first archdeacon of Taranaki, a post he held until his retirement in 1898. Unlike Bolland, Govett worked closely with Riemenschneider in Taranaki and did not attempt to prevent the Anglican Māori from attending the German missionary's services.
26. RP IV, 105.
27. See *Taranaki Herald*, 28 December, 1853.

Chapter Eight

Puketapu Feud, 1854–1857

SINCE HIS ARRIVAL IN New Zealand, Riemenschneider had never expressed a particular interest in the politics of his new homeland unless they impinged on him personally, like, for example, the Mōkau *tapu*. In July 1847, Riemenschneider writes to Hamburg:

> I imagine that you are sufficiently acquainted with the political situation of this country from other sources. I must also confess honestly that I really don't have the time or inclination to write about it at length.[1]

In April 1854 the missionary's illness, his inability to appreciate Māori sentiments about land and his lack of interest in political issues combined to blind him to the significance of a meeting taking place in Manawapou in Ngāti Ruanui territory. It was an inter-tribal meeting, which had been called to discuss European colonisation and its effect on Māori sovereignty and tenure of the land. There had been a number of movements within various tribes to ban the sale of land to Europeans. However this meeting was of particular importance because it brought together, for the first time, a number of tribes in an attempt at organised resistance to further land sales.[2] The missionary was certainly aware of the meeting, but he does not seem to have regarded it as particularly significant.

The ailing Riemenschneider had gone to New Plymouth to stay with his in-laws[3] and to seek medical treatment. In spite of his long and close association with his Māori parishioners, he appears to have been unable to understand the depth of feeling, which had led to the calling of the Manawapou meeting. He certainly gives no indication that he was aware of the full significance to

---

1. Riemenschneider Papers, RP II, 155.
2. See Keith Sinclair, *The Origins of the Maori Wars*. Wellington: New Zealand University Press, 1957, pp. 70–72.
3. William Woon, ill and depressed, had abandoned his station and moved with his wife to New Plymouth in October 1853. Two months later, the mission station at Heretoa was destroyed by fire. The Woons later moved to Whanganui.

Māori of the subject, which had been the main topic of discussion. Despite being ill, he spent a Sunday with some of the Taranaki people who had come to town to earn money and conducted divine service. His description of the conversation after the service shows the gap between the missionary's concerns and those of his congregation:

> As soon as the service had finished some of them immediately began to talk about their daily work, as well as about money, profit and about the meeting concerning their land which was being held at Ngati Ruanui. I showed them that this was clearly a desecration of the Sabbath which should be devoted entirely to thinking about God's word and about heavenly things and in particular about the sermons which they had heard.[4]

The missionary had been aware for some time that there was great anxiety among Māori about the loss of their land to European settlers, and he writes about frequent meetings and agreements that appear to have been concluded in 1853. At the end of 1853 he reports:

> Along this entire coast, all the way down to Wanganui, [the Maori] have held large tribal meetings in the course of this year. They have concluded collective protection and defiance agreements, having sworn most solemnly that not a foot's breadth of Maori land between New Plymouth and Wanganui should be sold to Europeans from now on, that none of the various tribes should presume to break this agreement. Every district should enjoy the defensive protection of the whole federal might of the various tribes.[5]

The pastor of Taranaki clearly could not remain totally aloof from his congregation's worldly concerns. His apolitical stance changed dramatically in 1855 when his Taranaki people became embroiled on the fringes of a conflict that over the next few years was to have far-reaching consequences for the region, the country and for him personally.

The initial cause, as in so many conflicts between Māori and Māori, or Māori and Pākehā, was a dispute over the ownership of land. In 1848, a block of land between the Mangatī and the Wataha streams, north of the settlement of New Plymouth and in the territory of the Puketapu *hapū* of Te Atiawa, was offered for sale to the Government by some of the Puketapu chiefs, led by Rāwiri Waiaua. Another group of chiefs opposed the sale. The chief who led this faction was called Te Waitere Kātātore. The sale of the land, which would later become known as Bell Block after the New Zealand Company Agent, F. Dillon Bell, was agreed. When the boundaries were to be cut, however, a

---

4. RP IV, 267.
5. RP IV, 184. Sinclair, *op. cit.*, p. 84, cites a letter, written by Donald McLean to the Colonial Secretary on 20 February 1854, as the earliest document that refers to a Māori land league. Riemenschneider's report is not only earlier, it could well be that McLean's letter may, in part, be based on information from his friend Riemenschneider.

bitter fight developed between Rāwiri Waiaua's and Kātātore's parties. This confrontation led to an incident in which there was considerable physical violence between the antagonists, although lethal blows were carefully avoided.[6]

Six years later, in July 1854, Riemenschneider reports, Rāwiri Waiaua and Kātātore again came into conflict about a piece of land near the Waihonga Stream. Rāwiri had sown wheat on the block of land in question, and Kātātore claimed that it was his to use.[7] When no agreement could be reached about who had the right to use the land, Kātātore and his party went out to the disputed field, threw dry fern onto Rāwiri's cultivation and burned the young seedlings. The furious Rāwiri, who wanted revenge and knew what would inflame Kātātore's anger most, offered the whole area around the Waihonga Stream to the Government for sale. The settlers in and around New Plymouth immediately and enthusiastically welcomed this offer. They were starved for land and were smarting from the refusal of the Māori to sell more. Rāwiri's offer was seen as the breakthrough they had been waiting for with growing impatience.

The missionary took the view that Rāwiri's offer was an elaborate bluff since he would have known that he would never have been able to obtain the consent of the tribe to sell. This consent was vital, however, since Māori land ownership was tribal ownership. Individuals, even if they were of chiefly rank, did not 'own' the land in the European sense; they exercised stewardship over it, and could therefore not sell land without having obtained the consent of their tribe after wide consultation.

While the initial conflict had essentially been an internal quarrel within the Puketapu *hapū*, the Ngāti Ruanui to the south of Taranaki took a keen interest in it and made it known that they strongly sympathised with Kātātore's stance in the dispute. They were firmly opposed to the sale of any more land to Europeans. Their support for Kātātore and their passionate opposition to land sales, had led to some ugly brawls in New Plymouth when Ngāti Ruanui people had come there to trade and had encountered members of the Te Ātiawa land-selling faction.

Matters were further inflamed in November of 1854. One of Rāwiri's successors, Īhāia, apparently had good reason to suspect his wife of having an adulterous relationship with a Ngāti Ruanui man, named Rīmene, who at that time was staying with Kātātore. Īhāia arranged to have Rīmene shot by a man called Hōri. Riemenschneider, who dispatched long and meticulously

---

6. See B. Wells, *The History of Taranaki*. New Plymouth: Edmundson & Avery, 1878, p. 144.
7. The following account is taken mainly from the writings of Riemenschneider (RP V, 7–23. For a description of the various phases of the quarrel, see Ian Church, *Heartland of Aotea*. Hawera: Hawera Historical Society, 1992, pp. 119–124.

detailed reports of the feud to his superiors in Bremen, writes that in his view Īhāia was entitled to this act according to traditional Māori law.[8]

The Ngāti Ruanui took the killing of Rīmene as a welcome pretext to attack Īhāia and in December of 1854, 180 of them marched from the south of Taranaki to the *pā* Te Mamaku, on the Waitara River, where Īhāia had entrenched himself with about 30 followers. They used the inland route, called the Whakaahurangi trail,[9] a track that led around the eastern side of Mount Taranaki so that they did not have to cross either Taranaki or European territory. They had, however, written to Taranaki to ask for military support in case that should be needed. On Monday, 18 December, the Ngāti Ruanui stormed and took Te Mamaku in a fierce battle, which resulted in the loss of seven lives and 14 wounded on their side, and six dead with 11 wounded on the side of the defenders. Īhāia escaped.

Riemenschneider, who was in New Plymouth for rest and medical treatment, followed the news about the unrest, as it was reported in town, with increasing alarm. The Wesleyan missionary Turton, was absent from New Plymouth and Bolland's successor as Anglican priest in New Plymouth, Henry Govett, did not appear to be able to deal with the warring Māori. Finally the missionary, who had received reports from Warea that the Taranaki people were arming themselves and were keen to join in, rose from his sick bed and went to Waitara. Before his departure he wrote to Āperahama in Warea urging him and his Taranaki people to stay home at least until they would be called to battle by their Ngāti Ruanui relatives. This call for assistance, which would inevitably widen and intensify the conflict, and strengthen the hand of the settlers who were calling for military protection, was, of course, precisely what the missionary hoped to avoid. After several 'stormy debates' he managed to convince the Ngāti Ruanui that they had extracted enough *utu* (revenge, payment) and that they should not insist on hunting down Īhāia.

Riemenschneider may have won this particular battle, but the war of wills was not over. A new problem now arose. The Ngāti Ruanui insisted that, instead of returning by the way they had come, around the back of Mount Taranaki, they would now march right through Īhāia's territory, New Plymouth and Taranaki, carrying their wounded, thus courting further trouble. Riemenschneider was very concerned that this would jeopardise the safety of the European settlement of New Plymouth, because the town would then be between the two home bases of the two warring parties, particularly if Taranaki would decide to join Ngāti Ruanui against their northern adversaries the Puketapu *hapū* of

---
8. Sir Peter Buck's account of punishments for adultery describes a less bloodthirsty practice of *utu* (revenge, payment). See Te Rangi Hiroa (Sir Peter Buck), *The Coming of the Maori*. 2nd edn, Wellington: Maori Purposes Fund Board; Whitcoulls Limited, 1987, pp. 370–371.
9. For the history and the naming of the Whakaahurangi trail, see John Houston, *Maori Life in Old Taranaki*, Wellington: A. H. & A. W. Reed, 1965, p.45.

Te Ātiawa. On 5 February he writes to the *Verwaltungsausschuß* (executive committee of the North German Mission Society) in Bremen:

> Finally, on Christmas Day [1854], after I had negotiated with them for a long time, I conducted worship for them. I preached about Christ as the prince of peace, showed them how His kingdom was a kingdom of love, justice and peace, and what was required of those who wanted to have part of it. Then they broke camp and set off with bags and baggage and with nine wounded. One of them, who had been hit by four bullets, was left behind in the protection of Katatore. They left along the same road *around the back* of the mountain, along which they had come, and I thanked God with all my heart when I saw them enter the forest track.[10]
>
> Afterwards I preached at Te Hawhetaoai pa where Ihaia was staying. The next day I had an opportunity to send word of the retreat of Ngati Ruanui, on hearing this the Taranaki had dispersed at once.
>
> This long period of mental stress as well as the physical and mental effort which I had suffered at a time when I had hardly enough strength to sit on my horse and needed a stick to walk, sent me back to my sickbed, once peace and quiet had returned. I had been here in medical care for seven weeks and I felt compelled to return to Warea to my family and my people. On 6 January I left New Plymouth while I was still very weak, and in the evening of the 7th I arrived home to my wife and children.[11]

What the missionary describes as 'more misery and trouble' followed in the form of a disturbing rumour that swept Taranaki in the middle of January 1855. It was claimed that the Puketapu had exhumed some of the Ngāti Ruanui dead who had fallen in the taking of Te Mamaku *pā* and had subjected their corpses to indignities. Riemenschneider, who never put much trust in Māori rumours and often chided his parishioners for their gullibility, found them to be justified in this instance. The Ngāti Ruanui, understandably, were looking for *utu*, but before sending a *taua* (war party) to the Waitara they intended to come to Warea to mourn the dead from the measles epidemic of the previous year. This would provide a convenient occasion to discuss the issue of a further expedition to Puketapu with their Taranaki relatives. The anxious pastor had made considerable efforts to extract a promise from the Taranaki people that they would discuss the matter calmly and rationally.

The Preacher of Taranaki felt weary. On 8 February he writes:[12]

---

10. Riemenschneider does not mention that on the day before, 24 December, Provincial Superintendent Charles Brown, Dr Peter Wilson and Sergeant Halse had visited the Ngāti Ruanui camp. The Ngāti Ruanui informed the three concerned prominent inhabitants of New Plymouth that, since blood had been spilled, the matter was now closed and that they would now return via the mountain route. (Cf. Ian Church, *op. cit.*, p. 119.)
11. RP V, 17–18.
12. Riemenschneider actually dated this section of his report 8 January. Since he commenced writing it on 5 February I assume that this is a mistake.

As far as my physical condition is concerned, I *really* need a longer period of rest and recuperation, however the way things stand I cannot permit myself to take it, least of all in these restless and unstable times. I don't have any help and cannot ask for any either, because there are few people and the maintenance of the mission here is far too expensive to warrant a double occupancy of this post.[13]

Riemenschneider, who saw himself as a sentinel of peace, attended the meeting of Taranaki and Ngāti Ruanui. His task was difficult, particularly since he had to concede that Ngāti Ruanui had just reason to be aggrieved. Restraint, no matter how Christian, was not easy for Māori or Pākehā.

In this instance, the missionary achieved his goal. He reports that he managed to convince Ngāti Ruanui and Taranaki not to send a *taua* to Puketapu, in spite of the extreme provocation they had suffered. This is all the more remarkable as it appears, at least from the missionary's reports, that among both Ngāti Ruanui and Taranaki the feeling initially was overwhelmingly in favour of a war expedition.

Although a further armed conflict between Puketapu and the southern tribes had been avoided in this instance, the tensions continued within Puketapu between those wishing to sell land and those opposing any further sales. Reinforcements for both parties started to trickle in from the south, with a few Ngāti Ruanui among them, and sporadic skirmishes continued to the north of New Plymouth. In what appears to have been a rather ill considered move, the Wesleyan missionary and pastor Turton invited the northern Ngāti Maniapoto and Waikato tribes to come to the Waitara and settle matters.[14] These two tribes had for some time been archenemies of Taranaki and Ngāti Ruanui because they had been responsible for the disastrous invasions in the 1830s. Their arrival on the scene thus intensified rather than eased the tension.

Meanwhile the inhabitants of New Plymouth were growing increasingly alarmed by the unrest in their vicinity, even though they had been assured by the Māori that this was a Māori conflict and no harm would come to them. In March 1855, following a public meeting, it was decided to send a memorial to the Queen, pointing out to her that the town was completely unprotected, and in August the whole of the male adult population was sworn in as special constables.[15] The Colony's Administrator, Colonel Wynyard, finally agreed to the urgent requests for a military garrison at New Plymouth and by the end of August about 500 soldiers had been landed in the town. Riemenschneider describes the arrival of one detachment of soldiers:

---

13. RP V, 21.
14. Turton may have lacked political astuteness, but he certainly did not lack courage. He at one stage set up his tent between the opposing parties to prevent them from engaging in battle. See Ian Church, *op. cit.*, p. 122.
15. B. Wells, op cit., p. 156.

I myself had just arrived in New Plymouth when the ship *Duke of Portland* anchored with the first detachment of troops numbering 250 men. The beach was crowded with people (it was Sunday evening) who were watching the landing. For a start three boats landed together with more than 100 officers and men, all soldiers had their *bayonets at the ready* and were equipped with live ammunition. And *why this*? Because no other conclusion could have been drawn from the reports going between here and Auckland, except that they would have to face gunfire as soon as they landed here, because the natives, who had already taken New Plymouth, would try and prevent them from landing by firing on their boats. They therefore were most surprised when they found both Māori and Europeans in a peaceful mix on the beach and the *Māori* even helped them to disembark.[16]

However the peaceful picture of Māori helping European soldiers to step ashore on the beach of New Plymouth could not hide the rising tension between Māori and Pākehā. According to the missionary the arrival of troops in New Plymouth considerably added to the unrest among the Māori who understandably felt threatened by this action. This was despite the fact that Colonel Wynyard had sent a proclamation to the Māori in which he stressed that the soldiers were nothing more than a protective force for the settlers in New Plymouth. Thoughtless and antagonistic Europeans in New Plymouth put around the story that as soon as the new Governor would arrive, he would use the soldiers to make war on Kātātore and his ally, the senior Te Ātiawa chief, Wiremu Kingi Te Rangitaake. He would then proceed to take the lands from the Māori by force and settle European colonists on them, thus disinheriting the Māori population.

Riemenschneider shared at least some of the views of many Europeans with regard to Māori land. He believed that it was a sin in God's eyes that so much Māori land lay there uncultivated and unproductive, while the colonists were crying out for it. Nevertheless he was adamant that under the Treaty of Waitangi,[17] which many Māori chiefs had signed with the Crown in 1840, Māori had the absolute right to refuse to sell land if they so chose. In the missionary's view, any attempt to take land away from them by force would be not only a calamity for the whole country but also a crime.

The new Governor, Thomas Gore Browne, arrived in New Zealand on 4 September 1855. As part of the briefing of the Crown representative in the Colony, Riemenschneider's old friend, Donald McLean, who was now Chief Commissioner of Lands and therefore an important adviser to the new Governor, asked the missionary to write a report on Māori feeling in Taranaki. Riemenschneider wrote a long document in which he set out

---

16. RP V, 116–117.
17. Riemenschneider placed great emphasis on the Treaty of Waitangi. He includes a full transcript of the English text of the treaty as an appendix to the report in which he describes the Puketapu quarrel.

the events as he saw them and his interpretation of them. He concludes by stating that, as long as the soldiers are not used against Māori, the Taranaki people would take no action. As soon as European forces were used against Kātātore and his allies, however, a general war would erupt, in which case the outlying European settlers would have to be removed to New Plymouth to ensure their safety. Colonel Wynyard sent the missionary's letter on to the new Governor for his information.[18]

On Saturday, 27 October 1855, the new Governor arrived in New Plymouth. Riemenschneider had already been in the town for a week awaiting his arrival. The Taranaki Māori had sent him. His task was to find out from the Governor in person what his intentions were. McLean had preceded Gore Browne in New Plymouth and had told the missionary that his report about feelings among the Taranaki Māori had made an excellent impression and was being copied to the Foreign Secretary in Britain. On Monday, 29 October, at 10 o'clock in the morning, Riemenschneider, who was one of a privileged group of people to receive an invitation, had a private audience with the new Governor. The missionary describes him as very friendly and affable, and the Governor assured him that his intentions were peaceful and that he was not planning to use troops against Kātātore.

Riemenschneider had not left the Governor's lodgings when he came face to face with the new leader of the land-selling faction among the Puketapu *hapū*, Arama Karaka. After a conversation with him, the missionary was more than ever convinced that Arama Karaka was not so much interested in selling land as in inflicting a defeat on Kātātore and his party.[19]

The Taranaki people's emissary's mission to New Plymouth had been successful. He writes about the reaction of his flock:

> The message of peace, which I had to transmit to our natives on my return from New Plymouth, was received throughout the whole district here with great and general joy. All mental tension seems to have been dissipated since then and a more desirable, quieter mood has prevailed again throughout.[20]

✣

The Puketapu feud and its associated problems was not the only matter that was exercising Riemenschneider in 1855. Another major quarrel in which he was asked to mediate had broken out between the North German Mission Society and their former mission assistant Heine, who was now Lutheran pastor in Nelson. Heine had left the service of the mission in 1849, but he

---

18. The correspondence and and extract from Riemenschneider's letter is in the New Zealand National Archive, Colonel Wynyard to Governor, G13, 2, 1855/12.
19. RP V, 122.
20. RP V, 126.

had continued to act as an 'agent' of the Society in Nelson and had looked after land and money matters for them. When the news of the transfer of the seat of the North German Mission Society from Hamburg to Bremen, and the withdrawal of the strict Lutheran societies, reached Nelson, Heine, as has been described in chapter 7, felt that the time had come to cut all ties with the Society. There appears to have been some informal agreement between the Society and Heine that the latter should get some compensation for the work he had done on the Society's behalf. In the absence of any written agreement, however, there were wide discrepancies in what Heine considered fair compensation and what the Society was willing to pay. To complicate matters further, the mission land in Nelson had been transferred to Heine's name since any compensation money from the New Zealand Company in respect of unallocated land could be paid only to New Zealand residents and not to absentee owners, such as the North German Mission Society. Settling the issues in dispute was clearly a task that would be very difficult if it had to be carried out entirely by means of correspondence between Bremen and Nelson.

In the course of 1855 the *Verwaltungsausschuß* therefore asked Riemenschneider to investigate the matter and then visit Heine in Nelson in an attempt to reach a final settlement. The missionary felt that in the current political turmoil he was unable to leave his post in Taranaki and Heine himself seems to have been reluctant to receive a visit from Riemenschneider. The explanation for this reluctance seems to have been that, in addition to the dispute with the Mission Society, the unfortunate Heine had become involved in a serious quarrel with his Lutheran congregation. Riemenschneider heard of this quarrel not from Heine, but from the German congregation who wrote to him in October, informing him that Heine had submitted his formal resignation as pastor, and asking Riemenschneider to accept a call to take over. The missionary may have been tempted by what would certainly have been a much easier task in more congenial surroundings. Nevertheless, his sense of order and duty prevailed. His response was that firstly he was not a Lutheran, but Reformed and thus could not accept a call to a Lutheran congregation, and secondly his current congregation was in need of his services. He therefore felt unable to leave Taranaki.

While the missionary's reports to Bremen for this period are full of Māori politics and Society matters in Nelson, there are glimpses of his personal affairs, often tucked away after all the weighty issues have been debated and described from every possible angle. At the end of the March/June report he asks for some extra money for himself for some extraordinary expenses. He claims a total of £24-16-6 for medical expenses during his illness in 1854, for his board and lodging in New Plymouth while he was there for treatment, for a McIntosh raincape and leggings, and for an 'Enema Apparatus - £1-15-0'.

In a report written to the *Verwaltungsausschuß* in November 1855 there is another bit of personal news:

> On 25 ultimo (October) two further letters arrived from my dear homeland. One of them is from Pastor Müller, dated 11 May and brings both sad and glad news. The death of my dear old mother and the sadness this brought to my old father and my suffering sister was of course a bitter blow for me. I submit to the will of the Lord and say to my soul: *Be still*. I praise God that I know that my old father as well as my poor, weak sister are provided for.[21]

While the year 1855 had, in many respects, been traumatic for Riemenschneider and his people, he did not rest from his other labours. Just keeping his family dry and warm was a major and never-ending task. The missionary had to work hard to prop up his house that was threatening to collapse around their ears because all its posts had rotted in the ground.

But private buildings, while important and necessary, were only part of his ambitions. The preacher of Taranaki had started to suggest to the people at Warea that they should build a new church. It would have to be a major edifice, because it was in the village where the senior chief and the missionary lived, thus it would be the main church for the area. A supporter of the North German Mission had already sent a bell as a gift for the new building.

In addition to his pastoral work which, as always, also included a great deal of medical care of his flock, Riemenschneider sought to 'reform' Māori practices. In the 1850s he had decided to concentrate particularly (and, with no subsequent success) on land tenure. He strongly felt that a land tenure system in which an individual had rights to numerous small plots over a large stretch of country was not only inefficient, but also inimical to law and order. He also knew from personal experience as a mediator that it caused endless quarrels.

To achieve this idealised vision of Europeanised Māori, the missionary suggested a rationalisation of land tenure. In his plan, the many small holdings would be aggregated into a single plot for each tenant who would then become permanently settled on it instead of migrating from plot to plot over a period of time. This was clearly more in keeping with the methodical German mind, whose model was based on the farming practices of his native North Germany. The flaw with such a rational and orderly scheme was, however, that it did not take into account the strong emotional bond between Māori and their land. Even land-owning Pākehā found it difficult to appreciate this bond; for Riemenschneider, the son of a landless family, it would have been even more difficult. By the end of 1855 the missionary had hopes that the chief of

---

21. RP V, 101.

Te Umuroa, Wiremu Kīngi Matakatea, would move to implement his plans. Not surprisingly, nothing appears to have come of it at that time.

By the end of 1855 things had become sufficiently settled in Riemenschneider's parish so that the missionary could seriously contemplate going to Nelson to adjudicate the North German Mission Society's financial affairs with Heine. The Puketapu feud seemed to have been settled in the meantime, and the Governor's assurance of peaceful intentions appeared to have calmed the fears of the Taranaki Māori. Thus when he set off for Nelson in March 1856, the missionary neither foresaw nor even suspected that much worse developments were yet to come.

*

Although Riemenschneider had planned to travel to Nelson in January 1856, he had to be patient because the regular steamer service had been suspended. The Governor had chartered the only available ship for visiting the various provinces of his new area of responsibility. In the second week of February, the steamer finally arrived in New Plymouth from Auckland, and after an uneventful journey of 27 hours the missionary arrived in Nelson on Sunday morning, 17 February.

He obviously did not have any friends left in Nelson whom he could have asked for a bed for a few weeks, since he writes:

> I had to take refuge in an inn for the time being. However, staying in a public house is not only extremely expensive but also most inappropriate and repugnant for the likes of us because in this country such houses always have noisy bars associated with them. I therefore made it my first task the next day (Monday) to find lodgings in a decent private boarding house. Since in this country everything is extraordinarily expensive, people neither can nor wish to provide board and lodging for strangers for almost any price. The normal rate is from £2 to £2-10/- per week for a man. I therefore considered myself lucky when I managed to find a position for £1-15/- because the room which I was content to rent was in reality a storeroom half filled with goods, thus it could not be charged for at a higher rate as it was not considered a *dwelling*.[22]

Riemenschneider met Heine by accident in town on the day after his arrival. Heine, who had established himself as a farmer in Moutere, since his German congregation could not support a full-time pastor, had come to Nelson to attend to some business. Ever since he had been a student at the Mission School, Heine had been handicapped by deafness, and this had been the reason why he had not been ordained after his training in Hamburg. Since then his hearing appeared to have deteriorated. Riemenschneider writes that he found

---

22. RP V, 179.

it impossible to discuss any business matters with him in a public place because the only way to communicate with Heine was to shout at the top of his voice. This handicap added yet another barrier to the negotiations, which were already proving a very difficult and delicate process. The practical difficulties were compounded by the fact that Heine was not very co-operative and at one stage made his brother pastor wait a whole week in Nelson before coming to town to sign some documents.

Another aggravation, which coincided with his visit, were the festivities associated with the anniversary of the founding of Nelson, which seems to have been celebrated very thoroughly. Riemenschneider was most surprised when he heard that all public offices were closed for the whole week. If he had previously compared New Plymouth unfavourably with Nelson, when he first went north, he now compared Nelson unfavourably with New Plymouth. In his opinion the work ethic was obviously more pronounced in the Taranaki settlement than in Nelson. In New Plymouth, the founding anniversary was also celebrated, but offices and businesses remained open during the festivities.

After he heard from his Māori contacts in Nelson that armed conflict once again appeared imminent in Taranaki, the pastor was in a hurry to return to his flock, but the delays caused by the Nelson celebrations affected his departure. The steamer left Nelson Harbour at two o'clock on the afternoon of Thursday, 13 March, but then anchored in the bay until eight o'clock that evening. The captain, whose priorities obviously differed from those of the missionary, had remained behind in Nelson to see the finals of the horse races so that he could report the results when the ship reached Auckland.

Refreshed by his sojourn in Nelson, Riemenschneider resumed his work in Taranaki. The rumours of war, which had reached him in Nelson, had, as usual, been exaggerated, but there was still cause for concern and plenty of work to be done to keep the peace.

The Puketapu feud was still simmering. At the communion *hui* in Pungairere on 19–21 April the main topic of discussion had been whether Taranaki warriors should go and help Ngāti Ruanui avenge the death, in a skirmish, of one of their chiefs, Piripi of Ōhāngai. The unanimous decision was that, since Piripi had gone to Waitara against the advice and wishes of the senior chiefs of his tribe, his death was a just retribution from God for disobedience and therefore did not require revenge. Even though a rumour that Piripi's body had been hacked to pieces by his adversaries turned out to be untrue[23] Ngāti Ruanui decided to return to Puketapu. Again, Riemenschneider worked very hard to prevent the Taranaki warriors from joining their Ngāti Ruanui relatives and to prevent another war expedition. Two of the senior Ngāti Ruanui chiefs, Tāmati Hōne Ōraukawa and Rawenata were in favour of a peaceful settlement, provided that Āperahama

---

23. It was not Piripi, but one of his companions, Mohi, who had been treated in this way (RP V, 227).

of Warea would join them in a war dance and armed muster of their warriors.²⁴ With a heavy heart, Riemenschneider watched Āperahama and his warriors depart for Weriweri, where the muster was to be held. He knew that there were still plenty of Ngāti Ruanui and Taranaki who vociferously advocated bloody revenge. For precisely this reason, the northern sub-tribe, the Ngā Māhanga under their chief Paratene, had not been invited by Āperahama because he feared that Paratene would seek to involve Taranaki in war. The missionary felt that he himself should not go to Weriweri, and that it was better if he remained behind to keep an eye on the Ngā Māhanga people. At the same time he was aware that these were anxious times and his presence in Warea gave the women and children who remained behind, and who daily feared an attack from the Puketapu sub-tribe of Te Ātiawa, some sense of security. During the fortnight in which the men were absent, Riemenschneider reports, 20 to 30 women gathered every day at the missionary's station in Warea, 'like a flock of chickens who see the hawk circling above them'.²⁵

On this occasion, the pastor's view that no further warlike action should be taken had prevailed, and this was mainly because he still enjoyed the trust of the majority of the Taranaki people. In a report to the *Verwaltungsausschuß* he records a speech made to him by Āperahama of Warea:

> When the military came last year and we became alarmed, you told us to sit still and you did not lie to us and they have not touched or harmed either us or our property. When the new Governor arrived and we were filled with apprehension about what would happen to us from him, you became our representative and the words which you brought to us from him were sufficient for us, because they were words of goodness and peace and you assured us that they were true words and that we could trust them. When the commanding officer of New Plymouth, Major Nugent, visited you out of friendship here in Warea and stayed in your house for two days and was friendly to all us Maori we felt even more that the Governor and all those in his employ mean well, since they showed so much love towards you, our pastor.²⁶

Later events were to show that while the trust the Māori placed in Riemenschneider was not misplaced, the missionary's naive trust in the civil authorities was.

The authorities themselves appear to have had considerable faith in Riemenschneider's powers of persuasion. When the Ngāti Ruanui appeared to threaten Waitara again in May 1856, one of the Provincial Councillors, Rundle, asked the missionary and Whiteley, who had just replaced Turton as

---

24. Riemenschneider uses the Māori word *pūkana* for the event. According to the Williams dictionary this word refers to the distortion of the countenance in dances, such as the *haka*. H. W. Williams. *Dictionary of the Maori language*. 7th edn. Wellington: GP Publications Ltd, 1992.
25. RP V, 420.
26. RP V, 234.

Wesleyan pastor in New Plymouth, to go and persuade them to return home. On this occasion, Riemenschneider and Whiteley's intervention was not required. On the first day of their march around the back of Mount Taranaki the Ngāti Ruanui had received a rumour that Te Ātiawa was invading their territory from the sea. They had turned back at once to defend their territory, only to find that the rumour lacked substance, like so many rumours that were beginning to swirl around Taranaki in the increasingly unstable political environment.

Another sign of confidence in the missionary's judgement on the part of the authorities was demonstrated by the request from the Governor for a report on a political issue. The 1852 Constitution Act, which had brought parliamentary democracy to the European population in New Zealand, had excluded native affairs from the authority of parliament and had left them solely in the hands of the Governor. On July 31, 1856, the Governor, Thomas Gore Browne, wrote to Riemenschneider (as well as to a number of other missionaries and Pākehā experts in matters Māori).[27] He was seeking an opinion as to whether the conduct of native affairs could be 'conceded to the governor's responsible Advisers – consisting of a Ministry chosen from the elected Representatives of the Europeans'.[28] The missionary responded at once and in the course of August produced an enormous report in which, like the overwhelming majority of the respondents, he strongly urges that the Governor should retain sole control of native affairs.

He also makes the point that the Constitution Act, if it were to be applied to 'both nations' in New Zealand, would amount to a disenfranchisement of the Māori who had no vote and therefore had no say in who would 'manage' their affairs. At the same time he seems to have overlooked the fact that the Governor, even though he represented the Queen of England, was also subject to considerable political pressures from the settlers, and would, in time, have to bow to such pressures. In particular, Gore Browne was dependent not only on parliament for funds to carry out his policies, but also on his newly appointed Native Secretary and Chief Land Purchase Commissioner, Riemenschneider's old friend, Donald McLean, for advice.[29] In the event, between 1855 and

---

27. The Governor's request was sent to a total of 38 persons, among whom were several of Riemenschneider's friends and acquaintances, such as Govett, Turton, Whiteley, McLean and Dr Peter Wilson. The responses are printed in full in the British Parliamentary Papers with the one exception of Riemenschneider's. The explanation reads: 'The Rev. J. F. Riemenschneider wrote from the Mission House, Warea, Taranaki, under date 29th August 1856, but as his letter was unusually long (upwards of sixty pages) a précis only is forwarded:'. (*British Parliamentary Papers, Colonies, New Zealand*, Shannon: Irish University Press, 1968-, vol. 10, 387–88.
28. RP V, 301.
29. McLean became Native Secretary in place of Francis Dart Fenton, when the Land Purchase Department and the Native Secretariat were amalgamated. See Keith Sinclair, *The Origins of the Maori Wars. op. cit.*, p. 101.

1859, the percentage of the general revenue spent on Māori declined from 6% to 3%.[30] The lack of adequate finance was not assisted by the fact that the Governor himself, in whose wisdom Riemenschneider placed so much trust, was not an expert in things Māori. One historian describes him as follows:

> Unlike Grey, Gore Browne never learned to speak the native language, was ill at ease in the presence of Māoris, and, as they often complained, seldom visited them.[31]

The missionary's great respect for authority may have clouded his judgement about Gore Browne's ability to guide Māori policy wisely, handicapped as he was by his inadequate knowledge of Māori language and culture, combined with frequent sabotage and opposition from parliament. With the benefit of hindsight, the missionary was sharply critical of Gore Browne's Māori policy, once the Governor had left New Zealand.

During this time, constant travel, in an attempt to keep the peace, in addition to normal pastoral activity and writing, did not permit Riemenschneider to look after his station and in August 1856 he paints a rather sad picture of his home:

> Being overrun continually by herds of [the Maori's] pigs horses and other cattle, our station in this place has, during the last four years, looked most sad and neglected. All my many and laborious attempts to keep even the smallest part of our garden fenced with the remains of the previous fence so that we can at least grow some vegetables for our needs, particularly as the natives don't grow any, have been useless. The rotten posts have been broken by pigs etc., the garden has been rooted up and laid waste, and the reed walls of our old, rickety house have been torn down again and again by the cattle and are hanging down in tatters. In addition to all this several of our small number of goats on which we depend completely for milk for our children have been killed and eaten by the dogs of the Māori, who have also destroyed [our] chickens and eggs.[32]

It is not surprising that in the face of these conditions the missionary on a number of occasions contemplated moving his station to a more hospitable location. Because of a strong sense of his vocation to serve the Māori, he had not taken up the invitation of the Tataraimaka settlers and, on this occasion, when he had again considered his options, he ended up convinced that the message from God was:

> Stay where you are and remain firmly and without moving from the post where you have stood so far and are standing now.[33]

---

30. Keith Sinclair, *op. cit.*, p. 92.
31. Keith Sinclair, *op. cit.*, p. 89.
32. RP V, 252.
33. RP V, 254.

Having once again made the decision to stay in Warea, Riemenschneider entered negotiations for the building of a new house for which the Society had finally sent him some money.[34] After protracted discussions, he finally came to an agreement with Kereopa, the chief and teacher of Hōpāiaia and his three brothers.

As well as building a new house, the people of Warea had decided to commence building a new church. They had asked Ngāti Ruanui for help because this tribe had a reputation for being skilled in the erection of large buildings and they had already deposited some cartloads of hewn posts. However the Puketapu feud and their agricultural duties had intervened and the Māori in the meantime were making no progress. Riemenschneider, for his part, had brought some church windows with him when he returned from his visit to Nelson and had also acquired some sawn timber. In May 1856 he was occupied with making door and window frames, an altar, altar rail and pulpit. It was to be some time before they would be needed in the new building.

While the year 1856 had been one of hard work for the missionary, towards the end he is able to report on two pleasant events.

The first one was the arrival, in October, of no fewer than five chests containing gifts from the North German Mission Society. Riemenschneider writes:

> My wife and I would like to thank you very particularly for the two pictures of my dear hometown of Bremen. Oh, how many dear memories are connected with and are awoken by the view of my dear home-town with its various steeples etc. When I then look through the Bremen 'Weser Zeitung'[35] with its various political and advertising columns which you so kindly sent me, I often feel that I have almost been transported to my homeland. Love for one's home never dies on this earth, even if we come, after years, to feel at home in a strange country.[36]

While the arrival of the goods from Germany was a private celebration for the family, he was also invited to take part in a public festivity. The new Wesleyan church in New Plymouth was being opened on the first Sunday of October 1856, and the German Reformed missionary, who was obviously counted as one of the Wesleyan clerical establishment in the town, was invited to contribute by preaching at the evening service.

No matter how integrated Riemenschneider may have been in the clerical

---

34. The amount set aside by the Society for building a house for Riemenschneider and his growing family was a very modest £100 (RP V, 250). More than 10 years earlier, in 1843, the Church Missionary Society missionary Robert Maunsell had been allocated £600 for the same purpose by his society. (Church Missionary Society Papers, Index to the Minutes of the CMS, p. 369.)
35. A newspaper, published in Bremen.
36. RP V, 294.

establishment and also the social scene of New Plymouth, he still remained unmistakably German. A little later in the same report he writes:

> On Monday afternoon, at 4.30, a public "tea party" took place in the *old*, abandoned and emptied church building (which is for sale for demolition since the last earthquake has damaged it irreparably). Each ticket cost 1/6d. However, although I was admitted free of charge, I did not take part, because I still have not been sufficiently acclimatised to the English way in order to enjoy such occasions.[37]

Nevertheless, in spite of his aversion to tea meetings, Riemenschneider's standing in New Plymouth society seems to be confirmed by the invitation to speak at the public opening of the new church on Monday night. The other speakers were the Resident Magistrate, Josiah Flight, a prominent church member who had also laid the foundation stone, the Primitive Methodist preacher, Pastor Long, and the Wesleyan pastors Whiteley and Turton.

The *Taranaki Herald* did not describe the opening of another church in New Plymouth that took place a few months later. On 19 July 1857 a weatherboard Māori chapel was opened in the *pā*.[38] Riemenschneider was invited to preach in Māori at 10.30 a.m. and in English at 6.30 p.m. The opening of the chapel was also an occasion for the missionary to meet his old friend Schnackenberg, who preached in Māori at 4.30 p.m. while the Rev. Long, the Primitive Methodist preacher, officiated at the English service at 3.00 p.m.

The opening of the new Wesleyan church in New Plymouth made the old building available for cultural pursuits and on 7 January, 1857, the Taranaki Institute was formed under the presidency of Dr Peter Wilson. Among others, the Revs Samuel Ironside, Henry Govett and John Whiteley were elected to serve on the committee. The early activities of the Institute consisted of weekly evening lectures on a variety of topics, dictated mainly by the persons available to deliver them. Riemenschneider was soon called upon to contribute to the proceedings of the Institute. On 10 June 1857 he shared the speaker's platform with John Whiteley, who spoke on 'Māori Superstition'. The missionary spoke 'on the nature of the tapu, and the means recently adopted by an enlightened Native of the Puketapu tribe for its removal'.[39] In November he followed a series of lectures on Morocco given by Dr Peter Wilson with one on Germany. Like most of the missionary's lectures and sermons, it was definitely not a model of brevity. The *Taranaki Herald* reports:

> On Thursday evening the Reverend Mr. Riemenschneider delivered an

---

37. RP V, 298.
38. This was most probably the Kawau pā at the site of the present Centre City complex in New Plymouth. It was abandoned in 1860, due to the Taranaki War. (Information from Mr Kelvin Day, Puke Ariki.)
39. *Taranaki Herald*, 13 June, 1857.

interesting discourse on Germany having more immediate reference to the free and Imperial cities of the empire, and whose rise and fall, and various political vicissitudes, he depicted in a very lucid manner, greatly to the satisfaction and instruction of a very attentive audience, though the lecture occupied the space of nearly two hours.[40]

Riemenschneider's relationship with his Taranaki people had also developed. In a report written in June 1857 he describes aspects of it as follows:

> For [the Māori], their missionary is their spiritual and physical father and caregiver. They are convinced that he lives and works among them out of free and disinterested love which they look at in wonder and admire but which they can't possibly find in themselves; that in everything he tells them or undertakes, even where it does not accord with their views or please them, he has their temporal and eternal welfare in mind and tries to achieve it; that at the same time he is also their spokesman and representative looking after their interests against all real or imagined interference from outside, and that therefore he is not only worthy of their whole love and their full confidence, but also that, "maringanui e noho ana a Rimene[41] ki konei he matua mo tatau ('Fortunately we have Rimene living among us here as our father'). The mission station is the people's refuge and emergency gathering place where the sick and the well, the old and the young, can turn with their spiritual and physical needs and requirements, in order to take advantage of and receive the counsel and help of our love.[42]

In 1856 and 1857 the missionary in many ways reached the zenith of his labours. His health had greatly benefited from the journey to Nelson, he was established as a respected member of New Plymouth society, and his opinion on matters Māori was requested by the highest authorities in the land. Above all, he enjoyed the full trust and confidence of the great majority of his Māori parishioners. They saw him as their father, teacher and pastor and on a number of occasions, if his reports can be relied upon, he had managed to persuade them to change their mind and to follow his guidance in secular matters such as the Puketapu feud. The feud, however, was indicative of major tensions within Māoridom and between Māori and Pākehā. These tensions, and the as yet largely hidden disaffection of the Māori with European settlement, combined to make Riemenschneider's position among the Taranaki people increasingly difficult and, in the end, untenable.

---

40. 14 November, 1857.
41. Māori, who would have had great difficulty in pronouncing Riemenschneider's German name, used the name Rimene for their missionary.
42. RP VI, 81–82.

Pl.17: *Riemenschneider. Warea.* [1847]
Walter Baldock Durrant Mantell, ink on paper, 98 x 172 mm, Alexander Turnbull Library, Wellington, New Zealand (C-103-044-2)

Pl.18: *Mr Riemenschneider's [?], Warea, Jan 16/57* [16 January 1857]
Richard Taylor, pencil sketch on paper, 70 x 130 mm, Alexander Turnbull Library, Wellington, New Zealand (E-296-q-138-3)

Pl.19: *Reverend Richard Taylor* [c. 1860–1873]
Photographer unknown, half-plate glass negative, 165 x 115 mm, Alexander Turnbull Library, Wellington, New Zealand (C-14302-1/2)

Pl.20: *Taranaki region showing sites mentioned in the text*
Terralink International

Pl.21: *The Grey Institute* (c. 1855)
Artist unknown, watercolour on paper, 150 x 220 mm, collection of Puke Ariki, New Plymouth (A75.419)

Pl.22: *Grey Institute Mission Hall* (n.d.)
Williamson & Co, New Plymouth, carte-de-visite, 64 x 89 mm (standard 2.5 x 3.5"), collection of Puke Ariki, New Plymouth (A64.074)

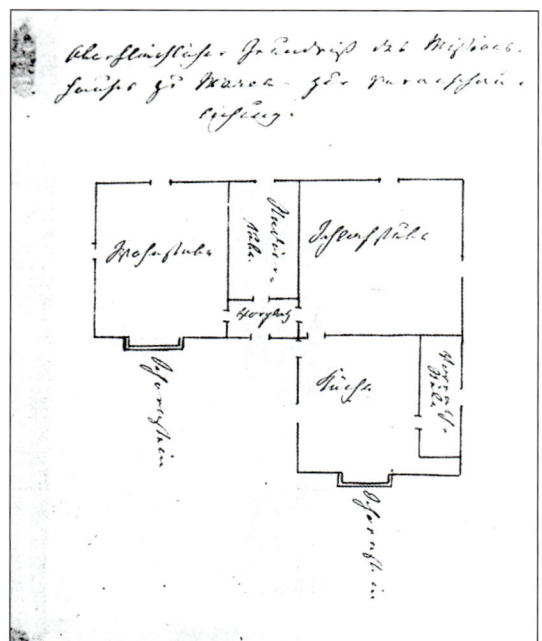

Pl.23: *Riemenschneider's floor plan of mission house*
[January/March 1854. RP IV, 241]

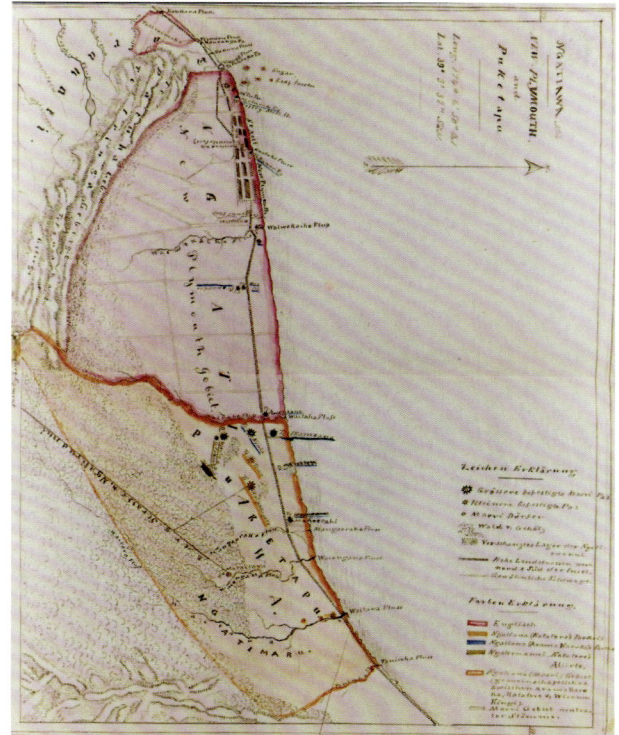

Pl.24: *Riemenschneider's map of Taranaki*
Riemenschneider papers, Staatsarchiv Bremen, 7.1025, Germany

Pl.25: *Catherine Garland Riemenschneider, nee Woon* (n.d.)
Photographer unknown, black & white negative of original photographic print, 102 x 127 mm, collection of Puke Ariki, New Plymouth (PHO2007-228); location of original unknown

Pl.26: *Reverend Johann Friedrich Riemenschneider 1859*
Ambrotype in leather case with velvet internal and copper and brass matting, 120 x 95 x 15 mm, collection of Puke Ariki, New Plymouth (A82.030)

Pl.27: *Reverend Johann Friedrich Riemenschneider*
Staatsarchiv Bremen, 1025-Foto-1803, Germany

Pl.28: *Johann Friedrich Heinrich Wohlers* (1880s)
Photographer unknown, Alexander Turnbull Library, Wellington, New Zealand (F-37421-1/2)

Pl.29: *Johann Wilhelm Christoph Heine* (1900s)
Alexander Fletcher, S Natusch Collection, Alexander Turnbull Library, Wellington, New Zealand (F-66177-1/2)

Pl.30: *Carl Sylvius Völkner*
John Kinder, half-plate negative, Alexander Turnbull Library, Wellington, New Zealand (F-59698-1/2)

Pl.31: *Te Whiti o Rongomai (sitting) – taken in Nelson* (c. 1882–1883)
Photographer unknown, half-plate glass negative, 6 ½ x 5", reproduction courtesy of the Trustees of Parihaka Pā

Pl.32: *Te Ua Haumene* (n.d.)
Photographer unknown, black and white photograph mounted on card, 151 x 107 mm, collection of Puke Ariki, New Plymouth (PHO2007-258)

Pl.33: *Untitled (Wreck of the 'Lord Worsley', Opunake)* (n.d.)
John Gully, watercolour on paper, 260 x 420 mm, collection of Puke Ariki, New Plymouth (A75.460)

Pl.34: *Parihaka* (1881)
W A Collis, black & white photograph, 220 x 586 mm, collection of Puke Ariki, New Plymouth (A64.034)

Pl.35: *St Stephen's Māori Church, Taiaroa Head* (c. 1920)
Photographer unknown, Alexander Turnbull Library, Wellington, New Zealand (G-2322-1/2)

Pl.36: *Port Chalmers grave of Johann Friedrich Riemenschneider* (2007)
Max Oettli, digital photograph, private collection

Chapter Nine

Rift between Riemenschneider and his People, 1857–1859

THE YEAR 1857 BEGAN auspiciously for the Riemenschneider family. The missionary reports the birth of their fourth child, yet another daughter, Amanda Helene, on 30 January. Both mother and child were well although on this occasion the mother took a fortnight to recover from her confinement.

Catherine Riemenschneider had only just been restored to health when about 120 Ngāti Ruanui builders arrived, together with their families, to commence building the church at Warea. The particular *hapū* that had undertaken to build the church at Warea was Mananiakai under their chief Tāmati Hōne Ōraukawa.

The church, the shell of which was finished and handed over on 23 March 1857, was certainly an imposing building. All the Taranaki Māori had made contributions towards its cost of £200, because it was to be the main parish church for Taranaki. It was 11 m. long, 7.3 m. wide and almost 5 m. high, with seating for 200 worshippers.

The building was in the traditional Māori style, with a grass roof and reed-clad walls. Its roof beam was supported by the end walls and two octagonal support pillars. All the wooden framing was planed smooth and painted in red ochre. The spaces between the timbers were decorated with *arapaki* work, artfully woven ornamental lattice panels. The European influence in the appearance of the building consisted of two mullioned arched windows, measuring 1.7 m. by 0.46 m., set 0.5 of a metre apart into the west facade of the church above the entrance porch, and a mullioned arched window, 2.6 m. by 0.46 m., in the east wall above the choir. Riemenschneider reports that he would have liked to have larger windows but that he could not afford them. The Ngāti Ruanui builders for their part complained about the windows being too large and detracting from their *arapaki* work decorating the interior walls. In the end, when the finished work was inspected, both parties agreed that the mixture of traditional and European features was aesthetically pleasing.¹

Once the shell of the building had been completed and handed over, the missionary went to work on his part of the endeavour. He encouraged Āperahama to build a small entrance porch for which he constructed an arched door. He then built a hexagonal pulpit, an ambitious undertaking even for a skilled cabinet maker, particularly since he had never seen one made before and had to learn as he went along. On completion of the pulpit Riemenschneider constructed a communion table, a communion rail, a reading desk for the Māori catechist and a special pew, which was set aside 'for the family of the missionary'.² Finally, the artisan missionary laid a wooden floor and installed the furniture. He reports that he completed the whole task after 26 days of strenuous work.

Thus the new church was a co-operative venture between Riemenschneider and his Māori congregation. The Māori had provided the shell and the ornamentation of the building, the missionary had provided the windows, laid the wooden floor, and manufactured the furniture. He now felt that a 'ladies' touch' was needed. After a discussion with his wife he drew up a list of 23 'English ladies in New Plymouth with whom we are acquainted'. At the top of the list he wrote the heading 'Ladies' contributions towards the decoration of pulpit & Communion table in the North German Missionary Society's Māori Church at Warea in Taranaki'.³ When he had drawn up the list, he went to New Plymouth to collect subscriptions. He was distracted from this task as some of his wayward parishioners had yet again become entangled in the Puketapu feud, and he tried to negotiate a peace between the hostile parties in this quarrel. He was thus able to contact only 13 ladies. However he collected more than the shilling per lady that he had requested from them. With that money he managed to buy 4 yards (2.3 m.) of best quality crimson damask, fringes and yarn from which his wife made up the necessary coverings. The new church was ready for worship on Saturday, 15 May although in fact a year would pass before it was formally consecrated.

Riemenschneider had not been so fortunate with his new home, which had been in the planning and building for even longer than the church. Once the money had been paid over and accepted by Kereopa and his people, the work was due to start. But now a quarrel broke out between the builders because some of them did not agree that the money that was paid to them as a group, should be used to purchase a plough and a team of oxen. The idea was that this would then benefit all of them in their farming. The dissidents wanted to use it to buy muskets and ammunition for themselves and therefore requested

---

1. Riemenschneider Papers, RP VI, 214.
2. *ibid.*
3. RP VI, 216.

their share in cash. If their wish was to be granted, it would of course have the effect of making the communal purchase impossible. After lengthy and at times acrimonious negotiations failed to bring about a solution, Kereopa and his brother Hōhepa decided to exclude from the contract all those who were not willing to work towards the common goal. This meant, in effect, that the two men were left to carry it out themselves.

The two brothers had saddled themselves with an enormous undertaking. Quite apart from building the missionary's house they had obligations in respect of the church building and the feeding and housing of the Ngāti Ruanui builders and their families. In addition to all these tasks they were also caught up in the Puketapu feud. On the personal front, they were stricken by various illnesses that were prevalent, and they also had to look after their own agricultural pursuits to ensure food and shelter for their families. Building a house virtually on their own in addition to all these tasks and distractions was obviously almost beyond their strength.

Finally, by September 1857, the timber for the new house had been felled and roughly dressed but now planting time for the Māori farmers intervened and it was January 1858 before Kereopa and Hōhepa finally began with the preparation of the site and the erection of the wall supports.

By May the frame of the house was finally in position, but now the cold and rain were beginning to cause the builders severe discomfort, particularly as they did not have adequate clothing. Riemenschneider and his wife,

> … bought for each of them a pair of good, strong work trousers (@ 2/9), 1 blue woollen shirt (@ 8 shillings) and 1 cotton shirt (@ 4 shillings) and for the two of them a woollen blanket for the night (£1).[4]

By May 1858 the building finally had made sufficient progress to enable Riemenschneider to engage a European builder to put on the roof, which consisted of boards covered in painted canvas. The carpenter, called Reddy, was a former sailor who had been shipwrecked in northern New Zealand in a whaler. He had married a Māori woman from Taranaki who had been a slave in the north. He had worked on several mission stations as a carpenter and handyman before settling with his family in his wife's home territory at Ōmata, south of New Plymouth. Riemenschneider complains that Reddy did not work as hard or as well as a German tradesman, but then the thrifty missionary did not pay top rates and could therefore not expect a top performance either. One of the New Plymouth builders who quoted for the work demanded eight shillings per day as well as board and lodging plus three glasses of brandy per day. Reddy was happy to work for four shillings per day plus board and lodging, and as a teetotaller he required neither brandy

---
4. RP VI, 190.

nor beer. In addition he did not swear and curse and quarrel, nor did he cause any 'vexing problems with the womenfolk'.[5] In spite of Reddy's leisurely pace the house progressed sufficiently for the missionary to be able to report in December of 1858:

> At the beginning of October the bedroom as well as the kitchen of the new house were sufficiently finished so that they were habitable. We thanked God that we could finally leave the old tumbling down house and move into the new one. We turned the kitchen into our living room, but during the first three days of occupation, it was minus a door or windows. Since then I have finished the bedroom, put in the kitchen door and windows, and made a floor for the children's bedrooms. But the living room is not habitable yet and my study has neither floor nor door nor window. I first had to make beds etc and other things and the timber is so rare and expensive and so difficult to get hold of that I often don't know how to apportion what is available in the best way just so as to make the most necessary household furniture. So far we have been so poor and so extremely needy that we have suffered real deprivation.[6]

The deprivation to which the missionary refers was the result of him continually trying to save money for the North German Mission Society. The paupers' son felt guilty all his life whenever he had to draw funds for himself and his family. His correspondence with Bremen is full of excuses and justifications for expenditure, even though what he did spend was perfectly normal and necessary for him to survive and work, and only just barely adequate to maintain his growing family.

Housebuilding and money problems were not the only worries with which Riemenschneider had to contend in the course of 1858. He also found it necessary to petition the New Zealand Legislative Council. The Marriage Act of 1854 had provided for a register of clergy licensed to conduct marriage ceremonies as Officiating Ministers. Schedule D to the Act listed the churches whose ministers could be licensed. The Act also made it possible for a minister who was not in one of the listed churches to be declared an Officiating Minister if 24 householders resident in a district signed a document declaring him to be their minister. The Lutheran church, represented in New Zealand by Wohlers at Ruapuke and Heine at Nelson, was listed in Schedule D, but Riemenschneider's 'Protestant Reformed Church of Germany' had been left out. It appears that the civil servants of the day considered that the designation 'Lutheran church' would cover any protestant denomination from German-speaking Europe.

On 17 June 1858 the Legislative Council debated a petition from the missionary, asking that his church be included in the list of Officiating Ministers in Schedule D to the Act. After some desultory procedural sparring

---
5. RP VI, 205.
6. RP VI, 343–344.

and some misinformation to the effect that all denominations operating in New Zealand had been included in the Act of 1854 and that the Protestant Reformed Church of Germany 'had sprung up since', the petition was declined by seven votes to six. Chief Justice Arney expressed the view that 'the Council should not, by adding the Church to the schedule, confess themselves as of the opinion that the importance of the Church warranted its insertion in the schedule, especially when it appeared that Mr. Riemenschneider could not obtain a certificate from twenty-four householders that he was their officiating clergyman'.[7] The fact that Riemenschneider ministered to a large body of Māori did not count; the Act did not apply to them.

John Whiteley now took up the issue on his colleague's behalf. On 19 July 1858 he wrote to C. W. Richmond, who at the time was a member for New Plymouth in the House of Representatives as well as colonial treasurer and minister of native affairs. Whiteley respectfully tried to set matters right by pointing out that the church, which the legislators had dismissed so lightly was, in fact, the church of which the husband of the Princess Royal, was a member, and that Riemenschneider regularly performed duties as a minister to the settlers in New Plymouth and Tataraimaka.[8] Whiteley's letter also contains the information that the missionary had been a guest at the wedding of the Wesleyan missionary's daughter in March 1857, and had been invited to perform the ceremony. He had however been unable to do so because at the last minute it had been discovered that he was not an Approved Officiating Minister. Some hasty re-arrangements had to be made and, in the end, Whiteley had been obliged to officiate himself.[9]

A final appeal to the Governor was also declined and Riemenschneider does not appear on the list of Approved Officiating Ministers until April 1861. His church however never became an approved church in New Zealand. He is listed under the *Free Church of Scotland*!

The forces of lawful government were, in the Christian pastor's view, much less dangerous to his and his flock's spiritual welfare, however, than the forces of darkness that the missionary saw working among the Taranaki Māori. The new church at Warea had been completed in May 1857 and had been in use ever since, although the formal opening, together with a regional *hui* and communion service, did not take place until a year later, on Sunday 16 May 1858. The reason for this long delay was that a religious movement had taken hold among the Taranaki Māori, which had incurred Riemenschneider's grave displeasure.

---

7. Parliamentary Debates (Hansard), House of Representatives. Wellington: Government Printer, 1856–1858.
8. Whiteley does not mention that the husband of the British Princess Royal was, in fact, Frederick III of Hohenzollern, the German Emperor.
9. *The Richmond–Atkinson Papers*, vol. 1. Ed. Guy H. Scholefield. Wellington: Government Printer, 1960, pp. 415–416.

The Wāhi Tapu movement, as it came to be called, appears to have been a Māori attempt to come to terms with the disastrous effect on the Māori population of introduced diseases, the new religious concepts preached by the missionaries and the old teachings about *tapu*. The fact that neither the missionaries nor the European doctors had been able to prevent the disastrous decline in the Māori population caused by illness and epidemics had given rise to the view that there were certain illnesses that were specific to Māori, and therefore could not be understood or treated by Europeans. Tamati Te Ito and others taught that these illnesses were due to Māori unwittingly breaking a *tapu* and they set about making sites on which a *tapu* had been imposed, common, i.e. no longer spiritually significant, so that they would no longer be a danger to the lives of Māori. Te Ito, a member of the Puketapu sub-tribe of Te Ātiawa, had for this reason been in great demand among the Ngāti Ruanui in spite of the vigorous opposition of Richard Taylor, the Church Missionary Society missionary who looked after them from his base in Whanganui. Before moving south, Te Ito had been visiting the settlements of the northern sub-tribe of Taranaki, the Ngā Māhanga, where he had also attracted a large following.

While Te Ito was not anti-missionary, he was pro-Māori. Riemenschneider had a different perspective on the situation, and he made it clear in his reports to Bremen that he saw Te Ito's activities as a threat and a challenge to his teaching, even though they had actually produced an increase in church attendance. In May 1858 the missionary writes that the religious movement had also assumed a political dimension. On 9 January, while Te Ito was active in Taranaki, the prominent Puketapu chief, Kātātore, who had opposed land sale, was murdered. This brought some relief to the besieged missionary, because Te Ito left Taranaki at once with his followers to 'become the bloodthirsty oracle of the war party that would avenge the murder committed on Kātātore'.[10] There was, however, an ominous aspect for Riemenschneider and his work. In spite of all his efforts to keep the Taranaki people neutral in the threatening armed confrontations in Puketapu, between 70 and 100 Taranaki warriors followed Te Ito to Puketapu to support him in a possible war of revenge against Kātātore's killers.

The Taranaki people were greatly troubled. While some of their warriors were at Waitara, laying siege to the *pā* of Kātātore's murderers, others were at home, bitterly opposed to those who had gone. In addition, many New Plymouth settlers were only too keen to keep agitating in order to justify the stationing of further troops in the settlement, thus increasing the likelihood of armed intervention and the subsequent seizing of Māori land. Riemenschneider reports that the distressed Taranaki people held *rūnanga* (council debate) after *rūnanga* to debate the situation, many of which he attended. Their anxiety made them prone to believe some of the most

---

10. RP VI, 224.

unlikely rumours. The missionary tried, often in vain, to counteract the pernicious effect of European agitation. He worked and travelled continually among his people in Taranaki but did not neglect the contingent at Waitara, which he visited regularly for divine service and counselling. He describes the atmosphere and his work:

> Being spread over a wide area, and being, as it were, hunted and hounded with all sorts of frightening rumours both from the side of the Europeans as well as from Waitara, and thus kept in a constant tension and changeable mood and excitement, the people needed constant attention and a firm counterbalance. It often really became almost too much and too difficult for me, so that, in spite of all my travelling and working among them, I hardly knew where to turn first, and became almost weaned of my house and my family.
>
> On several occasions where the mad antics of European schemers had brought things to such a pass that only a hand's breadth remained from a hot, bloody conflict between the natives and the whites, I had to throw myself into the fray against the latter, and as a guarantor of peace for and in the name of the Governor and his government.[11]

From the beginning of the Puketapu feud and throughout the fifties, the preacher of Taranaki's message had consistently been one of peace and non-involvement in any warlike activity among Māori or between Māori and Pākehā. While this message represented the missionary's strong conviction based on his interpretation of the Bible, there was also a pragmatic motive for his stance. He was well aware of the threat to the Taranaki people from settlers who would exploit Māori unrest and belligerence to provoke a war. Riemenschneider sets out his thinking, in which he appears to have been supported by many Taranaki Māori:

> The first and best thing that is generally wished for and most seriously sought here is the quick restoration of the neutrality (in its full integrity) of this whole tribe with respect to all current external conflicts, and their further developments and results, so that the name 'Taranaki' would disappear completely from them; and therefore this whole district with its people would present itself to the outside again in the unity of peace within itself as well as in its peaceful attitude against everybody outside. In this way both all other Māori tribes as well as all *Europeans* would once and for all have taken from them all further reason, pretext and opportunity to cast suspicion on Taranaki for having hostile intentions, and thus persecute it.[12]

While Riemenschneider was clear in his message of peace, he was also aware that the move of a substantial group of warriors to Puketapu had produced a polarisation within Taranaki between this group and those who had stayed

---

11. RP VI, 285.
12. RP VI, 243.

home and desired peace. The missionary reports that the peace party went as far as to seriously consider expelling the warriors who had gone to Puketapu from both their church and their territory by closing the border to them. He managed to dissuade them from taking such draconian measures by pointing out that these would be just as unchristian as the actions of the people they were trying to punish.

The Wāhi Tapu movement and the renewed trouble in Puketapu were two of a number of signs of unease and alarm at the inexorable encroachment of European settlement and European dominance over Māori territory and Māori culture. A few days before Riemenschneider held the first communion service in over a year, after having received an assurance that Taranaki would renounce Te Ito and his teaching, he received a letter from Hopaiaia, his teacher at Hauranga, which he had written together with the Anglican teacher of Haurāpari, Hoani. The missionary translated part of the letter into German for transmission to the *Verwaltungsausschuß* (executive committee of the German Mission Society):

> The clouds are thickening all the time, the peril is getting more and more pressing. The anxiety among us is growing stronger and stronger like an overwhelming flood and with it the general excitement and confusion is increased. This is the result of our deviation from God and our following of the old, vain delusion. Your *early warnings* and *admonitions* were ignored, now your *threats* are being fulfilled.
>
> Our people here feel as if they had been rejected by God. We would like to be assured again of His grace and His protection, to be controlled and ruled by Him in order to sit and remain here in peace and joy, but everybody here is anxious because of doubt and fear, and with all good will there is no strength of faith and trust.[13]

The missionary was aware of the suffering of his people. He finally relented and responded to their plea. He invited his flock back to the Lord's table from which he had banned them as a punishment for following what he considered a false prophet and forsaking the true faith, which he had preached to them. While he had compassion on his people when he saw their suffering, he did not realise that the malaise among the people of Taranaki was far deeper than he could see or understand. He also was not aware that things had progressed too far for the solutions that he offered them in all sincerity, to be effective. The clouds were indeed gathering, and a confrontation between the Pākehā settlers and the Māori landowners looked increasingly inevitable. The events over the next two years would show that Riemenschneider had neither the insight nor the resources to protect the Taranaki people or himself from the violent storm they portended.

---

13. RP VI, 287.

※

On 1 June 1858 a large number of Māori representing tribes mainly from the Waikato and Taupō area gathered at Ngāruawāhia, at the confluence of the Waikato and Waipā rivers. On the following day the meeting proclaimed the old and highly respected Waikato chief Te Wherowhero as King – a title and office in which he was confirmed at a further meeting held later in the month at Rangiaowhia, near present-day Te Awamutu. The Taranaki tribes did not support his election. They remembered him as the chief who directed the disastrous Waikato invasions of their territory in the early decades of the century.

The idea of a Māori King was not new. It had been discussed and advocated at a number of meetings that had been called to consider the Māori response to European immigration, and in particular the increasing threat to the Māori ownership of land. The meeting at Manawapou in Ngāti Ruanui territory in April 1854,[14] and a large meeting at Taupō in late 1856 had been precursors to the Waikato meetings, which finally resulted in the appointment of a Māori King.

There is little comment in Riemenschneider's papers on the political manifestations of the rising tide of Māori nationalism. He shows a preoccupation with local parish matters and the minutiae of the Puketapu feud and its effect on the Taranaki people. The wider issues, which were influencing local developments, seem to have eluded him. In a major report, which he began in May 1858 and on which he wrote for most of that year, he writes, however:

> I speak simply and with all considered conviction right from a consideration of the current conditions when I say that it appears as if hell and the world have united with the express purpose of frightening, tormenting, seducing and confusing this people until, physically and spiritually ruined and destroyed it will be totally extinguished in a general flood of ruination.[15]

The 'ferment', as the missionary calls it, which expressed itself in the meetings, and which ultimately led to the formation of what became to be called the King Movement, reached Taranaki in 1858. Letters arrived from the new King, who called himself Pōtatau I, inviting the Ngāti Ruanui and Taranaki to join his cause and acknowledge him as King. In a report written in May/June of 1859, Riemenschneider describes the feeling among the Māori as he sees it. He picks up the theme of the year before and expands on it:

> The whole [Maori] people is as if it were suffering from the rising delirium of a burning fever. They are engaged in a desperate struggle about two points, which for them are closely connected and of the same magnitude, namely:

---

14. See chapter 8, footnote 2.
15. RP VI, 290.

1. The assured continuation of their national existence; and
2. An inviolable and permanent securing of their continuing, independent possessions as a people, i.e. of all the lands with uncurtailed rights and claims on it.[16]

The missionary, not surprisingly, interprets the mood of his people and the remedies they seek in religious terms. In one sense, he was right. The Māori, for whom the distinction between the sacred and the profane is artificial and irrelevant, invested their King with messianic qualities. Riemenschneider, with his narrow 19th century European interpretation of the Christian faith, saw the Māori King as a rival to the Christian prince of peace, and opposed him on these grounds as well as on the grounds of political expediency. The Māori perspective, which he may have never fully understood, was different. To them, the King Movement represented a possible solution for their increasingly desperate situation. It would have seemed all the more attractive in view of the fact that all other solutions, such as local agreements to prevent the sale of land or dependence on missionaries to protect their interests, appeared to have failed.

The seeds sown by King Pōtatau's letters clearly found fertile soil among both the Ngāti Ruanui and the Taranaki people, in spite of the fact that they came from a former enemy. The initial reaction of the two *iwi* was, however, different. The missionary reports in 1859:

> Just like in all blunders which have been committed over the last few years, the unfortunate Ngati Ruanui in this new issue also set the initial tone and provided the first example. As soon as the first letters from Potatau had arrived last year, in which they were requested to do homage to him, they held a large meeting and drew up a document. In it they declared that they were handing over themselves and all their lands to Potatau as their king and dictator. They sent this off to him at once.
>
> At the same time as the Ngati Ruanui, our Taranaki had also received their letters from Potatau, in which they were requested to do homage to him. Instead of acting like the Ngati Ruanui however, the letters were presented in an open meeting for me to express an opinion.[17]

The meeting was tense and emotional, with many impassioned speeches. According to Riemenschneider, opinion among the participants was divided, with a number being undecided. At Āperahama's request the missionary gave his opinion. As usual he spoke at length, over two hours, he writes, and gives a brief summary of his speech:

> I discussed the matter according to Scripture, reason, and all the various considerations and connections both spiritual and secular-political. I reminded

---
16. RP VII, 7.
17. RP VII, 34.

them of Pharaoh, Egypt and Israel and how Israel was delivered from their house of bondage through God's might and merciful hand, how they wished they were back in Egypt and the consequences of their ungrateful rebellion against God their saviour. I compared this with the earlier history of Taranaki and its neighbouring tribes in relation to Waikato and their deliverance from their bondage there. I warned them not to rebel against the God of mercy and faithfulness who had thus delivered them, and not to entrust themselves again into the arms of Pharaoh and the power of the Egyptians. If they did this, they would again provoke God's anger and become the servants of man, and indeed the slaves of a heathen and despisers of God etc. etc. etc.[18]

By escalating a political question of this magnitude (and Riemenschneider himself makes it clear that he saw it as a question of continued existence for the Māori people) to a question of faith, meant that he had staked his credibility as a missionary on an issue that was bound to be stronger than him. He asked his congregation to place their faith in God, the God of the Pākehā who were taking more and more Māori land and whose behaviour, particularly in Taranaki, was becoming increasingly threatening. Unlike the Ngāti Ruanui, the Taranaki people, on Riemenschneider's advice, rejected the first approach from the King, but their feelings of insecurity in the light of threats from the Pākehā did not diminish, and the matter did not end there. The missionary was aware that agitation from the supporters of the King, both in Taranaki and from Waikato continued, even though attempts were made to keep news of any further discussions secret from him. In February 1859 a delegation from the King was sent to Ngāti Ruanui to bring them a flag. The delegation was to pass through Taranaki and intended to hold a meeting at Warea.

Riemenschneider's report of how he tried to 'prepare' the people for the arrival of the delegation shows how he had manoeuvred himself into a situation in which the credibility of his message was closely linked with the credibility of the Governor. If the latter failed, then the Christian pastor's teaching must inevitably become suspect:

> I sought to prepare and equip my people [for the visit of the king's delegation] in every possible way and for every eventuality by proving to them from Holy Scripture as well as from history and experience what a dangerous game it was to make a despot king over themselves. This was against God's counsel and providence, who had granted this country a Christian and benevolent government which would not interfere at all in the independence of the Māori, but would do everything for the continuance of the people's existence and for their recovery in prosperity, civilisation and well-being.[19]

---

18. RP VII, 35.
19. RP VII, 36.

Probably as a consequence of his 'preparation', Riemenschneider was not invited to take part in the *hui* that had been called to consider again the question of whether Taranaki should join the King Movement. He himself did not feel that it was prudent to attend and he reports that in his sermons he did not refer to the question at all, even though the King's emissary, Wī Toko, and his party regularly attended his services. However, against the impassioned advice of their missionary, the Taranaki people decided to accept the Māori King in an attempt to ensure their continued existence.

In spite of the fact that Riemenschneider was opposed to the King Movement, he was prepared to act as advocate on Taranaki's behalf and to assure the Governor that Taranaki's allegiance to the Māori King did not imply either hostility or disloyalty to the British crown, which he represented. When Gore Browne visited New Plymouth in February/March 1859, the missionary waited upon him and tried to explain his people's attitude. The Governor's response was singularly unhelpful. He took the view that the matter was beneath the dignity of the representative of her majesty the British Queen. Riemenschneider was unable to take back a clear indication of the Governor's views. The Taranaki people were later to argue that any accusations of disloyalty to the crown or rebellion against lawful government had no foundation. After all, the Governor had been informed of their loyalty, and he had chosen not to make a statement on the proposition that adherence to the Māori King was incompatible with loyalty to the Government of the British Queen.

Riemenschneider attributes the change of attitude among the Taranaki people towards the Māori King to an incident that occurred late in 1858. A minor chief, named by the missionary as Tāmati Wiremu, had offered to settle a dispute about the southern boundary of New Plymouth by accepting a payment of £200 from the European authorities. However, instead of settling matters with his tribe by sharing the purchase price of the disputed land, he had kept the money for himself without informing the tribe of the deal. When Europeans then settled the land in the belief that it had now been legally purchased, a *taua* (war party) set out in January 1859 to evict them. Riemenschneider, who had heard of the matter only after they had already departed, succeeded in restraining the warriors, but only with great difficulty. He managed to catch up with them nine miles from Warea.[20] The supporters of the King Movement were not slow to point out that such incidents would be prevented in the future by a strong Māori authority, such as the King.

When the King's emissary, Wī Toko, and his party left Warea in order to hand over the King's flag to the Ngāti Ruanui, the Taranaki people proceeded to erect an enormous flagpole and a fortnight later, on the return of the party

---

20. RP VII, 37–38.

from the south, a royal flag was hoisted on it. The preacher of Taranaki had been outmanoeuvred by his own congregation. He bitterly remarks on the fact that the flag for Taranaki had obviously been brought down together with the one for Ngāti Ruanui, indicating that the King's supporters among the Taranaki people clearly expected to prevail in this instance and that they had informed Wī Toko of this in advance.

From now on, the village of Warea was dominated by two structures: the new church, and across from it the new flagpole from which the King's flag flew. They were symbolic of a deepening rift between Riemenschneider and his people, a rift that hurt the missionary deeply but which was not acknowledged by either side at this time. The missionary saw it as a personal victory that the people of Warea refused to accept a cask of rum, that Wī Toko was going to send them to celebrate their joining the King Movement. He also managed to dissuade Āperahama from providing a guard of honour to conduct the King's emissary south to Wellington. At the same time, while carefully avoiding any public statements about the King, the text for one of his sermons at this time could nevertheless be taken as a veiled threat that he would leave if his people did not pay heed to his message. He preached on Mark 6,11: 'If you come to a town where people do not welcome you or will not listen to you, leave it and shake the dust off your feet. That will be a warning to them'. The fact remained, however, that Riemenschneider and his message was no longer the dominant authority among the people of Taranaki. A new and powerful movement had arisen to lay claim to the hearts and minds of the deeply troubled Māori.

∗

Riemenschneider's domestic life provided the usual background of personal joy and sorrow to the momentous events in which he had become involved. On 11 August 1859, while carting earth to the site of the old house, which had been demolished, he suffered an accident that injured him severely in his chest. Vinegar compresses and a pressure bandage failed to ease the unbearable pain, so the missionary pushed a piece of cardboard inside the bandage to prevent the broken bones from moving. Two days after he sustained the injury, the missionary, still in great pain, delivered his fifth child, another daughter, Augusta Frederica. He reports that his wife came into labour at half past eight in the evening and:

> ... at 10 o'clock everything had already been put away and tidied, so that I could soon go to bed. It was a blessing that it did not go further into the night. I could hardly have lasted much longer.[21]

---

21. RP VII, 87.

On 3 October Riemenschneider was in New Plymouth and finally decided to have his injury examined by a doctor, more than six weeks after he had incurred it. The diagnosis was a fractured sternum with two broken ribs at the point where they were attached to the sternum. They had started to heal somewhat irregularly because of continuing movement since the accident. The doctor advised the wearing of a bandage and rest for the next few weeks. The missionary, as usual, ignored the advice and carried on working.

A festive occasion for the whole family was the arrival, in November 1859, of another chest from Bremen, filled with gifts for the missionary, his wife and children. Of particular note among the presents was a photograph of Riemenschneider's father, the first he had received since his departure from Bremen. Riemenschneider writes:

> You have kindly taken care that on this occasion a most welcome photograph of my dear old father has arrived here safely and in good condition. You can imagine how most dear and precious it is to me and all of us here. Oh, how much the dear old man has aged in his features over the last 17 years in which I have not seen him face to face! But of course each of you over in the dear homeland, just as we here, have had similar signs of increasing age engraved on his face during that long time ...[22]

In the report in which he makes these remarks, Riemenschneider encloses a photo, which he had taken of himself in New Plymouth, as well as a photo of his wife, which she had taken at the request and expense of her mother. Copies of both portraits have survived and are now in the custody of Puke Ariki (formerly the Taranaki Museum).

Another tantalising snippet of domestic news that is found in the correspondence of 1859 is a reference to a Māori child who appears to have been brought up in the missionary's household. On 3 October he reports that he had been able to keep household expenses for the quarter, including horse fodder and shoeing, to £30 13/4d, 'which includes feeding and clothing our little native pupil Matakine whom we have in our care now for two years'.[23] Apart from this enigmatic sentence, no further reference can be found to Matakine anywhere in Riemenschneider's papers.

The missionary's parish work had increased over the last few years because the Anglican Māori had also adopted him as their preacher and many of them had, in fact, joined his 'German' church. Their missionary, Archdeacon Govett,[24] had been less strict than his predecessor Bolland and had not prohibited them from attending North German Protestant worship although he insisted that they did not take communion. He had been absent in England

---

22. RP VII, 117.
23. RP VII, 111.
24. Govett was made Archdeacon after his return from England in 1859.

from 1856 to 1859 and had, according to Riemenschneider, made no formal provision for his Māori congregation in Taranaki. Riemenschneider had looked after Govett's flock and in his report of December 1859 he comments on how much things had changed since his arrival in Taranaki when he was politely but firmly told by Episcopal Māori that his services were not required. Now, he writes, 'there is no place and no hut in all of Taranaki where we and our word and work are not welcomed gladly and with open arms'.[25]

In spite of an apparent increase in church attendance, however, Riemenschneider was clearly aware of the grave threats to peace between the Māori and the settlers. In May 1859 he quotes a statement of Colonel Wakefield that he had heard in 1843, 'It is my opinion that Taranaki on some future day will become the battle field of New Zealand'.[26] In July of the same year the missionary refers to the visit, in March, of Governor Gore Browne and Native Secretary McLean in New Plymouth; of Te Tēira's offer of a small parcel of land on the Waitara and of Wiremu Kīngi's objection to the sale.

The situation in New Plymouth and Taranaki was tense. Pākehā provocation and Māori mistrust combined to bring about an atmosphere of increasing tension and uncertainty.

The warclouds were now gathering over the Waitara and they were casting their shadow over the whole Taranaki region and beyond. Riemenschneider's personal sincerity and integrity were not in question among the majority of his Māori congregation. But he counselled faith in a God that had been brought into the country by the very people who had done harm to the Māori and were now threatening their very existence. He also taught that the British Queen, her Governor and his officials were instituted by God to bring about God's will, the great benefit, as he saw it, of colonisation of Māori land by Europeans. Āperahama and his people, in the face of pressure and threats by the Pākehā, a shrinking population and dwindling land holdings, sought refuge in a specifically Māori response both in religious and in political terms. Neither of these approaches was able to avert the disaster that was about to overwhelm Taranaki.

---

25. RP VII, 132.
26. RP VII, 8.

Chapter Ten

War and Exile, 1860

THE YEAR 1860 OPENED with a celebration for Riemenschneider. The settlers belonging to the various Christian denominations in Tataraimaka had always been willing to co-operate as far as the provision of church services was concerned. They had now built a small 'Union Chapel', and the missionary had been invited to preach the morning sermon on its opening Sunday, 1 January. It was to be one of very few celebrations in that year.

On 6 February 1860 he arrived in New Plymouth on one of his periodic visits to town. Just as he arrived, the postman was setting out for Wellington with the overland mail. He handed the missionary a letter that he had been intending to deliver in Warea on his way south. It contained fateful news:

Confidential
New Plymouth, February 6, 1860
My dear Sir;
I write to you by this morning's Mail to inform you, that the Government have determined to proceed with the survey of Teiras land at Waitara at once, & should there be any opposition (which I feel certain there will be) the survey will then be carried on under the protection of the Troops, who will occupy the block of land, not with any intention whatever to commence hostilities against the natives, but to enforce the Governors determination to conclude the purchase of Teiras offer.

The natives of Taranaki & Ngati Ruanui will put a very different construction upon any movement of the troops, & I fear Sir, we shall have a very tedious time of it.

I should very much like to have seen you before anything was done, but I am so busy, I cannot get to your place.

I am afraid that unless great caution is used we shall have a critical time of it yet in Taranaki, but the Government have prepared for the worst.

Be pleased to keep this private at present.
I am my dear Sir
Yours etc. etc. etc.
[To:] The Rev. Mr Riemenschneider[1]

---

1. Riemenschneider Papers, RP VII, 153–154. Although Riemenschneider does not give the signature in his transcript, it is clear that the letter is from Robert Parris, the Government Land Purchase Agent.

Up to this point, the missionary's belief in the integrity, fairness and good will towards the Māori by the European authorities had still not been shaken. A few weeks later, on 2 March, he comments in a letter to his superiors:

> After nine months of careful and indefatigable investigation of the question, and after exhaustive consideration of all circumstances connected with it, the Governor had become sufficiently convinced that he could conclude the deal with Teira justly and with good reason, and the purchase price was paid to the latter and his supporters.[2]

While the fears of extermination were certainly exaggerated, the fear that the Government was intent on acquiring more land, particularly in Taranaki where the Pākehā pressure was greatest and the opposition to land sales perhaps fiercest, was certainly justified. It has since been shown that the Governor's 'indefatigable investigation' and 'exhaustive consideration' of the matter, which the Governor based on information supplied to him by Donald McLean and Robert Parris, rested on a misconception about the right of chiefs to have their opinions taken into account in the question of land sales, and on grossly biased information supplied by McLean and Parris.[3] Riemenschneider himself makes it clear in one of his many retrospective reflections on the origin of the war, that in his view the Governor, while not guilty of ill-will, had not been adequately informed. When the hostilities broke out, the Governor was not sufficiently aware of the background for his decisions and not in a position to foresee the likely consequences.[4]

With a heavy heart, Riemenschneider returned to Warea before the survey took place. While he had been informed of the impending action, the general public and the Māori were in the dark and rumours were circulating everywhere. The missionary writes:

> I went back home to my excited tribe with a heart heavy with portents. As soon as I returned, having been expected with the greatest anxiety by my people, I called them together the next morning and simply presented them with the whole plan and intended action of the government. No raging and fulminations arose, but a deep, oppressive and dreadful ferment of all minds could be read in their faces and heard in their firm speeches.[5]

---

2. RP VII, 158.
3. See Keith Sinclair, *The Origins of the Maori Wars*. Wellington: New Zealand University Press, 1957, pp. 136–180. About McLean's investigations into any absentee claimants, Sinclair writes, 'McLean's investigations were, in fact, a sham, designed to aid Teira's case and not to seek the facts' (p. 159). When McLean fell ill, George Parris took over the examination of Teira's right to sell. Sinclair shows, 'that his evidence was dubious and his arguments almost worthless (p. 171). See also New Zealand Waitangi Tribunal, *The Taranaki Report: kaupapa tautahi: WAI 143 nuaru me te raupatu*. Wellington. GP Publications, 1996, p. 67: '[Gore Brown's] decision to challenge Kingi and to push the purchasing into Waitara was probably due more to bad advice than to his own assessment'.
4. RP VII, 280–281.
5. RP VII, 159.

In informing the Warea Māori, Riemenschneider broke the confidentiality under which Parris had advised him of the coming survey. He justifies himself in his report to the *Verwaltungsausschuß* (executive committee of the German Mission Society). His position is that, given the state of feverish emotional excitement in which he found the people at Warea, he felt that it was better to tell them the truth and take the consequences, rather than to leave them in further uncertainty and prey to rumours, which were far worse than the truth. After the meeting, the missionary also wrote to the settlers in Tataraimaka asking them to stay calm and not to do anything to increase the tension.

On 20 February 1860 the surveyor Octavius Carrington, accompanied by Parris, attempted to survey the disputed land on the Waitara. He was prevented from carrying out his task by the non-violent obstruction of about 60 to 80 Māori. On the following day the military commander, Colonel Murray, gave Wiremu Kīngi 24 hours in which to change his stance and when he did not receive a reply that he considered satisfactory, he declared martial law on Wednesday, 22 February. This declaration of martial law rested on dubious grounds. One New Zealand historian has summarised the situation as follows:

> The important fact was that the proclamation had been signed and sent down before a single act of any description had been committed against the peace, had been published before a single Maori was known to be in arms against the Crown or even to contemplate resistance, and before any offence had been given except the unarmed obstruction of a survey by people who were actually living on the land concerned. The Governor, who was charged with protecting the interests of the Maoris, would certainly not have condoned, far less authorised, such proceedings against Europeans in similar circumstances.[6]

There has been some debate about the tone of the declaration of martial law. The Māori text, it is argued, was so badly translated that it read like a challenge, a declaration of war. Although Robert Parris, a resident magistrate, as well as two missionaries, stated that in their view no Māori regarded it as such,[7] Riemenschneider unequivocally takes the opposite view in a letter to his superiors in Bremen, written some months after the event. He had access to the document, he was by now clearly very skilled in Māori, and he writes to Bremen:

> They stand forfeit to the government as criminals by reason of rebellion without admitting this. They say that the Governor has declared war on them and has made war against them, and indeed they have strong grounds for this assertion because of an error committed by the Governor, in that his proclamation of martial law [issued in] February in the Maori translation clearly reads as a firm, unequivocal declaration of war.[8]

---

6. Keith Sinclair, *op. cit.*, p. 189.
7. *ibid.*
8. RP, VII, 198.

The missionary rushed to New Plymouth on the day after the proclamation. He arrived on the morning of 24 February, spent the day gathering information on the situation and returned to Warea straight away.

In Warea, Āperahama had decided to call a *rūnanga* (council meeting) of the whole Taranaki tribe, but in deference to their pastor, had waited with determining the day until the missionary had returned from New Plymouth. He arrived back at the station on Saturday, 25 February, held a district communion service on the Sunday and agreed that the *rūnanga* should be held on Wednesday, 29 February.

The meeting took place on the village square in Warea, which was symbolically framed on one side by the new church, on the other by the flagpole from which the flag of the Māori King was flying. Riemenschneider's brief description of the *hui* shows the tragedy of the situation of Taranaki. Buffeted by rumours and conflicting advice, troubled by the unfolding events and convinced that their very existence as a people was at stake, they were desperately seeking for the best way to cope with the events.[9]

The final decision was that the Taranaki people would not go to war against the Pākehā even if the Government and Wiremu Kīngi should come to blows on the Waitara. Instead, they would wait for advice from King Pōtatau's court to which 10 Taranaki people had been sent a fortnight before. It is significant that Riemenschneider, who in the past had been able to sway the councils of the Taranaki people, ended up with just three people on his side. At least as far as political issues were concerned, the advice sought by the Māori of Taranaki was no longer only that of the missionary, but also that of the Māori King.

The missionary remained, however, a useful contact for the Taranaki people with the European authorities. Once the *rūnanga* was over and Riemenschneider was satisfied that no hasty action would be taken, he returned to New Plymouth to await further developments. He arrived on the afternoon of 1 March, the same day on which the Governor and Colonel Gold, the new commander of the army, had arrived. On the following day, he was received by Gore Browne. As on the previous occasion, Riemenschneider found the Governor an affable man and the meeting reassuring. He reports:

> His last words with which he left me were, "Believe me when I assure you that, even though I am a man of arms (the Governor is a Colonel in the British army) and hold a position which is different from yours, this does not make me in any way inclined to use force, as long as I find it in my power to bring about peace and to achieve its goal and purpose by amicable means. ... But if it were to happen that Wiremu Kingi drives me to the brink with his persistent opposition, I am the Governor and no matter what happens then, I will intervene with a firm hand and nothing shall prevent me from carrying out my task to the limit".[10]

---

9. RP VII, 162.
10. RP VII, 164.

A number of New Zealand historians, most recently James Belich,[11] have made the point that it is an oversimplification to see land as the sole cause of the Taranaki (and later Waikato) conflict. They argue that an important motive on the European side was the assertion and imposition of British sovereignty over those parts of New Zealand where Māori still governed themselves. Riemenschneider's reports of Māori feelings, and Browne's parting words to him ('I am the Governor'...) indicate that both the Governor and his Māori opponents understood very well that land, while important, was not the sole issue at stake.

Riemenschneider was in the Waitara area with his friend and fellow missionary John Whiteley when the first hostilities of the Taranaki war broke out on 17 March 1860. They watched the European bombardment of the Te Kohia *pā* until about 5.00 p.m. when they returned to New Plymouth. Riemenschneider, who was familiar with Māori war tactics, was not surprised to learn, on the following day, that Wiremu Kīngi and the occupants of the *pā* had escaped during the night without having suffered any casualties.

Three days after the action the missionary, together with the Wesleyan Whiteley and the Anglican Govett, rode out to the *pā* where Wiremu Kīngi had retreated and had a conversation with him. Kīngi repeated his view that the war had been imposed on him by the Governor, that he did not wish to continue it, and that it would end as soon as the Governor decided to give up his claim to the land at the Waitara. After their visit, the three reverend gentlemen went to look over the Te Kohia *pā* (or 'L' pā, as the Europeans called it because of its shape). A close inspection of the *pā* and its earthworks led Riemenschneider to the conclusion (which apparently escaped the military commander, Colonel Gold), that 'the natives know how to protect themselves safely and how to escape unscathed even against the best [European artillery] fire.[12]

In the meantime, the Taranaki and Ngāti Ruanui people had decided to intervene in the war. On the day before their missionary's return, the Warea people had already taken action to defy Government authority. The *Taranaki Herald* reports:

> News arrived from Taranaki that the Warea natives had taken and detained the mail for the South, which started on Monday at 1 p.m. Aperahama, chief of the Patukai natives, had forcibly detained the bag. It is hoped that the Niger on her return will be sent down to shell and destroy Warea – as the pa is conveniently situated for the purpose near the beach.[13]

---

11. *The New Zealand Wars and the Victorian Interpretation of Racial Conflict.* Auckland: Auckland University Press, 1986, pp. 76–80.
12. RP VII, 200. James Belich makes the point that Gold did not seem to recognise anti-artillery bunkers in the L pa. See *The New Zealand Wars, op. cit.*, p. 83.
13. 24 March 1860.

Two days later Porikapa, another of the mission teachers at Kaihīhī and a supporter of the policy of peaceful neutrality in the conflict, which was being advocated by Riemenschneider, prevailed on Āperahama to send the post bag south after all. It never arrived at its destination however. On 21 April the *Herald* reports that after consultations between the Taranaki and the Ngāti Ruanui people, the letters were burnt and the newspapers were used to make cartridges.

Taranaki was a divided people. Some chiefs and teachers favoured armed conflict with the Europeans before the latter could muster further armed forces in the New Plymouth area. Others followed their pastor's counsel to stay neutral in what was essentially a conflict between the northern Puketapu people and the Governor, which, in the missionary's opinion, the Governor would surely win. The recent events at Waitara however had made the pendulum swing towards war among the people of Taranaki, and brought about an increasing polarisation between the two parties. Riemenschneider's simple and naive advice to have faith in God and the Governor, no matter how passionately advocated, could no longer satisfy his anxious and angry parishioners. He describes the mood at the Sunday service:

> On Sunday I preached about the parable of the sower and the weed on the field (Matthew 13) in the simplest way possible and without further confronting the question that was on everybody's mind. Nevertheless the consciences were so restless and the irritation of the mood which did not want to give in to the advice of the conscience was so great that several times a loud grumbling broke out and threatening expressions were directed at me which would have made me tremble if I had not stood in God's name on the ground of divine truth and on the post on which He had ordered me to stand; where it was therefore a matter of speaking gladly and confidently, whether it was a matter of life and death or not.[14]

The warriors from southern Taranaki had gathered at Warea on Wednesday, 22 March in order to wait for the Ngāti Ruanui contingent before setting out for the Waitara. They had decided not to take the route behind Mount Taranaki as they had done during the Puketapu feud, but to march straight through the European territory of New Plymouth. After all, they argued, the Europeans had marched through Māori territory to get to the Waitara from New Plymouth. According to Riemenschneider it was Āperahama's intention to march towards New Plymouth on the high road and to fight the Europeans in an open, pitched battle. The missionary reports that the southern Taranaki people were in agreement with this strategy.

The situation was, however, more complicated among members of the northern sub-tribe, the Ngā Māhanga. Riemenschneider's teacher, the chief

---

14. RP VII, 214.

Porikapa and all his church members among the Ngā Māhanga declared themselves opposed to any warlike action against the Europeans; a stance for which some of them were later sent into exile in European territory by their own people. Another Ngā Māhanga chief however, Paratene Te Kōparu, mindful of the proud and warlike history of his *hapū* (sub-tribe),[15] felt strongly that Āperahama's plan to fight his way through to the Waitara, was not the traditional Māori way to wage war. With a group of like-minded Ngā Māhanga warriors and some Ngāti Ruanui who had joined him, he therefore marched towards Ōmata on Saturday, 25 March, without waiting for the main Taranaki/Ngāti Ruanui contingent and his commander in chief, Āperahama. When Āperahama learned of Paratene's independent advance, he set out on Monday morning, 27 March with his party from Warea without waiting for the Ngāti Ruanui, who still had not arrived.

Before Āperahama had caught up with the Ngā Māhanga contingent, they had killed two European boys. Riemenschneider, while not condoning the action, explains that such an act was not considered murder because, according to the traditional Māori code of war, any living thing encountered by a *taua* (war party) on the march is killed as a legitimate victim of war.[16]

In addition to a farmer called Ford and the two boys, two other adult Europeans were killed by the advancing Māori. The European reaction was swift. On 28 March 1860 a British force under Lieutenant-Colonel G. F. Murray marched south and attacked the Māori force in what became known as the battle of Waireka. Contemporary sources estimated the number of Māori confronted by the Europeans as between 460 and 600, and the number of Māori casualties between 70 and 150. A more recent historian, James Belich, has stated that the Māori 'are unlikely to have exceeded 200 warriors',[17] and that 'the 70–150 warriors said to be killed in fact numbered about one.[18] While Belich is right in his analysis of the contemporary accounts as a wild exaggeration of the truth, Riemenschneider, who met the Taranaki war party in Warea on the morning after the action, states that the *taua* numbered about 400, and that they had suffered 15 dead and 16 wounded. Among the dead were Paratene Te Kōparu as well as Paora Kukutai, the old chief of

---

15. In a celebrated incident during the incursions into Taranaki from the north in 1820, the Ngā Māhanga successfully defended their *pā* Ngāweka, in present-day Ōkato, against a superior force of Ngāti Toa and Ngāpuhi warriors. This was one of only four defeats inflicted on the northern raiders who were armed with muskets, by the Taranaki, who at that time had no such weapons. See John Houston, *Maori Life in Old Taranaki*. Wellington: A. H. & A. W. Reed, 1965, pp. 52–56.
16. See Sir Peter Buck (Te Rangi Hiroa), *The Coming of the Maori*. 2nd edn, Wellington: Maori Purposes Fund Board; Whitcoulls Limited, 1987, p. 388: 'A war-party on the march had to kill anyone whom they met, such a victim being termed a *"maroro kokoti ihu waka taua"* (a flying fish which crosses the bows of a war canoe). Unless this was done, the war-party would be defeated'.
17. *The New Zealand Wars*. Auckland, *op. cit.*, 1986, p. 84.
18. *ibid*, p. 88.

Warea and uncle of Āperahama, who had been a loyal supporter and faithful parishioner of the missionary ever since he arrived in Taranaki.[19] Āperahama himself had been wounded in the shoulder.

Five years later, Riemenschneider still vividly remembers the arrival of the *taua* in Warea. He writes to Bremen:

> On the very day after the engagement by the Waireka, the Taranaki warriors returned to their own district and arrived at Warea, having left behind 15 dead while others had returned wounded. As soon as they had arrived in Warea I went among them. Reproachfully I rested my glance on Arama Karaka [the chief of Matakaha or Waiaua] and Wiremu [Kingi te Mataka[a]tea [the chief of Umuroa]. At once the latter rose, stepped up to me, took my right hand into both of his hands, bent his noble, tattooed face onto my shoulder (he is of considerably taller and much stronger stature than I), burst first of all into strong sobs, and, at his first attempt to speak, into a stream of heartfelt tears of remorse which completely overcame him.[20]

When he was finally able to speak, the missionary reports, Wiremu expressed his deep regret at having allowed himself to be carried along by the others into the war expedition. He now saw it as being the work of Satan rather than the Christ about whom their pastor had been preaching to them as the Prince of Peace.

In Riemenschneider's view there was still a small chance that there could be negotiations leading to peace after the Waireka engagement. He describes how, in the evening of the day on which the Taranaki *taua* had returned to Warea, about 470 Ngāti Ruanui arrived. Since the Taranaki had returned home, however, and in view of the fact that, in the missionary's judgement, they 'had come to their senses and were in no hurry to make another attempt',[21] the Ngāti Ruanui, who did not wish to attack New Plymouth without their Taranaki relatives and allies, returned home again. However, the conflict had now taken on a momentum of its own, which neither the desperate missionary nor the small peace faction among the Taranaki people could control. Just after the arrival of the defeated *taua* with its dead and wounded the barque-rigged screw-corvette *Niger* arrived off the coast and bombarded the *kāinga* - without doing any damage, however.

The bombardment of Warea by the *Niger* appears to have been the catalyst uniting Taranaki against the Pākehā. Only a small handful of the Ngā Māhanga now wanted peace and Riemenschneider, who visited them on 1 April, took a letter from one of their chiefs, Kōmene, to New Plymouth, in which Kōmene offered peace to the Governor. Porikapa continued vigorously to advocate

---

19. RP VII, 210.
20. RP VIII, 225.
21. RP VII, 210.

peace. Some of his followers were no longer able to live among their people and moved to New Plymouth, a fact duly noted by the *Taranaki Herald*.

As far as the rest of Taranaki was concerned, the tribe was now united in defiance against the Governor and his troops. At a *hui* that was held on 13 April, a prominent Taranaki chief made a speech directed, via their missionary advocate, to the Europeans in which he voiced his disapproval of the Ngā Māhanga killings on the day before the battle of Waireka. The missionary then records the continuation of his speech:

> We Maori do not consider that we are the only guilty ones in this matter [the killing of defenceless individuals], since the Governor has shown us that he and his white people do exactly the same thing. We did not know this before, but now we know for we have seen it, and the only difference is that the Maori finish their plunder and murder expeditions against their enemies and thus give the enemy an opportunity to defend themselves against us. The Governor and his people, on the other hand, undertakes his expeditions of destruction at sea with warships and their guns, where he knows that we cannot put up any defence against him and his superior power.[22]

The bombardment of Warea by the *Niger* clearly demonstrated to the Taranaki people that punitive measures would be taken against them and that their unfortified coastal settlements would not afford them any safety against attack from either land or sea. As they had done during the raids from the north in the 1820s and 30s, they therefore constructed fortresses deep in the impenetrable bush towards the foothills of Mount Taranaki. One of them, constructed mainly for Ngā Māhanga, Riemenschneider reports to Germany, was at Hangatahua, 14 km. north of Warea, the second, central fortress, for the population of Warea and the villages immediately south of it, about eight km. inland from Warea, while a southern fortress was erected at Okaha (Te Tekapu), about 20 km. south of Warea. The fortresses, like most Māori *pā*, were completed within a few days and virtually the whole population of Taranaki withdrew into them, leaving the coastal strip, the North German Mission Society parish, once again depopulated and desolate, just like it had been after the depredations of the Waikato in the thirties.[23]

A few days after the return of the Taranaki and Ngāti Ruanui from Waireka, the missionary visited New Plymouth in order to find out what was to happen next. On Maundy Thursday, 5 April, he rode over to Waitara with his colleague and brother missionary Whiteley. On the way out they discovered a burning Māori village some distance away. It turned out to be the *kāinga* of Tāmati Te Ito of the Puketapu sub-tribe who had caused Riemenschneider so much grief in Taranaki. Te Ito himself asked the missionaries for details when they

---
22. RP VII, 212.
23. RP VII, 214–215.

encountered him in one of the Waitara *pā* but they had no further information. It was only when they returned to the British camp at Waitara that they heard that the village had been fired by a force of Māori and European irregulars, which had been established under a Captain Brown for escort duties, etc. They had been sent out to recapture draught animals that had escaped and were wandering around the countryside, and they had set fire to the *kāinga*, which consisted of 'five miserable reed huts',[24] without orders to do so and in reckless disregard of the consequences. The consequences were not long in coming. By the evening of the same day, five European farmhouses were burned to the ground. Riemenschneider comments that this thoughtless and senseless act of destruction widened the gulf between Māori and Pākehā considerably.

There was no prospect of a settlement of the dispute in the south either. The missionary soon found out from hints given to him by the authorities and his friends that, as the Taranaki people had suspected, a punitive expedition was being planned that might go as far south as Warea, which would place his family in immediate danger. With a heavy heart he finally decided to evacuate them to a place of safety. Āperahama and the Taranaki Māori made it clear to him that New Plymouth was not safe and that it might soon become the focus of a concerted Māori attack. Quite apart from that, New Plymouth had become hopelessly overcrowded as a result of the influx of settlers who had sought refuge there from their farms in the countryside The *Taranaki Herald* of 31 March reported that the Superintendent of Taranaki, George Cutfield, had written to Governor Gore Browne that accommodation, which had hitherto housed 800 people, now had to house approximately 2,500. Three days earlier, the Superintendent had issued a proclamation, offering free passages to Nelson, with a free return passage once hostilities ceased, to any people willing to be evacuated.

In the light of this information, the worried missionary reluctantly decided to send his wife and children to Nelson, the place where he and his fellow North German missionaries had first landed 17 years ago, and where he still had friends and acquaintances, particularly among the German settlers.

The parting took place at dawn on Friday, 13 April, 1860. The Riemenschneider family and their baggage travelled in three ox carts, one of which was driven by Tamihana, Āperahama's son, as far as the 'border' at Ōmata, where the Taranaki drivers were replaced by neutral Māori who took the family to New Plymouth and later returned the carts to Ōmata.

On the afternoon of Saturday, 21 April Mrs Riemenschneider and her five children embarked on the steamer *Airedale* for Nelson. The missionary writes:

On that afternoon I took leave of my most faithful and best life companion

---

24. RP VII, 178.

together with my dear children, commending her into God's care with a heavy heart without knowing when we would see each other again. It happened in God's name and according to our innermost conviction according to God's will, and so we could submit to the cross, no matter how utterly bitter and painful our parting was.[25]

He himself was keen to return to Warea at once. He conducted four services of worship for the Māori in *pā* surrounding New Plymouth on the Sunday, and then set out for home on Monday morning, 23 April. He only got as far as Tātaraimaka however, where he was turned back by the Army Commander Colonel Gold. Gold, as always, treated the missionary with great politeness and cordiality, but he did not tell Riemenschneider that he was commanding a punitive expedition to the south. He made some strong hints, however, which implied that the German missionary's presence at Warea could be embarrassing for both of them.

Riemenschneider was in a difficult position. If he insisted on going to Warea, he would be seen as a Pākehā spy if the European expedition was successful, or as a Māori informer if it was unsuccessful. During his stay in New Plymouth he had already been accused by several people of being responsible for the failure of the Warea bombardment by warning the Māori to evacuate the village. In reality it had in fact been the Māori who had warned the missionary and his family to keep out of the way. Nevertheless the rumours of Riemenschneider being a Māori spy enjoyed wide circulation.

After his conversation with Colonel Gold at Tātaraimaka, the missionary decided reluctantly to return to New Plymouth in the meantime.

The military expedition reached Warea on the Friday of that week, 27 April. But the Taranaki people had retreated to their safe forest hideouts and when Riemenschneider arrived back in Warea on Sunday, 29 April, to his dismay he found the village burned to the ground. All that was left was the church, the mission house and the flour mill, which the troops had not been able to find. The missionary, whose health had suffered considerably as a result of his exertions and who reports feeling deeply depressed in almost every letter sent to Bremen in the first half of 1860, was returning to a scene of destruction and desolation. His dream of a flourishing village community of Europeanised Māori, trading and working harmoniously with the colonists and learning useful skills from them, had literally turned to ashes. It was only a matter of time before he would have to admit defeat as well.

✻

---

25. RP VII, 221–222.

In the course of May 1860, Riemenschneider wrote a long letter to his wife in several instalments. What makes it particularly remarkable is that it is one of the very few private documents found in the mission archives, destined not for his superiors in Bremen or other official use, but for a person with whom the missionary had an intimate relationship. In it he describes, in English since Catherine knew no German, the solicitous farewell he received from his friends when he left New Plymouth to return to Warea after his family had left for Nelson, and the arrival at the bleak and lonely mission station:

> Mrs Flight said, "Even let us suppose that your life is all safe with the natives only just think how very miserable & lonely you will be & feel yourself there all by yourself alone without either your dear wife or children. Do stay with us yet a while before you venture to go."
> "Kati na, tempt me not, mother Eva," I replied.
> "Well if you must go, then promise at least that you will not stay there very long before you come back. I am sure you will get worn down & ill there all by yourself; when shall we see you back again here with us on Monday – surely not later than Tuesday? we shall be so anxious about you until we see you again." again Mrs Hood said "but what have you got at home & for the journey in the way of kai [food] & comforts to live on?" & then, kind soul, she wanted to load me with all manner of good things, none of which I could take. On Sunday morning I gave Mr Whitely my letter for you (which I had written in last part during the night) to post by the Airedale.[26]

On the day after his arrival back at Warea, the missionary, who had announced the fact that he was now in residence again by tying a white handkerchief to the highest fencepost near the gate, travelled inland to visit his congregation in their forest stronghold. He reports to his wife that he was well received:

> With the exception of Erueti, Ahitone & several others of the young folks who had gone to Hangatahua & have not as yet returned from thence, I found all the Patukai & Upokomutu in the pah just having their Kai No sooner did I appear at the entrance of the pah when I was received with such a tangi & karanga of welcome as never before; men women & children all wept tears of aroha & this not merely because they saw me back among them but because it made them think of you.[27]

Some historians have accused Riemenschneider in rather harsh and censorious language of having been a 'spy' for the military and thus having betrayed the people whose pastor he was and who trusted him.[28] While he certainly would

---

26. RP VII, 231.
27. RP VII, 234.
28. See, for example, Dick Scott, *Ask That Mountain. The story of Parihaka*. Auckland: Reed/Southern Cross, 1975, pp. 14–15. Scott also claims that Riemenschneider 'had shared the people's bread for fourteen years but had abandoned his mission and moved to New Plymouth at the first hint of trouble'.

have passed on some information, like virtually all missionaries appear to have done, and while he certainly was on friendly terms with Colonel Gold, his description of their interactions indicate that they carefully avoided a formal exchange of information that related to the armed conflict between Māori and the Governor's troops. There is, however, no doubt that the missionary was a keen observer of Māori military installations and several detailed descriptions of *pā*, some with sketches, have survived. They are, however, not in the archives of the colonial armed forces, but rather in the papers that he sent to Bremen. It appears therefore that Riemenschneider, at least, described the *pā* because they were of interest to him rather than because he was gathering information on behalf of the military.

It is not surprising that the missionary felt lonely and depressed in his mission station, surrounded by the ashes of the destroyed dwellings of the Warea people. He also missed his wife and family, as he writes in his letter:

> I have tried to take my meals as usually in the parlour but could not endure it – in fact I rarely ever enter it except to wind up the clock at night – it is too large & lone for my single self empty & vacant of all whom I love its void & stillness makes me too sad to like being in it. I take my meals in the kitchen, surrounded by cats & dog the only living creatures that keep always about me …[29]

Riemenschneider's relations with his congregation, while cordial and even affectionate, were clearly deeply strained by the events of the war and by the gulf that the conflict had opened up between him and his people.

Loneliness, depression, lack of adequate diet and constant worry about his flock, combined to afflict the missionary, who had never had a strong constitution, with another severe bout of illness. He reports that on Friday, 4 May he was beginning to suffer from severe stomach cramps and diarrhoea. For several days he battled the illness, unable to even light a fire and make himself some tea. He lay wrapped in his blanket on the sofa in the bleak and empty house. No Māori came to visit because the atrocious cold and rainy weather that prevailed at the time had caused the Hangatahua River, which lay between the *pā* and the mission station, to rise to a point where it could not be forded. Because he was too weak and ill, and because the river was still too dangerous to cross, he was not able to go inland and conduct worship on Sunday. In his letter he paints a rather sad picture of himself amid the ruins of a war that he could not understand and that he had been unable to avert from his flock:

> In the afternoon when for a little while the sun began to shine out I took a slow walk to the desolate village, all had been swept clean by the devouring flame no vestige of any house or hut (church excepted) from Keretape down to the beach

---

29. RP VII, 240.

remained except the ash covered spots of where but a few days before all had yet been standing – I counted about 31 [house sites].[30]

On Thursday, 10 May, the lonely missionary had recovered sufficiently to travel and he decided that he had no option but to return to New Plymouth until his health improved sufficiently to allow him to continue with his work. He found ready hospitality and kind care with the Whiteleys and as soon as he was partially restored he accompanied Whiteley on his journeys to the Māori encamped in the various *pā* on the Waitara River.

Quite apart from the wretched state of his health, Riemenschneider's life was not easy in New Plymouth, nor for his colleagues Whiteley and Govett. The town was overcrowded with refugees from the outlying countryside, and living conditions were difficult. But that was only part of their troubles. The missionaries also encountered public opposition to their actions with respect to the conflict with the Māori, in particular to their pastoral visits. On 12 May the editorial in the *Taranaki Herald*, the paper owned by the missionary's brother-in-law, Garland Woon, contained a vitriolic attack on the three clergymen whom he styles a 'meddling triumvirate'.

Ironically, the very issue of the *Taranaki Herald* in which this attack appeared was suppressed by the order of Colonel Gold on the grounds that it contained sensitive military information.[31] It appeared two days later with the offending paragraph blanked out. Riemenschneider was not slow to see this irony, particularly as he and Whiteley had been to visit the Māori on the Waitara with a special pass issued by Colonel Gold for the purpose, on the very day that the paper called on the military to stop the missionaries from having any further dealings with the Māori.

When the missionary returned to Warea towards the end of May he was, as usual, by no means fully recovered. During June he continued to labour among the Taranaki people in spite of the fact that he did so in what could be described as a war zone, and therefore frequently his life was in considerable danger.

However, he reports that the attitude of the Māori to him was changing. The Government had closed access to New Plymouth for them and Riemenschneider became more and more the focus of resentment against all Pākehā. He describes the process:

> At first they began to blame the Government, then me personally because *I, of all people, had not succeeded in persuading the Governor* to give up Waitara and thereby avoid the war, that I had permitted the closing of the border [with New Plymouth], and finally, that I observed it which clearly demonstrated that I was more of a friend and ally of the Europeans than a friend and father

---

30. RP VII, 248.
31. For a brief account of this incident, see Murray Moorhead, 'The man who censored the Herald', *Tales of Old North Taranaki*. New Plymouth: Murray Moorhead, 1991, pp. 64–65.

of my own *Maori* ... They demanded that I should fully approve and justify all this wild and depraved behaviour, all this murder and arson of the Maori and that I should attribute all the blame for it totally and exclusively to the Government ...

... In short, they demanded nothing less than that I should become a rebel against my lawful authorities and a twister and falsifier of God's word and divine truth, and thus become a heretic and seducer for them for their own and my destruction and damnation; and all this only so that I would grace their present hatred, revenge and bloodthirst against the Europeans with approval, support and a certain semblance of justice and sanctity.[32]

The deep tragedy of the situation was that the Māori had trustingly invested Riemenschneider with more power and authority than he could legitimately claim and exercise, and that, because of the paternalistic nature of his role, he had naively accepted the power. He had come to the people of Taranaki as a missionary, preaching the Gospel. But over time he had been asked, and had agreed, to be their judge and political adviser and advocate without considering the implications of doing so. The *iwi* had invested him with powers that the Europeans were unable to exercise in areas that they did not occupy, and that the traditional political and judicial Māori infrastructure would or could no longer exercise. The vacuum created by the weakening of traditional Māori power structures may have been exacerbated in the case of the Taranaki because of their defeats in the inter-tribal wars in the 1830s. These had resulted in a large proportion of their population, including chiefs, being made slaves. Riemenschneider certainly thought so and quotes some Māori opinion to support his view. The problem was that the Taranaki people endowed him with some of the power that may rightfully have belonged to their chiefs. This was no different from what happened to missionaries elsewhere, but in most of those cases defeat and humiliation had not damaged the *mana* of the chiefs. Riemenschneider sincerely had the welfare of the people at heart but was unable to escape his narrow ideological interpretation of political events. As a result he assumed a theocratic leadership, which in the end he was unable to exercise and which his people were unable to accept. The political events of 1860 showed that he too was powerless in the face of forces that were much stronger than any he could marshal and direct. The people who felt oppressed had turned against their oppressor, and their own advocate was unable to prevent the disaster.

In addition to the change in the attitude of the Taranaki Māori, which was exacerbated by the expected arrival of reinforcements from the Waikato tribes who were strongly of the view that no missionaries should be tolerated on Māori territory, Riemenschneider was also becoming the subject of rumours

---

32. RP VII, 259–260.

which, if acted upon, could bring about further hostilities. He writes that it was rumoured in town that he was a prisoner of the Māori at Warea, or that he was lying on his deathbed. The missionary was most concerned that if one of his friends in town, John Whiteley, for example, would come to Warea to visit him in order to obtain reliable news of his condition, he might be killed by the Māori. Among the Taranaki people, on the other hand, rumours were circulating that a military expedition was going to be sent out from New Plymouth to 'rescue' their missionary. Riemenschneider's condition, the political situation and the rumours associated with his safety all combined to increase the tension that had been created by his preaching of peace and accommodation in a situation which, in the collective judgement of the Taranaki people, called for war and resistance.

The final confrontation occurred on Sunday, 8 July. Riemenschneider was on his way from Warea to New Plymouth to get some badly needed supplies and stopped at Kaihīhī to hold a church service with the people who, a week earlier, had raided Tātaraimaka and had burned down three abandoned farmhouses there. He reports that he preached 'simply and plainly'[33] on Psalm 4, that during the sermon he saw 'the storm brewing'[34] and that it broke straight after the sermon. The missionary describes the meeting:[35]

> They attacked my sermon, accused me that my admonition to do penance and work for peace and justice was treachery against them, my own flock, and designed to lead them astray into the teeth of the wolf (the Governor) ... "Your own emaciated figure and appearance shows us that you are ill and weak. We know that you suffer great privations among us. But why are you suffering privations? Is it not your own fault? Why did you not prevent the closing of the border, or, since it is now in force, why do you not break it by force? But either you are scared of the Government or else you approve of their plan and their hostile behaviour towards us, or if they are really too strong for you, why don't you turn to us and ask us to get by stealth from town what is needful and useful for you and your flock (Rahui)"?[36]

The final conversation between pastor and the people at Kaihīhī (of which the above quotation is an extract) clearly shows the gulf and lack of understanding that had opened up between them. Riemenschneider felt constrained by his vocation to play the role of an Old Testament prophet among a people who

---

33. RP VII, 261.
34. *ibid.*
35. The Māori reaction to Riemenschneider's sermon is not altogether surprising. The short Psalm 4 contains verses such as: 'How long will you people insult me?/How long will you love what is worthless/and go after what is false?' (v. 2) This Psalm seems to have been a favourite of Riemenschneider's whenever he felt that his people had gone astray. He used the same text, concentrating on v.2, when it appeared that the Taranaki were going to join the Ngāti Ruanui in the Puketapu feud (RP V, 436).
36. RP VII, 261.

had forsaken their God,[37] in other words, he felt bound to interpret their behaviour almost exclusively in Christian religious terms. The people, on the other hand, saw themselves engaged in a struggle for life and death as a people. They felt that they had been forced into a radical position in which a judgement of their actions from the standpoint of a Pākehā gospel could no longer be tolerated.

Riemenschneider continued on his way to New Plymouth, determined to return to Warea as soon as possible. However, during his stay in town, further rumours reached him to the effect that if he were to return, he would be taken prisoner and used as a hostage by the Māori against the Government. So he decided that it was his 'positive duty towards God, the Government, myself and my family'[38] that for the time being he should go to Nelson to await the outcome of the conflict. The missionary decided not to stay in New Plymouth, he says, because he did not want his Taranaki people to think that he was in collusion with the Europeans and the Government officials there.

He had another good reason for his decision to go to Nelson. While he had worked closely with John Whiteley, particularly over the opening months of the war, he nevertheless found it necessary to clearly distance himself from Whiteley's stance, which was uncompromisingly pro-settler. Already at the beginning of the war, Riemenschneider had chosen not to sign a letter that Whiteley had written to Wiremu Kīngi, urging him to acquiesce to the survey of the disputed land at Waitara. Six clergymen of New Plymouth and its neighbourhood had signed. Whiteley expressed his sympathy with the settlers symbolically by moving from his mission station to New Plymouth, and clearly states his position in the diary entry for Wednesday, 28 March 1860, the day of the Waireka engagement, when he made the decision to move:

> ... I thought it best that we should be all together with our daughter and her family in Town. Moreover I considered that under the circumstances I ought to let the settlers of the Town see that I was one with them and prepared to share their fate in the time of threatening danger. I am a Missionary to the Natives and as such am bound to stand by them in all that is right but in this case my duty is clear to turn my back upon them to set my face against them and by every means to testify my disapproval and disavowal of their conduct. Otherwise, as I do not think it was necessary on the ground of danger, to leave my residence, I had resolved to remain with my family at the Mission House.[39]

Riemenschneider's removal to Nelson, 14 July 1860, even though it was the result of careful consideration and at the request of the Māori leaders at Warea,

---

37. Cf. also his reference to the Taranaki people as the people of Israel in connection with the King Movement, in chapter 9 (RP VII, 35).
38. RP VII, 264.
39. Whitely Journal, (typescript), Alexander Turnbull Library, Ms, qMS-2212-2213, p. 70.

appears to have been severely criticised, particularly in Church Missionary Society circles. On 15 May 1861, Riemenschneider's former assistant Carl Sylvius Völkner writes to Heine from Tauranga:

> There is now peace again with the Taranaki tribe so that Riemenschneider can go back there. People have been very indignant that in the time of need he has left the tribe so completely to its own devices. He is the only missionary in New Zealand who has left his natives because of the war. This has not happened from the time the first mission stations were founded here until the present day. Our missionaries went there from Auckland and have managed to speak with the natives and to preach the Gospel to them. Mr Wilson[40] has visited Riemenschneider's Maori and has had long conversations with them and has also made an impression on them. Mr Wilson said that he could see no reason why a missionary should leave New Plymouth while many families lived there who had no vocation to be there.[41]

It is a tragic irony that four years later, on 2 March 1865, Völkner was killed by Māori in Ōpōtiki where he had returned from Auckland in spite of warnings that it was not safe to do so.

Riemenschneider's decision to withdraw to Nelson for the time being was certainly not the act of a coward. He had shown in many instances during the Puketapu feud and the present conflict that he was not afraid of staying at his post and facing hostile opponents. 'His' people had asked him to go and not to take up residence in New Plymouth. Unlike Whiteley and the Anglican clergy in New Plymouth, he did not have a supporting congregation and many months had to pass between the missionary asking advice from his superiors in Bremen and him actually receiving it.

The brief entry in the shipping news of the *Taranaki Herald* of 14 July 1860, which announces the departure of the S.S. *Airedale* for Nelson, with the Rev. J. F. Riemenschneider listed among the cabin passengers, masks the sadness and heartbreak of the missionary's departure from Taranaki. He still hoped to be able to return after hostilities ceased and salvage some of the work of 16 years among the Taranaki people. But when he left New Plymouth on 7 July, Riemenschneider was sick, depressed, and rejected both by the majority of the Māori and the Pākehā settlers. The one bright spot for him was the prospect of being reunited with his wife and family.

---

40. J. A. Wilson (1809–1887) joined the Church Missionary Society as a lay missionary after a career in the Royal Navy and arrived in the Bay of Islands on 11 April 1833. He served in Pūriri (Thames) and at Matamata. He was ordained deacon in 1852. Wilson may have felt that he had justification for his censorious stance towards Riemenschneider. In March 1836 when he and his family were at Tauranga and the station was raided by Māori, he sent his family to safety in Pūriri while he remained at his post.

41. Heine Papers, Nelson Provincial Museum.

Chapter Eleven

Final Parting from Taranaki and New Beginning in Otago, Mid-1860 to Mid-1863

R IEMENSCHNEIDER'S temporary retreat to Nelson did not mean that he could now take some months of well-earned and badly needed rest. He was certainly not in good health, either physically or mentally. In December 1860 he excuses his lack of major reports to the *Verwaltungsausschuß* (executive committee of the North German Mission Society) by stating that since his arrival in Nelson he had been suffering from 'total exhaustion of both body and mind'.[1] On 11 January 1861 he writes:

> Because of the continuing tension when I look at the present and the immediate future of New Zealand and its population, and particularly with regard to the work and kingdom of the Lord, my mind is almost ground down and all my physical and mental strength almost exhausted. One attack of illness follows another. The day before yesterday I have got up again after having been confined to bed by illness for five days. Our doctor's bill from 1 January to 31 December 1860 amounts to £17-13/5d.[2]

The Nelson doctor who treated the missionary, himself a Prussian, repeatedly suggested to him that a trip to Bremen would be most beneficial for his health and would allow him to recover. The doctor suggested that this would be a good time to go, since it would take some time for the political situation in New Zealand to settle down. The missionary seems to have considered the suggestion seriously but finally rejected it on the grounds that it would be too expensive for his Society and, above all, it would prevent him from being on the spot to return to Taranaki as soon as there was an opening for him to do so.

In spite of his illness and exhaustion, Riemenschneider was unable to rest. He felt driven to continue working in his vocation, as a preacher, teacher and pastor. He was frequently asked by the local Wesleyan and Presbyterian ministers to preach for them in the Nelson churches, and the Germans at

---

1. Riemenschneider Papers, RP VII, 287.
2. RP VII, 293.

Waimea and Moutere also asked him, with Heine's knowledge and support, to conduct church services in German for them.

It did not take long for the local Māori to find a way to the missionary family's door. Many of them were originally from the Taranaki and Te Ātiawa territories and had been displaced by the Waikato raids in the thirties. They were eager to hear whether Riemenschneider intended to return to his old parish. When he confirmed this, they tried to persuade him to change his mind and to settle permanently among them as their pastor. While he would not consider this, he was prepared to work among them while he was in Nelson because he considered that his real vocation was work among the Māori wherever they were. In April 1862 the missionary writes to his superiors in Bremen that he felt much less constrained by the fact that the Māori in the Nelson area were 'claimed' by the Anglicans than he felt when he had first arrived in New Zealand.[3] His aim was not to proselytise, but to feed the hungry with the words of the Gospel, regardless of their church affiliation, and he travelled through the area, preaching, teaching and doing pastoral work. Neither the Wesleyans, who had withdrawn from work among the Māori in the area and who counted him as one of 'theirs' anyway, nor the Anglicans took any exception to the German missionary's help. Indeed the Anglican Māori missionary, who had been consulted by the Anglican Māori, encouraged them to attend Riemenschneider's services. No doubt he welcomed some help in looking after an estimated 908 Māori and six Māori chapels.[4] The Bishop of Nelson, Edmund Hobhouse, who had arrived in February 1859, appears to have tacitly agreed to the arrangement. The missionary reports that the matter was never discussed between them, since the Bishop would not have been able to give official support to his parishioners attending the services of a North German Reformed clergyman. Hobhouse had established a good relationship with the German settlers in Moutere, spending evenings with them and occasionally conducting prayers.[5] Personal relations between the two clergymen were most cordial, and the missionary was an occasional dinner guest in the Bishop's house.

The friendship between Riemenschneider and Heine does not appear to have suffered from Heine's quarrel with the North German Mission Society in which Riemenschneider had acted on behalf of the Society. A number of letters from the missionary to Heine, written in 1861 and 1862, are testimony to a continuing friendship, with their two wives also developing a friendly relationship. The Riemenschneiders seem to have benefited from the fact that

---

3. RP VIII, 8–9.
4. H. F. Ault, *The Nelson Narrative: The Story of the Church of England in the diocese of Nelson, New Zealand, with an account of the years 1842–1957*. Nelson: Standing Committee of the Diocese of Nelson, 1958, p. 217.
5. *op. cit.*, p. 34.

Heine and the Germans in Moutere were farmers. Letters of thanks for gifts of sausages, apples and even a goose show that the preacher's work among the Germans did not go unrewarded.

One of the less pleasant duties that the missionary undertook during his time in Nelson was the preparation of a Māori prisoner for his execution. The Māori had been found guilty of the murder of his wife. While the decision to carry out the execution was sent to Auckland to be confirmed by the Governor (a process that took three weeks), Riemenschneider visited his charge daily. He not only came to genuinely like the prisoner, but he reports that he was also instrumental in bringing about a classic conversion experience in him. When the sentence was commuted to three years' imprisonment with hard labour, the story even had a relatively happy end and thus was eminently suitable for publication in the North German Mission Society publication, *Monatsblatt*, where it appeared in the April issue of 1862.[6]

In spite of the fact that the missionary found more than a full workload among the Māori and Europeans of the Nelson district, he writes in every letter back to Bremen that his heart yearned to be back with the Taranaki people at Warea. Both he and his wife were also in regular correspondence with many of the Warea people. He reports that with every mail steamer they receive, 'three, four, indeed 10 letters at once from several of them, in particular however from our senior chief Āperahama, his son Tamihana, his nephew Erueti and others'.[7] No trace of this extensive correspondence appears to have survived.

Besides writing to the Warea Māori, Riemenschneider also kept up a lively correspondence with a number of influential figures in New Zealand politics. One of them was Sir William Martin, the former Chief Justice of New Zealand. Martin had written a pamphlet about the Waitara conflict.[8] In an appendix,[9] Martin had published part of a letter from the missionary to Donald McLean, then Chief Land Purchase Commissioner, dated 24 September 1855, in which the missionary describes the feelings of the Taranaki people about possible Government interference in the Puketapu feud. He had sent a copy of the pamphlet to his superiors in Bremen with the comment:

> I have sent you this book because it presents the clearest and most faithful and true state of the 'Taranaki Question'. I am an old Maori missionary and have lived in the midst of the Maori for 17 years, 15 of them in Taranaki. I am thoroughly acquainted and familiar with all their conditions, affairs, laws and

---

6. pp. 505–506.
7. RP VII, 324.
8. *The Taranaki Question*. Auckland: Melanesian Press, 1860 (reprint Dunedin, 1967).
9. *ibid.*, pp. 131–136. Riemenschneider is styled 'The Rev. J. T. [sic] Riemenschneider, (of the Lutheran Church [sic])'. Martin wrote to Riemenschneider and apologised for the errors. This may well have been the beginning of the correspondence between the two men.

customs as well as with the whole sequence of events surrounding their King as well as Wiremu Kingi and the Waitara question. I also know the Treaty of Waitangi and its high old and originally pure and true meaning. According to all this I can in all conscience confirm and vouch for everything both *what* and *how* Sir W. Martin has set it down.[10]

In December 1861, Riemenschneider, who had by then returned to Taranaki (in August 1861) and was residing in New Plymouth, quotes a letter from Martin to him, dated 6 November 1861. The former Chief Justice thanks him for a letter and enclosures, which he intends to put before Sir George Grey, who had returned to New Zealand in September of that year to take over as Governor from Gore Browne. The missionary's letter, dated New Plymouth, September 30, 1861, sets out his view of the war mainly from the perspective of the Taranaki people. Martin writes:

Thanks, most hearty thanks for your last letter & its enclosures.
That letter supplies full & accurate information on a subject which has been consistently & grossly misrepresented of late. That misrepresentation it was possible to detect but to constitute for it the true story was beyond our power. I shall avail myself of the permission you have given, & shall lay the whole before the Governor on his return from the north.

The enclosures are interesting. They consist of three pieces written by his favourite former pupil and friend, Erueti Te Whiti o Rongomai, together with three others, in which they accuse the Governor of bad faith in land matters, and provide an eloquent and carefully argued defence of the Taranaki people against accusations of having held up the Queen's mail and murder.

Sir William Martin did submit a copy of Riemenschneider's letter to Sir George Grey, who in turn forwarded it to the Duke of Newcastle, the British Secretary of State. Copies of the Te Whiti documents have survived in the National Archives of New Zealand.[11]

All through the early part of 1861, however, the preacher of Taranaki's heart was not in his work in Nelson. He was constantly and impatiently looking for an early opportunity to return to his people at Warea and to resume his work among them. His desire, which appears to have been genuine, gives lie to those of his critics who maintained that he left his people in a cowardly way.

In April 1861 an opportunity to return to Taranaki appeared to present itself when active hostilities ceased and peace terms were signed between the Te Ātiawa and the Governor. The southern tribes were not included in the same peace process however. In a letter to the 'Chiefs of the Taranaki (or

---

10. RP VII, 312.
11. Erueti Te Whiti o Rongomai, document defending Taranaki against accusations by the Governor. National Archives of New Zealand, MA 1 (Box 3).

Ngāti Ruanui) tribe', the Governor made it clear that in his view they were in a different category from the Te Ātiawa because they had interfered in a matter with which they had 'no concern'.

Riemenschneider reports that he received letters advising him not to trust the peace. One of the Warea people wrote to him with regard to his own position that, 'since the candlestick has now been removed from its place, it will never be permitted to assume its former position among us'. Riemenschneider responded that, unless it was contrary to God's will, he would return to be among them and let the light of the word of God shine in their midst.[12]

The missionary's departure for Taranaki was delayed by a number of factors, not least among them the fact that his wife was expecting their sixth child. She was safely delivered of a daughter, Frances Mary Adolphine, on 22 July. Riemenschneider booked a passage on the August steamer from Nelson to New Plymouth but almost missed this opportunity to go north. On the day before his departure his wife fell gravely ill and the doctor, who had called every few hours, advised the missionary not to travel. However his wife Catherine insisted that he should go and he embarked for Taranaki.[13] After five anxious weeks in the North Island he received the good news that his wife had recovered and was now well.

Riemenschneider was uncertain of what reception he would find at Warea. He had heard that when the Episcopal minister, Archdeacon Govett, had tried to visit the Taranaki Māori in late April after the terms of peace had been signed, he had been sent home by his Anglican parishioners without even being permitted to conduct a church service. In the wake of Govett's unsuccessful visit a meeting of the Taranaki people had been called to discuss the question of visits by missionaries and they had reached the unanimous decision that no missionaries would be permitted to enter Taranaki under any circumstances, and that the authorities in New Plymouth should be informed of this decision. Riemenschneider was later told that the question of whether he should be treated as an exception had been raised and that this had caused an uproar in the meeting. The final decision was that he could not be treated as an exception, first because this would weaken the principle behind the decision, that no subject of the British Queen should be allowed on the territory of the Māori King; and secondly, because they could not guarantee his personal safety in view of the fact that the war had brought a number of non-Taranaki warriors into the area.

---

12. RP VIII, 22.
13. When Riemenschneider described these events for the *Verwaltungsausschuß* he appears to have been a month out. He puts the birth of his daughter into June, while her birth certificate gives July, and he gives the month of travel to New Plymouth as July, when the passenger list of the steamer *Airedale* lists him among the passengers on the sailing of 26 August. (Copy in Riemenschneider Papers held in Puke Ariki, ARC2002-578.)

Riemenschneider decided to risk a journey to Warea in spite of the unfavourable reports and in spite of being warned against it by his colleague Govett and the authorities.[14] Accompanied by Tāmati, a neutral Māori who had been one of his parishioners and who had been driven out of Taranaki territory because he declared himself neutral in the conflict, he set out for his station. Nobody appears to have tried to hinder the missionary's progress and his arrival at Warea, after an absence of just over a year, was accompanied by emotional scenes, which still affected him deeply when he described the meeting for his superiors three months later:

> During the first greeting the mutual weeping was so loud and lasted so long that I finally lost consciousness and fell to the ground. When I came to I found myself in the arms of our chief Piripi, with my head leaning on his chest. Our senior chief Aperahama and his wife spent the whole day and the following night with me.[15]

Two days after the missionary's arrival a large meeting was held about two miles inland from the mission station to decide his fate among the Taranaki people. He had been given hints that the meeting might not find in his favour and he saw the arrival of emissaries from the Waikato as a bad sign. In the course of the discussion, which lasted a whole day, Piripi explained the position of the majority of the Taranaki Māori with regard to their pastor:

> The person we see before us is not just you as a private person, and we cannot simply regard you as an individual in your personal relationship to us. Such considerations are of secondary importance here. They are a matter for the heart and you must be in our hearts, there you are one of us. But here it is a matter of external questions, considerations and positions. According to these we regard you as an enemy belonging to the people who are against us Māori, a follower and loyal subject of the Governor who is our enemy, a civilian member of the hostile Europeans, a bearer of the same name ('minita' – minister) as those others who hold your office and who have besmirched the sacred name of their office.[16]

One of the chiefs, Ahitona, introduced the metaphor of the two houses. When Riemenschneider arrived in Taranaki, Ahitona said, the people lived in an old house. Now they lived in a new house and the pastor would have to decide where to live, because he could not live in two houses at once. The missionary picked up the metaphor when he summed up his position:

> As a Christian and as a subject and teacher of divine and human law and order, can and may I kick against the authority that has been ordained and installed lawfully for me and my country? Is it my task to depose and institute kings and

---

14. RP VII, 329.
15. RP VII, 348–349.
16. RP VII, 345.

governments? If you have built a new house for yourself and tied yourself to a new king, that is a *new* undertaking which is *completely yours*. In this point I cannot follow you. I have no choice, the old house to me is God's immutable law. As a citizen of the world I am and will always remain subject to the British queen and government. As a servant of Christ and as a messenger of His kingdom however I am your pastor and spiritual father who has long since been instituted by the Lord and recognised and confirmed permanently by your own hearts and consciences.[17]

Having made and announced his decision to leave, Riemenschneider left the meeting and went home. Half an hour later he was visited by two young chiefs, Heka and Kōmene, who had come to ensure that he was safe. After his departure some of the participants of the meeting had apparently suggested that they should at once go to the station, kill the missionary and burn down the buildings.[18] After the two young men had left, Tāmihana, Āperahama's son, arrived with horses so that the missionary could set out for New Plymouth early in the morning of the following day.

Riemenschneider reports that even though it was a sad evening for him he was, in one sense, relieved that a decision had now been made and he was confident that God would protect him from harm. At quarter past one in the morning, just as he was about to go to bed, Āperahama and his wife called to share with him their grief at his departure. The three talked for several hours. Āperahama reported to the missionary that they had continued with their religious observances. Both at home and in the war camps, the Taranaki people had held their church services, and they had gathered regularly for morning and evening prayers and communal reading of the Bible. The Sabbath had been strictly observed. While he had been expelled for political reasons, Riemenschneider's teaching and exhortations, repeated regularly in his letters from Nelson to Taranaki, appear to have been followed by the majority of the Taranaki people, putting their European neighbours to shame, in the missionary's opinion.

The parting on the following morning was hard for both sides. The missionary writes:

> Towards four o'clock in the morning, after I had read the first Psalm with Aperahama and prayed, I lay down for a little. At seven o'clock the natives were gathered in the courtyard again in large numbers. I held prayers with them and then took leave. Not one of us spoke a word because none of us was able to speak. Our hearts were too full. Tamihana accompanied me to the border.[19]

---

17. RP VII, 343.
18. RP VII, 352.
19. RP VII, 357.

All mission property and the family's personal effects, furniture and books had to stay in Warea, even though the books were being damaged by rats. The property was forfeited to the Māori King until peace had been made between him and the Governor.[20]

This time, Riemenschneider did not leave for Nelson at once, although he seriously considered retreating again immediately after his return from Warea. On 30 September he wrote a letter to the Superintendent of Taranaki asking for a free passage to Nelson.[21] The request was politely refused on the same day. So he remained in New Plymouth in the hope that he would be able to work on behalf of the Taranaki people with the local authorities and making a number of visits to his Taranaki people.

During October the missionary also wrote a major report for Sir George Grey about the situation in Taranaki. This and other reports written by Riemenschneider to the authorities on Māori views and feelings were written partly in response to Māori wishes. In their final conversation, Āperahama had said to him:

> You alone are our friend. You alone can we trust for truth and justice. Tell the Governor whatever you want and what seems right and true to *you*, as long as he hears it from *you yourself*. Inform him of our thoughts, wishes and requests so that they are not presented to him in a distorted form by the ignorant Europeans; then let him say what he thinks about it and let him sheath the sword or pull it out again.[22]

It was also while the missionary was in New Plymouth that the news reached him of the death of his father who had died in the poor house in Bremen, aged 80.

Riemenschneider's stay in New Plymouth was not easy. He was again dogged by illness, and he found his forays into Taranaki on pastoral visits difficult. The missionary attempted to be the advocate for the Taranaki people but increasingly they tried to dictate to him what he should say and how he should say it. Increasingly he found himself unable to defend views which, to him, were too radical to be consistent with his interpretation of the Gospel. He was also blamed for not preventing anti-Māori views being printed in the newspaper. In April 1862 the missionary looks back on this difficult period in New Plymouth after he had been expelled for the second time from Warea. The description shows how the relationship between the pastor and his flock deteriorated. Riemenschneider, with all his good will and

---

20. Riemenschneider appears to have received at least part compensation for the losses he suffered. In his Last Will and Testament of 20 July 1864, he bequeaths to his wife, 'a Balance of Compensation Money still now remaining due to me on the part of the Taranaki Compensation Commission for losses sustained by me through the war'. See chapter 14.
21. Riemenschneider Papers, Puke Ariki, ARC2002-578.
22. RP VII, 357.

love for the Taranaki people, found himself unable to gauge and understand the mood of his parishioners. He was unable to appreciate that the context was inappropriate for a rigid, paternalistic and uncompromising stance, and unable to reconcile his interpretation of God's word with the political realities in which he and the Taranaki people found themselves:

> It was not right and feasible to agree with everything and in addition to fulfil all their wishes. As far as I found that it was necessary and advisable and desirable to accede to their wishes I did this, in order to help towards the reaching of a mutual clear understanding between the Governor and them for the common good. But quite often I had to send the pages back to them with some enclosed instruction and admonition regarding the spirit, meaning and tone of their thoughts and writings in which I required changes. In return I received bitter reproaches and instead of improving it, they seemed intent on becoming increasingly strident. Finally I was obliged to clearly intimate to them that I was not only their preacher, but also their paternal mediator and representative, but that I could only exercise this role in the spirit and meaning of the Gospel of Christ, and not in the spirit of a quarrelsome and disputatious diplomat.[23]

In February 1862 the missionary returned to Nelson. He was leaving New Plymouth for the last time, although he did not know this. He still had hopes that a permanent peace would be made between the Taranaki Māori and the Governor and that he would then be able to return to his beloved flock. In this hope, he was to be disappointed, but a new door was opening for him, far away from the troubled district where the missionary had lived and worked for the last 15 years.

*

In August 1859, while Riemenschneider was suffering from his fractured sternum, and struggling to keep up with his work among the Māori of Taranaki as well as the demands of a growing family, a meeting was held in Dunedin in the South Island, some 600 km. south of Warea. He was, of course, not aware that this meeting was to have a profound effect on his future career in New Zealand. A public meeting, which had been called on 16 August, decided to establish a 'Society for the elevation of the physical, social and moral conditions of the Māories'. This interdenominational Society started with considerable vigour and energy. The Superintendent of the Province accepted the presidency and the Governor, Thomas Gore Browne, was asked and agreed to accept the office of patron. The initial committee of the Society consisted of no fewer than four clergymen and six laymen. In order to avoid any possible sectarian conflict its initial work was to concentrate on secular education.

The justification for the formation of the Society was the real concern

---

23. RP VIII, 14.

felt by a number of prominent citizens of Dunedin for the welfare of the Ngāi Tahu Māori population along the Otago coast and particularly at Otago Heads (Ōtākou). In the early 1830s the Weller brothers had established a shore whaling station at Ōtākou. This commercial venture had ended in bankruptcy a decade later. Many of the unemployed whalers stayed on, however, and a good number of them intermarried with the Māori population. Whalers from other declining stations also moved to Ōtākou, which had been the centre of the whaling industry along the Otago coast. As McLintock describes it in his history of Otago, 'Otakou had become the rendezvous of the derelict whaling fraternity, cast, like flotsam and jetsam, upon the pleasant shores of Otago Harbour'.[24] While the Scottish settlement of Dunedin was being established from 1848 onwards by the earnest and sober settlers, Ōtākou 'continued to be the centre of turbulence and vice'.[25]

The missionaries had attempted to be a moderating and 'civilising' influence among the Māori. But they were powerless in the face of disease and alcohol, the most pernicious imports accompanying the whalers. The Wesleyans had worked among the Otago Māori from their base at Waikouaiti since 1841, but they ceased their activities with the withdrawal of the last missionary, George Stannard, who had arrived in Waikouaiti in November 1857, but had shifted to Port Chalmers almost immediately after his arrival. When a Presbyterian minister arrived in Port Chalmers, he moved across the harbour to Ōtākou and established his station there in May 1859.[26]

Already in 1857, the Presbyterian church felt that something had to be done to improve the lot of the Māori at Ōtākou. It commissioned a report on the 'condition of the Aboriginal and Half-Caste population'.[27] The report recommended the establishment of an Industrial School at Otago Heads to raise the condition of the Māori there. It was to be led by a married couple. One of the persons consulted commented as follows:

> ... a proper person to perform these duties is very much wanted at the Native Reserve at the Heads of the Harbour – as I do not think that from the Northern to the Southern point of New Zealand there could be found Natives leading a more heathenish, shocking course of life; their Sabbaths being spent in horse-racing, playing cards, drunkenness, and every other kind of vice.[28]

---

24. A. H. McLintock, *The History of Otago: The origins and growth of a Wakefield class settlement*. Dunedin: Otago Centennial Historical Publication, 1949, p. 146.
25. op. cit., p. 147.
26. See Donald Phillips, 'Methodism', in: Booth, Ken et al., *The Farthest Jerusalem. Four lectures on the origins of Christianity in Otago*. Dunedin: Faculty of Theology and Hocken Library, University of Otago, 1993, pp. 49–50. Stannard must have left Ōtākou after 3 April 1859, the date on which he baptised the senior chief Taiaroa and his wife Karoraina and married the couple. (T. A. Pybus, *Maori and Missionary: Early Christian Missions in the South Island of New Zealand*. Wellington: A. H. & A. W. Reed, 1954, pp. 134–135.)
27. Otago Provincial Council, *Votes and Proceedings of the Provincial Council*, Session VI, 1857, Appendix, p. 43.
28. op. cit., p. 48.

A married couple to lead the proposed school at Ōtākou came forward in late 1858 in the form of a Mr Thomas Parry and his wife. They were recommended by George Stannard to John Gillies, a member of the Provincial Council, as fit persons to open a private school in case the provincial government lacked the funds to initially establish such an institution. Once set up, it could then find ongoing funding from a sum of £7,000 set aside for native education by the general (central) government. Parry also managed to get a letter of recommendation from Captain William Cargill, one of the founding fathers of the Otago settlement, while chief Taiaroa wrote to Governor Gore Browne requesting permission to lease a piece of land to Parry for the purpose of setting up the school.[29]

Less than a year later, a two-man mission of inquiry that had been sent to the Māori village of Ōtākou reported to a meeting of the newly established Otago Society on 6 October 1859. The committee reports that it was,

> ... much struck with the improvement in the social condition of the Natives, who, instead of being huddled together amongst the sand hills on the beach as formerly, are scattered in various localities along the margin of the bush at the foot of the hills, each house having the owner's cultivation around it, laid out with some degree of regularity, and substantially fenced, according to European ideas.[30]

Nevertheless, the committee was less impressed with the provisions for schooling the population. After inspecting the school run by Mr and Mrs Parry, the two commissioners found that,

> ... we saw nothing which would warrant us in recommending to the Committee the employment of these parties as teachers. The Natives are fully aware of their incompetence, though they have nothing to allege against their moral character.[31]

After a 'long discussion' the meeting decided to establish a school at the 'native settlement of Otago for the education of the natives of that locality, and any others who may choose to resort or send their children there to be educated'.[32] A married couple who could speak the Māori language was to be appointed as teachers,[33] plans and estimates for the school buildings were to be obtained and the Governor was to be asked for financial assistance, while in addition, fundraising was to be conducted in Dunedin and the Otago Province.

---

29. Fulton Papers, Collection of the Otago Settlers Museum, 2/1/2/1, 2/1/2/5; 2/1/3/1–2/1/3/3.
30. *Otago Witness*, 15 October 1859, p. 6.
31. ibid.
32. ibid.
33. In spite of strong representations from the Māori community at Ōtākou who preferred the Parrys to any new appointee, the Society decided that they were not satisfactory and had to be replaced. (McGlashan papers, Hocken Library, Dunedin, MS 463/7.)

The Government agreed to subsidise the philanthropic venture, and the Society appointed a married couple, Mr Charles Pratt Baker and his wife, from Auckland, to be the first teachers at Ōtākou. With that, however, its energies seem to have been exhausted. In March 1861, when Riemenschneider was in what he called his 'exile' in Nelson, the *Colonist* printed an editorial that was sharply critical of the Society's inaction. The writer comments on the fact that more than a year had passed since the founding of the Society and that there had not yet been an annual meeting in which the Society accounted for its actions. The Society is likened to a '... high-pressure engine, which soon burst and became useless from too much steam'.[34]

Mr Baker and his wife seem to have found it difficult to work for a Society that was clearly not functioning properly. Early 1862, when Mr Baker was offered the position of Resident Magistrate in Tauranga, he and his wife resigned their position as teachers and left Dunedin.

While the Otago Society was taking its first, rather inadequate steps, to do something for the Otago Māori, Riemenschneider was working among the Māori people in the Nelson area and also helped out, when required, among the European congregations. His focus however was still Taranaki and he was fully expecting to return there, as soon as the hostile feelings stirred up by the war had subsided enough for him to once again become effective as a pastor and teacher in the area. There appears to have been no shortage of offers for him to work elsewhere. Both at the General Assembly of the Presbyterian Church in November 1861 and at the General Synod of the Anglican church in February 1862 his name had been mentioned in informal conversations as a possible worker. During the Anglican Synod, which had been held in Nelson, he was repeatedly approached with indications that there would be plenty of work for him with the Church Missionary Society. However, this would have meant giving up his connection with the North German Mission Society and joining the Anglicans. Riemenschneider, while flattered by the attention, was no more tempted by these offers than he had been by a similar suggestion by the Anglican missionary, Richard Taylor, in 1845. His loyalty and commitment to the Reformed Church and the North German Mission Society were for life, and prevented him from changing his mind at this time as well.

The two major churches and their missionary sections were not the only bodies interested in securing the services of the unemployed missionary. In March 1862, to Riemenschneider's considerable surprise, he received a private approach from Dunedin with the question as to whether he would consider accepting the position of missionary teacher at Ōtākou under the sponsorship of the 'Otago Society for the elevation of the Māories'. This preliminary

---

34. *The Otago Colonist*, 8 March 1861.

discussion led to an official invitation, which the missionary reports to his superiors in April 1862. After outlining the work of the Society, as he knew it, and the established position at the Otago Heads, he continues:

> ... yesterday I received the *official* invitation from that society to come to Otago and to take up that teacher's position. It has just become vacant because the person who has been the teacher there so far has accepted a position with the Government. The arrangement would be that I would exercise my *ministry* independently of the *Otago Society* and any of the churches there, according to my own wishes and discretion in the service of my original Society, so that all church and congregational matters of the natives there would belong to me and our North German Mission Society completely and independently of the *Otago Society*, while the latter would only have an interest in school matters among the natives there and would support me in this. In this sense, therefore, the Otago Society would be and act as an auxiliary society to our North German mission.[35]

The missionary then informs his superiors that the proposal from the Otago Society would also have financial advantages, since his total family's upkeep in Nelson cost Bremen 'close on £300'. Otago was guaranteeing a salary of £200, so that the North German Society would only have to find another £80 to £100 to sustain its work in the new field.

The Otago Society had closed its letter with the words: 'The Committee most earnestly requests you to communicate to it at your earliest convenience & with as little delay as possible your decision in reference to the appointment which is now placed at your disposal'.[36] So Riemenschneider once again found himself having to make a major decision regarding his activities as a missionary of the North German Mission Society without being able to consult with his superiors in Bremen because of the time factor.

Riemenschneider was able, however, to consult with his friend and colleague the Wesleyan minister, Whiteley. Whiteley at first was opposed to the idea because he was under the misapprehension that the German missionary would have to leave his North German Mission Society and join the Presbyterians in Otago. When Riemenschneider informed him of the proposed arrangement with Otago, which safeguarded his association with Bremen, Whiteley changed his view. The missionary reports that he received a second letter from Whiteley after he had informed the Wesleyan that he had accepted the call to Otago:

> In it he not only fully agreed with the step I had taken, but also offered that as long as our Taranaki would remain unoccupied by our Society he would look after and preserve it for the latter as far as conditions would permit, and that as soon as it would become possible, he would extend his care over it. According to

---

35. RP VIII, 16.
36. RP VIII, 29.

his suggestion I have written an official letter to him in which I have transferred to him the care of our Taranaki mission in the name of our Society, until further decisions will be made in due course. I have also sent a letter to the natives there by his hand, in which I inform them of the arrangements I have made, mentioning all the reasons, and referring them to him as my current deputy until they have called me back again and have either me or another new missionary from our Society sent to them.[37]

Whiteley was not the only one of Riemenschneider's colleagues who feared that the shift to Ōtākou meant that the missionary had changed his allegiance. Soon after his arrival in his new parish, Riemenschneider had an opportunity to write a quick note to his North German Mission Colleague, Wohlers. Wohlers' response shows that the missionary, in his hurried correspondence, cannot have been very clear about the new position. Wohlers writes:

> ... Recently I heard from Honoré[38] that Völkner had written to him that you had joined the Scottish Presbyterian Church and that this church had sent you to Otago, as if you had severed your relationship with the North German Mission Society. But I cannot think that this is true because how could you, a child of Bremen, give up your link with Bremen? I don't have the slightest objection to you being in a friendly relationship with the Scottish Presbyterian Church, but please write to me who is your master on earth; the Mission Committee in Bremen or the Scottish Presbyterian Church in New Zealand. At times the people in Dunedin have *begun* to *want* to do something decent for the elevation of the Māori, but their zeal has always faded after a very short time. If they were your earthly masters, I fear that you would soon be neglected by them.[39]

Wohlers's words were prophetic, although at this early stage in his association with the Otago Society, Riemenschneider could not know how acutely his older colleague and brother missionary had apparently been able to observe the situation in Dunedin from the isolation of Ruapuke Island.[40]

As a final gesture, the exiled preacher of Taranaki wrote to his Māori

---

37. RP VIII, 32.
38. In 1848 the North German Mission Society sent Abraham Honcré as an unordained assistant to Wohlers. Honoré subsequently moved to the North Island and was ordained in Riverton on 24 February 1869.
39. RP VIII, 108–109, note 2.
40. Wohlers had, in fact, been invited to become a member of the 'Extraordinary Committee' of the Society. On 8 October 1859, he responded to the invitation as follows:
   > ... For myself I am willing to become a subscriber to the above mentioned Society, but the inhabitants of this District are still too poor to contribute to funds for the benefit of the Maories within the Province of Otago.
   > There are however some Maories under the charge of this Mission Station, residing within the Province of Otago, that is to say, on the Banks of the

New River [Oreti River], old and young, about		30 persons
Jacobs River [Aparima River] "	"	70 persons
Oranga and neighbourhood (West of Jacobs R.)		70 persons
Total about		170 persons.

   (McGlashan Papers, Hocken Library, Dunedin, MS 463/7.)

congregation in Warea, asking them whether they would welcome him back and when he could hope to return to work among them. He received no reply.

*

Having accepted the position, on Friday, 13 June 1862, Riemenschneider and his family left Nelson by steamer and on Saturday, 21 June, they crossed over from Port Chalmers to their new station at Ōtākou. On the following day the new pastor of Otago preached his inaugural sermon to a large congregation, which had gathered from all over the neighbourhood. What he does not mention in his papers but what becomes apparent from a letter his wife wrote to Bremen after his death is that on their journey from Nelson to Ōtākou the Riemenschneider family was accompanied by one of Catherine's sisters, Emily Jane. She died on the day on which the missionary preached his inaugural sermon and was subsequently buried at the Port Chalmers cemetery. As always, personal events, no matter how tragic, could not be allowed to take precedence over the matters Riemenschneider felt duty bound to report to his superiors in Bremen.

Riemenschneider must have been relieved to find that the atmosphere among his new parishioners was much less politically charged and radical than in polarised, war-torn Taranaki. The missionary's initial message to the Māori of Otago had nothing to do with politics. It was an exhortation to simplicity. He reports that at each of the preaching places he visited on his inaugural visits, children were brought to him for baptism. At each place, therefore, he used the same text for his first sermon. He felt that it had been supplied to him by God in the words of Jesus as recorded by the gospel according to St Mark, 10,15: 'Truly I say to you, whoever does not receive the kingdom of God like a child shall not enter it'.[41]

The Otago Society, who had recruited him, was also anxious to introduce their new missionary to the inhabitants of Dunedin. On 9 July they held a public meeting at which Riemenschneider was the principal speaker. The newspaper report of the meeting reveals that the missionary had lost none of his preponderance for lengthy orations. The reporter writes:

> Short addresses were delivered by the Ministers and other Gentlemen, and the Rev. Mr. Reimsneider [sic!] gave an account of his early experience among the Māori Tribes, which was listened to with much interest, but as it was found that the evening was far advancing, and the Rev. gentleman had yet much to say, it was resolved to adjourn the meeting to an early day when it is hoped that the state of the weather will enable many to attend, who were prevented being present on this occasion.[42]

---

41. RP VIII, 75.
42. *The Otago Colonist*, 9 July, 1862.

Riemenschneider found that in his new field of labour a few things needed to be put on a proper footing as well. Just as in Motukaramū and later in Taranaki, denominational disputes accompanied the missionary's settling in. Riemenschneider reports that his predecessor had been appointed as a teacher rather than a missionary because this arrangement relieved the Otago Society from having to face the question of which denomination was to work in the field. The Bakers, Riemenschneider's predecessors, had been Anglicans and the Anglican Bishop Harper in Christchurch, in whose diocese they were, had bestowed on the teacher Mr Baker the ecclesiastical title 'catechist', without, according to the missionary's account, consulting him or the Otago Society. Riemenschneider was concerned that the Bishop might now use Baker's 'clerical' status to lay claim to all the Otago Māori for the Anglican church. He therefore wrote to Harper on 25 August 1862 in an attempt to clarify the situation and to stake his own claim on behalf of the North German Mission Society.

Harper's response, while polite, was not encouraging. The Bishop pointed out to Riemenschneider that he had had plans to ordain Barker and that some money had been donated to him by the British Society for Propagating the Gospel in Foreign Parts. He intended to supplement these funds with donations from Otago Anglicans to provide an Anglican minister to either Waikouaiti or Moeraki. The choice of the two possible locations, according to Harper, was so that the work of the Anglicans would not interfere with Riemenschneider's work at Ōtākou and any Māori parishes south of Riemenschneider's station. Harper was clearly under the impression (or at least chose to adopt the stance), that any Māori north of Ōtākou were his responsibility, while Riemenschneider's territory would run south from the Heads. The bishop concludes his letter as follows:

> Reserving to myself therefore the liberty to act among the Māori in your District, according to my own judgement and sense of duty, and as circumstances may enable me to act, I bid you God speed in your endeavours to bring them to the knowledge of the truth as it is in Jesus and I pray God, that while we show each in our own way for the faith of the Gospel, we may be kindly affectionate one to another with brotherly love.[43]

The newly arrived missionary, who felt strongly that all the Māori in the area had been entrusted into his pastoral care and resented what he saw as the Bishop's interference in his patch, informed the Otago Māori of the contents of Harper's letter. The congregation at Moeraki, followed by Waikouaiti, and then Ōtākou and Taieri, held *hui* to discuss the matter. The missionary

---

43. Harper to Riemenschneider (Bishop Henry James Chitty Harper Correspondence, Christchurch Diocesan Archive). I am most grateful to Jane Teal, the Christchurch Diocesan Archivist, for her transcription of parts of this letter

reports that all of them ended with unanimous decisions to the effect that Riemenschneider and his church were regarded as the only Christian denomination to which the Otago Māori would henceforth be affiliated. And a major factor in the decision, according to the missionary, was that the Māori of the area felt that they had been abandoned by the Wesleyans while Wohlers, the North German missionary, had faithfully remained with his flock in the Foveaux Strait area.[44] They knew, of course, that Riemenschneider came from the same Mission Society and expected him to remain with them and not abandon them as the Wesleyans had. And they were not to be disappointed.

While he was trying to protect his parish against what he saw as inroads from the side of the Anglicans, Riemenschneider was not aware that the Society for the Elevation of the Māories had, without his knowledge, entered into discussions with Bishop Harper about the placing of an Anglican catechist/teacher in Moeraki and Waikouaiti. When he discovered this, a furious Riemenschneider lodged a vigorous protest with the Otago Society. Since the Otago Society had indeed given Riemenschneider the right to be active as a missionary in the two villages, and since a majority of the executive committee was unwilling to grant the Bishop full control over whoever might be sent there from the Anglican side, the Anglicans withdrew from the Otago Society and Bishop Harper sent a Māori teacher to make occasional visits to Moeraki and Waikouaiti.[45] Riemenschneider reports that this action did not appear to have any effect on the firm allegiance of the Māori to him and his German Society, but that it provoked the Presbyterian members of the committee of the Otago Society into considering the establishment of a specifically Presbyterian presence in the Māori villages north of Dunedin.

---

44. The Otago Māori had some grounds to be unhappy with the treatment they had received in recent years from the Wesleyan missions. When Charles Creed departed from Waikouaiti in January 1853, they were left without a pastor for a whole year, while his replacement, William Kirk, looked after the needs of the Wesleyan Europeans in Christchurch. His successor Stannard closed down the Waikouaiti station almost immediately after his arrival, and spent no more than a year at his new station at Ōtākou before leaving. (See Phillips, *op. cit.*, pp. 48–50.)

45. As he wrote to Riemenschneider, Bishop Harper had received a sum of money (£80) from the Society for the Propagation of the Gospel to station a missionary among the Māori of Otago and Southland. On 24 June, 1862, the Bishop informed the Otago Rural Deanery Board of this and suggested that the Otago Anglicans contribute a further £50 to enable an Anglican teacher to be sent to either Moeraki or Waikouaiti, in view of the fact that the 'Presbyterian teacher' was going to be working at Ōtākou. Further correspondence between Harper and the Board suggests that the Anglican representative on the executive committee of the Otago Society had made application for the £50 subsidy to come from the Society. The Otago Society not only declined the request, but in turn requested that the Bishop pay over the £80 from the Society for the Propagation of the Gospel, presumably as a subsidy towards Riemenschneider's salary. The Bishop refused on the grounds that he could not pay the money to a Society which was 'in effect, composed chiefly of Presbyterians', for the stipend of a clergyman that would not be under his control. (Papers of the Anglican Church, Otago Rural Deanery Board, Archives of the Diocese of Dunedin, Hocken Library, AG-349/1/1.)

The Otago Society's negotiations behind the missionary's back were not an isolated instance of the Society's inept handling of relations with their teacher/missionary. Riemenschneider was to be bitterly disappointed in his dealings with his new employers. He had been very careful, before accepting the position at Ōtākou, to make sure that his association with the North German Mission Society would not be regarded as a hindrance, and he had been assured that, on the contrary, it might well be an advantage in his dealings with the disaffected Otago Māori. He had also obtained the agreement of the Society to continue in his work as a missionary and Christian minister. As far as practical arrangements were concerned, the Otago Society had promised him that in addition to his stipend it would refund his travel expenses and would make generous provision for enlarging the small house that his predecessor had built at Ōtākou. This was certainly necessary. The Bakers, a childless couple, had built the cottage to accommodate only themselves. The Riemenschneiders now had six children, one boy and five girls, and were expecting their seventh. The missionary complains, among other things, of the lack of a study. He used the upstairs girls' bedroom during the day and the small kitchen at night to do his writing.

The Otago Society was unable to deliver on its rather rash promises and seemed unable to reconstitute itself into an effective organisation. In October 1862 Riemenschneider travelled to Dunedin to try and mobilise his supporters into fundraising. The missionary, who had looked forward to having local support and advice for the first time in his career, had to organise his own support. He describes his efforts in a report to the Administration Committee of the North German Society written in the following December:

> I succeeded with difficulty in getting together a committee meeting for half an hour and even then only five members [of 19] were present. The treasurer declared that there were no funds, only some debts. They could hardly raise the money for my quarterly stipend. ....
>
> ... It was decided to invite 12 ladies by circular for the following Friday in order to ask them to collect contributions for the mission. A sub-committee was appointed to be present and to conduct the meeting and I was asked to be there as well to bring some life and fire into the meeting.[46]

Riemenschneider withdrew to Port Chalmers to await the appointed day and on Friday he attempted to return to Dunedin for the promised meeting. This proved to be difficult as the morning steamer had broken down and he had to be at the meeting at 2 p.m. So he walked to Dunedin, the journey taking five hours, and arrived just in time for the meeting. One member of the sub-committee, two other committee members and a total of three ladies attended it. There was no quorum, therefore no meeting took place, and the

---

46. RP, VIII, 48–49.

exhausted and frustrated missionary had to leave Dunedin without having achieved anything.

By January 1863 the Society found itself unable to pay Riemenschneider's salary and seems to have searched for a pretext to dispense with his services. It finally formally required him to give up his connection with the North German Mission Society and regard the Otago Society as his sole employer; indeed, the secretary harshly criticised him for having kept his links with the North Germans.

The German missionary teacher was baffled. He had agreed to work for the Otago Society only in school matters and with the express proviso that he would continue to work in his Christian ministry as a member of the North German Society. Now the conditions of his contract were suddenly changed and he was asked to throw in his lot entirely with a Society that was unable to pay his salary and did not appear to be capable or even interested in carrying on the work among the Otago Māori. Riemenschneider's analysis of the situation was that after the departure of the Anglicans, the remnants of two factions remained: a secular group who were looking for a schoolteacher and who strongly disapproved of his Christian ministry among the Māori, and a Presbyterian group who wanted to establish its own Māori congregations and who therefore also objected to his work as a minister of the German Reformed church. When he pointed out to his critics in the Otago Society that he had agreed to work for them on the clear understanding that he would be permitted to continue as a pastor and missionary, they replied that their understanding of this stipulation had been that he would conduct the occasional church service in his spare time while working full-time as a school teacher. It is not surprising that Riemenschneider opted to remain with the North German Society that had looked after him for 25 years rather than throw in his lot with a Society that could not even pay for his keep, let alone keep its promises.

For most of 1863, the missionary attempted to communicate with the Otago Society regarding his employment. His repeated written requests for a meeting remained unanswered and no money was forthcoming so that he was forced to draw his full salary from the North German Mission Society again. Finally, on 12 October 1863, the Otago Society committee met and elected yet another sub-committee to negotiate with the German missionary. The meeting took place on 27 October in Dunedin. The members of the sub-committee once again put the view that Riemenschneider should cease his association with the North German Mission Society and that he should become nothing but a secular school teacher in their employ. When Riemenschneider reiterated his position, the sub-committee declared that it was not authorised to make any concessions, and the two parties left once again without any decisions having been made. After sleeping on it, the missionary submitted his resignation to the Otago Society on 29 October 1863 and informed his Māori congregations that he considered himself free of any obligations to the Otago Society. From now on they were to regard themselves as members of the North German church.

It took until February 1864 for the situation between Riemenschneider and the Otago Society to be finally settled. The missionary was reimbursed for expenses he had incurred while building his churches, which will be described in the next chapter. The Otago Society renounced any claim to the Māori in Otago, and Riemenschneider was permitted to live in the house built by the Otago Society. The cost of any improvements he made would be refunded to him.

The missionary's vexations with the Otago Society were not the only problems with which he had to grapple during his initial period in Otago. An appointment for Riemenschneider as interpreter in the Otago law court was far from straightforward. His predecessor, Mr Baker, had been considered for an official appointment as court interpreter, but left while the Superintendent of Otago was consulting with the Colonial Secretary's office about making a formal offer.[47] When Riemenschneider accepted the position with the Otago Society for the elevation of the Maoris, the Superintendent's office approached him and offered him the position of interpreter on his arrival in Otago. The missionary accepted, no doubt partly induced by the annual salary of £100 that went with the position, and the Superintendent approached the Governor, through the Colonial Secretary, to have the appointment ratified. Since Justice was the concern of the General Government, the salary would be paid from its coffers.

On 12 September 1862, the Colonial Secretary informed the Superintendent that the Governor would be advised to ratify Riemenschneider's appointment. Six weeks later, the Provincial Treasurer wrote to the sub-treasurer of the General Government, informing him that the missionary had begun his duties on 20 June, and was asking for the first instalment of his salary. This letter came to the attention of Francis Dillon Bell who had administered the Native Office since July 1861, and had taken office as Minister of Native Affairs under Alfred Domett, when the latter became premier, succeeding William Fox in August 1862.

Bell, who had been prominent in Nelson society in the early 1840s, and who had been the resident agent of the New Zealand Company in New Plymouth and Nelson from August 1847 until the demise of the Company in 1850, knew Riemenschneider. His reaction to the Treasurer's letter shows

---

47. The relevant correspondence is in the National Archives of New Zealand, IA1, 1863/2218. (Otago, Superintendent, correspondence with Colonial Secretary re. court interpreter.)

that the Minister clearly did not hold the missionary in high regard. It is possible that the two men may have clashed over the Waitara purchase, which Bell strongly supported, while Riemenschneider equally strongly condemned it. On 5 January 1863, Bell writes to his premier, seeking to have the appointment stopped, and recommending a reduction of salary payments to any court interpreter from £100 to £25. In his memorandum to Domett, Bell explains why he had not acted against Riemenschneider when the original application came through the Native Office in June 1862, when William Fox was premier:

> As the application was stated to have been made with reference to an authority from Mr Fox, I overcame my repugnance (which was very great) to giving any employment to Mr Riemenschneider, and said that he would be appointed when the Session was over.

Now that Bell had seen the correspondence, he felt that Fox had only generally approved the appointment of an interpreter, and both the person and the salary were, in his view, open for further negotiation.

An unseemly wrangle between the Superintendent and the Minister of Native Affairs followed, which lasted until late 1863, when the question was finally settled in the Superintendent's (and Riemenschneider's) favour.

Like all the beginnings of his missionary ventures, Riemenschneider's start in Otago had been difficult. He had felt hindered rather than helped by the Otago Society that had asked him to move south and he did not attempt to hide his justified exasperation with his new sponsors in his correspondence with Bremen. His work with the Otago Māori prospered, however, and was beginning to bear fruit in a number of respects over the few years of activity left to him.

Chapter Twelve

Teacher, Pastor, Counsellor, Builder, 1863–1864

By coming to Otago, Riemenschneider had taken on a huge parish for one person. While he estimated that it contained about 300 souls, they were scattered over a wide distance.[1] From his mission station at Ōtākou, on the south head of the Otago peninsula, he had to look after Taieri, 50 km. to the south and Māranuku, a Māori settlement on the Clutha River, 43 km. further south. In the north was Waikouaiti, 50 km. from Ōtākou and Moeraki, a further 28 km. to the north of Waikouaiti. These distances are as the crow flies and they do not reflect the difficult conditions under which the missionary had to travel. Most of his journeys involved crossing the harbour to Port Chalmers on the northern side by Māori canoe, whaleboat or the boat of the harbour pilots stationed at the nearby Heads. From Port Chalmers, the missionary would take a steamer to Dunedin or Waikouaiti, and then a ride on horseback to either Taieri and Māranuku, or Moeraki. Riemenschneider had occupied an extensive field in Taranaki, but there he had lived approximately in the centre of the coastal strip and not at the end of a long peninsula, which made access to his outlying districts difficult.

Riemenschneider's new field of labour differed from his previous one in another major respect. In Taranaki, the Māori population had lived in relative isolation from the Europeans who had been confined within the boundaries of the land that had been allocated to the New Zealand Company settlement. In Otago, its three major centres, Ōtākou, Waikouaiti and Moeraki, all had been the sites of shore whaling stations and there had therefore been small

---

1. In 1861, Charles Baker had provided an informal census of the Māori population he served for his sponsoring Society. He reported that there were 58 adults and 23 children under the age of 14 at Ōtākou, 53 adults and 11 children at Moeraki, and 67 adults and 33 children at Waikouaiti. This total of 277 does not include the settlements south of Dunedin. (Report on the Otago Society for the elevation of the Maories, McGlashan Papers, Hocken Library Dunedin, MS 463/8). Riemenschneider's estimate, made a year later, seems therefore to be fairly accurate. Later in his ministry, on 3 October 1865, he reports to Bremen that in his district there were 307 'baptised' and 32 'unbaptised' Māori. (Riemenschneider Papers, RP VIII, 216.)

European settlements alongside the Māori villages for several decades. This was not an entirely negative feature. When whaling ceased to be profitable and the stations closed down, the former Ōtākou whaler Octavius Harwood and the whaling entrepreneur Johnny Jones established themselves as farmers at Moeraki and Waikouaiti alongside other former whalers. In this way they provided examples of successful agricultural enterprises as well as employment for Māori who were of a mind to join them.[2] The fact that many of the former whalers had Māori wives helped them in the allocation of land for farming.

The situation at Ōtākou was not as favourable. The social and moral decline of the settlement after the bankruptcy of the Weller brothers has already been described. While many of the European inhabitants of the whaling station settlement had moved into the newly founded Dunedin at the head of the harbour, a remnant of Europeans remained.

After he had worked in the area for 10 months, the missionary describes his new field of work as 'one of the most extensive and difficult in all of New Zealand'.[3] His comment refers, of course, to the extensive travel required to visit his parishioners. Instead of day trips, as in Taranaki, he had to be absent sometimes for weeks. But these difficulties were insignificant compared with the spiritual neglect and decay that he saw in his parishioners. The 'old' heathendom had formed an amalgam with the 'new' European vices that was much more difficult to overcome than 'heathen superstitions'. In one of the more distant villages, Riemenschneider found to his horror that, 'the holding of all divine services, both in church and in the homes, both on Sundays and feast days as well as weekdays, had long ago ceased altogether'.[4] There were thus many challenges, but the missionary was secure in his conviction that he had been called to this place and that God would give him the strength to tackle what he saw as an enormous task. One very helpful factor was that his new parishioners were not engaged in war with the Government and he therefore was not asked to take sides.

In spite of his indifferent health, Riemenschneider commenced his work in Otago with vigour and enthusiasm. The Society for the elevation of the Māoris had received a grant of £150 from the Government to erect school buildings. It had allocated £50 each to Ōtākou, Waikouaiti and Moeraki for the purchase of timber for building school houses. Taieri had been left without provision for such a building. At Ōtākou, most of the timber had been used for the erection of the school teacher's house. Although in the 1840s the tip of the Otago Peninsula had boasted of no fewer than three Māori churches

---

2. See Harry Morton, *The Whale's Wake*. Dunedin: McIndoe for the University of Otago Press, 1982, pp. 307–308.
3. Riemenschneider Papers, RP VIII, 67.
4. RP VIII, 73.

in three distinct Māori settlements, they had fallen into disuse and neglect. When Riemenschneider arrived, church services were held in an old wooden hut that had previously been inhabited by a European living in the Māori community. When that became too dilapidated for religious services, the faithful gathered in the house of the mother of Te Mātenga Taiaroa, the senior chief who had died in February 1863.[5] At Waikouaiti the local chief, Matiti, had contracted a German cabinetmaker, called Ross, who had come south with his Māori wife to seek refuge from the wars in the North Island, to build a church 'as large as the timber would permit'.[6] At Moeraki the pile of timber had been left out in the open, so that a considerable amount of it had become unusable because of rot. Riemenschneider immediately drew up the plans for a church that could, if needed, also be used for a school. In all three centres he urged his parishioners, who were only too willing to do so, to organise regular special collections for the church building funds.

To fulfil the contract into which he had entered with the Otago Society, Riemenschneider also became very active in the field of education. But, as he had found in Taranaki, there did not appear to be much support for the establishment of schools among the adult Māori population. In addition, he found that in many localities there were not many prospective scholars. At the beginning of 1863 he reports that the populations of school-age young people (five to 18 years) was eight at Ōtākou, six at Māranuku, three at Taieri, 16 at Moeraki and between 30 and 40 at Waikouaiti.[7] It was clearly not possible to open a school in each of the villages and Riemenschneider considered the possibility of establishing a boarding institution. In the meantime, however, a more modest start could be made at least in some places. In March 1863 two Māori schools were opened, one in Waikouaiti, where the German Ross had agreed to teach for half a year in the hope that the Otago Society would eventually pay his salary, and one in Moeraki where a gifted Māori teacher, Herewini Ira, was appointed for a salary of £20. The schools did not flourish, mainly because the Otago Society was unable to find the money for the salaries of the teachers and for school supplies. The school at Waikouaiti was closed after the initial six months because no salary was forthcoming from the Otago Society,[8] Moeraki continued at the

---

5. For information on Taiaroa and his family see Bill Dacker, *Te Mamae me te Aroha. The pain and the love. A history of Kai Tahu Whanui in Otago, 1844–1994*. Dunedin: University of Otago Press, 1994.
6. RP VIII, 43.
7. RP VIII, 95.
8. The mission school at Waikouaiti was by no means the only school operating in the district. The Otago Education Board had established a school there as early as 1860, but as was the case with all Board schools, it charged tuition fees and would therefore not have been accessible to Māori, quite apart from the fact that under the existing legislation, Māori education was not the responsibility of the Education Board. (See Helen McComb, *125th Year of the Waikouaiti School, 1860–1895*. [Waikouaiti: J. Porter, 1985] p. 9.)

expense of the North German Mission Society until the end of 1864.[9]

In March 1864, the Parrys, the married couple who had established the first school at Ōtākou, and who had withdrawn to Port Chalmers during the tenure of the Barkers as teachers, returned to Ōtākou. Riemenschneider had different priorities from the two-man commission that had found them scholastically wanting. After having ascertained that they were firm in the faith and that they were known and liked by the local Māori, Riemenschneider engaged them as school teachers at a salary of £40. This arrangement and that at Moeraki were very tenuous, however, employment contracts for the teachers being for one year at a time and depending on sufficient funds arriving from Germany for their continuation. In spite of the difficulties, the school at Ōtākou seems to have been able to provide its pupils with a solid educational foundation. One of its star pupils, the youngest son of Te Mātenga Taiaroa, Hōri Kerei T. Taiaroa, later became a prominent member of Parliament and a tireless worker for his people.[10]

Riemenschneider's superiors in Bremen do not seem to have been particularly supportive of the missionary's school ventures. Indeed, the expenses that he incurred seem to have alarmed Inspector Zahn, and he must have written to Wohlers. On 6 November 1865, the older missionary, who had just returned from a visit to Riemenschneider who had been very ill, writes to Zahn:

> ... I do not consider it appropriate either if he uses mission funds for Māori schools, after he has drawn money for the support of himself and his family. Where school costs have to be met, they should be raised by the congregation.[11]

The missionary found himself in a very difficult situation. The Otago Society had given him the task of establishing Māori schools. He had done so in good faith, but had not been supported by the Society. Faced with the choice of either abandoning the work or continuing it with unauthorised North German Mission funds, he had chosen the latter path and then had to face the consequences.

Riemenschneider was more successful with his church building. The church in Moeraki was completed in December 1862. The missionary's description of the opening shows that it was not exactly a rest-day for him; between six o'clock in the morning and 10 o'clock at night he conducted no fewer than six church services as well as an extended catechism session.

The church building in Waikouaiti had also progressed well and Riemenschneider was able to preside over the inauguration festivities in March of 1863.

---

9. Herewini Ira seems to have continued to teach traditional Māori knowledge on an informal basis. (See Bill Dacker, *op. cit.*, p. 91.)
10. See Bill Dacker, *op. cit.*; T. A. Pybus, *Maori and Missionary: early Christian missions in the South Island of New Zealand*. Wellington: A. H. & A. W. Reed, 1954, p. 168.
11. Wohlers, Letters and Papers, Alexander Turnbull Library, Wellington, Micro-MS 98, reel 2.

Building the church at Ōtākou took longer, it was, after all, going to be the main church of the new North German Mission district. On 25 April 1863, the missionary convened a congregational meeting at Ōtākou and the parishioners agreed unanimously with the suggestion of their senior chief, Hoani Wetere Kōrako,[12] that there should be a special collection towards a building fund every Sunday. A sympathetic European resident of the area asked the missionary to write an appropriate document to collect subscriptions from the neighbouring Pākehā, and by the end of January 1864, Riemenschneider had raised enough money to be able to sign a contract with a builder for a church, again designed by him.

The missionary himself was actively engaged in the building of the church. He mobilised his parishioners to help him dig a level space where the church was to be built but complains that only he and his 13-year-old son in the end did most of the work with pick and shovel and handcart.[13] The shell of the building was completed by the beginning of March. Riemenschneider and his helpers took many weeks before they had finally completed the painting of the exterior, however, because the work appears to have stopped as soon as the missionary went on one of his journeys to visit other parishes and was not present to cajole his team into action.

Over the winter months Riemenschneider manufactured the choir rail and the pulpit – a considerable achievement since he had to continue all his other duties at the same time and as he was no expert cabinetmaker. Nevertheless, he had gained some experience in his youth, and when he built the furnishings for the church at Warea. Parts of the pulpit and the communion table have survived to the present day. A new church, which was erected in place of the one that he built, was formally opened on 22 March 1941. It is called the Centennial Church and commemorates both the signing of the Treaty of Waitangi and a hundred years of missionary endeavour in the Otago district. The pulpit in the new church was rebuilt on the pattern of the one designed and built by the missionary and contains parts of the original structure. The communion table was also taken over from the old building and carved in Māori designs for the new church. Completing the interior of Riemenschneider's church took several months as the missionary became seriously ill and was unable to work in July and August.

Because of the great interest taken in the building of the church at Ōtākou

---

12. Hoani Wetere Kōrako, who succeeded Taiaroa after the latter's death, was one of a group of younger chiefs who had accepted baptism comparatively early. He was baptised in 1843 at Ōtākou by James Watkin, the Wesleyan missionary who had settled in Waikouaiti in 1840. After his baptism, Kōrako built one of the three churches on the tip of the Otago Peninsula, on the slope of Tahakopa, where he taught and held services. Bill Dacker describes him as 'an important tohuka (learned man) of the new faith'. (*Te Mamae me te Aroha op. cit*, p. 39.)
13. RP VIII, 164.

on the part of Riemenschneider's Pākehā friends and acquaintances in Port Chalmers and Dunedin, the opening of the church was planned as a major festival with celebrations lasting two days. The actual dedication of the church was to take place on Christmas Day 1864, while for the following Tuesday, 27 December, a festival was planned to celebrate the completion of the work for a wider audience than just the local community. The Presbyterian minister at Port Chalmers, the Rev. W. Johnstone, had agreed to preach the festival sermon in English on Christmas Day, with Riemenschneider acting as interpreter. The church was named St Stephen's, after the St Stephani church in Bremen from which Riemenschneider had left to take up his missionary vocation.

The 'Mission Pic Nic in connexion with the opening of the church'[14] had been organised by an ad hoc committee under the chairmanship of the harbourmaster of Port Chalmers, Captain Thomson, and consisting of the Rev. Johnstone, Riemenschneider's doctor, Dr Niven, and Messrs Thuckwell and Fleming. It was to be a splendid occasion. Two days before Christmas, each committee member had sold 80 tickets for the festival, and the planning was completed for a festivity attended by 400 Pākehā and 150 Māori. The Māori too had planned ahead and on the day before Christmas they had slaughtered two fat oxen, four sheep and four pigs for the nourishment of their guests. Transport had also been arranged. Two passenger ships, the 'magnificent and powerful paddle steamer *Bruce*'[15] from Dunedin and the *Golden Age* from Port Chalmers, were to take the guests to the celebrations.

It was just as well that the day chosen for the public festivities was a Tuesday. In the course of 1864 the master of the *Golden Age* had been taken to court to be tried for the crime of trading on the Sabbath. He successfully defended himself by claiming that the Maritime Act did not specifically prohibit this and was discharged, albeit with a stern warning that he was not to sound his whistle when travelling on a Sunday. For many years after this, church groups refused to use the Otago Harbour steamers for events scheduled on Sundays.[16]

The opening festival clearly was one of the high points in Riemenschneider's career. It is obvious that he relished the occasion and he sent a very full description to Bremen. Representatives of the Dunedin newspapers also attended and filed reports.

The reporter of the *Otago Mail* was certainly impressed with the celebrations and the building, even though he erroneously calls it 'the first native church at

---

14. RP VIII, 191. The phrase is in English in the original.
15. Advertisement in *Otago Mail*, 24 and 26 December, 1864.
16. See F. H. McCluskey, *Down the Bay. The history of the ferries on Otago Harbour*. Wellington: New Zealand Ship & Marine Society Inc., 1995, p. 46.

the Maori Kaik'.[17] He is on firmer ground when he describes the building:

> The Maori church is a neat, simple edifice, 28 feet [8.5 m.] by 16 [4.9 m.], and is seated for 120. The chancel or communion is 8 feet [2.4 m.] by 8, the height of the building in front including the tower is 30 feet [9.1 m.], and the spire rises 10 feet [3 m.] above the roof and is 6 feet [1.8 m.] square.[18]

The newspaper account of the formal part of the proceedings provides a rare description of Riemenschneider exercising his public function:

> The Rev. Mr Reminsneider [sic] opened the proceedings by prayer in the Māori language, the people frequently responding, and joining with him in repeating the Lord's Prayer. The Maoris then rose and chanted a hymn, also in their own language, after which the visitors sang the fifty-fourth paraphrase,[19] and the Rev. Mr Connebee[20] engaged in prayer.
>
> The Rev. Mr Reminsneider [sic] then in broken but clearly intelligible English, and in simple, homely language, proceeded to detail the story of the mission, when he was interrupted by the chief of the tribe, who stepped forward, and, hat in hand, addressed the pakehas for about five minutes with great fervour. At the close of the chief's address, Mr Reminsneider [sic] stated that it embodied a hearty welcome on the part of the chief and his people, and an expressing of the joy the presence of the pakehas gave them, and that he thanked them that they (the pakehas), though far superior in many respects to him and his people, had yet condescended to fraternise with them, and further stating that his tribe was encouraged, by the presence of so many friends, to persevere in their good work.
>
> The rev. gentleman then resumed his narrative. ...[21]

The missionary had made it clear in his speech to the guests that he would dearly love to have a harmonium on which his wife who could play, could accompany the singing. A number of visitors had dropped strong hints that such a present would be forthcoming and the missionary started at once with the building of a choir and organ gallery in the new church, complete with an organ front of false wooden pipes, wrapped in tinfoil to make them look like tin pipes.

After some prodding from Riemenschneider the Dunedin friends were as good as their word. They collected enough money to purchase a harmonium, which was shipped to Ōtākou by steamer and whaleboat. From now on, it was played by Catherine Riemenschneider at every service and for some time there was even a choir that met twice a week to practise.

---

17. 28 December, 1864.
18. *ibid.*
19. A metrical setting of Second Timothy, 1, 12, 'But I am not ashamed, for I know whom I have believed and I am sure that he is able to guard until that Day what has been entrusted to me'.
20. The Rev. Richard Connebee was the first Congregational minister in Dunedin. He had arrived from Australia in October 1862.
21. *ibid.*

At Ōtākou and in his other preaching places, Riemenschneider had established Christian congregations on the European model, with European churches mainly designed by him, and worship and pastoral care along European lines. Although he claims otherwise in his reports to Bremen, his work as pastor among the Māori was very similar to that of a European pastor in a Pākehā congregation. His fights against what he calls superstitions, 'old ways', and secular modes of thought, which he sees as the specific 'missionary' components of his vocation, were fought just as hard and with equally tenuous success by his brethren in Pākehā congregations in Port Chalmers and Dunedin.

In addition to his work among the Otago Māori, the missionary pastor also exercised some pastoral functions among the Pākehā who lived in the vicinity of the Māori settlements. He not only invited his Pākehā neighbours to contribute financially to his Māori churches (and made sure that special 'English' services were held for them when the buildings were dedicated), but he also officiated at occasional Pākehā baptisms, weddings and funerals. On 16 May 1864, for example, Riemenschneider signed as officiating minister at the marriage of Edward Fairbrother, fisherman, and Constance Constant, dressmaker. The ceremony was conducted at the missionary's house. A few months later, George Ashwell, boatman, married Lavinia Watkins, widow, in the then still not formally consecrated 'Māori Church at Otago Heads'. Again, Riemenschneider officiated.[22] In his first year at Ōtākou, Riemenschneider reports that he baptised 39 people, '13 adults, partly Māori, partly half-caste; and 26 children, among them four Europeans, the others partly half-caste, partly Māori'.[23] In addition to these special services, Riemenschneider conducted a regular Sunday afternoon service for the Europeans living in the vicinity.

Although similar to the role of the Pākehā ministers, Riemenschneider's work was much harder in terms of the time and effort that he felt driven to devote to it. His parish required a great deal of travel. In November and December of 1862, for example, the missionary who was convalescing from an illness, spent a fortnight in Moeraki and Waikouaiti. He reached his home at Ōtākou on Saturday, 6 December. After having conducted the usual Sunday services and teaching sessions, Riemenschneider had to travel to Dunedin on Monday, 8 December, in order to be the interpreter in a court case that some of his Ōtākou parishioners were bringing against one of their Pākehā neighbours for horse stealing. (They won their case.)

After having spent the night in Dunedin, the missionary took the

---

22. Records of the Port Chalmers Presbyterian Parish. Marriage Register, Māori Kaik; 1864–1972. Hewitson Library, Knox College, Dunedin.
23. RP VIII, 93.

steamer to Port Chalmers but was prevented by bad weather from crossing the harbour by whaleboat until Friday, 12 December. When he had finally managed to cross, he spent the weekend at home, again conducting worship and teaching on Sunday. On Monday he commenced writing the report to the *Verwaltungsausschuß* (executive committee of the North German Mission Society) in which he describes his activities. He must have taken the unfinished manuscript with him because already on the following day, 16 December, he re-crossed the harbour in order to catch the steamer for Moeraki where he arrived on the following morning at two o'clock. His activities during the consecration of the church at Moeraki have already been described briefly. On the day after the festivities Riemenschneider took an early morning service and held school. This was followed by a *rūnanga* (council meeting), which lasted until four o'clock on the following morning. After two hours' sleep Riemenschneider rode the ca. 28 kms to Waikouaiti where he conducted the Christmas services. On Saturday, 27 December, he took the steamer back to Port Chalmers and crossed over to his station on the evening of the same day. After his usual Sunday duties, the missionary spent Monday at home, but already early on Tuesday morning, 30 December, he had to go to Dunedin where two Māori were waiting for him with horses to take him to Taieri. He finally returned home on 10 January 1863 and he ends the description of his journeys with the following comment:

> After such long and sustained travels both on land and on the sea which at least here is always stormy, and after the continuous work among the natives both day and night to which the few single days which fell in between here at Otakou gave no respite and still don't (because the Maori village is right at the foot of our hill here), I finally felt tired enough and in need of recuperation. However all that remains here for us is – work, work and more work as long as the day lasts.[24]

The report that describes all these activities and which he began writing during one of his rare sojourns at home on 15 December was completed at midnight on 13 January 1863, three days after his return from Taieri. It is 12,300 words long!

Another factor which made Riemenschneider's work more arduous than that of his Pākehā brethren was the extra duties that were expected of him over and above the work of a European pastor in a Pākehā congregation. His role as interpreter in the court has already been mentioned. Admittedly he received payment for these services, but they involved him in a great deal of time and effort with a trip to Dunedin being required in each case.

The missionary was also involved in the administration of Māori justice. The Native Districts Regulation Act and the Native Circuit Court Act of

---

24. RP VIII, 57.

1858 had given local *rūnanga* the jurisdiction over petty crime and minor civil cases between Māori. In one of his reports to Bremen Riemenschneider emphasises that he attends the sessions as a 'father' and 'advisor', not as judge. He does this to ensure that his superiors do not misunderstand and consider that he contravenes the spirit of Luke 12,14, where Jesus asks, 'who made me a judge or divider over you'.

As there was no resident doctor in Ōtākou, the missionary continued, as he had in Taranaki, to minister to his parishioners' medical needs, including acting as a midwife. In January 1865 he describes his manifold duties:

> Already at the beginning of autumn (of the previous year) there was a great incidence of sickliness all around us, particularly among the female sex and children generally. This lasted throughout winter. And as besides being a pastor I also hold the position of doctor and pharmacist, I had to be out and about frequently both by night and day and in all weathers, in order to provide my patients with physical and spiritual medicine. Besides this I had to work hard at home with axe, spade and also woodworking tools, preach three times every Sunday and hold a catechisation hour, and often on weekdays I had to participate in all sorts of negotiations of the natives in order to ensure a favourable outcome in everything that took place.[25]

Riemenschneider also considered the protection of the Ōtākou Māori against corruption by Europeans to be part of his pastoral duties. In the 1860s the Māori settlement at the Heads had become a popular destination for steamer excursions from Dunedin. The missionary observes:

> Frequently on festivals and general holidays large European pleasure parties come down here by steamship, but they come simply for their own sensual entertainment, in order to dance down here in the open air beside the Maori village and to gamble, to eat and to drink. But the worst feature is that on such occasions they always pour drinks for the Maori and raise their glasses to them until they become fools and let themselves be talked into displaying their old foolish practices for the entertainment of such parties, whereupon the latter go around and spread the word, 'what a degenerate set of savages those Maori are'.[26]

After a particularly bad incident in November 1864, in which the revellers had handed the Māori beer glasses filled with neat Brandy, the indignant Riemenschneider took his concerns to the police in Dunedin who agreed to send a constable along with each party to keep an eye on the proceedings.

Another issue that occupied a great deal of Riemenschneider's time was the perennial and recurring problem he had encountered in every locality and at every stage in his career: land. Late one night in October 1865 he writes to

---

25. RP VIII, 168.
26. RP VIII, 194. The final sentence, in quotation marks, is in English in the original.

Pastor Zahn. After describing what he saw as the main issue – the attempt by the local Pākehā government to deprive the Māori of reserve land, which they had agreed to when the land was sold – he continues:

> The way in which I proceed is that in every case in which they have to present a complaint or make an application, they write me a letter. I append to every such letter a translation into English, include my comments in a separate note, and then despatch the whole set – the original of the Maori letter with translation and my own added note – to the general government in Wellington. When I receive an answer I translate it into Maori and hand it to the natives concerned.[27]

In addition to his duties as a preacher, advocate, interpreter, doctor and pastor, Riemenschneider also made friends and acquaintances in accordance with his social status as a Reverend gentleman, as he had done in Nelson and New Plymouth. He appears to have had a very cordial relationship with the Presbyterian minister at Port Chalmers, the Rev. Johnstone[28], as well as with the harbourmaster of the same town, Captain Thomson, who was also an elder in Mr Johnstone's church. The missionary also had a number of friends in Dunedin, among them the famous doctor and amateur historian Dr T. M. Hocken. It was for Dr Hocken that Riemenschneider wrote a report on Māori health from the perspective of a missionary.

Like other contemporary descriptions of the general state of health among Māori, Riemenschneider lists some of the more prevalent diseases, and there seems to be a close relationship between his observations and those of mid-19th century doctors.[29] Unlike most of the medical writers, however, the German missionary paints a detailed and idealised picture of the Māori before European contact, and contrasts their former healthy lifestyle unfavourably with the changes brought about by the partial adoption of European ways.

As he had done in Taranaki, Riemenschneider did not spare himself, but drove himself to the limits of his physical and mental capabilities. Again he assumed every task that came his way and carried it out to the best of his ability without counting the cost to himself or to his family. In this way he became a key figure for all the activities in his extensive parish, as he had been in Taranaki. At the same time however the demands of his far-flung parish, which required frequent long absences from his home, seem to have prevented

---

27. RP VIII, 235. An example of a letter in Māori with Riemenschneider's comments has survived in the papers of Alexander Francis McDonnell, Alexander Turnbull Library, MS Papers 151:1. It is a letter from Te Mātenga Taiaroa to which is appended an explanation by Riemenschneider. It is addressed cryptically to 'Baker, Esqr. Wellington. The recipient was probably Charles Baker, who worked in the Native Secretary's office.
28. Riemenschneider's spelling of Johnstone's name is erratic. He sometimes adds the 'e' and sometimes omits it. I have used the spelling given in official documents in all cases.
29. See, for example, R. E. Wright-St Clair, 'Maori health in the mid-nineteenth century, *New Zealand Medical Journal*, 101 (1988), 14–15; Arthur S. Thomson, *The story of New Zealand*. London: John Murray, 1859, vol. 1, 211–222.

him from establishing close personal relationships with his parishioners. While his reports from Taranaki are full of names and accounts of conversations with individuals, very few names appear in his Otago documents. The Otago letters give the impression of a man who has overextended himself. The multiplicity of roles and the huge task seem to have overwhelmed the missionary both mentally and physically.

What remained to be done for the missionary was to ensure that when his work among the Māori of Otago ended, it was carried on in some form by whoever his successors would be.

Chapter Thirteen

A Legacy in Taranaki, 1846–1862

ALTHOUGH RIEMENSCHNEIDER devoted all his energy and work to his new field of labour in Otago, he never lost touch completely with Taranaki and at least some of his former parishioners there. The bitter conflict between Taranaki, Ngāti Ruanui and the Governor remained unsolved and the missionary reports on it frequently in his correspondence with Bremen, which in the 1860s increasingly consists of letters to Pastor Zahn rather than formal reports. While he had not been able to achieve what had been his particular vision of a christianised and europeanised Taranaki, he nevertheless felt that he had left a legacy. It consisted of people who were prepared to perpetuate his message of peace in the face of the more belligerent factions.

Not long after his arrival in Otago, the missionary found grounds for rejoicing in the report of a shipping disaster. He writes:

> The same steamship (the "Lord Worsley") in which I had made my final journey back from Taranaki to Nelson (1862) and in which we afterwards made our journey from Nelson here to Otago (in June 1862), stranded only a few months after our arrival here, towards the end of 1862 [1 September] on the coast of Taranaki between the two villages Te Umuroa (W[iremu] Matakatea's place) and Waiaua (Arama Karaka's place) and thus, although it stranded between two neutral villages, it was nevertheless in the middle of enemy territory, 45 English miles from the nearest European territorial border (New Plymouth). The entire crew as well as all passengers (a considerable number which I cannot now state precisely however [ca. 60]) and also the entire cargo thus fell into the hands of our Taranaki people.
>
> Wiremu Matakatea together with Arama Karaka, Horopapera Te Ua and others had at once gone to the spot [Namu Bay] in order to rescue the shipwrecked people and to extend to them their protection, and Wiremu Matakatea had lodged them in his village Te Umuroa, as it was the largest and most convenient. Soon however the whole tribe had assembled there in order to hold council and court martial about the victims of the accident. There was no lack of people who would have liked to satisfy their thirst for revenge against their enemies, the whites, on these unfortunates. Others had wanted to treat the

215

accident victims as prisoners of war, keep them in a kind of slavery and take all their possessions as rightful plunder.

Risking their lives, Arama Karaka, Horopapera Te Ua, Wiremu Matakatea had resolutely opposed every one of these plans, and they had finally prevailed so that the shipwrecked people with all their possessions were granted free withdrawal from Te Umuroa and free passage with a security escort through all the 45 miles of enemy territory (Taranaki) to the English border (New Plymouth). In addition our Taranaki tribe, their enemy, provided for them both horses and carts in order to transfer all of them, kith and kin, safe and sound from enemy territory and enemy hands, to safe friendly territory.[1]

One of the three people whom Riemenschneider mentions as the saviours of the crew and passengers of the *Lord Worsley*, Horopāpera Te Ua, was a former slave who had as a young boy with his mother spent some time on John Whiteley's mission station at Kawhia where he had been baptised by the Wesleyan missionary.[2] By the time Riemenschneider began his work in Taranaki, Horopāpera had returned to his native village, Waiaua, where he was, in the missionary's terminology, 'second teacher'. The missionary seems to have had a fairly close relationship with Horopāpera. Waiaua was the second largest *kāinga* in his district when he arrived and he had attempted to settle his assistant Völkner there. When this had failed, Riemenschneider visited frequently. It was, however, during one of Völkner's brief periods of activity at Waiaua, on 2 September 1850, that the young assistant missionary performed the marriage ceremony in which Te Ua married Erihāpeta Hine Kou.

Like so many Taranaki Māori, Te Ua seems to have suffered from the increasing polarisation between missionary teaching and Māori nationalism. He became a strong supporter of the King Movement but at the same time he appears to have retained his office in Riemenschneider's church. Although the Māori teacher took part in some fighting in the 1860 phase of the Taranaki war, it is likely that he withdrew from the fighting after the encounter at Waireka, together with his chief Wiremu Kīngi Matakatea, because Riemenschneider describes Te Ua as one of the few among the Taranaki who counselled peace when the majority wanted to go to war.

The stranding of the *Lord Worsley* and the subsequent heated discussions about how the passengers, crew and cargo were to be treated, appears to have caused a sharp conflict in Te Ua's mind. Riemenschneider was no longer with them, but his teachings were. At the same time, the former Māori teacher was also acutely aware of the plight of his people, brought about by the settlers.

---

1. RP VIII, 230–231. The added information in square brackets is based on C. W. N. Ingram, *New Zealand shipwrecks: 195 years of disasters at sea*. Auckland: Beckett, c. 1990, pp. 68–69.
2. Paul Clark, *'Hauhau' , The Pai Marire Search for Maori Identity*. Auckland: Auckland University Press, 1975, p. 5.

On 5 September, five days after the stranding of the *Lord Worsley*, Te Ua had a vision in which the archangel Gabriel appeared to him, commissioning him as a prophet.[3] Although he was at first considered mad by his family and others, and placed under house arrest, he became the founder of a powerful religious movement, which he called Hauhau, a name that was to strike terror into the hearts of the Pākehā settlers in the mid-1860s.

Te Ua's new church was an attempt to create a Māori church on Māori territory, free from the perceived errors of the missionaries. The prophet and his followers would therefore have seen their faith as something new and distinctively Māori, untainted by missionary error and distortion. There are nevertheless some aspects of the Hauhau religion that bear some similarity to the major emphases in Riemenschneider's teaching. One of the major themes in the missionary's teaching from the mid-1850s until his departure from Taranaki had been peace. Again and again, from the Puketapu feud onwards, he had preached peace. The two guiding principles of Te Ua's religion were pai marire, goodness and peace. Another similarity between Riemenschneider's teaching and the Māori prophet's lies in their emphasis on God as a punishing father. A passage from Te Ua's writings sounds like an echo from one of Riemenschneider's sermons

> [God] teaches us as we teach our children: through listening, he is called a child of yours. And if he does not, he is chastised, as He chastises us. Whereupon that chastisement remains as an example for the people. Understand that the striking of the lash is teaching you; if you do not listen, he increases the lash.[4]

Clearly the concept of peace is a central concept of the Christian religion and the idea of God using chastisement as a way to teach his people is widespread through the Old Testament. It is nevertheless interesting that both Riemenschneider and Te Ua, although dissimilar in their views about events in Taranaki, had remarkably similar views about at least two aspects of the interpretation of the Bible.

Given the country's political situation, which threatened the very existence of the Māori people, Te Ua Haumene's[5] 'good and peaceful' religion could not stay peaceful for very long. By encouraging its spread throughout the North Island and sending emissaries to other tribes, the prophet lost control over his followers and his teachings. His emissaries often would not, or could not, deal with local manifestations of the new faith, which would probably not have

---

3. See, *The people of many peaks. The Maori biographies from the Dictionary of New Zealand Biography*. vol. 1, Wellington: Bridget Williams Books and Department of Internal Affairs, 1990, pp. 283–286.
4. L. Head, 'The Gospel of Te Ua Haumene', *Journal of the Polynesian Society* 101 (March 1992), 25. Cf. Riemenschneider's extensive use of the book of Proverbs in his preaching, described in chapter 6, note 40, for example.
5. Te Ua Haumene abandoned his baptismal name Horopāpera when he commenced his activities as a prophet.

found approval in the founder's eyes. On 2 March 1865, Riemenschneider's former assistant, now the Church Missionary Society missionary at Ōpōtiki, Carl Sylvius Völkner, the man who had officiated at Te Ua Haumene's wedding 15 years earlier, fell victim to the prophet's followers. He was hanged, then decapitated and his eyes gouged out and eaten by Māori who had embraced the new creed.

For the Pākehā settlers in New Zealand, the killing of Völkner and other violent acts committed by followers of Te Ua, were seen as proof for the view that the Hauhau were bloodthirsty fanatics and rebels, intent on driving the Europeans out of the country no matter what the cost.

There appears to be some doubt about whether Te Ua still had any control over events by the end of 1865. He continued to preach peace while some Ngāti Ruanui, among whom he was living, favoured warlike measures in the face of European confiscation of their lands.[6] In the interest of peace, the prophet may have recanted and described his visions as an illness. In January 1866 Te Ua put his signature to a letter renouncing his religion and expressing loyalty to Queen Victoria and her Governor, and by February 1866, Te Ua gave himself up to General Chute, the commander of a force of Pākehā soldiers operating in Taranaki. At the suggestion of Donald McLean, Riemenschneider's former friend, the prophet was humiliated by being paraded around the North Island as proof that the Hauhau movement had been conquered by the Governor.[7] Riemenschneider suggests that already in mid-1865 Te Ua was no longer a completely free agent and that his followers rather than he were intent on perpetuating the anti-missionary sentiments expressed in his speeches and writings. In a letter to Pastor Zahn, dated 11 October 1865, the missionary writes:

> Several months ago I received through Tamati a pleasing message from Horopapera Te Ua (who is credited with having been the founder of the "Hauhau" fanaticism). He had passed on his message to Tamati *orally* and had asked him to write it to me after they had met in one of the strong forest pa of the insurgents in the vicinity of Warea, because he himself was not allowed to write and send letters to me. The message was that in a condition of mental impairment he had unfortunately had false dreams and visions and that he had promulgated false teaching based on them. However, others had misused and twisted and distorted them to the point where the Hauhau fanaticism with its atrocities had arisen from it. [He continued] that in the meantime the Saviour had taken mercy on him and had given him back his right mind and with it also his earlier faith and his seeking and striving after God's peace and justice. He felt an intense yearning to see me, his father in Christ, again and to pour out his whole heart in my presence and to hear my words like before.[8]

---

6. See Paul Clark, *'Hauhau' op. cit.*, Auckland, 1975, p. 24.
7. *op. cit.* pp. 25–26.
8. RP VIII, 229.

We may never know whether Te Ua Haumene was the victim of a movement that he started and which then got out of hand or whether his message to Riemenschneider was a less than sincere political move. The fact that at Christmas 1865 a meeting was held at Pūtahi to consecrate three new prophets and 12 new workers in the Hauhau faith[9] seems to suggest that the first explanation is more likely. Te Ua and his message of peace and subservience to the Queen and her Governor, was no longer acceptable to the people he served in the prevailing political situation. Like his mentor Riemenschneider before him, he was put aside and replaced. The prophet Te Ua, one of the first Māori to attempt to put a uniquely Māori stamp on Pākehā Christianity, died in October 1866 at Ōeo in South Taranaki.

Of the three new prophets created at the Christmas meeting at Pūtahi, two were former pupils of Riemenschneider. One of them, Tohu Kākahi does not figure in the missionary's writings although he had been a resident of Warea during his period of work there. The other, Te Whiti o Rongomai, Tohu's brother-in-law, has a prominent place in Riemenschneider's descriptions of his Māori parishioners. The young Te Whiti, whose baptismal name was Erueti, had been doing domestic chores for the missionary when he first settled at Warea and had received some instruction in the three Rs in return. This arrangement had ended soon after the arrival of Trost from Motukaramū when Te Whiti left Riemenschneider's service. A few years later Te Whiti appears to have spent some time in New Plymouth. The missionary writes:

> In 1848 he was drawn to New Plymouth in the course of Maori business, where he established relationships with Europeans and spent a full year among them and had dealings with them. Spiritually and morally this was a great disadvantage to him, because, although he was preserved from falling into grievous vice by the inner disciplinarian of divine truth which never left his heart completely, yet in overall attitude and behaviour he had in many respects fallen into bad habits. But towards the end of 1849 he returned here. This was as a result of an extremely strong eye infection which had befallen him in town and which almost cost him his sight. They had tried to persuade him to go with his illness to the hospital there and to seek medical attention. He had firmly resisted however, stating that indeed the local hospital with all the help and care offered there deserved all recognition, that he also might entrust himself to it if it were not the case that at home in his village of Warea he had his own white father who had treated and healed him in an illness before, and to whose care he would entrust himself all the more gladly as he knew that he was known and loved by him. [Erueti further stated that] the thought that he had for so long lived away from his dear spiritual father in a strange place made him depressed, his heart was heavy and restless, his love for his father was driving him to go home and seek help from him. If he then would become blind, so be it etc.

---

9. *Dictionary of New Zealand Biography: The people of many peaks. op. cit.*, p. 286.

> He was almost completely blind when a companion brought him here. I locked him into a dark hut and used all the possible care and remedies that were at my disposal.[10]

The condition either resolved itself or Riemenschneider's treatment was successful as was also his spiritual counselling. The missionary reports that not only Erueti's sight was saved, but he also underwent some kind of conversion experience. The incident appears to have strengthened the already warm and friendly relationship between the two men because Riemenschneider comments:

> His going in and out with us was and remains a perfectly normal thing and where we need a bit of help with this or that, and if he is not too far away (which admittedly is frequently the case with his scattered plantations and other manifold claims to which he is subject as a chief), it goes without saying that he helps us. He has now been married for several years and his wife does the washing for my wife, and thus she earns clothing for herself and her two little children, as she receives clothes from mother from time to time.[11]

A little later in the same document, written in June 1857, Riemenschneider gives his opinion on Erueti's faith:

> ... as far as human eyes can see and as far as human feeling and judgement can reach, we may joyfully say: he is faithful in his Christianity and in his Christian vocation, and the chastisement of divine truth and love never seems to be used on him in vain. In comparison with other native Christians he does not appear as prominently as far as religious verbosity and external pious appearance in the ordinary daily life is concerned; but as far as the inner innate power of Christianity and knowledge of divine truth is concerned, and where it is a matter of making a frank testimony and confession for the Lord Jesus, no matter under what circumstances and before what person, there Erueti is far ahead of most of the others. I have never found a Maori whose heart is more liberated or even as liberated from all the old, dark superstition, and who confronts it with greater dislike and decisiveness in the defence of the truth and honour of the Lord, than Erueti.[12]

Riemenschneider's judgement was no doubt partly based on Erueti's behaviour during the activities of Tāmati Te Ito and his Wāhi Tapu movement that reached Warea in March 1857. The missionary reports that even his protector and friend (and uncle of Erueti), Āperahama was supporting it, although, he hastens to add, 'with the best of intentions'.[13] Seeing their chief's behaviour, some of the Warea Christians also began to waver and finally follow Te Ito.

---

10. RP VI, 96–97.
11. RP VI, 99.
12. RP VI, 100–101.
13. RP VI, 114.

Not so Erueti Te Whiti. Riemenschneider writes:

> Only Erueti stood firm on the rock of his open confession of Christ as the only saviour; and when he could not achieve anything and could not yield to the demands that were made on him, he retreated for weeks into the solitude of his distant fields. He realised that Aperahama would not leave him in peace and therefore out of respect and in order to avoid an open conflict, he went out of Aperahama's way.[14]

Riemenschneider's concern at Erueti's absence from Warea was not only because he worried about his spiritual state, there was also a much more practical and prosaic reason for the missionary to wish for the return of his pupil and friend. Erueti had undertaken to build a fence around the mission station's gardens, to keep out Māori stock, and the longer he was away the longer the missionary had to wait for his fence. It was finally completed in September 1857.

The increasing Māori resistance to European settlement and the consequent emergence of the King Movement, which polarised opinion in Taranaki, saw Erueti and Riemenschneider in opposite camps. While they continued to share religious observance, and while they appear to have shared the view that secular authority was ordained by God,[15] Erueti saw the Māori King as the representative of this God-ordained authority, while Riemenschneider regarded himself as the loyal subject of the British Queen. The missionary must have been deeply saddened by what he would have seen as Erueti's error, but he never rejected him personally. Likewise, Erueti Te Whiti does not appear to have rejected Riemenschneider as a person. In the *rūnanga* which finally decided to expel Riemenschneider from Taranaki, the missionary reports that Erueti made it clear that it is political necessity, not personal sentiment, which compelled him to support his exclusion from Māori territory.[16]

Riemenschneider was no longer alive when Erueti Te Whiti o Rongomai, together with his brother-in-law Tohu, became a prominent leader of Māori resistance to the European land confiscations in Taranaki in the 1870s and 1880s. Together they founded and developed Parihaka, a model settlement, which was at the same time a symbol of Māori self-determination and an irritant for the European government. The German missionary was not able to observe the rise to fame, and the subsequent humiliation at the hands of an unscrupulous government, of the Māori prophet. While he would have been scandalised by some of the religious pronouncements of his former pupil and friend, he would certainly have felt, rightly or wrongly, that he had been

---
14. ibid.
15. See Bronwyn Elsmore, *Mana from Heaven: A century of Maori prophets in New Zealand*. Tauranga: Tauranga Moana Press, 1989, p. 250.
16. RP VII, 346–347.

a major influence in developing Te Whiti's philosophy. Like his friend and mentor Riemenschneider, Te Whiti advocated pacifism. He believed that in the end, God would intervene and overrule the oppressors of his people. Also, he was prepared to promote some key concepts, such as honesty, industry, cleanliness and peaceful living, which Riemenschneider had made major planks of his teaching while he had been the Preacher of Taranaki.[17]

Te Whiti's desire to isolate himself and his people from what he saw as the pernicious influence of the European settlers, his opposition to some European values and his anti-missionary stance, have been well documented. This does not mean, however, that the Māori prophet repudiated Riemenschneider himself and all his teaching.

A poignant meeting occurred in October 1881, when the Native Minister, William Rolleston, went to visit Te Whiti in an attempt to settle the dispute between him and the Government. He took with him, as an interpreter, Riemenschneider's son Wilhelm.[18] The missionary's son knew Te Whiti in his boyhood years in Warea. The matter of fact report of the business transacted cannot and does not refer to the emotions that must have been present at the meeting of two former friends. They had been separated by the events of 20 years ago when young Wilhelm Riemenschneider with his mother and sisters had been forced to leave what had been his childhood home in Warea.

Thirteen years after Te Whiti's meeting with Wilhelm Riemenschneider, in February – March 1894, two Lutheran missionaries, H. Dierks and F. K. G. Blaess, went to see the Māori leader in his village. Their visit is described as follows:

> At Parihaka they visited each Maori hut and also Te Whiti and Tohu. Te Whiti was at first very cold and not inclined to talk, but when Dierks began to enquire after his contact with Riemenschneider, Te Whiti became more friendly, even invited the missionaries to dine with him.[19]

Riemenschneider left Taranaki against his will and both he and some commentators on his work considered his work a failure. After all, he had been expelled by the people among whom he had worked for 16 years; they had ultimately rejected him and his teaching. While this may be true for some, perhaps for the majority of his former parishioners, the missionary did leave a legacy – the teaching of peace and Christian values.

---

17. See Daniel P. Lyons, "An analysis of three Maori prophet movements", in: *Conflict and Compromise: Essays on the Maori since colonisation*. Wellington: Reed, 1975, 64, 65 f.
18. For a description of the interview, see Keith Sinclair, *Kinds of Peace. Maori people after the wars 1870–85*. Auckland: Auckland University Press, 1991, pp. 122–123.
19. F. Blaess, 'Early Lutheran Church NZ'. Typescript, Alexander Turnbull Library, Wellington, MS Papers 2200, Lutheran Church of New Zealand, Folder CR 80/2, p. 11.

Chapter Fourteen

At Rest, 1865–1866

IN 1863 THE 46-YEAR-OLD Riemenschneider must have received a letter from the *Verwaltungsausschuß* (executive committee of the North German Mission Society) asking him for his opinion about the continuation or closure of the mission once he and Wohlers would retire. The missionary replied in November of that year that he had not yet reached a definite conclusion.[1]

By March 1865 the decision seems to have been made in Bremen that the North German Mission Society would cease its operation in New Zealand when Riemenschneider and Wohlers were ready to retire. The missionary responds:

> I have now had to wait for a *long time* for such enlightenment and I have received it only at the time of the resignation of the last government ministry. According to that understanding, the matter of our mission here is such that when the Lord recalls me, the current missionary, from this field of labour, our dear Society can regard its task here as having been honestly completed, and that it can withdraw from further activity in this post with as much joy in God's name as it entered it joyfully in God's name when it was requested to do so.[2]

The way in which the missionary intended to make provision for the spiritual care of his congregation after his death is detailed a little later in the same letter. He had been keeping the small school at Ōtākou functioning by paying the teachers, Mr and Mrs Parry, from mission funds. Together with the chiefs of the area he had applied to the Government for funds to continue the school, but he was not very hopeful that their representations would be successful. 'Waiting for help or counting on it from the Government', he writes, 'was like digging for a spring in a sand hill.'[3] Riemenschneider sadly came to the conclusion that if no help was forthcoming, the school at Ōtākou would have to be closed at the end of 1865. He would then have to

---
1. Riemenschneider Papers, RP VIII, 128–129.
2. RP VIII, 174.
3. RP VIII, 178.

make provision for the continuation of pastoral care:

> Then I have to do my best to instruct the young people at least in English, and draw some of them closer to me and educate them more closely and deeply in the Word of God, and train them in the spiritual ministry, so that they will be able to serve the old people and indeed all of them at the time when we will no longer be available to do it.[4]

In Bremen too, things were changing. Early in 1865 Riemenschneider was informed of the death of Pastor Hermann Müller, a nephew of the Hermann Müller who had been young Riemenschneider's pastor at St Stephani in Bremen. The younger Müller had been a member of the *Verwaltungsausschuß* and had corresponded regularly with the missionary after the departure of Inspector Brauer in 1851.

Riemenschneider, the tireless worker in God's vineyard, was getting tired. The years of toil, privations and worry were taking their toll. From June to August 1864 the missionary had suffered the most serious illness of his life. Almost a year later, in April 1865, he describes its course to his friend and mentor, Pastor Zahn of Bremen.

Riemenschneider and his doctor must have expected the missionary's death at any moment because during one of the doctor's daily visits in July he brought the Presbyterian minister of Port Chalmers with him. On 20 July 1864, the missionary made his last will and testament and the doctor and the minister signed it as witnesses. It is a simple document. Whatever else he had done, the paupers' son Riemenschneider had not made a fortune on this earth. The will, which is still preserved in the National Archives of New Zealand, reads:

> In the Name of God Amen!
>
> This is the last Will & Testament of Mr John Frederick Riemenschneider of the Mission House, at Otago Heads in the Province of Otago, Missionary.
>
> I will, give, devise & bequeathe unto my wife, Catherine Garland Riemenschneider all my real & personal estate including a Deposit of £100, at the Bank of New Zealand, Dunedin, & including further also Interpreter's Salary from the 1st April 1864 & including also furthermore a Balance of Compensation Money still now remaining due to me on the part of the Taranaki Compensation Commission for losses sustained by me through the war.
>
> And I hereby appoint my Wife Catherine Garland Riemenschneider sole Executrix of this my last will & Testament, as witness my hand this 20th day of July 1864
>
> John Frederick Riemenschneider.

It was certainly necessary that the missionary made what provision he could for his wife and family. Shortly before he succumbed to his illness, on

---

4. RP VIII, 179.

6 July 1864, his wife had been safely delivered of their seventh child. To the missionary's delight it was a second son, Ernest Edwin, after five daughters. The gravely ill Riemenschneider also asked his wife to write to his friend and brother missionary, Wohlers.

> to come here as quickly as possible in order to discuss our mission here with me if he still found me alive. In case I had departed this life, he was to take appropriate steps.[5]

Although the letter to Wohlers took two weeks to reach him, the faithful friend and fellow missionary set out at once and reached Ōtākou in mid-August. He stayed only three days. On the day after his departure Riemenschneider was once again stricken and the doctor had to be fetched across from Port Chalmers. The doctor suggested that the missionary should be brought across to Port Chalmers so that he could be treated more intensively. This was done and his eldest daughter Anna was sent across with him to nurse him. It took another fortnight during which Riemenschneider passed a number of gallstones before he was ready to be transported back to his home to convalesce.

Wohlers himself, who had denied Riemenschneider the chance to go South with Tuckett 20 years ago, was presiding over a peaceful but declining Māori congregation on Ruapuke Island. When he had arrived, in 1844, the island had been the largest concentration of Māori in the Southern part of the country. The former farmer Wohlers had introduced livestock and agriculture along with Christianity and the people had prospered as a result. But nearby Stewart Island and particularly the mainland to the South of it offered more contacts with Pākehā and better access to their resources than the isolated island. By the time Wohlers died, aged 73, on 7 May 1885, only a few old people lived on Ruapuke. Today, the island is no longer permanently inhabited.

The younger Riemenschneider does not appear to have ever regained his full strength and vigour. After the festivities associated with the inauguration of the new church at Ōtākou in December 1864 he had to spend a day in bed recuperating from his exertions in organising them. His papers from 1865 refer to various illnesses. In April he reports that he has still not recovered completely from the severe episode of the previous year,[6] and in October he had been ordered by his doctor to take a complete rest.[7] Needless to say, he ignored the doctor's advice.

By May 1866 Riemenschneider had given up all hope of ever returning to Taranaki. He ends a letter to Pastor Zahn as follows:

> Several of the missionaries have since [the wars] been completely released from

---

5. RP VIII, 187–188.
6. RP VIII, 189.
7. RP VIII, 219.

service among the Maori and have been assigned gospel ministry duties among the Europeans or have devoted themselves to it for the future. Others wait in their places of refuge for the time when they will be able to enter their fields of labour among the natives again and carry on their work among them.

As far as we are concerned, the Lord has assigned us this Maori field of Otago, and any prospect of returning to Taranaki has long since died in my innermost conviction. Partly because of war casualties and partly by natural dying out, the Taranaki tribe has dwindled to little more than 100 survivors; and before the Northern Island enjoys peace and the work of the missionaries will have become possible among the Maori there, there will be too few Taranaki left for us to find a field of labour there. Here in the Province of Otago, on the other hand, we have been entrusted with the care of a field of labour containing 300 souls; although admittedly they are scattered over a wide area and are difficult to reach. I must confess that if it were up to me to wish and to decide I would rather be stationed in Taranaki at some time than here, but the Lord seems to have decided otherwise for us. His will be done in this matter.

I must write you a particular and separate chapter about the "Hauhau" or "Pai Marire" fanaticism – it would lengthen this letter too much.

In order not to miss the approaching departure of the mail this month I cannot add anything except that I conclude the attached letter which I had already started on 2 August by adding a few brief remarks and requests concerning our house here.[8]

With kind regards to the whole Verwaltungsausschuß and all friends and brothers in Christ in the old homeland I remain in deep respect and love,
Your humble
J. Fr. Riemenschneider[9]

This is the last letter in the papers of the North German Mission Society written by Riemenschneider himself. The next letter is from Wohlers, dated Ruapuke, September 5, 1866, and reads as follows:

My dear Inspector Zahn

I am obliged this time to convey sad news to you. It has pleased God to recall our dear brother Riemenschneider at Otago from his labours. I have not received any letter from the widow yet, I assume she is too sad to be able to write, but a minister at Port Chalmers, Otago, has reported his death to me. The letter is dated 28 August and it reports that brother Riemenschneider fell ill on Saturday a week ago (that must have been 18 August) and that last Saturday (this must have been 25 August) he went to his eternal rest. Physically he had been in a lot of pain but there had been peace in his mind.

[The minister] further reported that he did not know how Riemenschneider's worldly affairs stood but he knew that a number of tradesmen's bills had not yet been paid and he asks whether the North German Mission Society would do something for the poor widow and the orphans. I answered him that I confidently hoped that the North German Mission Society would be able to

---

8. This letter has not survived in the Riemenschneider Papers.
9. RP VIII, 256–257.

do something for them and asked him to discuss with the widow how matters stand; whether she was in need at the moment and what would be desirable to do for the future. I asked him to then write to me so that I can report about it to the North German Mission Society.

I hope that it will not be necessary to make the journey to Otago because it costs far too much – the trip cannot be done for under £10. Also, I have no serviceable clothing for it and it costs too much to buy new clothes in this expensive country.

Since I expect to have an opportunity tomorrow to have letters transported to the post and since I have to write a few more letters I must end here. I am incidentally deeply moved by the news which I received last night of brother Riemenschneider's death and at the same time by the news that war has really broken out in Germany.[10]

In his final illness the missionary was attended by Dr Robert Urquhart of Port Chalmers. A small notebook belonging to Urquhart, now in the Port Chalmers museum, contains some hurried pencilled entries. They reveal that the doctor visited Riemenschneider on 22 and 23 August. Unfortunately the doctor's handwriting is very hard to decipher. The entry for August 25 reads (as far as can be ascertained): 'Riemenschneider. All day. [two words illegible] Died 4 p.m.'[11] The official death certificate lists the cause of death as 'disease of the heart'.[12]

While Riemenschneider died at home, in the circle of his family, his eldest son, Friedrich Wilhelm, was absent. Two months before the missionary's death he had been sent to his maternal uncle in Whanganui, E. T. Woon, to learn the draper's trade. In December of 1866, clearly homesick for Dunedin, he writes to the Rev. D. M. Stuart of Dunedin, asking the Reverend gentleman to please send him a Dunedin newspaper every now and again.[13]

The public acknowledgement of Riemenschneider's passing consists of three entries in the *Otago Daily Times*. The death notice appeared on 29 August 1866:

> DIED on the 25th August, at the Mission Station, Otago Heads, the Rev. J. F. Reimenschneider[sic], in the 49th year of his age.

On 31 August 1866, the paper carries a brief description of the missionary's funeral:

> The funeral of the late Rev. J. F. Reimenschneider[sic], Māori Missionary, took place at Port Chalmers yesterday. The coffin with the body had been previously

---

10. North German Mission Society Papers, BSA 7.1025.2/7. The war that Wohlers mentions is most probably the 'Seven Weeks' War' between Prussia and Austria, June to August 1866.
11. I am most grateful to Mr Ian Church, curator of the Port Chalmers Museum, for drawing my attention to the notebook and giving me access to it.
12. Copy in Puke Ariki, ARC2002-578.
13. Stuart family papers, Collection of the Otago Settlers Museum, AG-97.

brought to the Presbyterian Church, at which place the Rev. Mr Johnston[e], assisted by the Rev. Mr Stewart preached the funeral sermon to a large audience, after which, according to deceased's request, the Rev. T. S. Forsaith addressed the Maoris (a large number of whom were present from the Heads) in their native tongue, and afterwards conducted the service at the grave in the same language.

A week later, on 6 September, there is a report of a memorial minute passed by the Presbytery of Otago:

> On the motion of Mr Stuart, it was unanimously agreed to – "That the Presbytery record on its minutes the high sense which they entertain of the late Rev. Mr Riemenschneider's abilities, of the worth of his character, and of the important services he had rendered to the common faith as an earnest Christian Missionary to the Maoris of this country, during twelve years in the North Island, and five years in Otago; and also their profound sympathy with Mrs Riemenschneider and her family in their sore bereavement, commending them to the care and comfort of the Head of the Church, and direct that an extract minute be sent to Mrs Riemenschneider; and also to the Bremen Missionary Society, by which he was maintained."

The headstone on Riemenschneider's grave in the old Port Chalmers cemetery and the railing surrounding the grave were erected with the proceeds of a collection organised by and among his Māori parishioners, although it is likely that some contributions also came from European friends of the missionary.

A description of Riemenschneider's last days, death and funeral has survived. It is by the hand of his wife Catherine, who wrote to Pastor Zahn in Bremen nine months later, on 4 May 1867, in response to his letter of condolence:

> ... His death was rather sudden at the last, for he was ill only one week, but he had been suffering from disease of the liver for some time previous to the last severe attack which took him from us. He had been working for some time in the garden and over-exerted his strength. This, it would appear, was the immediate cause of his sudden death. I sent to Dunedin for the best doctor that I could get. As soon as it was possible for him to reach us he came. The doctor at once pronounced his case hopeless, and my dear husband was quite prepared to learn the worst, for he was well aware of the nature of his complaint. His sufferings were very severe, notwithstanding he was sensible to the last. I myself was not allowed to see him die, for I was expecting my confinement in a few weeks, and the Dr. was afraid of the consequences if I had been allowed to see him. I felt it very keenly for I wished so much to see him breathe his last ...
>
> ... My dear husband expressed a wish to be buried in Port Chalmers by the side of my dear sister, who died in Otago the day after we arrived there. This wish was, of course, carried out. Capt. Thomson of Port Chalmers of whom I dare say you have already heard, became my friend, and undertook to have everything done that was required. All the Natives from the station attended the funeral, as also did a great number of gentlemen from Dunedin as well as

the Port. He was greatly respected by all who knew him and his death deeply regretted. The Natives collected money among themselves and they have erected a very nice iron railing around the grave. Poor creatures, they felt it very much, for they were all greatly attached to their Pastor. They miss him much and I fear they will never get another minister like him, who took such an interest in their welfare. I trust that his labours among them may be abundantly blest.[14]

Riemenschneider's widow found herself in a difficult situation. She had seven children, ranging in age from 16 to 2, and she was seven months pregnant with her eighth child, another girl, Emily Catherine, who was born on 10 October. Catherine had no income and nowhere to live. Captain Thomson, the harbourmaster of Port Chalmers and a good friend of Riemenschneider, undertook to look after the widow's financial affairs. He used £100, which had been paid to Riemenschneider as compensation for the losses he had suffered in Taranaki, to pay off all outstanding debts. He then launched a subscription for the widow and her family and raised £167. Wohlers did his best to find some money for her continued support. On 1 November 1866 he writes to the *Verwaltungsausschuß* asking the Society to make provision for the widow who had moved with her family to Whanganui to live with her youngest brother, E. T. Woon.

In the event, Wohlers sent Mrs Riemenschneider an annuity of £40 from the Society and in later years, £45 or £50. It was little enough. Catherine Riemenschneider's brother in Whanganui contributed money towards the schooling of the children. However, all of this support proved inadequate for a family of seven non-earning children and the widow must have suffered poverty until her death in 1901. Little glimpses of her remain. On 18 June 1868 Wohlers writes to the *Verwaltungsausschuß*:

Widow Riemenschneider has asked me to ask the North German Mission Society to send her annually a chest with clothing as she finds it very difficult to equip herself and her many children with shoes and clothing with the annual £40. I hope that the friends of the mission will help so that a chest can be sent to her every year.[15]

Subsequent letters of Wohlers make it clear that a chest full of clothes was indeed sent to Mrs Riemenschneider for several years following this letter.

Catherine Riemenschneider also sought help from one of her late husband's former friends. In the correspondence of Donald McLean in the Alexander Turnbull Library there are three letters from her, dating from 1869, 1870 and 1876, outlining the plight of the family and asking for some financial help.[16]

---

14. RP VIII, 259–260.
15. *ibid.*
16. Donald McLean, MS Papers, 0032-0537, Alexander Turnbull Library.

There is no letter of thanks for any contributions received. Seven years later, in 1883, Friedrich Wilhelm wrote to McLean with the same plea.[17] He also appears to have been unsuccessful. In terms of material prosperity of Riemenschneider's family, the wheel had turned full circle. Riemenschneider had come into the world as the son of paupers, who appear to have depended on charity to make ends meet. He left his wife and children in poverty, again dependent on support from friends and family.

If Riemenschneider's immediate family keenly felt the loss of their husband and father, the Māori congregations in Otago were also bereft. Their beloved missionary had been taken from them prematurely, and the Otago Society who had so enthusiastically and patronisingly adopted their cause six years ago was no longer a functioning unit. It was again Riemenschneider's good friend Captain Thomson, who had taken steps to ensure the welfare of the widow and children, who took the initiative to look after the welfare of the missionary's congregation. On 9 January 1867, Wohlers passes on to the Inspector of the North German Mission Society, Pastor Zahn, a letter which Thomson had written to him. It reads:

> Will you kindly say whether or not your Society is likely to send another Minister to occupy this corner of our Lord's vineyard wherein the late lamented Rev. Riemenschneider laboured, or if you would recommend such a course. My opinion is that we should no longer be a burden on the home country. Send labourers by all means, but let us support them. I will be glad to hear what your views are in the matter. Meantime our Maories in this locality are quite neglected in their spiritual welfare, it must not continue so.[18]

Wohlers did not feel able to support Captain Thomson's request. He felt that it would be too risky to station a North German missionary at Ōtākou if he had to depend on financial support from the New Zealand community. If the Society did decide to send someone, it would also have to pay his stipend.

It was the Presbyterian church, which had originally shown concern for the Māori at Ōtākou, who decided to take an interest in the continuation of Riemenschneider's work. In December 1867, the Synod's Mission Committee received a letter from Captain Thomson, who would in the meantime have learned that the North German Society did not intend to continue Riemenschneider's work with one of their own missionaries. Thomson informed the committee that the Māori congregation at the Heads would welcome another missionary, and that they felt that they had certain rights with regard to the mission property.[19] At the request of the Synod, the

---

17. Donald McLean, MS Papers, 0032-0863, Alexander Turnbull Library.
18. Wohlers, Letters and Papers, Alexander Turnbull Library, Wellington, Micro-MS 98, reel 2.
19. Presbyterian Church. Minutes of the Mission Committee of the Synod of Otago and Southland, vol. 1, Feb. 20, 1867, to Dec. 15, 1880, p. 10., Hewitson Library, Knox College, Dunedin.

Committee had already written to Wohlers to find out what the intentions of the North German Mission Society were with regard to the establishment at Ōtākou. The reply had been that the Society was not planning to send any further missionaries to New Zealand, but that they considered that they had a claim for compensation for the work carried out by Riemenschneider, at their expense, in enlarging the missionary's house.[20] The Mission Committee's search for a Presbyterian successor for Riemenschneider had at first been unsuccessful. Finally, a letter to the Rev. Dr Duff, Professor of Evangelistic Theology in Scotland, produced a recommendation from the learned professor that they approach the Rev. Alexander Blake, a missionary who had been obliged to return from Madras for health reasons and was currently stationed in a parish in Wales. Blake arrived and took up his duties early in 1869. With his appointment, the changeover from the work of the North German Mission Society to the Presbyterian Church in Otago was complete.

Riemenschneider's fellow North German missionary in the South, Wohlers, soldiered on until his death, aged 73, in 1885. With his passing, the work of the North German Mission Society in New Zealand came to an end. The North German Mission Society continued its activities and has indeed continued them to the present day, with a significant partnership involvement with African churches.

✻

Johann Friedrich Riemenschneider, the man who lies buried on the hillside above the Presbyterian church in Port Chalmers, is not recognised as one of the great figures of 19th century New Zealand history. He came to this country not because he chose to come – he had wanted to go to Africa. He came in obedience to his Mission Society who sent him and his colleagues to New Zealand on a well-intentioned, but inadequately prepared and funded mission.

His first venture in Motukaramū ended in failure, again because of inadequate information, lack of support, lack of experience, and lack of preparation for the conditions he was to encounter in the isolation of the Upper Mōkau. In the end he was forced to deceive the people he had come to serve in order to effect his ignominious retreat from the first station of the North German Mission Society in the North Island of New Zealand.

The second venture in Taranaki, although begun with high hopes and with a much greater chance of success, also ended in failure. Riemenschneider and

---

20. *ibid*. Annual Report for 1867. The North German Mission Society's claim for £75 was finally settled by a payment of £50 to Riemenschneider's widow in March 1869.

the people he served became caught up in the bitter struggle for supremacy between the white settlers and the indigenous Māori population. The missionary, with his North German upbringing and his conservative theology, was unable to read the changing circumstances of the people whom he had come to serve. He found himself confronting a dynamic and emotionally highly charged social and political environment with the static concept of a religion that was seen by his flock more and more as an expression of the colonisers who were antagonistic to the Māori people. At the same time his identification of Māori views and aspirations as inferior and non- or anti-Christian, did not permit him to really identify with the people he had come to serve. Without being fully aware of it, and with the best of intentions, he had usurped the role of the chiefs and elders of Taranaki, and in the name of the God he served he had tried to direct and influence the political fortunes of the tribe. When his message became overwhelmed by the rise of Māori nationalism, fuelled by the increasing polarisation between settler and Māori in the Taranaki area, the messenger himself became a victim and was forced to leave the people he loved.

In some ways, Riemenschneider's work in Otago was successful. He built three churches and, at least for some time, ensured the provision of basic education for Māori in a number of localities. But when he died, his work was not carried on as he would have wished it to have been. The North German Mission withdrew from the field, and the Presbyterian and Anglican churches continued some activity among the Māori in Ōtākou, Waikouaiti and Moeraki. But the Māori in the Otago Province no longer had 'their' pastor, who looked after them with the dedication and zeal that Riemenschneider had devoted to them.

Apart from his legacy as a pastor and teacher, Riemenschneider has also left a wealth of writing that has yet to be fully appreciated and evaluated by New Zealand historians. He decided to live with his Māori flock as long as they tolerated him among them, and his observations about Māori society in the mid 19th century, in spite of his prejudices and value judgements, are an important and valuable record. The same is true for his commentary of the wars in Taranaki. They provide one of the very few Pākehā perspectives from outside beleaguered New Plymouth.

It is, however, Riemenschneider's dedication and zeal as a pastor, coupled with a genuine love for his Māori parishioners, whether in Motukaramū, Taranaki or Otago that characterise his ministry in New Zealand. Plagued by ill health and frequent bouts of severe depression, often neglected by his Society and his supporters, with inadequate resources, he refused to spare himself and toiled tirelessly for the welfare of what he saw as his *tamariki*. Throughout the difficulties and vicissitudes of his career he had remained true to his calling, mindful of the words of his mentor in the sermon preached at his ordination:

> Even if you cannot see any fruits of your labour, and even if not a single soul seems to pay attention to your voice – stand fast and remain *faithful*.[21]

Riemenschneider's legacy will never be fully known. The trauma and bitterness of the Taranaki wars and its aftermath obliterated much of it. It consists, without doubt, of his work with hundreds of individuals who were touched by him, in his advocacy of Māori causes, in his contribution to Māori health, and in the pastoral care, that he gave to his parishioners. It also consists of his passionate preaching of peace, which may have influenced Māori leaders and may well have prevented some bloodshed that would otherwise have taken place during the Puketapu feud and in the Taranaki wars.

The life and work of Johann Friedrich Riemenschneider may perhaps be summed up in the famous prayer of a Roman Catholic saint who would be at the opposite end of the Christian religious spectrum from the protestant missionary. Ignatius of Loyola (1491–1556), the soldier turned scholar and monk, who founded the order of the Society of Jesus, one of whose main tasks is to engage in mission to non-Christian lands, wrote:

> Teach us, good Lord, to serve thee as thou deservest;
> To give, and not to count the cost,
> To fight, and not to heed the wounds,
> To toil, and not to seek for rest,
> To labour, and not to ask for any reward,
> Save that of knowing that we do thy will.

---

21. RP III, 244.

Bibliography

Unpublished Manuscript Sources

Note: The signatures for the various documents, where given, refer to the actual material used. In many cases these materials are typescripts or microfilm copies of the originals. The originals themselves are sometimes held by the same archive or library under a different signature, or they may be held elsewhere.

Allgemeines Tagebuch der von der Norddeutschen Missions Gesellschaft ausgesandten Missionare Wohlers, Riemenschneider, Trost & Heine, auf der neuseeländischen Station in Moutere Disctrict. Nelson Provincial Museum, Heine Papers.

Anglican Church, Otago Rural Deanery Board, Papers, Archives of the Diocese of Dunedin, Hocken Library, AG-349/1/1.

Blaess, F., 'Early Lutheran Church NZ'. Typescript, Alexander Turnbull Library, Wellington, MS Papers 2200, Lutheran Church of New Zealand, folder CR 80/2, p. 11.

Church Missionary Society, Papers, Auckland University Library Microfilm Collection, 79.286–356.

Colonial Hospital, New Plymouth, 6th Annual Report, 1854. Puke Ariki, New Plymouth, ARC2002-21 Wilson, Peter (Dr), Letter Book. Containing Colonial Hospital reports 31 December 1849, 6 January 1851, 3 January 1852, 1853, 1854.

Curtis, George, Letter, Puke Ariki, New Plymouth, ARC2002-168

Fulton, James, Papers, Collection of the Otago Settlers Museum, 2/1/2/1, 2/1/2/5; 2/1/3/1 – 2/1/3/3.

Harper, Henry James Chitty, Bishop, Correspondence, Christchurch Diocesan Archive, Bishop Harper's Outward Letter Book No 1: pp 381-383.

——— Papers of the Anglican Church Otago Rural Deanery Board, Archives of the Diocese of Dunedin, Hocken Library, AG-349/1/1.

Heine, Johann Wilhelm Christoph, Letters and Papers, Staatsarchiv Bremen (BSA), 7.1025, folder 1/2.

——— Letters and Papers, Nelson Provincial Museum, series A, folders A, B, C.

McDonnell, Alexander Francis, Papers, Alexander Turnbull Library, Wellington, MS Papers 151: 1.

McGlashan, John, Papers, Hocken Library, Dunedin, MS 463/7 and MS 463/8 (Correspondence, reports and minutes relating to the 'Society for elevating the condition of the Maories within the Province of Otago'.

McLean, Sir Donald, Papers, Alexander Turnbull Library, Wellington (ATL), MS-Papers-0032. The correspondence with Riemenschneider is in MS-Papers-0032-0537.

——— Extracts from a journal kept during a visit to the tribes of the interior of the northern island of New Zealand, Alexander Turnbull Library, Wellington (ATL), fMS-140.

Marist Fathers, Letters received from Oceanea by the General Administration of the Marist Fathers during the Generalate of John Claude Colin, 1836–1854. Translated by Father R. O'Rielly S. M., Wellington, 1995. Typescript, Marist Archives, Wellington.

Morgan, John (Rev.), Letters and Journals of the Rev. John Morgan, missionary at Otawhao, 1833–1865. Alexander Turnbull Library, Wellington (ATL), qMS1390-1392.

North German Mission Society, Papers, Staatsarchiv Bremen (BSA), 7.1025, folders 81–83.

Otago, Superintendent, correspondence with Colonial Secretary re. court interpreter. National Archives of New Zealand (NA), IA1, 1863/2218.

Port Chalmers Presbyterian Parish, records. Marriage Register, Māori Kaik; 1864–1972. Hewitson Library, Knox College, Dunedin.

Presbyterian Church, Synod of Otago and Southland, Minutes of the Mission Committee, vol. 1, Feb. 20, 1867, to Dec. 15, 1880, p. 10, Hewitson Library, Knox College, Dunedin.

Riemenschneider, Johann Friedrich, Papers, Staatsarchiv Bremen (BSA), 7. 1025, folders 1/1–4. The majority of the Riemenschneider papers have been transcribed by the author. The references refer to the volume and page number of the typed transcript. Thus RP X, 83 refers to Riemenschneider Papers [transcript], vol. X, p. 83. Unless specified, the original text is in German, and all translations are by the author. A microfilm copy of the papers is lodged in Puke Ariki, together with a copy of the author's transcript. ARC2008-007

——— Papers, Puke Ariki, ARC2002-578. (These are mainly papers relating to Riemenschneider, rather than papers written by Riemenschneider.)

——— Extract of letter to Donald McLean, National Archives of New Zealand, G13,2,1855/12.

——— On Maori Habits of Health, MS 303, Hocken Library, Dunedin.

——— Last Will and Testament, National Archives of New Zealand, Dunedin Branch.

Schnackenberg, Cort Henry, Papers, University of Waikato.

Stuart family papers, Collection of the Otago Settlers Museum, AG-97.

Taylor, Richard, Journals, Alexander Turnbull Library, Wellington (ATL), qMS-1984–1999.

——— Correspondence, Auckland City Libraries GNZMS 297.

Te Whiti Orongomai, Erueti, document defending Taranaki against accusations by the Governor. National Archives of New Zealand (NA), MA1 (Box 3).

Tuckett, Frederick, Correspondence with William Wakefield, National Archives of New Zealand (NA), NZC 104/3.

——— Letters, Hocken Library, Dunedin, M.1,156++.

Urquhart, Dr, Notebook, Port Chalmers Museum.

Wesleyan Methodist Missionary Society Papers, containing correspondence between the Secretaries and missionaries stationed in New Zealand. Typescript copy, John Kinder Library, St John the Evangelist Theological College, Auckland.

Whiteley, John, Journal of the Revd John Whiteley, Missionary to New Zealand (typescript), Alexander Turnbull Library, Wellington, Ms, qMS-2212-2213.

Wohlers, Johann Friedrich Heinrich, Letters and Papers, Bremen Staatsarchiv (BSA), 7.1025, folders 2/6, 2/7. Microfilm, Alexander Turnbull Library, Wellington (ATL), Micro-MS 98.

Woon, William, Journal, Alexander Turnbull Library, Wellington (ATL), fMS-263.

Zivilstandsregister Bremen, Heiraten, 1812/473.

Zivilstandsregister Bremen, Sterbefälle, 1855, No. 618; 1861, No. 903.

Published Sources

Abel, Wilhelm. *Massenarmut und Hungerkrisen im vorindustriellen Deutschland*. Göttingen: Vandenhoeck und Ruprecht, 1972.

Abraham, Karl. *Der Strukturwandel im Handwerk in der ersten Hälfte des 19. Jahrhunderts und seine Bedeutung für die Berufserziehung*. Köln: Inst. für Berufserziehung im Handwerk an der Univ., 1955.

Albertz, Heinrich, Wilhelm Garlipp, Dieter Koch, Ernst Kramer, Andreas Röpke, Louis von Zobeltitz. *850 Jahre St Stephani-Gemeinde*. Bremen: Steintor, 1990.

Allan, Ruth. *Nelson: A History of Early Settlement*. Wellington: A. H & A. W. Reed, 1965.

Albertz, Heinrich, et al. *850 Jahre St Stephani-Gemeinde*. Bremen: steintor: BremenVerlagsgesellschaft mbH, 1990.

Alington, Margaret H. *Goodly Stones and Timber. A history of St Mary's church, New Plymouth*. New Plymouth: The Church, 1988.

Andrews, Ian. *Tataraimaka 1847–1993*. [Okato?]: Aries Print [1993]

Angas, George French. *Savage Life and Scenes in Australia and New Zealand: Being an artist's impressions of countries and people at the antipodes. With numerous illustrations*. 2 vols. London: Smith, Elder & Co., 1847 (Reprint Adelaide: Libraries Board of South Australia, 1969).

——— *Maori Scenes and Portraits, illustrated and described by George French Angas*. Ed. A. W. Reed. Wellington: A. H. & A. W. Reed, 1979.

Angel-Volkov, Sulamit. 'The decline of the German handicrafts: Another reappraisal'. *Vierteljahrsschrift für Sozial – und Wirtschaftsgeschichte* 61/2 (1974): 165–184.

Ault, H. F. *The Nelson Narrative: The story of the Church of England in the diocese of Nelson, New Zealand, 1858–1958, with an account of the years 1842–1857*. Nelson: Standing Committee of the Diocese of Nelson, 1958.

Bade, James N. (ed.) 'The Nelson German settlements.' *The German Connection: New Zealand and German-speaking Europe in the nineteenth century*. Auckland: Oxford University Press, 1993, pp. 52–59.

Barber, L. H. 'Maori societal responses to Pākehā entry in the Southern Waikato (1828–1870)'. *Proceedings of the symposium on New Zealand and the Pacific*. [Hamilton]: University of Waikato, 1987. 25.

Barber, L. H., and John Jensen. ' "Henare Minita": A neglected missionary of the second New Zealand war.' *Historical News* 52 (1986): 6–12.

Barrington, J. M., and T. H. Beaglehole. *Maori Schools in a Changing Society.* Wellington: New Zealand Council for Educational Research, 1974.

Bebbington, D. W. *Evangelicalism in Modern Britain. A history from the 1730s to the 1980s.* London; Boston: Unwin Hyman, 1989.

Beever, James. *A Dictionary of Maori Plant Names.* 2nd edn, Auckland: Auckland Botanical Society, 1991.

Begg, Alison. 'The conversion to Christianity of the South Island Māori in the 1840s and 1850s'. *Historical and Political Studies* 3 (1972): 11–17.

Belich, James. *The New Zealand Wars and the Victorian Interpretation of Racial Conflict.* Auckland: Auckland University Press, 1986.

Bericht von der am 6. März 1843 gehaltenen öffentlichen Jahresversammlung des Missionsvereins und der Bibelgesellschaft in Bremen. Bremen: Carl Schünemann, 1843.

Best, Elsdon. *Spiritual and Mental Concepts of the Maori.* 1922. Reprinted. Dominion Museum Monograph No. 2, Wellington: Government Printer 1978.

────── *The Maori School of Learning.* Wellington: Dominion Museum, 1923.

Bloomfield, G. T. *New Zealand: A handbook of historical statistics.* Boston (Mass.): G. K. Hall, 1984.

Booth, Ken et al. *The Farthest Jerusalem: Four lectures on the origins of Christianity in Otago.* Dunedin: Faculty of Theology and Hocken Library, University of Otago, 1993.

Borchardt, Knut. 'The industrial revolution in Germany, 1700–1914'. *The Fontana Economic History of Europe.* vol. 4, New York: Barnes & Noble, 1976-1977.

Bowden, G. R. 'Wairau – a massacre?' *Journal of the New Zealand Federation of Historical Societies* 1 (1981): 3–7.

Bremer Kirchenbote. Eine Zeitschrift. Herausgegeben von Friedrich Mallet, Pastor zu St Stephani. Vol. 1 (1832) – Vol. 16 (1847).

Briars, Jenny, and Jenny Leith. *The road to Sarau. From Germany to Upper Moutere.* Upper Moutere and Nelson: Jenny Briars and Jenny Leith, 1993.

British Parliamentary Papers, Colonies, New Zealand, Shannon: Irish University Press, 1968-, vol. 10.

Brown-Gore, Harriet Louise. *Narrative of the Waitara Purchase and the Taranaki War.* Dunedin: University of Otago Ptress, 1965.

Buck, Peter Henry (Te Rangi Hiroa). *The Coming of the Maori,* Wellington: Maori Purposes Fund Board; Whitcoulls Limited, 1987.

Budd, George. *The Story of Maori Missions.* n. pl: Presbyterian Women's Missionary Union, 1939.

Buddle, Thomas. *The Māori King Movement in New Zealand, with a full report of the native meetings held at Waikato, April and May, 1860.* Auckland: New Zealander Office, 1860, reprinted New York: AMS Press, 1979.

Burns, Patricia. *Te Rauparaha. A new perspective.* Auckland: Reed, 1980.

────── *Fatal success. A history of the New Zealand Company,* ed. Henry Richardson. Auckland: Heinemann Reed, 1989.

Buse, Dieter K. 'Urban and national identity: Bremen 1860–1920'. *Journal of Social History* 26.3 (1993): 521–537.

Butler, Fred B. *Early days in Taranaki*. New Plymouth: Printed for the author by Taranaki Herald, 1942.

Carey, Henry Ernest, *A Poem in Stone. Commemorating 100 years of endeavour in St Mary's parish New Plymouth*. New Plymouth Taranaki Daily News [1943].

Carter, G. G. *John Whiteley, Missionary Martyr*. [Auckland]: Wesley Historical Society of New Zealand, n.d.

Chambers, W. A. *Samuel Ironside in New Zealand, 1839–1858*. Auckland: Ray Richards Publisher, 1982.

Chappell, A. B. *Early Mission Days in South Taranaki*. Hawera: Wesley Historical Society, vol. 1, no. 4, 1942.

Church, Ian. *Heartland of Aotea*. Hawera: Hawera Historical Society, 1992.

——— "Frederick Tuckett: the father of Otago." *GRINZ Yearbook* (1994): 21–26.

Church Missionary Society London. *The Missionary Register*, 1–43, London: L. B. Seeley, 1813–1855.

Clark, Paul. *'Hauhau': The Pai Marire search for Maori identity*. Auckland: Auckland University Press, 1975.

Clover, Gary A. M. 'Christianity among the South Taranaki Māoris 1840–53; a study of the Wesleyan mission at Waimate South'. Thesis (MA), University of Auckland, 1973.

Conze, Werner. *Arbeiterexistenz im 19. Jahrhundert : Lebensstandard und Lebensgestaltung deutscher Arbeiter und Handwerker*. Stuttgart: Klett-Cotta, 1981.

Cowan, James. *The New Zealand Wars and the Pioneering Period*. 2 vols. Wellington: Government Printer, 1922 (reprint 1983).

——— *Sir Donald McLean. The story of a New Zealand statesman*. Dunedin, Wellington: Reed, 1940.

Craig, Dick. *Land of the Maniapoto: A brief history of the area now known as the Northern King Country, embracing the Otorohanga, Kawhia and Waitomo Counties*. Te Kuiti: King Country Chronicle, 1951.

——— *King Country: NZ's last frontier*. Te Awamutu: [Mount Maunganui, NZ: R.S. Craig], 1990 (Te Awamutu: Te Awamutu Couriers NZ Ltd), 1990.

——— *The realms of King Tawhiao: with review of causes of 1860-64 Maori Wars*. Tauranga: D. Craig, 1995.

Dacker, Bill. *Te Mamae me te Aroha. The pain and the love. A history of Kai Tahu Whanui in Otago, 1844–1994*. Dunedin: University of Otago Press, 1994.

Dalton, B. J. *War and politics in New Zealand 1855–1870*. Sydney: Sydney University Press, 1967.

Davies, John. *A History of Wales*. London: Allen Lane the Penguin Press, 1993.

Day, Kelvin. *Warea School and district Centennial, 1884–1894*. New Plymouth: Jubilee Booklet Committee, 1985.

——— "Iwi flour mills". *New Zealand Historic Places* 55 (1995): 26–28.

Devenish, Lucy Hannah. *The Story of St Mary's Church, New Plymouth NZ*. 2nd edn. New Plymouth: The Church, 1936.

Dictionary of New Zealand Biography. Volume 1: 1769–1869. Wellington: Allen and Unwin/Department of Internal Affairs, 1990.

Dieffenbach, Ernest. *Travels in New Zealand*. London: John Murray, 1843; reprint Christchurch: Capper Press, 1974.

Dieser Stat Armenhaus zum Bethen und Arbeiten. Geschichte des Armenhauses zu Bremen. Bremen: Senat für Soziales, Jugend und Sport, 1979.

The Dillon Letters. The letters of the Hon. Constantine Dillon, 1842–1853. Ed. C. A. Sharp. Wellington: A. H. & A. W. Reed, 1954.

Donnelly, Bernadette M. "The Māori King movement". Thesis. University of Auckland, Auckland, 1949.

Dow, Derek A. *Annotated Bibliography for the History of Medicine and Health in New Zealand.* Dunedin: Hocken Library, University of Otago, 1994.

Eberhadt, Wolfgang. 'Der Bremer Jünglingsverein'. *Christlicher Verein Junger Männer, Mitteilungen* 2 (1959): 6–9.

Eccles, Alfred, and A. H. Reed. *John Jones of Otago: whaler, coloniser, shipowner, merchant.* Wellington: A. H. & A. W. Reed, 1949.

Elliott, Gabriel. *Sowing the Seed in Pioneer New Zealand.* Auckland: Wesley Historical Society of New Zealand, vol. 16, no. 5, 1960.

Elsmore, Bronwyn. *Like Them That Dream: The Maori and the Old Testament.* Tauranga: Tauranga Moana Press, 1985.

—— *Mana From Heaven: A century of Maori prophets in New Zealand.* Tauranga: Tauranga Moana Press, 1989.

Entholt, Friedrich. *Bilder aus der Geschichte des bremischen Volksschulwesens. Ergänzt und fortgesetzt von Hinrich Wulff.* Bremen: G. Winters Buchhandlung [1928].

'Die erste deutsche Kirche in Neu-Seeland'. *Bremer Kirchenbote* 14.16, 26 April (1845): 61–62.

Festschrift zur fünfzigjährigen Jubelfeier der Norddeutschen Missionsgesellschaft, herausgegeben von der Committee. Bremen: Norddeutsche Missionsgesellschaft, 1886.

Firth, Raymond. *Economics of the New Zealand Maori.* 2nd edn. Wellington: Government Printer, 1959.

Gadd, B. 'The teachings of Te Whiti o Rongomai'. *Journal of the Polynesian Society* 75 (1966): 445–457.

Garrett, Helen. *Te Manihera. The life and times of the pioneer missionary Robert Maunsell.* Auckland: Reed Books, 1991.

Gavin, G. H., E. W. M. Lysons, and H. E. Carey. *The Taranaki Archdeaconry. Its history and associations.* Taihape: Taihape Times, 1955.

Geremek, Bronislav. *Poverty: A history.* Translated by Agnieszka Kolakowska. Cambridge (Mass.): Blackwell, 1994.

The German Family. Essays on the social history of the family in nineteenth and twentieth century Germany. Ed. Richard J. Evans and W. R. Lee. London: Croom Helm, 1981.

'Geschichte des Bremer Missionsvereins von seiner Entstehung bis zur Gründung der Norddeutschen Missionsgesellschaft'. *Bremer Kirchenbote* Heft 2.9 (1836): 105–110.

Gilbert, Thomas. *New Zealand Settlers and Soldiers, or, the War in Taranaki: Being incidents in the life of a settler.* London: A. W. Bennett, 1861.

Glen, Frank. 'Church Leaders and their First Taranaki War, 1860–1861: an exploration of their influence and theology'. Thesis. University of Waikato, Hamilton, 1992.

Glen, Robert (ed.), *Mission and Moko; Aspects of the Work of the Church Missionary Society in New Zealand 1814–1882.* Christchurch: Latimer Fellowship of New Zealand, 1992.

Gluckman, L. K. *Medical History of New Zealand Prior to 1860.* Auckland: Dr L. K. Gluckman, 1976.

Gorst, John E. *The Maori King, Or the Quarrel with the Natives of New Zealand.* Ed. Keith Sinclair, Hamilton and Auckland: Paul's Book Arcade; London: Oxford University Press, 1959.

Grayling, W. I. *The War in Taranaki, During the Years 1860–61.* New Plymouth: G. W. Woon, 1862.

Greenslade, W. W. H. *John Whiteley 1806–1869.* Auckland: Wesley Historical Society, 1968.

Greenwood, William. *Riemenschneider of Warea.* Wellington, Auckland, Sydney: A. H. & A. W. Reed, 1967.

Griffin, Erin Michael. *Tales of Te Namu and Hori Teira.* New Plymouth: Taranaki Newspapers Ltd [1972].

Hahn, Ernst Joachim, "Die Geschichte der Norddeutschen Missionsgesellschaft", Dissertation, Tübingen, 1943.

Hammer, G. E. J. *Pioneer Missionary, Raglan to Mokau, 1844–1880. Cort Henry Schackenberg.* Auckland: Wesley Historical Society, 1991. Proceedings of the Wesley Historical Society New Zealand, no. 57.

Hammond, T. G. *'In the Beginning': The history of a mission.* 2nd edn. Auckland: Methodist Literature and Colporteur Society, 1940.

Head, L. 'The gospel of Te Ua Haumene'. *Journal of the Polynesian Society* 101 (March 1992): 2 5.

'Die hiesige Sonntagsschule'. *Bremer Kirchenbote* No 11.13 (1838): 97–101.

Hill, Edward. *There Was a Taranaki Land League.* Wellington: Wellington Historical Association, 1969.

Hocken, T. M. *Contributions to the Early History of New Zealand (Settlement of Otago).* London: Sampson Low, Marston & Co., 1898.

Houston, John. *Maori Life in Old Taranaki.* Wellington: A. H. & A. W. Reed, 1965.

Howe, K. R., Missionaries, Maoris, and "Civilisation" in the Upper-Waikato, 1833–1863. A study in culture contact, with special reference to the attitudes and activities of the Reverend John Morgan of Otawhao. Thesis (MA). University of Auckland, Auckland, 1970.

Hubbard, William. *Familiengeschichte: Materialien zur deutschen Familie seit dem Ende des 18. Jahrhunderts.* München: Beck, 1983.

Hunwick, E. C. 'Missioner shouldered cross of a wilderness station'. *Footprints of History* 3 (1989): 49–51.

Hursthouse, Charles Jun. *An Account of the Settlement of New Plymouth, in New Zealand, from Personal Observation, During a Residence of Three to Five Years.* London: Smith, Elder & Co., 1849 (reprint Christchurch, 1975).

Ingram, C. W. N. *New Zealand Shipwrecks: 195 years of disasters at sea.* Auckland: Beckett, c. 1990.

Irwin, James. 'Some Māori responses to the Western form of Christianity'. *Religion in New Zealand.* Ed. Christopher Nichol and James Veitch. 2nd edn. Wellington: C. Nichol for the Tertiary Christian Studies Programme of the Combined Chaplaincies and the Religious Studies Department at Victoria University of Wellington, 1983. 54.

Jensen, J. H., and L. H. Barber. 'The Schnackenberg family papers'. *Auckland–Waikato Historical Journal* 51 (1987): 24–27.

Johnstone, J. C. *The Māories and the Causes of the Present Anarchy in New Zealand*. [Auckland]: Southern Cross, 1861.

Knight, Hardwicke. *Otago Peninsula: A local history*. 2nd edn. Broad Bay, Dunedin: Allied Press, 1978.

—— *Church Building in Otago*. Dunedin: H. Knight, 1993.

Köhler, Ernst. *Arme und Irre. Die liberale Fürsorgepolitik des Bürgertums*. Berlin: Klaus Wagenbach, 1977.

Kohlmann, Pastor. 'Bericht des Missionsvereins, abgestattet von Pastor Kohlmann'. *Bericht von der am 6. Maerz 1843 gehaltenen oeffentlichen Jahresversammlung des Missionsvereins und der Bibelgesellschaft in Bremen*. Bremen: Carl Schuenemann, 1843.

Lambert, Gail. *Peter Wilson, Colonial Surgeon*. Palmerston North: Dunmore Press, 1981.

Lambert, Gail, and Ron Lambert. *An Illustrated History of Taranaki*. Palmerston North: Dunmore Press, 1983.

Lash, Max D. *Nelson Notables 1840–1940. A dictionary of regional biography*. Nelson: Nelson Historical Society, 1992.

Laurenson, George I. *Te Hahi Weteriana. Three half centuries of the Methodist Maori Mission*. vol. 27, nos 1 and 2. [Auckland]: Wesley Historical Society of New Zealand, 1972.

Lawn, C. A. *The Pioneer Surveyors of New Zealand*. [Wellington]: New Zealand Institute of Surveyors, 1980.

Leadley, Alan. *A Brief History of the Kawhia Methodist Mission*. Kirikiriroa (Hamilton): Waikato-Bay of Plenty Bicultural Working Group, 1994.

Lehmann, Hans. *Geschichte des evangelischen Missionsvereins und der Norddeutschen Mission in Hamburg: Ein Beitrag zur Hundertjahrfeier der Norddeutschen Missionsgesellschaft am 9. April 1936*. Bremen: Verlag der Norddeutschen Missionsgesellschaft, 1936.

Lenger, Friedrich. *Zwischen Kleinbürgertum und Proletariat. Studien zur Sozialgeschichte der Düsseldorfer Handwerker*. Göttingen: Vandenhoeck und Ruprecht, 1986.

Lennard, Guy. *Sir William Martin*. Christchurch: Whitcombe & Tombs, 1961.

Lineham, P. J., and A. R. Grigg. *Religious History of New Zealand: A bibliography*. 3rd edn. Palmerston North: Department of History, Massey University, 1989.

Lyons, Daniel P. 'An analysis of three Māori prophet movements'. *Conflict and compromise: essays on the Māori since colonisation*. Ed. I. H. Kawharu. Wellington: Reed, 1975. 55–79.

McLean, Sally. 'A place of learning'. *New Zealand Historic Places* 43 (1993) N: 11–14.

Mallet, Friedrich Ludwig. 'Aufforderung'. *Bremer Kirchenbote* 3.6 (1833): 838–839.

—— *Altes und Neues*. Bremen: Müller, 1865.

Mandeno, J. F. 'The Rangiaowhia Mission of the Holy Angels'. *Footprints of History* 3 (1988a): 52–57.

—— 'Wesleyan missions on the West Coast and inland'. *Footprints of History* 1 (1988b): 15–18.

Martin, Sir William. *The Taranaki Question*. Auckland: Melanesian Press, 1860. Reprint Dunedin: Hocken Library, University of Otago, 1967.

McAloon, J. *Nelson, a Regional History*. Auckland: Cape Catley, 1997.

McCluskey, F. H. *Down the Bay. The history of the ferries on Otago Harbour*. Wellington: New Zealand Ship & Marine Society Inc., 1995 (reprint, 1996).

McComb, H. *125th Year of the Waikouaiti School, 1860–1985.* [Waikouaiti: J. Porter, 1985].

McDonald, K. C. *City of Dunedin. A century of civic enterprise.* Dunedin: Dunedin City Council, 1965.

McKean, John. *The Road to Secularisation in Presbyterian Dunedin: The first fifty years of the Otago settlement.* Dunedin: Presbyterian Historical Society, 1993.

McLintock, A. H. *The History of Otago: The origins and growth of a Wakefield class settlement.* Dunedin: Otago Centennial Historical Publications, 1949.

——— *The Church in a Special Colony. A history of the Presbyterian Synod of Otago & Southland 1866–1991.* Dunedin: Synod of Otago & Southland, 1994.

Metge, Joan, and P. Kinloch. *Talking Past Each Other.* Wellington: Price, Milburn, 1979.

Meurer, Wilhelm Hermann. *Zur erinnerung an Friedrich Ludwig Mallet, weil. Dr. theol. Und Pastor prim. An St. Stephani zu Bremen: eine biographische Charakteristik des Verstorbenen aus dessen hinterlassenen Briefen und Schriften.* Bremen: Müller, 1866.

Mission and Moko: The Church Missionary Society in New Zealand, 1814–1882. Christchurch: Latimer Fellowship, 1992.

Mittheilungen von der Norddeutschen Missiongesellschaft, herausgegeben von Johann Hartwig Brauer, Inspector. Hamburg, 1–16, 1845–1850.

Monats-Blatt der Norddeutschen Missions-Gesellschaft. [Bremen, Hamburg], 1–10, 1840–1850; 1–25, (New Series), 1851–1875; 1- (New Series), 1876-.

Moorhead, Murray. *Tales of Old New Plymouth.* New Plymouth: Taranaki Branch, N.Z. Founders Society, 1990.

——— *Tales of Old North Taranaki.* New Plymouth: Murray Moorhead, 1991.

Morgan, B. *Historic Māori Place Names from the Waipa River to Mokau.* Taumarunui: King Country Chronicle [1976].

Morton, H. *The Whale's Wake.* Dunedin: McIndoe for the University of Otago Press, 1982.

Mullon, Herbert D. *These Hundred Acres. The story of Whiteley township, city of New Plymouth.* New Plymouth: H. D. Mullon, 1969.

Murray, Janet. 'A missionary in action'. *The Feel of Truth.* Ed. Peter Munz. Wellington: A. H. & A. W. Reed, 1969. 197–218.

'Nachrichten'. *Bremer Kirchenbote* 11.43 (1842): 170–172.

Natusch, Sheila. *Brother Wohlers. A biography of J.F.H. Wohlers of Ruapuke.* Wellington: Nestegg Press, 1992.

——— *Hell and high water. A German occupation of the Chatham Islands, 1843–1910.* 2nd edn, Christchurch: Caxton Press, 1992.

Neale, June. *Pioneer Passengers: To Nelson by Sailing Ship, March 1842 – June 1843.* Nelson: Anchor Press, 1982.

——— *The Nelson Police.* Nelson: New Zealand Police, Nelson District, 1986.

Newport, J. N. W. *A Short History of the Nelson Province.* Nelson: Nikau Press, 1991.

The New Zealand Journal. London: H. H. Chambers, 1840–1850.

New Zealand Waitangi Tribunal, *The Taranaki Report: kaukapa tautaki: WAI 143: muru me te raupatu.* Wellington: GP Publications, 1996.

'Norddeutsche Missionsgesellschaft'. *Bremer Kirchenbote* 11.41 (1842): 162–163.

Nottingham, I. M. 'The Coming of the missionaries. A study of evangelical beliefs and Maori understandings'. Thesis. University of Waikato, Hamilton, 1980.

Oehler, Wilhelm. *Geschichte der evangelischen Mission.* Vol. 1. Baden Baden: Fehrholz, 1949.

Oettli, Peter, 'Two early Māori travellers in Germany', *Archifacts* (October 1991): 1–11.

——— "'Please excuse the dark smudges, dear Fathers'. The Papers of Johann Friedrich Riemenschneider", *Archifacts* (April 1993): 1–13.

——— 'The Taranaki Bible-burying incident – A footnote'. *Turnbull Library Record* 29 (1996): 85–90.

Olssen, Erik. *A History of Otago.* Dunedin: John McIndoe, 1984.

Otago Provincial Council, *Votes and Proceedings of the Provincial Council*, Session VI, 1857.

Owens, John. 'The unexpected impact. Missionaries and society in early 19th century New Zealand'. *Religion in New Zealand.* 2nd edn. [Wellington]: Published by C. Nichol for the Tertiary Christian Studies Programme of the combined chaplaincies and the Religious Studies Deptartment at Victoria University of Wellington, 1983. 14–53.

Owens, J. M. R, *The Mediator. A Life of Richard Taylor, 1895–1873.* Wellington: Victoria University Press, 2004.

Parliamentary Debates (Hansard), House of Representatives. Wellington: Government Printer, 1856–1858.

Parr, J. C. 'Maori literacy'. *Journal of the Polynesian Society* 72 (1963): 211–234.

——— 'Before the Pai Marire'. *Journal of the Polynesian Society* 76 (n.y.): 35–46.

Partridge, C. *Calumny Refuted, the Colonists Vindicated and the Right Horse Saddled: A brief review of mis-government in New Zealand. The cause of the native rebellion.* Auckland: Creighton and Scales, 1864.

Peart, J. D. *Old Tasman Bay. A story of the early Maori of the Nelson district.* Nelson: Lucas, 1937.

The People of Many Peaks. The Māori biographies from the Dictionary of New Zealand Biography. Vol. 1, Wellington: Bridget Williams Books and Department of Internal Affairs, 1990.

Pezant, Father Jean. Letters received from Oceania by the general administration of the Marist Fathers during the generalate of John Claude Colin, 1836–1854. Translated by Fr. R. O'Rielly S.M., n. d.

Phillips, Donald. 'Methodism'. *The Farthest Jerusalem. Four lectures on the origins of Christianity in Otago.* Dunedin: Faculty of Theology and Hocken Library, University of Otago, 1993.

Pool, D. Ian. *The Maori Population of New Zealand 1769–1971.* Auckland: Auckland University Press, 1977.

Pratt M. A. Rugby. *Nelson Methodist Centenary Souvenir.* Vol. 2, no. 1. Nelson: R. W. Stiles, 1942.

Prickett, N. *Excavations at Warea redoubt, January–February 1978.* Auckland: Auckland University Archaeological Society, 1977.

——— *Historic Taranaki. An archaeological guide.* Wellington: GP Books, 1990.

Prüser, Friedrich. *Achthundert Jahre St Stephanikirche. Ein Stück Bremischer Geschichte.* Bremen: Arndt Verlag Melchers & Boettcher, 1940.

Pybus, T. A. *It Happened in Otakou: A centennial souvenir, 1840–1940.* Dunedin: Star Print, 1940.

Pybus, T. A. *Maori and Missionary: Early Christian missions in the South Island of New Zealand.* Wellington: A. H. & A. W. Reed, 1954.

Rakena, R. *The Maori Response to the Gospel.* Auckland: Wesley Historical Society of New Zealand, 1971.

Raumer, Kurt von, and Manfred Botzenhart. *Deutsche Geschichte im 19. Jahrhundert. Deutschland um 1800: Krise und Neugestaltung. Von 1789 bis 1815.* (Handbuch der deutschen Geschichte, neu herausgegeben von Leo Just, vol 3./1a.) Wiesbaden: Akademische Verlagsgesellschaft Athenaion, 1980.

Reed, A. H. *Annals of Early Dunedin: Chronicles of the eighteen-sixties.* Wellington: Reed, 1973.

Richards, Rhys. 'Plans for a German Colony on the Chatham Islands'. *The German Connection: New Zealand and German-Speaking Europe in the nineteenth century.* Ed. James N. Bade. Auckland: Oxford University Press, 1993, pp. 46–51.

The Richmond-Atkinson papers. Guy H. Scholefield (ed.) Vol. 1. Wellington: Government Printer, 1960.

Riemenschneider, J. Fr. 'Nachricht'. *Bremer Kirchenbote* 12.5, 11 Feb. (1843): 20.

——— 'Aus einem Briefe des Missionspredigers Riemenschneider.' *Bremer Kirchenbote* 14.50 (1845a): 198–200.

——— 'Aus einem Briefe des Missionspredigers Riemenschneider (Schluß)'. *Bremer Kirchenbote* 14.51 (1845b): 201–204.

Rosenbaum, Heidi. *Formen der Familie: Untersuchungen zum Zusammenhang von Familienverhältnissen, Sozialstruktur und sozialem Wandel in der deutschen Gesellschaft des 19. Jahrhunderts.* Frankfurt am Main: Suhrkamp, 1982.

Ross, C. Stuart. *The Story of the Otago Church and Settlement.* Dunedin: Wise, Caffin & Co, 1887.

Rutherford, J., and W. H. Skinner. *The Establishment of the New Plymouth Settlement in New Zealand 1840–1843.* New Plymouth: Thomas Avery & Sons Ltd, 1940.

Sargison, A. J. 'The multi-racial society 1855–60. A vision destroyed'. *Historical and Political Studies* 3 (1972): 18–24.

Scanlan, A. B. *Historic New Plymouth.* Wellington: A. H. & A. W. Reed, 1968.

Schnabel, Franz, (ed.). *Die protestantischen Kirchen in Deutschland.* Vol. Deutsche Geschichte im neunzehnten Jahrhundert, vol. 8. Freiburg i. Br.: Herder, 1964.

Schöck-Quinteros, Eva and Dieter Lenz (eds). *150 Jahre Norddeutsche Mission.* Bremen: Norddeutsche Mission, 1986.

Schwarzwälder, Herbert. *Geschichte der freien Hansestadt Bremen.* Vol. 2 of 4 vols. Bremen: Röver, 1976.

Scott, Dick. *Ask That Mountain. The story of Parihaka.* Auckland: Reed–Southern Cross, 1975.

Sechzehnter Bericht des evangelischen Missionsvereins in Hamburg vom Jahre 1839. Hamburg: Evangelischer Missionsverein, 1839.

Sheehan, James J. *German History, 1779–1866.* Oxford: Clarendon Press, 1989.

Shortland, E. *Tradition and Superstitions of the New Zealanders.* 2nd edn. London: Longman, Brown, Green, Longmans & Roberts, 1856.

Simpson, Tony. *Te Riri Pakeha – the white man's anger.* Auckland: Hodder and Stoughton, 1986.

Sinclair, Keith. *The Maori Land League. An examination into the source of a New Zealand myth.* Auckland: Auckland University College, 1950.

Sinclair, Keith. 'Maori nationalism and the European economy 1850–1860'. *Historical Studies, Australia and New Zealand* 5 (November 1951 – May 1953) N: 119–134.

——— *The Origins of the Māori Wars.* Wellington: New Zealand University Press, 1957.

——— 'Te tikanga pakeke: The Māori anti-landselling movements in Taranaki' 1849–59. *The Feel of Truth. Essays in New Zealand and Pacific history.* Ed. Peter Munz. Wellington: A. H. & A. W. Reed, 1969: 79–92.

——— *Kinds of Peace. Maori people after the wars 1870–85.* Auckland: Auckland University Press, 1991.

Skinner, W. H. *Pioneer Medical Men of Taranaki, 1834–1880: With an account of the establishment of hospital accommodation at New Plymouth.* New Plymouth: Thomas Avery, 1933.

Smith, Ailsa. 'Ko Tohu te Matua: the story of Tohu Kakahi'. Thesis. University of Canterbury, Christchurch, 1991.

——— *Songs and Stories of Taranaki. He tuhituhinga tai hau-a-uru.* Christchurch: Macmillan Brown Centre for Pacific Studies, University of Canterbury, Christchurch, 1993.

Smith, Dawn. 'Cow herding in the Moutere'. *Journal of the Nelson and Marlborough History Societies* 2, no. 2 (1988): 39–40.

Smith, Percy S. *An 1858 Journey into the Interior.* New Plymouth: Taranaki Herald, 1953.

——— *History and Traditions of the Maoris of the West Coast North Island of New Zealand prior to 1840.* Christchurch: Capper Press, 1984.

——— 'Clairvoyance among the Maoris'. *Journal of the Polynesian Society* 29, no. 115 (September 1920): 149–161.

Sole, Tony. *Ngati Ruanui. A history.* Wellington: Huia Publishers, 2005.

Sorrenson, M. P. K. 'The Maori king movement'. *Studies of a Small Democracy.* Ed. Robert Chapman and Keith Sinclair. Auckland: Blackwood and Janet Paul Ltd, 1963. 33–55.

Springer, Randal. 'William Woon – printer and missionary'. *Historical Record. Journal of the Whanganui Historical Society* 25, no. 2 (1994): 2–8.

Statistics of New Zealand for the Crown Colony Period, 1840–1852. Auckland: Department of Economics, Auckland University College, 1954.

Stokes, Evelyn. *Mokau: Maori cultural and historical perspectives.* Hamilton: University of Waikato, 1988.

Swainson, William. *New Zealand and the War.* London: Smith, Elder & Co, 1862 (reprint Christchurch: Capper Press, 1984).

Taylor, Richard. *The Past and Present of New Zealand: With its prospect for the future.* London: William Macintosh, 1868.

Te Whiti o Rongomai of Parihaka as seen by his contemporaries. [Hamilton: Printed for the Waikato Museum by the Hamilton Printing Works [1973].

Thomson, Arthur S. *The Story of New Zealand.* London: John Murray, 1859.

Thomson, Jane. 'Some reasons for the failure of the Roman Catholic mission to the Māoris, 1838–1860'. *The New Zealand Journal of History* 3 (1969): 166–174.

Tiesmeyer, L. *Eine deutsche Missionsarbeit auf Neu-Seeland. Lebensgeschichte des Missionars J. Fr. Riemenschneider.* Bremen: W. Valett & Co., 1875.

——— *Die Erweckungsbewegung in Deutschland während des 19. Jahrhunderts. 10. Heft: Die drei Hansestädte Bremen, Hamburg, Lübeck, Kassel.* Kassel: Röttger, 1908.

Treue, Wilhelm, *Wirtschaft, Gesellschaft und Technik Deutschlands im 19. Jahrhundert.* Munich: dtv, 1999. (*Handbuch der deutschen Geschichte,* ed. Bruno Gebhard, vol. 17).

Treviranus, G. G. 'Wie wurde Bremen aus einer lutherischen Stadt eine reformierte?' *Bremer Kirchenbote* 1, Heft 2 and 3 (1832): 10–104, 163–180.

Troup, Mary. 'A church divided'. *Archifacts* 24 (1982): 669–671.

——— 'Stones of contention' *Archifacts* 25 (1983): 13–14.

Tucker, Sarah. *The Southern Cross and Southern Crown, or, the Gospel in New Zealand.* London: J. Nisbet, 1855.

Tullett, J. S. *The Industrious Heart. A history of New Plymouth.* New Plymouth: New Plymouth City Council, 1981.

Wake, C. H. 'George Clarke and the government of the Maoris: 1840–45'. *Historical Studies, Australia and New Zealand* 10 (Nov. 1961–May 1963): 339–356.

Wakefield, Edward Jerningham. *Adventure in New Zealand from 1839–1844.* London: J. Murray, 1845, reprint Auckland: Wilson & Horton, 1971.

Ward, Alan. *A show of Justice. Racial 'amalgamation' in nineteenth century New Zealand.* Auckland: Auckland University Press, 1973.

Ward, J. P. *Wanderings with the Maori prophets, Te Whiti and Tohu.* Nelson: Bond, Finney & Co., 1883.

Ward, Robert. *Life among the Maories of New Zealand: being a description of missionary, colonial and military achievements.* Ed. Rev. Thomas Lowe and Rev. William Whitby. London: Lamb, 1872.

Wards, Ian. *The Shadow of the Land: a study of British policy and racial conflict in New Zealand 1832–1852.* Wellington: Historical Publications Branch, Department of Internal Affairs: A. R. Shearer, Government Printer, 1968.

Warren, John. *The Christian Mission to the Aborigines of New Zealand. Its connection with the colonization of the country, and the results which have followed. A lecture delivered at the Odd Fellows Hall, Auckland, to the Y.M.C.A., July 9, 1863.* Auckland: Creighton & Scales, 1863.

Wells, Benjamin. *The History of Taranaki.* New Plymouth: Edmundson & Avery, 1878.

Wenig, Otto. *Rationalismus und Erweckungsbewegung in Bremen Vorgeschichte, Geschichte und theologischer Gehalt der Bremer Kirchenstreitigkeiten von 1830 bis 1852.* Bonn: Bouvier, 1966.

White, John. *Lectures on Maori Customs and Superstitions.* Wellington: Government Printer, 1861.

Wilkens, Cornelius August. *Friedrich Mallet, der Zeuge der Wahrheit. Eine Biographie aus handschriftlichen und gedruckten Quellen zur Stärkung des Glaubens.* Bremen: Müller, 1872.

Williams, H. W. *Dictionary of the Maori Language.* 7th edn. Wellington: GP Publications Ltd, 1992.

Williams, William. *Christianity Among the New Zealanders.* London: Seeley, Jackson & Halliday, 1867.

Wilson, Ormond. *From Hongi Hika to Hone Heke. A quarter century of upheaval.* Dunedin: John McIndoe, 1985.

Wiltgen, Ralph M. *The Founding of the Roman Catholic Church in Oceania, 1825–1850.* Canberra: Australian National University Press, 1981.

Wohlers, J. F. H. 'On the conversion of the Maoris in the South of New Zealand'. *Transactions and Proceedings of the New Zealand Institute* 14 (1881): 123–134.

Wohlers, J. F. H. *Memories of the Life of J. F. H. Wohlers, missionary at Ruapuke, New Zealand. An autobiography.* Translated from the German by John Houghton. Dunedin: Otago Daily Times and Witness Newspapers, 1895.

Wolf, Stuart Joseph. *The Poor in Western Europe in the Eighteenth and Nineteenth Centuries.* London, New York: Methuen, 1986.

Wood, R. G. *From Plymouth to New Plymouth.* Wellington: A. W. Reed, 1959.

Wright-St Clair, R. E. 'Maori health in the mid-nineteenth century'. *New Zealand Medical Journal* 101 (1988): 14-15.

Zobeltitz, Louis von. 'Theologische Hauptströmungen in St Stephani von der Reformation bis ins 19. Jahrhundert'. *850 Jahre St Stephani-Gemeinde.* Bremen: Steintor, pp. 25–73.

Index

Ahitona 187
Ahitone 175
Ahuahu 71
Airedale 173, 175, 181, 186 n13
Aldred, J 35, 39–40, 49
Angas, George French 75 n48
Anglican 35–36, 39, 41, 46, 48 n10, 49, 51, 65, 67, 76, 78, 81–83, 85–87, 90, 114, 122, 130, 134, 156, 162, 168, 181, 183, 186, 193, 197–198, 200, 232
Anglicans 39, 45, 48 n10, 49, 76, 81, 86, 183, 193, 197–198, 200
Anglo-Catholic 40, 81, 88
Aotea 71 n38
Aparima River 195 n40
Āperahama *see* Te Reke, Āperahama
Ashwell, George 210
Atlantic 27, 29
Auckland 65, 81 n10, 82 n11, 85, 125, 137, 141–142, 181, 184, 193
Australia 35, 54, 75 n48, 209 n20,

Bahia 29–32
Baker, Charles 213 n27
Baker, Charles Pratt 193, 197, 201, 203 n1
Basel 9–10
Bay of Islands 17, 123, 181 n40
Beit, John Nicholas 19, 27–31, 34, 37–38, 41, 43
Belich, James 168, 170
Bell, Francis Dillon 132, 201–202
Bell Block 132
Berlin 10, 15, 17
Blaess, F. K. G. 222
Blake, Alexander 231
Bolland, William 51, 66, 81, 85–86, 90–91, 130 n25, 162, **Pl.13**
Border Maid 125

Brauer, Johann Hartwig 11–19, 31, 33, 36 n24, 37, 105–106, 108 n20, 125–126, 224
Brazil 29
Bremen 1–12, 14–16, 19, 22–25, 27, 50–51, 57, 104–105, 106 n14, 113–114, 116, 118, 123, 126–129, 134–135, 139, 146, 152, 154, 162, 166, 171, 174–176, 181–184, 189, 194–196, 202, 203 n1, 206, 208, 210, 212, 215, 223–224, 228
Bremen Mission Society 10
Bristol 35 n20
Brown, Captain 173
Brown, Charles 135 n10
Browne, Thomas Gore 137–138, 144–145, 160, 163, 167, 173, 185, 190, 192
Bruce 208
Burns, Patricia 29
Butt, Henry Francis 46, 52, 69, 72–73
Buttle, George 70–71

Calvin, John 3
Calvinist 40, 66 n22, 92, 113
Calvinistic 130
Cambridge 40, 51 n17
Canterbury 35 n20
Carbon 108
Cargill, William 192
Carrington, Octavius 166
Catholic 3, 55–56, 63, 65, 68–69, 75–76, 83, 91, 233
Catholicism 81, 84
Chatham Islands 16, 19
Church Missionary Society 15–16, 18, 52, 65–66, 69, 83, 87 112, 117, 125–126, 146 n34, 154, 181, 193, 218
Chute, Trevor 218
Cloudy Bay 19, 33, 35
Clutha River 203

Connebee, Richard   209 n20
Constant, Constance   210
Cook Strait   32, 50
Cornwall   *119 n2*
Cotton, W. C.   83
Creed, Charles   198 n44
Cutfield, George   173
Cuxhaven   15

Dacker, Bill   207 n12
Devon's Hotel   51–52
Dickenson, W (also spelt Dickinson)   43, 48
Dieffenbach, Ernst   71 n36
Dierks, H   222
Dillon, Constantine   29
Domett, Alfred   201–202
Duff, Rev. Dr   231
Duke of Portland   137
Dunedin   1, 19, 35 n20, 190–193, 195–196, 198–200, 203–205, 208–213, 224, 227–228

East Frisia   4
East India   15, 126
Egmont, Cape   86
Egypt   159
Egyptians   159
Elbe River   12 n34, 26
England   4, 7, 15, 27, 36, 41, 70 n35, 71 n38, 80, 99 n5, 108–109, 144, 162
English Channel   27
Episcopal   51, 66, 75, 85, 92, 163, 186
Episcopalian   90, 130 n25
Episcopalians   71, 85
Eton   40
Evangelical   4 n5

Fairbrother, Edward   210
Fenton, Francis Dart   144 n29
Fitzroy, Robert   82
Fleming   208
Flight, Josiah   147
Flight, Mrs   175
Ford, Samuel   170
Forsaith, T. S.   228
Foveaux Strait   49, 107, 198
Fox, William   43, 47, 51, 201, 202
Free Church of Scotland   153
Fricke   39
Friendly Islands   86 n22
Fritze, W. A.   16–17

Geneva   3, 65

German   2, 2 n2, 3, 4, 4 n8, 5 n11, 7 n15, 11 n31, 13, 15–16, 18–20, 21 n63, 23–24, 26, 27 n2, 29–31, 33–49, 51, 57–58, 61, 63–71, 75, 80–81, 84–85, 87–88, 90, 94, 99, 106, 108 n20, 115, 119, 121–122, 137, 139–141, 146–147, 148 n41, 151, 153, 156, 162, 173–174, 183, 194, 200, 205, 213, 221
Germans   17, 30, 35–39, 42–44, 47–48, 50, 51 n15, 54, 57, 66, 74, 182, 184, 200
Germany   2–3, 4 n7, 5–6, 9–10, 16, 40, 49, 70, 72, 97, 105–106, 108, 126–127, 140, 146–148, 152–153, 172, 206, 227
Gillies, John   192
Glückstadt   26
Göders, Dr J. F.   27, 30, 33–34
Gold, C. E.   167–168, 174, 176–177
Golden Age   208
Gossner, Johannes Evangelista   17
Govett, Henry   80 n25, 84, 130, 134, 144 n27, 147, 162–163, 168, 177, 186–187
Grey, Sir George   119, 145, 185, 189

Haase   34
Hakopa   82
Halse, Sergeant   135 n10
Hamburg   4 n8, 5–6, 10–16, 18–20, 23–24, 26, 28, 30, 34, 42, 57, 67–68, 72, 91, 98, 100, 104–106, 114, 116, 118, 121,126, 131, 139, 141
Hamburg Mission Society   10
Hangatahua   172, 175–176
Hannover   10
Hanseatic League   2, 4 n8
Harper, Henry James Chitty   197–198
Harwood, Octavius   204
Hauhau   217–219, 226
Hauranga   83, 85, 99, 102, 156
Haurāpari   156
Heine, Johann Wilhelm Christoph   9 n27, 12, 18, 20–22, 26–27, 29, 31–32, 36, 39, 43, 45 n2, 46 n4, 48 n6, 50, 52 n19, 55 n30, 57, 74, 78, 107 n19, 108, 127, 138–139, 141–142, 152, 181, 183–184, **Pl.29**
Heka   188
Hēnui   83
Heretoa   82, 86–87, 107, 116, 131 n3
Heskin   108
Hesse   4
Hoani   156
Hobhouse, Edmund   183
Hocken, T. M.   213
Hōhepa   151
Hokianga   35 n20

'Holy Trinity, St Georg', church   23, **Pl.3**
Hōne Ōraukawa, Tāmati   142, 149
Honoré, Abraham   32 n11, 52 n19, 195 n38
Hood, Mrs   175
Hōpāiaia   146, 156
Hōri   133
Hoyerhagen   15
Hutt   35 n20

India   15, 18, 21 n64
Ira, Herewini   205, 206 n9
Ireland   7
Ironside, Samuel   19, 35, 147
Israel   159, 180 n37

Jacobs River   195 n40
Johnstone, W   208, 228
Jones   69 n33
Jones, Edward   69
Jones, Johnny   204
Jung, C. F. W.   45

Kaihihi   102, 169, 179
Kākahi, Tohu   115, 219, 221–222
Kapoaiaia   87
Karaka, Arama   138, 171, 215–216
Kātātore, Te Waitere   132–133, 135, 137–138, 154
Kawhia   64–65, 70–75, 80, 81 n10, 216
Kereopa (of Hōpāiaia)   146, 150–151
Keretape   176
King, Henry   110
King Movement   157–158, 160–161, 180 n37, 216, 221
Kīngi, Wiremu Te Rangitaake   102, 137, 163, 166–168, 180, 185
Kīngi, Wiremu Matakatea   141, 171, 215–216
Kirk, William   198 n44
Knight, Hardwicke   48 n10
Kōmene   171, 188
Körber   39
Kōrako, Hoani Wetere   207
Kororareka   17
Kou, Erihāpeta Hine   216
Kukutai, Pāora   80, 86, 94, 96 n1, 119–120, 123, 170

Lampe, Friedrich Adolf   4
Lawry, Walter   65
Lemon Point   71 n37
London   15, 30, 64, 81, 124
London Missionary Society   15
Long, Pastor   147

Lord Worsley   215–217, **Pl.33**
Lower Saxony   10
Lübeck   4 n8
Lüneburg   7
Luther, Martin   3
Lutheran   3–4, 10–11, 15 n44, 23, 36, 65, 66 n22, 69, 71, 78 n55, 95, 108 n20, 127, 138–139, 152, 184 n9, 222

McLean, Donald   66, 68, 78–79, 88, 91, 97–98, 122, 137–138, 144, 163, 165, 184, 218, 229–230, **Pl.12**
McDonnell, Alexander Francis   213 n27
McLintock, A. H.   191
Mallet, Friedrich Ludwig   5–6, 10, 12, 16, 23–24, 42
Manahiakai   149
Manawapou   92 n43, 131, 157
Mangaharekiekie   77
Mangapehi Stream   63
Mangatī Stream   132
Māngungu   86 n22
Maniapoto, Rewi   92 n43
Manukau   71 n38, 86 n 22
Māranuku   203, 205
Marburg   3
Marlborough   46 n3
Martin, Sir William   184–185
Matakaha   103, 171
Matakatea, Wiremu *see* Kīngi, Wiremu Matakatea
Matakine   162
Matamata   68, 181 n40
Maunsell, Robert   117, 125, 146 n34
Mautoti   102
Meierdirks   9
Mengert   17
Merritt, J. J.   128
Methodism   4 n5
Methodist   39, 63 n16, 147
Middle Island   56
Miller, Frederick   63–65, 67, 74
Mitai   123
Moeraki   48, 197–198, 203–206, 210–211, 232
Mohi   142 n23
Mōkau and Region   41, 59, 61, 63–64, 68, 70 n35, 71, 73–77, 79–81, 83–84, 88–89, 131, 231
Mōkau River   20, 52–54, 62–63, 67, 72, 74–75, 77, 83
Morgan, John   65–67, 69, 112
Morocco   147

251

Moutere (includes Upper Moutere, the Moutere) 8 n22, 34, 36, 38–39, 42–48, 50, 52, 57, 112–113, 141, 183–184
Moutere River 42
Motueka 42
Motukaramū 45, 52 n19, 55, 57, 59, 62–65, 67–69, 72–81, 83–86, 88–90, 94, 103–105, 111, 197, 219, 231–232
Mukau 55
Müller, A.W. 17–18
Müller, Hermann 4–5
Müller, Hermann (Jnr) 140, 224
Murray, G. F. 166, 170

Napoleon Bonaparte 2, 4 n8, 7
Nassau 4
Nelson 19, 25–26, 28–29, 32–43, 45–48, 50–52, 57, 69, 72–73, 78, 91, 107–108, 119, 127, 138–139, 141–142, 146, 148, 152, 173, 175, 180–186, 188–190, 193–194, 196, 201, 213, 215
New Caledonia 35, 49, 117
New Munster 19
New Plymouth 49–52, 66, 69, 70 n35, 71 n38, 74–77, 79–86, 88–90, 97–99, 101, 102 n9, 103, 107–114, 118–119, 122–123, 125, 127–128, 130–139, 141–144, 146–148, 150–151, 153–154, 160, 162–164, 167–169, 171–175, 177, 179–181, 185–186, 188–190, 201, 213, 215–216, 219, 232
New River 195 n40, **Pl.5**
Netherlands 4
New Zealand 1–3, 5–11, 13–14, 15 n44, 16–23, 26 n1, 30, 32–36, 38, 40, 44, 46 n3, 48, 51 n17, 62, 63 n16, 65–66, 70 n35, 71, 77–78, 81 n9, 82 n11, 83–84, 86 n22, 90, 95, 97 n4, 104, 106, 108, 116, 118, 121, 127, 129, 130 n25, 131, 137, 139, 144–145, 151–153, 163, 166, 168, 181–185, 190–191, 195, 204, 218, 223–224, 230–232
New Zealand Company 16, 19–20, 26–30, 32–34, 37–39, 41–43, 46–47, 50–51, 71, 132, 139, 201, 203
Ngāi Tahu 191
Ngā Māhanga 122–123, 143, 154, 169–172
Ngāpuhi 75, 81, 170 n15
Ngā Rauru 86
Ngāruawāhia 157
Ngāti Maniapoto 53, 136
Ngāti Ruanui 53 n22, 86, 88, 92, 94, 96, 101–102, 115 n44, 123, 131–136, 142–144, 146, 149, 151, 154, 157–161, 164, 168–172, 179 n35, 186, 215, 218

Ngāti Toa 170 n15
Ngā Ture 69
Ngāweka 170 n15
Niger 168, 171–172
Niven, Dr 208
North German 1, 2, 11, 41, 90–91, 99, 162, 183, 201, 206, 231–232
North German Mission Society 3, 7–12, 15–17, 19–20, 23–24, 34–37, 40, 45–46, 52, 56, 59, 65, 67, 72, 78 n55, 89, 95, 98, 100, 105, 107 n19, 108 n20, 109, 112, 122, 125–127, 129, 135, 138–139, 141, 146, 152, 172, 182–184, 193–195, 197, 199–200, 206, 211, 223, 226–227, 229–231
North Island 19–20, 32, 36, 41, 49–50, 51 n17, 71 n38, 83, 87, 186, 915 n38, 205, 217–218, 228, 231
North Sea 26
North Taranaki 53
Nugent, Major 143

Ōeo 219
Ōhāngai 142
Okaha 172
Ōkato 170 n15
Okawa 87
Okawha 96, 102
Ōmata 97, 151, 170, 173
Ōpōtiki 181, 218
Oranga 195 n40
Ōraukawa, Tāmati Hōne 142, 149
Oreti River 195 n40
Otahuhu 70 n35
Otago 191–208, 210, 214–215, 226–228, 230–232
Ōtākou 191–193, 195–197, 198 n44,45, 199, 203–207, 209–212, 223, 225, 230–232
Ōtāwhao 65
Ōtūmatua 82, 87, 103

Pai Marire 217, 226
Paratene 143, 170
Parihaka 115, 221–222, **Pl.34**
Parininihi 53
Parris, Robert 164 n1, 165–166
Parry, Thomas 192, 206, 223
Patea 64
Patea River 86
Patukai (hapu) 168, 175
Petrie, Captain 30
Pezant, Father 68–69
Pharaoh 159
Pietism 4
Piripi 85, 142, 187

Piritoko 75
Poirama 119
Porikapa 169–171
Port Chalmers 1, 191, 196, 199, 203, 206, 208, 210–211, 213, 224–229, 231
Port Nicholson 35 n20, 49–50, 96, 102
Pōtatau I 157–158, 167
Presbyterian 1, 66, 182, 191, 193, 195, 198, 200, 208, 210 n22, 213, 224, 228, 230–232
Protestant 3, 4 n7, 23 n68, 55, 66–69, 83 n18, 152–153, 162, 233
Protestantism 4
Pukeko 102
Puketapu 131–136, 137 n17, 138, 141–143, 146–148, 150–151, 154–157, 159, 172, 179 n35, 181, 184, 217, 233
Pungairere 87, 102, 111, 142
Punihangarua 69
Pūriri 181 n40
Pūtahi 219

Quaker 41, 46
Queen Charlotte Sound 101

Raglan 70 n35
Rangiaowhia 63, 68, 112, 157
Rangihuia 67, 73, 83
Rangitukia 35 n19
Rationalism 4
Rauhes Haus 18
Rawenata 142
Reay, C. A. 35–36, 39–40, 51
Reddy 151
Reformed 3–4, 10–11, 40, 65, 127, 139, 146, 152–153, 183, 193, 200
Revivalist Movement 4–5, 12
Rhine 4 n8
Richmond, C.W. 153
Riemenschneider, Anna Dorothea Leonore 7
Riemenschneider, Anna Jane 128
Riemenschneider, Anna Metta 7
Riemenschneider, Anton Conrad 6–7
Riemenschneider, Augusta Frederica 161
Riemenschneider, Catherine Garland 107, 149, 173, 175, 186, 209, 224, 228–229, **Pl.25**
Riemenschneider, Emily Catherine 229
Riemenschneider, Emma Eleonora *129*
Riemenschneider, Ernest Edwin *225*
Riemenschneider, Frances Mary Adolphine 186
Riemenschneider, Friedrich Wilhelm 116, 222, 227, 230
Riemenschneider, Justus Werner 7
Rimene (for Riemenschneider) 148

Rīmene 133–134
Ritzebüttel 15
Rolleston, William 222
Ross 205
Ruapuke Island 48, 107, 152, 195, 225–226
Rundle, Councillor 143

St George, G. H. F. 99–100
St Martini 6
St Michaelis 5
St Pauli 26–27, 29–30, 32, 36 n24, 37
St Paulidorf 38, 48
St Stephani 3–5, 7–8, 23, **Pl.1**
St. Stephen's church, Otakou 208, **Pl.35**
Sanders, Johann Hinrich 7
Schacht, Captain 26, 30, 34–35, 38, 43
Schachtstal 38
Schnackenberg, Henry Cort 54, 60, 62–64, 69 n33, 74, 76–77, 79, 106, 109 n29, 147
Schneider 34
Schneppel, Johann Friedrich 7
Schniedewine, J H 24
Selkirk, Captain 30
Selwyn, George Augustus 35 *n19,* 40, 46, 67, 81, 88, [122–123], 125, 130 n25
Seon, Father 63
Seven Stars Inn 50
Sieveking, Karl 16, 19
Sinclair, Keith 165 n3
Sixtus 36
Skevington, John 82, 86
Smith, S. Percy 77
Society Islands 16
South Island 11, 19, 32, 46, 190
South Taranaki 219
Spencer, [Seymour?] 66
Stade 10–11, 16
Stewart, Rev. 228
Stewart Island 225
Stannard, George 191–192, 198 n44
Stuart, D. M. 227–228
Suffert, E. G. 9 104–105
Suffert, Leonore 105–106
Sydney 49, 51 n17

Tahakopa 207 n12
Taiaroa, Hōri Kerei T. 206
Taiaroa, Karoraira 191 n26
Taiaroa, Te Mātenga 191 n26, 192, 205, 213 n27
Taieri 197, 203–205, 211
Tainui 53
Tāmati 116, 187, 218
Tāmati Wiremu 160

Taonui 61, 67, 75–76
Tarakihi 85, 91, 96 n1
Taranaki 41, 52–53, 80–92, 95, 101–103,
 108, 110, 112, 115–118, 122–123, 125,
 129–130, 132–135, 137, 139–140, 142 144,
 149–151, 154–155,157, 159, 161–162–165,
 168–169, 173, 178, 181–190, 193–197,
 203–205, 212–219, 221–222, 224–226, 229,
 231–232–233
Taranaki Herald 147, 169, 172–173, 177, 181
Taranaki Institute 147
Taranaki, Mount 32, 50, 123, 128, 134, 144,
 169, 171–172
Taranaki people 53, 74, 80–82, 85–87, 94,
 101, 111–113, 115, 121, 128–129, 132,
 134–136, 138, 141–142–143, 148–149,
 153–161, 164, 167–168–174, 177–181,
 184–190, 215–216, 226
Tasmania 49
Tataraimaka 127–128, 145, 153, 164, 166,
 174, 179
Taupō 55, 66, 75 n48, 77 n54, 78, 157
Taupō, Lake 49, 52
Tauranga 68, 181, 193
Taylor, Richard 51–52, 66–68, 78, 83, 86, 88,
 115 n44, 154, 193, **Pl.19**
Te Aharoa 96
Te Araroa 35 n19
Te Ātiawa 75, 80, 86, 92, 101, 133, 135, 137,
 143–144,154, 183, 185–186
Te Āti Awa 53 n22
Te Awamutu 63, 65, 112, 157
Te Hawhetaoai Pa 135
Te Ikapārua River 96 n1, **Pl.15**
Te Ito, Tāmati 154, 156, 172
Te Kapa 59
Te Kirikumara, Īhāia 133–135
Te Kohia pā 168
Te Kōparu, Paratene 143, 170
Te Kurī 59–62, 67, 74, 77, 83
Te Mamaku Pa 134–135
Te Namu 103
Te Oharoa 102
Te Pawa 73
Te Reke, Āperahama 96 n1, 112, 134, 142–
 143, 150, 158, 161, 163, 167–171, 173, 184,
 187–189, 220–221
Te Reke, Tamihana 173, 184, 188
Te Tēira (also Tēira) 163, 165
Te Turu 53, 58
Te Tekapu 172
Te Ua Haumene (Horopāpera) 215–219, **Pl.32**
Te Waitara 73
Te Waitere 71 n 37, **Pl.8, 9, 10**

Te Wati (also E Wati) 55, 57
Te Wherowhero 157
Te Whiti o Rongomai (Erueti) 115, 175, 185,
 219, 220–222, **Pl.31**
Thames 181 n40
Thompson, Henry Augustus 38 n29
Thomson, Captain 208, 213, 228–230
Thuckwell 208
Tiesmeyer, L 13
Tipoka 87, 96, 102
Toko, Wī 160–161
Tongapōrutu 53
Tongapōrutu River 53
Treviranus, Georg Gottfried 5–6, 9–10,
 105–106, 116
Triton 35 n20
Trost, Johann Heinrich 9 n27, 12, 18, 20 n62,
 26–27, 30, 32, 34, 36, 39, 43, 46 n4, 50,
 55 n30, 57,62 n13, 72–75, 78, 84, 89, 94–95,
 97–101, 103, 107 n19, 108–111, 118, 219
Tonga 86 n22
Tuckett, Frederick 38 n30, 41, 46–47, 49,
 78 n55, 225
Turton, Henry Hanson 71, 79–83, 85–86,
 88, 93, 95, 98, 101, 109, 113, 134, 136, 143,
 144 n27, 147

Ullrich, Berthold 36, 39, 49
Umuroa 87, 103, 141, 171, 215–216
'Unser lieben Frauen', church 23, **Pl.2**
Upokomutu 175
Upper Moutre *see* Moutere
Urgent 49
Urquhart, Robert 227

Vallé, Philip 41, 45
Verwaltungsausschuß (Administration
 Committee) 11–12, 16, 19, 30, 34, 39, 41,
 45, 48 n8, 52, 72, 75, 89–90, 98, 100, 102,
 104–109, 116, 121, 125, 128, 135, 139–140,
 143, 156, 166, 182, 186 n13, 211, 223–224,
 226, 229
Viard, Father 68
Vietor, C. R. 112, 127
Völkner, Carl Sylvius 103, 109, 116–117,
 125–126, 181, 195, 216, 218, **Pl.30**

Wāhi Tapu Movement 154, 156, 220
Waiaua 87, 103, 116–117, 125, 216
Waiaua, Rāwiri 132–133
Waihonga Stream 133
Waikato 53 n23, 69, 75, 81, 87, 92, 112, 117,
 125, 136, 157, 159, 168, 172, 178, 183, 187
Waikouaiti 19,191, 197–198, 203–207,

210–211, 232
Waima   86 n22
Waimate   97, 110, 128
Waimea   34–35, 183
Waipa   70–71, 74, 82 n11, 157
Waipu   35 n19
Wairau River   33, 36–37, 41
Waireka   170–172, 180, 216
Waitara   79, 86, 92 n43, 102, 134–136, 142–143, 154–155, 163–164, 165 n3, 166–170, 172–173, 177, 180, 184–185, 222
Waitōtara   53
Wakefield, Arthur   33, 36–37, 39 n32, 41, 51
Wakefield, Edward Gibbon   19
Wakefield, William   37–38, 51, 163
Walsall, Mary Ellen   106, 109 n29
Wanganui   88, 94, 132
Warea   79–80, 82–83, 85–86, 88–92, 94, 96, 98–103, 107 n19, 108, 114–115, 117–120, 122 n10, 123, 125, 129, 134–135, 140, 143, 144 n27, 146, 149–150, 153, 159–161, 164–177, 179–180, 184–187, 190, 196, 207, 218–222, **Pl.15**
'Warea Delusion'   83
Wareatea   96
Wataha Stream   132
Watkin, James   19, 207 n12
Watkins, Lavinia   210
Weightman, W. A.   43, 48–51, 54–55, 57–60, 62 n13, 66, 72–73, 77, 78 n55
Weller Brothers   191, 204
Wellington   16, 35 n20, 37, 49, 51, 78, 107–109, 16–117, 123, 161, 164, 213
Wells, B   80, 102 n9, 119 n2
Weriweri   143
Weser   15
Wesley, John   4 n5
Wesleyan   19, 35, 39, 41, 46–47, 49, 53, 55–56, 62–63, 65–66, 70–72, 74–75, 73–82, 85–90, 94–95, 101, 109 n29, 110, 113–114, 134, 136, 144, 146–147, 153, 168, 182, 194, 198 n44, 207 n12, 216
Wesleyan Methodist Missionary Society   64 n17, 71 n39, 81 n6, 82 n13
Wesleyans   39, 46–47, 49, 56, 63 n16, 65, 71, 76, 81–82, 86, 183, 191, 198
Wesleyan Missionary Society   15, 18
West Africa   9, 19
Wetere Kōrako, Hoani   *see* Kōrako, Hoani Wetere
Whanganui   51–52, 86, 88, 97, 125, 131 n3, 154, 227, 229
Whakaahurangi Trail   134
Whakatumutumu   63–64, 66, 70, 74, **Pl.6, 7**

White Cliffs   53
White, George   38, 43
Whiteley, John   62–65, 70–72, 74, 77–78, 81, 85, 99, 106, 143, 144 n27, 147, 153, 168, 172, 177, 179–181, 194–195, **Pl.11**
Wicksteed, John Tylston   51
Williams, H. W.   53 n23, 70, 143 n24
Wilson, J. A.   181
Wilson, Dr J. F.   34–35
Wilson, Dr Peter   97–100, 107, 124, 128, 135 n10, 144 n27 147, 181, **Pl.14**
Wiremu   84
Wiremu, Tāmati   160
Wittemberg   3
Wohlers, Johann Friedrich Heinrich   9 n25, 12–15, 18–23, 26–28, 30–31, 33–36, 39, 41, 43, 45–49, 107–109, 117, 127, 152, 195, 198, 206, 223, 225–226, 227 n10, 229–230–231, **Pl.28**
Wolters, F. H.   29
Woodstock   108
Woon, Catherine   107, 110
Woon, Emily Jane   196
Woon, E. T.   227, 229
Woon family   107
Woon, Garland   177
Woon, William   86–87, 94, 109–110, 131 n3

Zahn, Franz Michael   206, 213, 215, 218, 224–226, 228, 230
Wynyard, Robert   136–138
Zürich   3
Zwingly, Huldrych   3